WITHOUT
PRECEDENT

ALSO BY JOEL RICHARD PAUL

Unlikely Allies

WITHOUT PRECEDENT

JOHN MARSHALL AND HIS TIMES

Joel Richard Paul

RIVERHEAD BOOKS

NEW YORK

2018

RIVERHEAD BOOKS
An imprint of Penguin Random House LLC
375 Hudson Street
New York, New York 10014

Library of Congress Cataloging-in-Publication Data

Names: Paul, Joel R., author.
Title: Without precedent : John Marshall and his times / Joel Richard Paul.
Description: New York : Riverhead Books, 2017. |
Includes bibliographical references and index.
Identifiers: LCCN 2017016049 (print) | LCCN 2017022497 (ebook) |
ISBN 9780525533276 (eBook) | ISBN 9781594488238 (hardcover)
Subjects: LCSH: Marshall, John, 1755–1835. | Judges—United States—Biography. |
United States. Supreme Court—Biography
Classification: LCC KF8745.M3 (ebook) | LCC KF8745.M3 P38 2017 (print) |
DDC 347.73/2634 [B]—dc23
LC record available at https://lccn.loc.gov/2017016049
p.   cm.

Printed in the United States of America
5   7   9   10   8   6   4

BOOK DESIGN BY MEIGHAN CAVANAUGH

For my friend and teacher Robert Gross

and for Charles Uehrke, who kept me waiting

CONTENTS

INTRODUCTION

Ｎone of the founding generation of American leaders had a greater impact on the American Constitution than John Marshall, and no one did more than Marshall to preserve the delicate unity of the fledgling republic. As chief justice of the United States, Marshall led the Supreme Court for thirty-four years, longer than any other chief justice, and he single-handedly established its importance and supremacy in American life. What George Washington was to American politics, John Marshall was to American justice. Buffeted by political adversaries prepared to do almost anything to stop him, Marshall brilliantly outflanked his rivals. Against a torrent of forces that threatened to shatter the fragile union, Marshall defended his vision of a strong national government. Armed with nothing more than his eloquence and his gift for invention, Marshall triumphed against all odds.

This is the story of the life and times of an exceptional man who mastered the art of self-invention and applied it to everything he did. At a time when all the leading southern statesmen—men such as Washington, Jefferson, Madison, Monroe, Randolph, Pinckney, and Lee—were wealthy patricians from prominent landholding families, Marshall grew up in a two-room log cabin shared with fourteen siblings on the hardscrabble frontier of Virginia. His only formal education consisted of one year of grammar school and six weeks of law school. Yet in the space of two decades he went from being a poor, unschooled frontiersman to become a military officer, an influential lawmaker, a successful attorney, a foreign diplomat, a national hero, Washington's biographer, a congressman, secretary of state, and chief justice.

How does a man from such modest beginnings reinvent himself so successfully? And how does a judge transform an insignificant and impotent court into a powerful coequal branch of the federal government and breathe meaning and life into an untested constitution?

As a young officer at Valley Forge, Marshall witnessed how Generals George Washington and Baron von Steuben transformed the Continental Army from a hungry, bootless band of undisciplined and demoralized men into an effective fighting force by kindling faith in their fight. Marshall learned early from his experience in the Revolutionary War that reality sometimes follows appearances. Marshall loved the theater. Wherever he traveled, he attended performances frequently and often wrote about them. Perhaps the power of illusion and the possibilities of one actor playing multiple roles were what drew him to the stage. Marshall played many parts so well because he was at heart a master actor. In the end his gift for illusion transformed not only himself but the Court, the Constitution, and the nation as well.

Later, while serving as a diplomat and secretary of state, Marshall negotiated on behalf of the United States when France, Britain, Spain, and the Barbary pirates threatened war. How does an infant nation lacking a powerful army or navy demand to negotiate as an equal with powerful adversaries such as France and Britain? Diplomacy was, in one of Marshall's pet phrases, "an extravagant pretense." But Marshall depended on this extravagant pretense to defend America's territorial sovereignty and right to trade against the ambition of great powers. His diplomatic maneuvers success-fully avoided war and maintained the country's foreign commerce.

President John Adams nominated Marshall as chief justice after a hu-miliating electoral defeat—and only after Adams's preferred nominee for the post demurred. At that time the Supreme Court was regarded as noth-ing more than a constitutional afterthought. The Court had few cases, little dignity, and no genuine authority. In designing the new capital, no one had even planned a building to house the Supreme Court: It ended up in the basement of the U.S. Capitol. From the outset, Marshall confronted a hos-tile President Jefferson and a Republican Congress that plotted to impeach Marshall and much of the federal judiciary. Despite these impediments, Marshall established over the course of his tenure the principle of judicial review and elevated the dignity of the Supreme Court as the final arbiter of the Constitution's meaning.

During Marshall's tenure from 1801 to 1835, the Court issued more than one thousand decisions—nearly all unanimous—and about half that num-ber were written by Marshall. No other chief justice comes close to that record, and no Supreme Court before or since has issued even a majority of its decisions unanimously. What makes this record of unanimity even more incredible is that Marshall was a Federalist, and for his entire tenure, every Supreme Court justice was appointed by a Democratic-Republican president who opposed Marshall. Nonetheless, Marshall forged a consen-sus on nearly every issue by sheer personality and intellect. His humanity and warm laughter helped to win over even the most resolute colleague. He rejected a strict construction of the Constitution and insisted on reading the Constitution broadly as a living document that responded to the needs and demands of a growing nation. Marshall envisioned a modern national economy under a strong federal government. He conceived virtually every foundational doctrine of constitutional law that has guided the United States for two centuries.

While Marshall's contributions to American constitutional law are well-known, his contributions to international law were just as important. On the Court, he confronted a stream of cases for which there were no clear rules or precedents. He was compelled to create new precedents. Cases involving pirates, slaves, and Indians were especially thorny, and Marshall continually crafted new doctrines for deciding these cases.

For thirty-four years on the Supreme Court, Marshall resisted the centrifugal forces of regionalism and parochialism. He eschewed rigid ideology. His was a consistent voice for moderation, compromise, and pragmatism in the face of ideologues and adversaries. In an era without precedent, Marshall invented the legal principles that form the foundation of American constitutional and international law today. He defended the independence of the judiciary and the sanctity of property and contract. He jealously guarded the separation of powers. And he dared to imagine a dynamic interpretation of the Constitution that could accommodate the nation's progress from a backward localized agrarian economy to a modern national industrial economy.

In a revolutionary time, against myriad enemies both foreign and domestic, Marshall held the Court, the Constitution, and the union together.

CHAPTER ONE

THE FRONTIER SOLDIER

Lieutenant General Baron von Steuben could not believe his eyes. At great risk and personal expense, he had traveled four thousand miles across the Atlantic from Prussia to join the Continental Army. Arriving at Valley Forge, Pennsylvania, in February 1778, he surveyed the desperate condition of this pathetic army with a mixture of alarm and disgust. He felt deceived.

Under a gunmetal sky, he came on horseback from the town of York, eighty miles west, where Congress had fled after the British captured Philadelphia. After weeks of bitter cold, the weather had improved in late February, and the Schuylkill River had begun to melt. From a distance, Steuben could see one thousand cabins crowding the hills. Smoke curled out of a forest of chimneys. As he approached, Steuben could not discern in the waning light the crimson tracks left by barefoot soldiers. But he could not miss the stinking carcasses of horses lying in the snow.[1]

General Washington met him on horseback outside the camp. The handsome, imposing Virginian and the plump Prussian with bulging lips and thick eyebrows rode side by side in awkward silence. Steuben, who was naturally ebullient, spoke French and German and very little English; Washington, who was characteristically reserved, spoke neither.[2] It was an inauspicious beginning.

Steuben soon realized that Washington's army was a chimera. The Continental Army was melting away faster than the snow. He had expected to join a force of 40,000 men, but fewer than 14,000 remained and only half that were fit for duty. Nearly 7,000 were sick or not equipped to fight. Over the winter, nearly 2,500 men died from disease and around 15,000 deserted, sneaking across enemy lines into Philadelphia twenty miles southeast along the Schuylkill.[3] "With regard to their military discipline," Steuben noted, "I may safely say that no such thing existed."[4]

"The men had been left to perish by inches of cold and nakedness," Washington admitted.[5] Without adequate food, the soldiers baked "fire cakes" made out of flour and water on a hot stone placed in the hearth.[6] In some cases, starving men roasted their leather shoes to provide one more meal.[7] One officer complained that "Congress have let it in the power of the States to starve the Army at pleasure."[8] The camp needed 30,000 pounds of bread and an equivalent amount of meat daily. In addition, the men were promised a gill (four ounces) of whiskey a day. Rarely did the camp have anything approaching that amount.[9] Angry soldiers chanted, "No bread, no soldiers!"[10] The local farmers refused to accept the nearly worthless Continental dollars. They preferred to sell food to the British soldiers for pounds sterling.[11] The situation was so desperate that Washington told his troops to steal whatever food they could find and "make an example" out of farmers who sold to the British.[12]

The next day Steuben surveyed the troops with his large wolfhound, Azor, sniffing alongside.[13] Half-naked men with skeletal bodies stared back in wonder at his well-fed figure in a smart Prussian blue tunic bedecked with medals. The men were awed by the general. "Never before, or since, have I had such an impression of the ancient fabled God of War," wrote one young private.[14] Few soldiers owned more than one shirt, and many had none. More than 3,000 men were barefoot or partly naked.[15] France had sent the army tens of thousands of boots that were too small for most Americans, and those that fit fell apart after marches across hundreds of miles.[16] The scarcity of supplies forced many to cannibalize what little they had. The lucky few who had blankets cut them into tents; the ones with tents sewed the fabric into shirts.[17] Most soldiers suffered from scabies or lice, which drove men to tear madly at their own flesh.[18] As Steuben inspected the troops, men stood shivering with open sores covering their bodies. Medical care was almost nonexistent. Thousands lay in camp hospitals without doctors, food, or drugs.[19]

Given all this, Steuben could not be surprised at the poor morale. Nearly all the enlisted soldiers were in their teens and twenties; most were poor and more likely to be motivated by the promise of a steady wage than revolutionary ideology. Soldiers had been promised forty shillings a month in hard coin, but wages were paid irregularly in rapidly depreciating paper money instead. By the winter of 1777, the Continental dollar had lost more than three-quarters of its value. With it, soldiers could barely afford a cheap bottle of rum.[20] While soldiers starved, the senior officers feasted on mutton and veal and toasted their commander's health with General Washington's favorite Madeira.[21] Still, even the officers found the conditions intolerable.[22] As many as fifty officers resigned their commissions in a single week.[23] Washington suffered deprivations of his own: He complained to Congress that his servants were not dressed properly.[24]

Amid this landscape of misery and disorder, one man seemed unaccountably upbeat. John Marshall was a twenty-two-year-old lieutenant from the Culpeper regiment of rural Virginia. Steuben's roving eye could not have missed this handsome young man: Rail thin with a tangle of brown hair and intense dark eyes, and more than six feet tall, Marshall towered above his contemporaries. He had a rugged complexion; a round, friendly face; and an infectious grin. Long dangling arms and legs made him appear ungainly, yet he was exceptionally athletic. Harsh weather and small rations never dampened his humor and good spirits. When other officers groused about conditions, Marshall teased them until they had no choice but to laugh with him. He loved practical jokes, even at his own expense, and turned every mishap into an excuse for laughter. Once, when his bedding caught fire, Marshall made fun of his own clumsiness. He delighted in challenging other soldiers to games. He could jump farther than almost anyone, and he was a master at quoits, a popular game involving tossing a donut-shaped discus onto a stake.[25] The men who served with Marshall loved him like a brother, and in all Marshall's prolific writing years later, he hardly ever complained about the conditions at Valley Forge.

Marshall impressed his superior officers with his even temper, fair-mindedness, and intelligence. Washington knew Marshall's father and appointed Marshall deputy judge advocate even though he had no legal experience or education. As a judge advocate, Marshall arbitrated disputes between soldiers and litigated violations of Washington's stern orders: Deserters and cowards were hanged, and even women living in the camp were flogged for minor infractions.[26]

Marshall also paid attention to how Steuben quickly transformed the Continental Army into a highly disciplined force by combining rigorous training with paternal affection. Steuben wrote the first regulations for the army, borrowing the best practices of the French and Prussian armies. Unlike with his Prussian soldiers, it was not enough to tell these Americans to do something; he had to explain why. Steuben decided to serve as drillmaster himself. He addressed the troops in a mix of German and French, and his translator, who had no familiarity with military terms, turned the general's words into a mishmash of fragmentary English. He drilled them relentlessly with fast-paced, highly stylized routines adapted for the unconventional guerrilla warfare that Washington favored. Soldiers struggled to keep up. Even when Steuben lost his patience with them and swore at them in a jumble of German and baby English, they found him endearing.[27]

Within a month, Steuben had transformed the ragtag shadow of an army into a disciplined fighting force. He reorganized the army into provisional regiments, reformed the quartermaster's office, improved sanitation and medical care, and demanded better food and uniforms. No one had done more to build the Continental Army, and Washington appointed the Prussian inspector general with the rank of major general.[28] At the same time, Steuben, like Marshall, appealed to the soldiers' sense of fun. He served the officers flaming whiskey drinks and organized costume parties that lampooned their conditions.[29]

MARSHALL WORKED CLOSELY WITH STEUBEN, and the two forged a great friendship. Marshall thought that Steuben and Washington, as different as they were, complemented each other. Steuben formed intense emotional relationships with his soldiers and insisted that his officers bond with their men as well. And Steuben's affection was reciprocated by officers and enlisted men alike.[30]

Steuben's unconditional love could not have been less like Washington's reserve. To his men, Washington was a remote father figure who demanded respect and discipline. He had a rigid sense of hierarchy and propriety. Officers were punished just for eating with enlisted men.[31] Still, Marshall thought that Washington was "the greatest Man on earth." He later wrote, "When I speak or think of that superior Man my full heart overflows with gratitude."[32] And Marshall credited Washington with saving the Continental Army from defeat.[33]

Washington and Steuben gave Marshall an early lesson in two styles of leadership: Washington demanded unquestioning deference to authority while Steuben fostered collegiality. These two heroes came to represent the twin attributes of Marshall's professional success: Marshall's influence as a statesman and jurist derived from his ability to command respect for the authority of the law and his talent for finding common ground.

GIVEN THE IMMENSITY of the challenge of turning these untrained men into an effective fighting force, one might wonder why on earth Steuben did not return to the Prussian army. The truth was he couldn't. Lieutenant General Baron Friedrich Wilhelm Ludolf Gerhard Augustin von Steuben was neither a general nor a Prussian baron. Though his maternal grandfather may have been a German noble, Steuben possessed neither a title nor a fortune. He never rose above the rank of captain in the army of Frederick the Great. His military career in the Prussian military was aborted in his early thirties when it was rumored that he preferred young boys.[34] After his discharge from the Prussian army, Steuben could not find work and eventually ended up in Paris, where he met the French playwright Pierre Augustin Caron de Beaumarchais, who was engaged in selling arms to the Americans. Beaumarchais introduced the Prussian to two American commissioners, Silas Deane and Benjamin Franklin, to see if they could offer him a military commission. They were impressed with him, but Congress had already complained that they were commissioning too many foreign officers, which enflamed jealousy within the ranks of American officers. Deane and Franklin thought that all they could offer was to send Steuben to America without pay or rank. To make Steuben more salable to Congress, Deane and Franklin concocted an over-the-top twenty-year record of military service in combat as a lieutenant general, an aide-de-camp, and a quarter master general to Frederick the Great.[35]

With his fictionalized curriculum vitae, Steuben was received by Americans as if he were a world-famous warrior. In Boston, John Hancock, the former president of the Continental Congress, gave a huge party in his honor for the leading citizens of the city. The Continental Congress set aside its collective suspicions of foreign mercenaries to welcome him warmly to York. Congress offered him a commission as a captain and agreed to pay him six hundred pounds annually for life if the revolution succeeded.[36]

Steuben thought he had pulled off a great subterfuge until he arrived in Valley Forge and realized that Washington's army was a far more extravagant deception: He was the one who had been fooled. But Steuben did not return to Europe. He and Azor had no place to return to. Instead, Steuben decided to make the best of a bad situation. He knew that reality often follows appearances. Marshall, too, learned that lesson early.

VALLEY FORGE LEFT an indelible mark on Marshall and laid the foundation of his political and legal career. He developed personal ties to Washington, Steuben, the Marquis de Lafayette, and Alexander Hamilton, among others, that served him well later in life. And the hardships at Valley Forge shaped his views about government. The Continental Congress and the thirteen state governments proved incapable of providing adequate support to the army. The near collapse of the army convinced Marshall that the Articles of Confederation were unworkable. Only a strong central government with the power to tax, regulate commerce, and raise an army could defend the nation effectively, he concluded.

Marshall was born on September 24, 1755, in Germantown, Virginia, in what was then the western frontier and is now Fauquier County—about sixty miles southwest of Washington, D.C. He was the eldest of fifteen—seven boys and eight girls. For the first decade of his life, the family lived in a rough-hewn two-room log cabin. They wore homespun—a coarse handwoven fabric—farmed their rocky soil, and survived primarily on cornmeal mush.[37] When Marshall was nearly ten, the family moved farther west to a valley known as the Hollow, now called Markham, in the shadow of the Blue Ridge Mountains. This is where he lived until age eighteen. He and his family shared a wood-framed two-room cabin measuring barely four hundred square feet with a half-story loft. There were few neighbors, and the nearest towns, Warrenton and Winchester, were more than twenty miles away, roughly a day's trip on horseback. At a young age Marshall was schooled in the conservative values of self-reliance, individualism, and property ownership that shaped his jurisprudence.

Marshall's father, Thomas, came from a modest background. Lord Fairfax, the largest landowner in Virginia, hired Thomas and his friend George Washington to survey Fairfax's more than five million acres in the Northern Neck of Virginia. The two young men worked side by side surveying and selling plots. Fairfax then became the patron of the Marshall family, and Thomas slowly acquired more land. Before John Marshall turned eighteen, the family moved to a larger farm at Oak Hill, a short distance away. As Thomas prospered, he became a respected leader in Fauquier County. Eventually, he was elected to the House of Burgesses.[38]

Marshall's mother, Mary Keith, was descended from two of Virginia's leading families, the Randolphs and the Ishams. She was the granddaughter of William and Mary Randolph, the "Adam and Eve" of colonial Virginia society. Marshall's relation to the Randolphs was tainted by scandal, however. His maternal grandmother, Mary Isham Randolph, was a free spirit who could not be constrained. At sixteen she eloped with a poor Irish workman, with whom she had a child. Members of her family chased her down and allegedly killed her husband and child. The trauma caused Mary to suffer an emotional collapse. Later, she had an affair with an unsavory Scottish minister, James Keith, who was seventeen years older than she was. After they were caught in flagrante delicto, the Randolphs banished Keith from his parish. When Mary was old enough to marry Keith without her parents' permission, she did so. The Randolphs refused to pay her dowry and cut Mary out of any inheritance. The cloud of scandal turned darker when rumors swirled that Mary's first husband was, in fact, still alive, casting doubt both on the legality of her second marriage and the legitimacy of her eight children, including John Marshall's mother. Perhaps as a consequence of this scandal, John Marshall rarely acknowledged his relationship to the Randolphs.[39] His grandmother's shame and the lack of a dowry undoubtedly made it more difficult for his mother to find a suitable husband.

Marshall's mother was a first cousin of Thomas Jefferson's mother, so Thomas Jefferson was Marshall's second cousin. Jefferson's father, Peter, was, like Marshall's father, a farmer and surveyor. Peter Jefferson befriended William Randolph, the eldest brother of Marshall's maternal grandmother. When William Randolph died in 1746, he did something unexpected: Rather than naming one of his relatives as his executor, he chose his friend Peter Jefferson and placed him in charge of the family's ancestral home, Tuckahoe. This was where Marshall's grandmother had been raised. In addition, William Randolph explicitly disinherited Marshall's mother and grandmother, so much of the Randolph property that otherwise might have flowed to John Marshall's family ended up in the hands of the Jefferson family. As a result, Thomas Jefferson grew up at Tuckahoe with five hundred slaves. There he enjoyed enormous privilege and wealth. His cousin John Marshall and his fourteen siblings grew up on the frontier working the stony soil on their father's modest farm.[40]

It is one thing to grow up poor. It is another to grow up bearing the shame of an ancestor and the knowledge that your family's wealth was irrevocably in the hands of a distant cousin. Yet Marshall responded to these circumstances without resentment. His upbringing allowed him to identify with the common man and also gave him the aplomb to associate with his social superiors. He did not become a prisoner of either his bloodline or the economic class he was born into. He moved fluidly between classes. The narrative of the Marshall family's fall from grace also endowed him with the boldness to lift himself up and the confidence of knowing that this was possible.

Marshall's father taught him to read and write, and his mother, Mary, who, unlike most frontier women, was literate, inspired an appreciation for reading in all her children. By the age of twelve, Marshall could transcribe Alexander Pope's *Essay on Man*. Lord Fairfax provided Thomas with books for his oldest son. One of Marshall's favorites as a young man was William Blackstone's *Commentaries on the Laws of England*, which may have influenced his decision to practice law. When Marshall was fourteen, he was sent to a grammar school about one hundred miles away in West-moreland County that was run by a strict Anglican minister, Reverend Ar-chibald Campbell. That was the only year of formal education that Marshall received. Campbell's school stressed mathematics and Latin. It was there that Marshall befriended his classmate James Monroe, whose friendship would turn bitter in later years. The next year John Marshall returned home, presumably for financial reasons. The local minister, Reverend James Thompson, moved into the Marshall household and tutored Marshall and his siblings in exchange for bed and board. From Thompson, Marshall mastered Latin and read Horace and Livy. After that, Marshall had no teacher other than his dictionary and the few books his father brought home from Lord Fairfax's library.[41]

Growing up in the relative isolation of the frontier, Marshall had little opportunity to socialize outside his family. His peers were his younger sib-lings, who looked up to him. At a young age Marshall had to assume sub-stantial responsibility for raising the other children. Other boys his age were, he thought, "entirely uncultivated," but he enjoyed spending time with them in "hardy athletic exercise." He patterned himself after his fa-ther, whom he once described years later as "my only intelligent compan-ion" and "affectionate instructive friend."[42] Marshall's characterization of his father is curious given the reality. His father may have been a strong role model, but he was neither affectionate nor encouraging. By modern stan-dards, both parents were distant and strict, which is understandable—with fifteen children to raise on a struggling farm, his parents had little time to spare. After Marshall left his family home to join the Continental Army, there is little evidence he corresponded with or visited either parent. Yet, over the course of Marshall's life, his expression of admiration for his father, like his attitude toward Washington, suggests that at an early age Marshall attached himself to authority figures. These two qualities, a natural predisposition for leadership and a respect for authority, shaped his philosophy and his career in public service.

Marshall's childhood was influenced by the French and Indian Wars, which ended when he was eight. Virginians on the frontier were made uneasy by the proximity of Indian tribes and French garrisons. Even boys as young as fourteen typically carried guns slung over their backs for protection.[43] Though the triumph of Britain in the war removed the French threat, the war also taught people living in the Piedmont that they needed to be ready to defend themselves and that they could not rely on the British army to protect them. Thomas Marshall took this lesson to heart. He prepared his oldest son for service in the local militia unit and taught him to be an excellent rifleman. When they heard the news that the first shots of the Revolutionary War had been fired at Lexington and Concord in 1775, Thomas and John Marshall volunteered for the 3rd Virginia Regiment.[44]

WHY WOULD MEN such as John and Thomas Marshall, living in the isolation of the Virginia frontier hundreds of miles from Massachusetts and struggling to support their families, concern themselves with colonial politics? Why would stamp taxes or tea concern men who had little use for either? And why would the events in a place as remote as Boston raise any alarm to someone who had never ventured beyond the western edge of northern Virginia?

Virginians living in the Piedmont were motivated by local concerns to join the struggle for independence. Virginia in the 1770s was struggling with a long-term economic crisis triggered by a steep drop in tobacco prices and a string of bad weather that devastated crops. As immigration surged, there was a shortage of land, and after George III decreed that settlers could not move farther west into Indian territory, many Virginians felt that their opportunities were limited. On top of that, poll taxes were raised to support the presence of British forces, squeezing the middle class especially hard.[45] Most Virginians in the northern and western counties resented the wealthy gentry who owned the Tidewater plantations and dominated colonial politics.[46] The Tidewater elite lived like the British gentry, and they were obsessed with wealth, gambling, drinking, and horse racing. By the 1770s, many of them were living far beyond their means, and their indebtedness to the Scottish traders who controlled the tobacco market threatened the colony's economy. All this was alien to the toilsome life of the Piedmont. Most Virginians did not aspire to ape the affectations of upper-crust Englishmen. They blamed the Tidewater gentry for the colony's moral decline.[47] By the 1770s, nearly one in five Virginians had joined Presbyterian, Baptist, or Methodist congregations. They resented the taxes they were required to pay for the support of Anglican ministers, whom many saw as immoral.[48]

These frustrations of ordinary Virginians were ignited by the appointment of Lord Dunmore as royal governor of the colony. Lord Dunmore was only the second royal governor to reside in Virginia, and he was ill-suited to the job. He was an obstinate bully with no patience for the people's elected representatives in the House of Burgesses.[49] Given the hostility Virginians felt toward the Scottish tobacco traders, it hardly helped that the governor was a Scotsman. Dunmore, one wit commented, "was as popular as a Scotsman could be" in Virginia.[50]

In March 1775, Lord Dunmore canceled the colony's elections for representatives to the Second Continental Congress called in Philadelphia to discuss British colonial policy. The following month, Dunmore seized fifteen barrels of gunpowder from the public magazine in Williamsburg to keep them from falling into the hands of rebels. These two incidents sparked fears that the unpopular governor was planning some sort of military action against Williamsburg. The fact that this happened as British troops marched on Concord and Lexington to seize colonists' arms inflamed the public. Confronted by angry colonial leaders, the governor impetuously threatened to arm slaves against white Virginians. White Virginians had a longtime fear of a slave insurrection: Some slaves had already revolted, hoping to win their freedom in exchange for supporting the British Crown.[51] When Dunmore ordered the arrest of Patrick Henry, one of Virginia's popular political leaders, local governments resolved to prevent Henry's arrest by force of arms. Some Virginia politicians, such as Richard Henry Lee, fanned public outrage by falsely alleging that the British planned to kidnap members of the Continental Congress to prevent them from meeting in Philadelphia.[52]

By June, Governor Dunmore had lost control of the situation. He fled Williamsburg on a schooner and returned later with a British fleet to suppress the incipient rebellion. Though many Virginians still hoped for reconciliation with Britain, the final straw came when Lord Dunmore issued a proclamation in November 1775 that freed all slaves who were willing to bear arms against the rebels. John and Thomas Marshall and their fellow Virginians were now prepared to fight for their independence. Like most white Virginians, they saw no irony in defending both freedom and slavery under the same flag.[53]

ON A WARM SPRING MORNING in May 1775, nineteen-year-old John Marshall arrived by foot at the local militia's first drill in Germantown. He carried a tomahawk and a rifle and wore a beaver hat, hunting shirt, and white-fringed pants that were a faded shade of periwinkle blue. The regiment met on a quiet farm field twelve miles from the county courthouse. When the regiment's captain failed to appear, Marshall, who had practiced with his father, volunteered to lead the drill. He assumed the leadership of the company with a naturalness that seemed remarkable for such a young man. After the drill, Marshall extolled the men to join the newly formed regiment to defend the colony against Lord Dunmore. He described the recent outrages imposed on Bostonians and warned the men that the same could happen in Virginia. Though Marshall had probably never traveled much farther than twenty miles from his home, he already had a sense that Americans shared a common destiny.[54]

Later that summer the Virginia convention met illegally to plan the defense against the British regulars commanded by Lord Dunmore. They formed battalions of minutemen. The most important of these were the Culpeper minutemen, who were charged with the defense of the western frontier in Fauquier County. Marshall quickly volunteered for the Fauquier Rifles, a company of about three hundred sharpshooters, and he was commissioned as a first lieutenant. The company marched under a flag bearing the warning "Don't Tread on Me" and an image of a menacing rattlesnake. The men did not have cannons, bayonets, or uniforms like the British redcoats. Instead, they carried their own tomahawks and muskets. They wore homespun osnaburg hunting shirts embroidered with the words "Liberty or Death," fringed deerskin trousers, and Indian boots. Their rustic appearance left no doubt that this was a homegrown battalion of local farmers and craftsmen.[55]

In September, under the command of his father, who had been commissioned as a major, Lieutenant Marshall and his men marched to Williamsburg where Patrick Henry, the commander of the Virginia militia, was preparing to attack Lord Dunmore's forces in Norfolk, Virginia's largest city, which was sixty miles south, near the mouth of the James River. Norfolk seemed impenetrable. As the city was surrounded by water and marshland, the only way to attack Norfolk would be to storm across the Great Bridge, a narrow 150-yard wooden trestle that crossed the Elizabeth River. At one end was a British fort guarded with a dozen cannons.

In early December, Lieutenant Marshall took part in a lightning-quick raid across the bridge, but they were easily repulsed by a hail of British fire. Five days later, the British launched a poorly executed counterattack. Marshall and the Culpeper sharpshooters positioned on the high ground above the river shot dozens of redcoats as they charged over the bridge. After suffering massive casualties, the British withdrew and ultimately abandoned Norfolk. The Great Bridge was Marshall's first taste of combat and was a signal victory for the Virginians. While the city was now back in the hands of Virginians, the townspeople were Loyalists, and a significant British fleet remained in the harbor. Marshall's regiment fired on the fleet but could do little more to drive them away. On New Year's Day 1776, Lord Dunmore gave the order to the British fleet to bombard the city. Cannon balls ripped apart the great port. It was a terrifying attack. Before the rebels retreated, they joined in the destruction by setting fire to the homes of wealthy Loyalists. Marshall watched helplessly as British and American forces together incinerated Virginia's largest metropolis. Soon black smoke blotted out the sun. Not a single residence was spared.[56] Marshall later described the burning of Norfolk as "one of those ill-judged measures, of which the consequences are felt long after the motives are forgotten."[57]

The Revolutionary War was a formative experience for the young frontiersman. It brought Marshall out of the isolated valley of his rural upbringing and exposed him to the wider world. He experienced firsthand the failure of state government and the need for a strong national government to defend against foreign adversaries. The ghastly image of that once great city reduced to smoldering rubble disabused him of any romantic notion of warfare or revolution. Instead, the young frontiersman, so skilled in the use of a gun, would later pursue the art of diplomacy.

Death and destruction demonstrated to Marshall the essential fragility of the social contract. It was easy for Jefferson to write about revolution since he had never experienced war firsthand. Marshall's military experience taught him to eschew facile ideologies and resort to violence. The elements of Marshall's conservatism were now formed—a belief in ordered liberty and a respect for property, national defense, moderation, and the need for reconciliation.

CHAPTER TWO

A REVOLUTIONARY CAPITAL

I n 1776, Richmond Town was an indistinct village along the James River. At the time, it consisted of a rope factory, a tobacco warehouse, and an open-air market in a pasture along Shockoe Creek. The town had little more than one hundred households, two brick buildings, one homely church, no paved streets, and herds of cows and pigs. Visitors were greeted by an insalubrious odor that rose from a slaughterhouse. Out of six hundred inhabitants, about 40 percent were enslaved, many of whom toiled at the warehouse to earn wages for their masters. There were also about forty free black tradesmen.[1] There were no rich or poor neighborhoods, white or black. Houses were scarcely more than shacks scattered over two hillsides. Only a handful of the whites could afford to own more than three or four slaves, and only seventy households could afford a horse. The town included five barbers, one schoolteacher, two doctors, one chemist, and one lawyer.[2] In short, Richmond was an unlikely location for the capital of the largest state in the confederation when Governor Thomas Jefferson decided to move Virginia's capital there.

Jefferson despised the colonial capital of Williamsburg when he was a student at the College of William & Mary. He was intimately familiar with the governor's palace there. As a student, he was a frequent guest of the royal governor, who was a family friend. In fact, Lord Dunmore retained Jefferson to redesign part of the interior of the palace. Neither man could have imagined how soon fate would cast them on opposite sides of a revolution. But the charm of the college town and the pomp of the royal governor's palace suited neither Jefferson's aesthetic ambitions nor his republican tastes. As governor, Jefferson scribbled a damning indictment of the capital city in a marginal note to himself: "Wmbsgh. nevr. cn. b. grt. __100 y. xprce." (Williamsburg never can be great [after] one hundred years' experience.) Jefferson dreamed of building a "magnificent" classical capital cleansed of fussy Georgian buildings.[3] Privately, Jefferson also hoped that moving the capital to a more central location would reduce the power of the Tidewater gentry.[4] And there was another personal consideration: Richmond was half the distance of Williamsburg from Monticello.[5]

The threat of a British invasion of Williamsburg convinced some legislators to move the capital farther west, and so Jefferson's proposal squeaked through the General Assembly by a single vote in 1779. One might imagine that in the midst of war the last thing on the governor's mind would be constructing a new capital. But Jefferson loved architecture, and his preoccupation with the design of the capital may explain his utter failure to prepare the state's defenses against a British invasion.

AFTER FIGHTING in the fierce but unsuccessful battles at Brandywine, Germantown, and Monmouth, Marshall was promoted to captain in the 11th Virginia Regiment. By the end of 1779, his men had all quit the army. Marshall had to be furloughed while the army tried to enlist more soldiers. Marshall visited his family in Yorktown, where his father was temporarily stationed. Their neighbor was Jaquelin Ambler, who was soon to be the state treasurer. Though the Amblers had lost much of their wealth as a consequence of the war, they were still considered the cream of the colony's social and political elite. Ambler introduced the lanky captain to his three eligible daughters, and Marshall, now twenty-four, instantly fell for the charms of Mary, the youngest, a pale, shy girl of only thirteen who was known as Polly. Marshall impulsively decided he would wed her when she was old enough. First, he needed a suitable profession. Since he had served as an advocate general in the army, he decided to enroll in law school in Williamsburg. It also gave him a convenient excuse to remain near Polly.[6]

Marshall began at William & Mary in the spring of 1780. He attended the lectures of the university's venerable chancellor, George Wythe, the first professor of law in America and a signer of the Declaration of Independence. Wythe, a classics scholar, Virginia attorney general, and judge, trained many of the great Virginia lawyers for a generation, including two of Marshall's friends, James Madison and Bushrod Washington, and the men who would become his rivals, Spencer Roane and Thomas Jefferson.

The basic texts for the course were British: Matthew Bacon's *A New Abridgment of the Law* and Blackstone's *Commentaries*. Blackstone had transformed legal education in Britain by presenting the common law as a unified and rational system of rules. In addition to Blackstone, Marshall read Montesquieu and David Hume. Marshall was particularly influenced by the latter, who rejected Blackstone's idea of a natural law and argued instead that society's rules derive from state power and common experience rather than an abstract idea of justice.[7]

This was Marshall's only exposure to higher education. He worked hard, diligently copying rules almost verbatim from his textbooks, but he had little patience for law school. His mind was restless and his thoughts kept turning to the prospect of marrying Polly Ambler. In the margins of his notebook, he frequently scribbled her name over and over as if it were a mantra. Six weeks into his studies at William & Mary, Marshall abruptly quit when Ambler announced that he was moving his family to the new capital of Richmond. Marshall decided that he, too, would move to

Richmond. But first, he took an examination for the bar and was granted a license to practice law. The license was signed by Governor Jefferson, who would rue the day that Marshall became an attorney.[8]

THE GOVERNMENT IN VIRGINIA dithered for months over how, and whether, to raise more troops. Governor Jefferson had little interest in such mundane subjects. And Marshall soon lost patience with the state's ineffectual government. He decided to rejoin the army in Philadelphia, and he walked the 250 miles from Richmond to there. When he arrived, General Washington could spare no men to defend Virginia, but he sent General Steuben to command the local forces in Virginia. Together, Marshall and Steuben lobbied the Virginia legislature to expand the militia, but Governor Jefferson and his advisers were not sympathetic. The legislature refused to appropriate money for arms and uniforms. Yet by Christmas of 1780, Marshall and Steuben, acting on their own initiative, somehow managed to recruit fifteen hundred volunteers.[9]

That same month, sixteen hundred crack British troops under the command of General Benedict Arnold, who by now had defected to join the British, sailed up the James River to attack Richmond. Marshall and Steuben were stationed in Petersburg with only eight hundred men available to defend the commonwealth. Governor Jefferson had advance warning of the attack, but he gave it no credence. He did not summon the militia, and he waited almost until it was too late to evacuate the city. He and the legislature frantically fled to Charlottesville, leaving behind most of Richmond's terrified residents. Arnold was astonished to find the capital of the largest state in the confederation undefended. Not a single shot was fired at the British. British troops blew up a powder magazine; torched four thousand barrels of tobacco, public buildings, factories, and homes; and looted the governor's extensive wine cellar. Many slaves escaped with Arnold's troops. After the British withdrew, the looting started. People smashed homes and looted their neighbors' furnishings. By then, Marshall and his forces had finally arrived. It took days for them to restore order to the capital.[10]

Jefferson and the General Assembly remained in Charlottesville as Arnold's forces continued to rampage through Virginia. When General Steuben demanded the governor's support to build fortifications to defend the capital, Jefferson procrastinated. Jefferson was too distracted, perhaps still sketching plans for his classical new capital, to worry about a foreign invasion. Besides, he had only a few weeks left before the end of his term in May 1781. He was preparing to leave office just days before the British forces stormed Charlottesville. Instead of focusing on the defense of the temporary capital, Jefferson made arrangements for sending away his family and most of his slaves and horses. He spent the day before the British arrived hiding his personal papers and silver at Monticello. When the British reached the undefended provisional capital, Jefferson took off.[11]

The British spared his home at Monticello, and only a few of Jefferson's more than one hundred slaves escaped. But Jefferson's reputation was badly damaged by neglecting the defense of the commonwealth. The General Assembly, spurred on by Patrick Henry, voted to investigate Jefferson's failure of duty. After General Charles Cornwallis surrendered at the Battle of Yorktown, the General Assembly abandoned the inquiry, but Jefferson never again sought state office.

In February 1781, Marshall resigned from the Continental Army in frustration. He felt thwarted by the state's complete failure to raise sufficient troops for its own defense. His military service taught him that a nation of thirteen independent sovereign states could not defend itself. Marshall's disillusionment with state government led him to conclude that the nation's survival depended on a strong federal government.

As the courts remained closed due to the war, there was little opportunity to practice law. With few prospects for earning a living, Marshall decided to run for the Virginia House of Delegates in the spring of 1782. He was elected to represent Fauquier County, which his father had also represented. There's no evidence that Marshall had political ambitions prior to that, but it gave him a convenient excuse to remain in Richmond, where he could pursue Polly.

At twenty-seven, Marshall did not quite cut a dashing figure as a suitor to the youngest daughter of one of Virginia's leading families. He dressed casually in ill-fitted clothing, and his manners were polite but unrefined. But Marshall's intense dark eyes, winning smile, and genial personality overcame his lack of social graces. He won Polly's heart with poetry and humor. When she turned sixteen, he asked Polly to marry him, and to his shock, she refused. Devastated, he left her home and began riding back to Fauquier County. Almost as soon as Marshall disappeared, Polly abruptly changed her mind and began sobbing hysterically. Her cousin John Ambler galloped after Marshall and persuaded him that she regretted her decision. To prove her sincerity, Ambler gave Marshall a lock of Polly's hair. Marshall returned to Polly's house, and in January 1783, Marshall and Polly were married at the Amblers' home in Richmond. Marshall gave Polly a locket containing that tress of hair, which she wore until the day she died.[12]

As a young lawyer with few clients, the only home Marshall could afford for his bride was a small two-room wood-frame house down the hill from the Amblers. As a wedding gift, Thomas Marshall gave his son three horses and a slave, Robin Spurlock, who would serve as Marshall's manservant his entire life and would become a close confidante as well. Despite his humble origins and awkward manners, Marshall was welcomed into the Ambler family. He quickly adapted to his new circumstances. As the son-in-law of the state treasurer, he settled comfortably into the highest social circles in the capital.[13]

In the House of Delegates, Marshall found common ground with the conservative Virginia Tidewater establishment. The gentry understood the need for a strong military and a centralized national government to protect property and contract rights. Marshall's military experience taught him that the bonds of society are brittle and that men need government to curb their natural passions. He often found himself allied with the Lee family and their circle, especially Richard Henry Lee, as well as his schoolmate James Monroe. Monroe and Marshall enjoyed the theater together and discussed politics over cards in their favorite tavern. During this period, Monroe and Marshall were the closest of friends despite any political differences.[14]

Marshall's colleagues acknowledged his geniality and intellect early in his legislative career. Governor Randolph thought Marshall was "a promising young gentleman of the law."[15] After only a year of service, he was elected to the powerful Council of State. It did not hurt that he had the backing of his influential father-in-law. The council functioned as Virginia's executive branch with the power to approve or disallow any action by the governor. The council was generally reserved for the wise old men in the House of Delegates. Marshall was the youngest man ever chosen, and some of the establishment, such as Edmund Pendleton, the president of the Virginia Supreme Court, grumbled that he should wait his turn. Though Pendleton thought that "young Mr. Marshall . . . is clever," he felt that Marshall "should rather have earned [the position] as a retirement and reward by 10 or 12 years hard service in the Assembly."[16] This frontier soldier seemed like a bit of an upstart to some. Still, no one doubted his intellect and judgment.[17]

One of the first issues to confront the council during Marshall's tenure concerned the power of the governor to remove a justice of the peace, John Price Posey, for misappropriating the assets of an estate he was responsible for overseeing.[18] The governor's action was authorized by an act of the General Assembly, but Marshall argued that the act violated the spirit, if not the letter, of the state's constitution. In Marshall's view, the commonwealth's constitution was supreme over any state statute. The Virginia constitution represented the supreme permanent will of the people rather than merely a transitory act by the people's representatives. His colleagues on the council concurred and issued a strongly worded rebuke to the legislature; the council would not permit the removal of the local magistrate. Some people questioned the power of the council to strike down legislation, but the legislature and the governor ultimately deferred to the council. Though Posey proved unworthy of the council's respect—he was later hanged for burning down a jailhouse and a county clerk's office—the idea that a legislative act is subordinate to a constitution was now established as the foundational principle of judicial review. Marshall would later inscribe that principle into the federal Constitution in his most famous opinion as chief justice, *Marbury v. Madison*.[19]

For the first year of his married life, Marshall struggled to support his wife on the small salary as a legislator. And he had few legal clients who were able to pay. Since becoming the capital, Richmond had quickly doubled its population, but the capital, like the rest of the country, was in a deep recession.[20] Marshall's cousin and fellow legislator Edmund Randolph became the state's governor in 1786, and he sold Marshall his more established law practice, which Randolph had in turn purchased from their cousin Thomas Jefferson after Jefferson became governor. Ironically, Marshall became the proprietor of a law practice started by Jefferson.

Marshall's practice ranged from simple transactions such as leases, deeds, wills, and contracts to complex criminal and civil matters before judges throughout the state. He soon earned a reputation as a talented oral advocate. He could closely tailor an ungainly argument to appear more elegant and seductive. Just as important, he was always generous to his opponents in court and never condescended to juries or judges. He quickly became known as a rising star in the Virginia bar. When James Monroe was considering a legal career, he was strongly advised that "you will find it a disadvantage to come after" Marshall.[21]

During this period after the Revolutionary War and before the Constitution, one fertile area of litigation concerned the indebtedness of many Virginians to British creditors from transactions that had preceded independence. By the end of the war, Virginians owed around $15 million to British creditors (equivalent to around $270 million today). This created a lucrative opportunity for lawyers, and by 1790, Marshall was considered the most successful attorney in Virginia in the defense of debtors.[22]

Under the 1783 Treaty of Paris, state courts were obligated to enforce the rights of British creditors over U.S. debtors. Marshall's willingness to defend debtors from discharging their legal obligations was inconsistent with his strong belief in property rights. But Marshall desperately needed work, and he appreciated the fact that it would have devastated Virginia's economy to repay this staggering amount. Virginia merchants and tobacco farmers who owed money to British subjects felt that they had been unfairly exploited by British traders who had underpaid them for their goods. And many Virginians felt that they should not have to repay debts to the British, who had refused to compensate them for the loss of hundreds of slaves freed by British soldiers.[23] Marshall was a hired gun. His advocacy of debtors' rights was not based on principle; he was equally comfortable representing British creditors seeking to enforce their rights against Virginia debtors. (Needless to say, this latter role was not a popular position in post-Revolutionary Virginia.)

Marshall's most significant client was the estate of Lord Fairfax, the largest landowner in Virginia, who was his father's former employer. During the Revolution, Fairfax was sympathetic to the American cause. Nevertheless, the General Assembly expropriated the property of British Loyalists, including five million acres of Fairfax's land in Virginia's Northern Neck between the Rappahannock and Potomac Rivers. Fairfax, a lifelong bachelor, died in 1781, leaving this property to his nephew, Denny Martin, who lived in Britain. Under Virginia common law, Martin, as a nonresident alien, was ineligible to inherit property, so the property arguably passed to the state. In 1785, the General Assembly confiscated the property in direct contravention of the Treaty of Paris, which guaranteed the property rights of British Loyalists after the war. From England, Martin retained Marshall to defend his property rights in Virginia in a series of cases that stretched on for nearly a quarter of a century.

One of these cases, which would eventually reach the Supreme Court, involved a dispute between Fairfax's estate and a tenant, Joost Hite, concerning the boundaries of Hite's leasehold. Hite's attorneys, including Marshall's law partner and cousin Edmund Randolph, challenged Fairfax's original title, which had been granted by King Charles II. While Marshall lost the case in court, the Virginia Court of Appeals implicitly acknowledged that Fairfax had good title to the rest of his property. By the time the legal question of Fairfax's title reached the Supreme Court two decades later, Marshall would be presiding over it. The Court's eventual decision would be one of the most important in its history.

As Marshall's political and social network grew, he established himself as a bright young man with a command of both the details of the law and oral argument. Within three years of beginning his law practice, Marshall emerged as one of the leading members of the Richmond bar with an active social and political life. He belonged to the Masons, the Formicola's Tavern Club, the Jockey Club, and the Quoit Club. Bit by bit, he acquired wealth and property. His father deeded him property in Fauquier County, and his father-in-law gave him a half-acre lot to build a home on in the Court End neighborhood of Richmond, where other state officers and delegates had settled. Marshall designed a handsome two-story Federal-style brick house. Marshall wanted his home to be a showcase where he could entertain the wealthiest and most powerful men in the state in a relaxed and informal atmosphere. The house featured an exceptionally large dining room that could accommodate as many as thirty guests. Marshall used the room as his law office until a separate brick structure was built behind the house. Once a month he invited all the prominent attorneys in Richmond to meet for dinner and cards. Marshall's new home announced that he had arrived as a significant figure in the social as well as the political life of the capital.²⁴

DESPITE MARSHALL'S SUCCESS, all was not as it appeared. His home life was complicated by the delicate state of Polly's health. Marshall's zest for entertaining and politics was too much for her frail emotional state. In July 1784, Polly gave birth to a son, Thomas, and the birth nearly killed her. She was bedridden for weeks afterward. A daughter, Rebecca, was born in 1786 and died days later. Polly never completely recovered from the loss of her first daughter. When she lost another child the following autumn, she had an emotional collapse. Her hysterical outbursts, which Marshall had first encountered when he proposed to her, now became a regular occurrence. Though Polly would eventually have five healthy sons and one daughter, she lost four children in infancy. For most of their married life, Polly's series of nervous breakdowns, severe migraines, wild mood swings, anxiety, and depression dominated their household. But Marshall devoted himself to her. He assumed most of the household responsibilities that usually fell to women, such as shopping and cleaning the home. Visitors describe his meeting them at the door with a broom and a dustpan. When Polly spent days in bed, Marshall insisted that everyone in the house must speak softly and avoid making any loud noises that could disturb her. Throughout their married life. Polly's emotional health remained a constant concern to him.²⁵

BY 1786, IT WAS APPARENT to Marshall and others that the country could not survive as a loose confederation of thirteen sovereign states with no power to tax or regulate commerce, no executive to enforce its laws, and no courts to adjudicate controversies between states. The nation was gripped by economic crisis. Each state imposed tariffs on the goods of every other state; tobacco shipped from Virginia to New York would be taxed each time it crossed state lines. Commerce was being strangled. States struggled to pay off the mounting interest on their war debt. Politicians responded either by printing paper money intemperately—as they did in Rhode Island—or by raising taxes, as they did in Massachusetts. Both strategies proved disastrous for different reasons, and the resulting controversies affected Marshall's views on the necessity for constitutional reform.

In 1786, the Rhode Island State Assembly was elected on a populist pledge to print paper money. The state issued a staggering quantity of paper money, which it lent at low interest to farmers to pay off their debts. As a result, Rhode Island's economy was inundated with worthless currency. Prices soared. Merchants wanted hard coins and refused to accept paper. To compel merchants to accept the state's paper, the state imposed a penalty of one hundred pounds that could be imposed by a judge without a jury trial. Many merchants preferred to close their shops, go into hiding, or flee the state.[26] Opponents in other states called for expelling Rhode Island from the confederation or dividing the state among her neighbors.[27]

One day John Trevett, a cabinetmaker, went into John Weeden's butcher shop in Newport to buy some beef. Trevett's pockets bulged with crisp bills freshly issued by the state's printing press. Weeden refused to accept Trevett's currency and demanded silver coin instead. Trevett filed an action against Weeden for violating the state's currency law. Weeden's attorney argued that the Rhode Island law was unconstitutional because it denied Weeden his right to a jury trial and that the court had the power to strike down such state statutes. This was a novel argument: Rhode Island had no constitution at that time, and Rhode Island's Royal Charter of 1663 did not mention either a right to a jury trial or the power of courts to review the constitutionality of legislation. Indeed, there was no precedent for courts striking down legislation.

Nonetheless, four of the five judges on the court voted to dismiss the case against Weeden on the grounds that the law was unconstitutional. The Rhode Island Assembly was outraged that judges would presume to strike down their law. After all, judges were appointed by the assembly for one-year terms and could be removed at its pleasure. The assembly retaliated by refusing to reappoint the four judges who voted for dismissal.[28]

Trevett v. Weeden shocked lawyers and the propertied classes throughout the country and had a profound effect on the creation of the American Constitution. First, the Rhode Island Assembly demonstrated that printing paper money with abandon would only create greater economic hardships. Second, by creating a precedent for what became known as "judicial review," the Rhode Island court demonstrated the value of an independent judiciary armed with a constitution that limited the power of government. By punishing the judges, the legislature only reinforced the value of lifetime tenure for judges. The controversy shaped the views of the men who drafted and ratified the Constitution, including John Marshall. For Marshall, the popular movement to deny creditors their rights was a sign of moral as well as political failure. Marshall later wrote of this period that

> [t]he restlessness produced by the uneasy situation of individuals, connected with lax notions concerning public and private faith, and erroneous opinions which confound liberty with an exemption from legal control, produced a state of things which alarmed all reflecting men, and demonstrated to many the indispensable necessity of clothing government with powers sufficiently ample for the protection of the rights of the peaceable and quiet, from the invasions of the licentious and turbulent part of the community.[29]

Trevett v. Weeden rumbled like a warning thunderclap across the nation. That same year, the outbreak of Shays's Rebellion in Massachusetts swept across New England with gale force. In Massachusetts, the legislature, confident that the economy would recover on its own, did nothing to relieve the suffering of the people. Instead, the legislature tried to balance the state budget by imposing onerous property and poll taxes. The taxes forced large numbers of farmers and businesses into foreclosure, and the number of bankruptcies tripled. Impoverished farmers petitioned the legislature and the courts for redress to no avail. Many Boston merchants ignored the gathering storm of protest, determined that they would not be driven out by the mob as the Rhode Island merchants had been.[30]

In the autumn of 1786, Massachusetts farmers surrounded the Northampton County Courthouse armed with muskets, swords, and bludgeons to prevent further foreclosures. That single incident inspired a spontaneous uprising throughout western Massachusetts. Daniel Shays, a farmer outside Amherst and a former officer in the Continental Army, emerged as one of the leaders of the uprising. Shays's Rebellion was aimed against the Boston elite who governed the state without representing the interests of the distant western counties. The rebels were known as Regulators because they wanted to reform the state government. They objected to the influence of moneyed interests in state government and the lack of accountability as much as they opposed the foreclosures on their land. Eventually, up to nine thousand Regulators took up arms. At the request of Governor James Bowdoin, the Continental Congress sent more than a thousand soldiers to suppress the uprising. Shays and his men boldly marched on the federal armory at Springfield. There the militia launched a decisive counterattack in the winter of 1787 and crushed the rebellion. The beleaguered rebels scattered across the barren hills of western Massachusetts. The Massachusetts legislature passed laws requiring that the Regulators be whipped thirty-nine times and imprisoned for twelve months. They imposed capital punishment against the militia officers, including Shays, who joined the uprising or even spoke in defense of it. Eighteen men would be sentenced to death, though most sentences were later reduced.[31]

Shays's Rebellion dramatized the urgency of reforming the confederation. To some, the rebellion was a "godsend" that would push popular

opinion in favor of a strong national government.[32] Others were less sanguine. Washington wrote that "I feel infinitely more than I can express for
the disorders which have arisen." James Madison later commented that
these popular outbreaks threatening landowners and merchants alike
"contributed more to that uneasiness which produced the Constitution,
and prepared the public mind for a general reform" than the impotence of
the confederation.[33]

When news of Shays's Rebellion reached Richmond in January 1787,
Marshall was sickened. "All is gloom," he wrote. He speculated whether
Shays was a British agent sent to overthrow the government or whether it
was an attempted coup by John Hancock and his supporters. Whatever the
cause of the rebellion, "they deeply affect the happiness and reputation of
the United States." And he feared that Shays's Rebellion was only the beginning of the end of the Republic. "These violent, I fear, bloody dissentions,"
he warned, "cast a deep shade over that bright prospect which the revolution in America and the establishment of our free governments had opened
to the votaries of liberty throughout the globe." Ordered liberty was under
threat. Sounding like the great British conservative Whig Edmund Burke,
Marshall concluded that the present unrest may prove "that man is incapable of governing himself" and another revolution was imminent.[34]

Both the assault on the judiciary in Rhode Island and the popular uprising in Massachusetts left a deep imprint on Marshall, whose conservatism
and skepticism of democracy were already apparent in his legislative record. These two incidents reinforced the lesson of Valley Forge: that only a
national government was equipped to secure the well-being of the people.
Marshall, like his colleague James Madison, was convinced that a mere
amendment to the Articles of Confederation would not do. A new federal
constitution must be formed to quiet the unruly passions of the masses.
Marshall believed that reason had to temper passion, that the radical ex-
tremes must yield to the center. And Marshall's conservatism would prove
revolutionary.

CHAPTER THREE

DEBATING THE CONSTITUTION

Purple buds on old English lavender signaled the start of a hot, dry summer. The long drought left fields of withered crops. The James River was low enough for a man on horseback to ford it. On Monday, June 2, 1788, with John Marshall in attendance, the Virginia convention call to ratify the proposed federal Constitution opened at ten a.m. in the hulking capitol designed by Thomas Jefferson. Marshall wore a new pair of breeches, a fresh linen shirt, a handsome new waistcoat, and shiny new shoes, yet still somehow looked characteristically rumpled. Fortunately, he attended more to his preparation than to his appearance. He had closely studied both the *Federalist* and Jefferson's *Notes on the State of Virginia*.[1] He had been elected as a delegate from Richmond, where his election as an outspoken supporter of the federal Constitution was far from assured. Richmond, like most of Virginia, was suspicious of the proposed federal Constitution. Marshall had barely defeated a staunch anti-federalist candidate by eleven votes out of nearly four hundred cast. Despite his controversial views, his local popularity helped push Marshall over the top.[2]

A formidable corps opposed the Constitution, including former governor

Patrick Henry; Marshall's boyhood friend James Monroe; Richard Henry
Lee, a signer of the Declaration of Independence; William Grayson, a prominent war hero and lawyer; and the legal titan George Mason. Marshall's
allies included James Madison, the principal draftsman of the federal Constitution; Edmund Pendleton, president of the Virginia Court of Appeals;
Governor Edmund Randolph; and George Wythe, Marshall's former law
professor at William & Mary. There were also some less well-known legislators supporting the Constitution, such as George Nicholas, Francis Corbin,
and Henry Lee. Anti-federalists, such as Patrick Henry, feared that a powerful federal government would threaten liberty and states' rights; federalists,
such as Marshall, believed that a strong federal government would strengthen
the nation's economy, fortify its borders, and protect property rights against
the popular will of the majority.

Richmond was packed with delegates and curious onlookers. Men of
property usually traveled by private carriage, but the city could not accommodate a large number of them, so some of the gentry were forced to
travel by stagecoach with the middling classes. To accommodate so many
out-of-towners, extra coaches were brought in from Williamsburg and
Fredericksburg, and coaches began arriving a day early.[3] As the delegates
gathered, a cloud of dust hung in the motionless air like a curtain. Behind it
the blazing sun glowed red. A line of carriages drew up to the capitol, and
somber-looking delegates climbed out. Their carriages and dress revealed
the social class of the delegates. Edmund Pendleton arrived in an elegant
phaeton wearing a powdered wig and a silk suit as if he were dressed to
attend Parliament. Most townspeople had never seen any vehicle grander
than a wagon, and many did not own a horse. Inside, the assembly chamber
was crowded and stuffy. There were too few windows for ventilation. In his
design of the building, Jefferson had been more attentive to the exterior appearance of the building than he had been to the interior comfort.[4]

Marshall and Madison were strange bedfellows with contrasting styles of argument. Madison was Jefferson's protégé and rarely acted without first consulting his mentor. At thirty-seven, Madison did not look or sound like a man of any importance. Unlike Marshall, he was painfully shy, dryly intellectual, and socially awkward. He seemed more like a philosophy professor than a politician. He had a pallid complexion, an oversize head stuck onto a short, reedy body, and a thin nasal voice that was barely audible. In this assembly of Virginia's finest, he could be easily overlooked. While Marshall was easygoing and gregarious, Madison was neither popular nor personable. Throughout his life, he was either sickly or hypochondriacal. He was easily exhausted and avoided physical exertion, stress, or travel, even to the Tidewater, where he feared the dampness. In addition to frequent stomach ailments, he suffered from blinding headaches and seizures that were erroneously diagnosed as epileptic fits. In brief, the father of the federal Constitution had a poor one of his own.[5] Given these shortcomings, it is surprising that Madison ever commanded anyone's attention. That he was elected to the Continental Congress and was able to persuade men of greater stature and experience to his point of view can be explained only by the fact that Madison was the most brilliant man in the room.

The Constitutional Convention in Philadelphia was originally called in 1787 for the narrow purpose of suggesting amendments to the Articles of Confederation to be considered by the Confederation Congress. Madison, however, ignored these instructions. He arrived in Philadelphia with a draft of a new constitution based not on the principle of state sovereignty but on the principles of federal supremacy and a separation of powers. The delegates in Philadelphia had no legal authority to consider a new constitution, let alone to propose a process of ratification that bypassed the Confederation Congress and went directly to popular conventions chosen in each state. The Articles of Confederation could be amended only by the Confederation Congress with the approval of all the state legislatures. Madison's proposed constitution provided that it would come into effect if it was approved by nine state conventions—not even nine state legislatures. For these reasons, anti-federalists could argue that Madison's constitution was literally *uncon-stitutional.*

"IT IS UNIVERSALLY UNDERSTOOD," Marshall later wrote, "that the great revolution which established the constitution of the United States, was not effected without immense opposition."[6] At the Virginia Ratifying Convention, it hardly looked like a fair contest: Madison and Marshall did not have the gravitas that men such as Henry or Mason could convey. While Pendleton and Wythe were persuasive speakers, Pendleton was elected president of the convention, and Wythe was chosen as chair of the committee of the whole, so they were both effectively sidelined for much of the convention. If only General Washington were there to defend the Constitution. He was by far the most popular man in Virginia and could have swayed most of the delegates. But Washington's absence was calculated. Everyone, except perhaps John Adams, assumed that Washington would be the first president of the federal government. He did not want to campaign openly for the Constitution because he did not want to appear to be campaigning for himself. (When asked if he was interested in the presidency, Washington coyly replied that "it has no enticing charms, and no fascinating allurements for me." But he added, "[I]t might not be decent for me to say I would refuse to accept or even to speak much about an appointment, which may never take place.")[7] If Virginia failed to join the union, Washington would not be eligible for the presidency. Without Virginia's ratification, the federal Constitution did not stand a chance. Washington was quietly working behind the scenes through Hamilton and Madison to coordinate support for the Constitution around the nation.[8] Marshall spoke only a few times on the floor of the convention, but he privately lobbied the other delegates with persistence and charm.

Jefferson, like Washington, was conspicuous by his absence from the

Virginia Ratifying Convention. He was then the U.S. envoy to Paris and witnessing the unfolding of the French Revolution. Both sides in the debate invoked Jefferson and claimed that if he were present he would be supporting their argument. Jefferson's own views on the Constitution were at best ambivalent. He was alternately hostile, neutral, or cryptic.[9] His initial response to the Constitution was chilly: "I confess there are things in it which stagger all my dispositions to subscribe to what such an Assembly has proposed." He thought that all that was needed were three or four simple amendments to the "good, old and venerable fabric" of the Articles of Confederation; there was no need for a whole new constitution.[10] In his view, a constitution was as superfluous as "setting up a kite to keep the henhouse in order."[11] Later, Jefferson would claim either that he had no opinion—on the single most important issue of his generation—or that he would have supported the Constitution but that he wanted it amended first to add a bill of rights.[12]

It was tempting to think that by adding a bill of rights the proposed Constitution would enjoy broader support. However, there were tactical considerations. Madison and Marshall recognized that in order to amend the Constitution there would have to be another national constitutional convention and then the revised document would have to be resubmitted to the eight states that had ratified before Virginia. This effort could postpone the Constitution indefinitely. Moreover, time was not on their side. By the end of June, the General Assembly would convene in Richmond, and it included more republicans who were hostile to the Constitution.[13] For these reasons, Marshall and Madison believed that the Constitution must be ratified first and then a bill of rights could be added later.

On the second day, the convention, now overflowing the capitol building with nearly 170 delegates, was convened at eleven a.m. in a more spacious building nearby that had been erected by the Chevalier Quesnay de Beaurepaire and modeled after the French Royal Academy of Sciences in Paris. In the Francophile style, it was pretentiously christened l'Académie des États-Unis de l'Amérique and was intended to foster arts and sciences. Here the fiercely independent Virginians debated their national constitution in a building dedicated to importing the ideas of the French Enlightenment at precisely the moment that France was descending into chaos.[14]

The air was heavy with the scent of honeysuckle and acrimony. The issue presented to the delegates on the second day was whether delegates could propose amendments to the Constitution before they voted on it. Patrick Henry argued that the Constitution was fatally flawed, that it "squints toward monarchy."[15] Against Henry's high-flown oratory, Madison, Marshall, and their allies carefully focused on one clause at a time, which played to Marshall's legal talent.[16]

Madison's intellect was breathtaking, but his speaking style tried the patience of the other delegates. He appeared unprepared and spontaneous when he rose to speak. He nervously shifted his weight back and forth from one foot to the other as he glanced down at a few scribbled notes hidden in the hat he clutched in his left hand. Madison was ill with the "bilious indisposition" that he frequently suffered from during stressful periods. He could barely raise his voice to be heard. But it hardly mattered. Even at the peak of health, Madison could not match the rhetorical heft of Henry. Fortunately, Madison could rely upon others, including Marshall.[17]

On the third day of their deliberations, Henry rose to lay out his broad argument against the Constitution as a whole. Virginia's most famous radical now fiercely defended the status quo. He argued that the people were tired of change. They were not demanding a radical new form of government. "Was the real existence of the country threatened, or was this preceded by a mournful progression of events? This proposal of altering our Federal Government is of a most alarming nature," he warned his fellow Virginians. "You ought to be extremely cautious, watchful, jealous of your liberty; for instead of securing your rights, you may lose them forever."[18]

When Henry spoke of "liberty," he was talking about more than a mere abstraction. Just as the federalists argued that a national government would best conserve the rights of landowners and creditors against popular uprisings like those in Rhode Island and Massachusetts, the anti-federalists were also concerned about how best to protect their property rights—in particular, their rights to hold slaves. "Liberty" to Henry included the liberty to enslave others. Though the word "slavery" rarely appeared in any ratification debates, Henry bluntly warned that if the federalists succeed, "[t]hey'll free your niggers!" Henry's outburst was discreetly excised from the records of the ratification debate.[19] Patrick Henry, the patriot who famously said, "Give me liberty or give me death," saw no inconsistency in opposing tyranny over white Americans in defense of slavery over others.

Marshall waited a week before responding to Henry's bombastic assault. He stood before the delegates in his customary dress, a wrinkled summer suit that hung limply on his tall, narrow frame. His manner of speaking was as casual and offhand as his dress and contrasted sharply with his piercing logic. When he spoke, he often shook one arm awkwardly as if he were scolding his listeners, or he would raise both arms over his head like a preacher calling on the heavens to punish the wicked. Other times he would lean so far forward into his audience that he appeared to be toppling over and had to grab hold of a chair for support. As his argument reached a crescendo, he would be so transported by his own words that he would screech in a high-pitched voice that jangled people's nerves. Yet, despite his careless dress, gawky manner, and sometimes shrill voice—much like those of another frontiersman, Abraham Lincoln—Marshall's eloquence and his dramatic flair transported his audience. Listening to Marshall, people could excuse his unceremonious appearance. He appealed to their intellect with such clarity and respect that even his opponents praised his arguments.[20] One of the leading anti-federalists, James Monroe, wrote to Jefferson that Marshall's "perspicuity and force were greater than ever."[21]

Marshall focused on two principal clauses: the president's powers as commander in chief under Article II and the authority of the federal courts under Article III. He stressed the need for a strong central government to defend the country. "Protection in time of war is one of its principal objects . . . [A] defenseless country cannot be secure." He warned the delegates, "The powers of Europe are jealous of us," and that "[i]f we invite them by our weakness to attack us, will they not do it?" His experiences in the Revolutionary War had proved to Marshall that the national army could not rely upon the states to provide voluntary support. "The inability of Congress, and the failure of the States to comply with the Constitutional requisitions, rendered our resistance less efficient than it might have been." The delegates gathered in Richmond needed no reminder that only seven years earlier British troops had burned the capital city and chased the General Assembly to Charlottesville.[22]

When the anti-federalists charged that Congress could pass laws that infringed on the rights of Virginians, Marshall asserted that if Congress adopted a law contrary to the Constitution a supreme court "would not consider such a law as coming under their jurisdiction. They would declare it void." Following the Rhode Island court's decision in *Trevett v. Weeden* that struck down a law denying a right to a jury trial, Marshall affirmed the principle of judicial review as a central feature of the federal Constitution. Though nowhere in the Constitution did the Framers mention judicial review, Marshall said such powers were implied. In essence, Marshall anticipated his own opinion asserting the power of judicial review in *Marbury v. Madison*.[23]

As the ratification debate dragged on, Marshall entertained many of the delegates in his nearby home with punch and ices. He would sometimes drop in on the delegates after dinner at one of the popular local taverns, usually Formicola's or the Swan, where a quart of Madeira cost only six shillings. Marshall amused them with his stories as he had amused his comrades at Valley Forge. Marshall understood that building personal relationships was essential to winning people's confidence. While Madison was the master architect of the Constitution, Marshall was a more effective salesman. Delegates would much prefer sharing a glass of Madeira with the gregarious Marshall than a pint of ale with Madison. Marshall targeted anyone he thought might be persuaded. The delegates from the Kentucky territory, for example, were still on the fence until Marshall convinced them that the Constitution would protect their property rights and open up the frontier for development.[24] By the end of June, Marshall's steady lobbying began to pay off as more and more delegates declared in favor of the draft.

On June 24, Patrick Henry made one last valiant effort to kill the Constitution. He gave one of the most passionate speeches of his career, opposing the document as an invitation to tyranny. It occurred during a swelling storm that pummeled the meeting place with ferocious gales and booming thunder, which rattled doors and windows and unnerved the delegates. As bolts of lightning illuminated the darkened chambers, Henry concluded his arguments against the Constitution with a dire warning.[25]

> I see the awful immensity of the dangers with which it is pregnant. I see it. I feel it . . . When I see beyond the horizon that bounds human eyes, and look at the final consummation of all human things, and see those ethereal mansions reviewing the political decisions and revolutions which, in the progress of time, will happen in America, and the consequent happiness or misery of mankind, I am led to believe that much of the account . . . will depend on what we now decide . . . We have it in our power to secure the happiness of one half of the human race. Its adoption may involve the misery of the other hemisphere.[26]

Henry's rant was in vain. The next day, the convention rejected his motion to ratify the Constitution only on the condition that some forty amendments be added to the seven articles that made up the original constitution.

Two days later, the Constitution was adopted by a razor-thin margin, 89 to 79. Proponents and opponents accepted the outcome with magnanimity and grace. "There was no bonfire illumination &c," Monroe reported. "[T]he opposition would have not only express'd no dissatisfaction, but have scarcely felt any at it, for they seemed to be governed by principles elevated highly above circumstances so trivial and transitory in their nature."[27]

According to Marshall, a critical number of delegates were persuaded in the end that with General Washington as the presumed chief executive they had nothing to fear. Conversely, if Virginia failed to join her sister states, the union would most likely be led by a northerner, possibly John Adams.[28] The vote to ratify the Constitution was, in part, a vote for Washington against Adams. The delegates appointed a committee to draft a list of recommended amendments to guarantee the rights of individuals and states. The committee included both Marshall and Madison. Within the week, Marshall and Madison drafted what became the First, Third, Fourth, Fifth, and Eighth Amendments to the Constitution. Though Marshall was never credited, he was as much the father of our Bill of Rights as Madison.

Though Madison, Pendleton, Wythe, and Edmund Randolph all deserve enormous credit, Marshall's role in winning ratification was critical. Not only had Marshall triumphed in these debates, but he had succeeded while maintaining his friendship with Henry and Monroe. He was relatively unknown beyond the narrow confines of Richmond when he entered the convention; he emerged weeks later as one of the national leaders of an inchoate and as yet unnamed political party. If Marshall had quit public life at that point, he would still deserve to be remembered as a champion of the federal Constitution.

Henry warned the delegates that Marshall was promulgating "a revolution as radical as that which separated us from Great Britain."[29] He was right about that. Marshall's defense of property rights, federal supremacy, and national self-defense labeled him a conservative, but his conservatism would prove more progressive than Henry's defense of states' rights. Henry feared that slaveholding could not survive a federal union, that the power of the states would be supplanted by Congress, and that the federal Supreme Court would always have the final word. Years later, Marshall's dynamic interpretation of the Constitution would prove that Henry's fears were well-founded.

CHAPTER FOUR

SLAVES AND HYPOCRITES

After the Constitution's ratification in 1788, Marshall's friends and colleagues urged him to run for the new Congress, but he resisted. The newly elected President Washington nominated him to be the U.S. attorney for Virginia, and the Senate approved his nomination even before Marshall was aware of it. But Marshall politely declined the appointment. He had a growing family, a sickly wife, and a burgeoning law practice that included some of the most prominent figures in Virginia. He had no interest in sacrificing his income or moving his family to Williamsburg or Charlottesville, where the federal courts met. Power and fame held no temptation for him. Marshall was content practicing law in a provincial capital like Richmond.[1]

In 1792, Hamilton again urged Marshall to run for Congress, and again Marshall declined. Marshall's popularity worried Jefferson. Though Jefferson was now secretary of state, he viewed Marshall as a rival for power. Jefferson confided to Madison, "I think nothing better could be done than to make [Marshall] a judge."[2] Words that Jefferson would no doubt later regret.

Marshall's professional success as a lawyer enabled him to avoid the more common route to wealth and influence in eighteenth-century Virginia as a slaveholding planter.[3] Still, slavery was an inescapable fact, and Marshall could not avoid involvement in that institution both personally and professionally. Managing a growing household without modern conveniences required a household staff. Marshall owned between seven and sixteen household slaves at any time, which was slightly more than the average household in Richmond had.[4] Nearly half the population of Richmond was black, and more than 90 percent of them were slaves.[5]

Virginians of Marshall's generation saw no contradiction in their fierce advocacy of equality and their dependence on slavery. Slavery made it possible to regard all white males as equal regardless of their social status. Tradesmen saw themselves as the social equals of wealthy plantation owners because they were both white. Unlike Europe, where class identity divided rich and poor and posed a constant threat to the social order, in eighteenth-century Virginia, the underclass was all black and mostly enslaved.[6]

The general condition of household slaves in a city such as Richmond was less constrained and less violent than that of most plantation slaves. Though they were still exploited and sold as chattel, urban slaves possessed certain freedoms unknown on plantations. Slaves in Richmond typically were able to enter and leave the master's property and were not subject to an overseer's capricious cruelty. Though urban slaves could not marry legally, they often lived together as married couples in their own houses that were no different from the houses that white working-class families lived in. Urban slaves could cultivate small plots of land where they raised vegetables, which they could sell for their own profit with permission from their masters. Slaves in Richmond often worshiped alongside their masters in church. Some slaves were educated to read and write, and some mastered a trade. Masters might permit their slaves to stay out late in the evenings and attend social events such as the theater. However, state law prohibited any blacks, free or enslaved, from visiting taverns, playing cards, gambling, or attending cockfights or horse races. Slaves who violated these prohibitions faced thirty lashes.[7] In this perverse way, the law held slaves to a higher moral standard than their masters and mistresses.

Marshall acknowledged that slavery was a terrible "evil" and that "nothing portends more calamity & mischief to the southern states." Yet he distinguished himself from most of his fellow Virginians, who "seem to cherish the evil and to view with immovable prejudice & dislike every thing which may tend to diminish it."[8] Marshall, like most southern federalists, opposed the slave trade, supported manumission, and wanted to outlaw discrimination and unnecessary regulations on African Americans.[9] As a member of the Supreme Court, he forcefully condemned the slave trade as a crime against natural law. Yet, paradoxically, Marshall upheld the right to own slaves in the slave states.[10]

Marshall was not free of racial prejudice, and he did enjoy the comforts that his household slaves provided to him. Marshall's attitude toward African Americans was paternalistic. He viewed his slaves as family members who needed his guidance and support. There is no evidence that Marshall ever separated families or mistreated or whipped his slaves—as Thomas Jefferson did.[11] It appears that Marshall treated his slaves humanely, and on at least one occasion, he paid for a doctor to care for a slave woman who was ill.[12]

But, like most white Virginians, Marshall feared what might happen if four hundred thousand slaves were suddenly emancipated. In 1791, slaves successfully revolted in a bloody revolution in Saint-Domingue. The very real threat of a race war was a constant fear of white Virginians. In August 1800, a slave named Gabriel Prosser, who worked as a blacksmith on a plantation just north of Richmond, conspired to lead hundreds of lightly armed slaves in an uprising to seize Richmond. The insurgents planned to kidnap the governor, James Monroe, and hold the capitol in exchange for their freedom. Another slave disclosed Gabriel's conspiracy only hours before the attack was to begin. Monroe sent the militia to crush Gabriel's army. At least seventy slaves were prosecuted, and dozens were hanged. Monroe's brutality toward the slaves threatened to become an issue in the 1800 presidential election.

Jefferson worried that hanging so many slaves would hurt his electoral chances in the North, and he persuaded Monroe to cease the executions. Calm was restored by year's end, but Gabriel's army had confirmed the worst fear of white Virginians—that there was no possibility of racial coexistence.[13] In response to Gabriel's conspiracy, republicans in the Virginia legislature proposed sweeping measures to crack down on the freedoms of all blacks. Federalists, including Marshall, opposed these measures.[14]

Marshall thought that ultimately the system of slavery must come to an end and that the federal government must take the lead, but he preferred a gradual end to slavery rather than a sudden and possibly explosive emancipation. Marshall believed that emancipated blacks would be best off if they were sent to Africa with support from the federal government. To this end, Marshall became active in the Society for the Colonization of Free People of Color of America, which was established in 1816. He founded the Virginia Society for Colonization and served as its president from 1827 until his death. When the society became insolvent in the 1830s, Marshall pledged five thousand dollars to support it. He hoped that a process of African colonization would provide an avenue for encouraging emancipation and giving slaves some restitution to help reclaim their lives. Many white Virginians defended slavery precisely because they feared the vengeance that millions of freed slaves might inflict against them. For just that reason, Marshall believed that African colonization offered a way to remove an obstacle to emancipation.[15] Of course, most slaves had no ties to Africa and had no reason to leave their homeland for a foreign country. Though today it seems unthinkable that the United States would have deported free blacks to Africa, to Marshall and his contemporaries it seemed just as unthinkable that whites would ever accept blacks as their social equals. More than 150 years after emancipation, it remains to be seen if Marshall was wrong.

Though Marshall did nothing as a member of the Virginia General Assembly to end slavery—that would have been a fool's errand in the 1780s— he did support some reforms that allowed masters to manumit (free) their slaves and offered emancipation to any slave who served in the U.S. army as a substitute for a white Virginian. In 1783, Marshall voted to define a state "citizen" to include all free persons, white or black, who were born in Virginia.[16] It may reflect on Marshall's own values that in 1832 his son Thomas, as a member of the General Assembly, courageously fought for emancipation.[17] Most significant is that Marshall believed in the federal power over the states while knowing that one day the federal government might choose to end slavery. Despite his hope for ending slavery, Marshall did not manumit any of his slaves until after his death, and then he offered freedom to his trusted valet, Robin Spurlock, only if he would settle in Liberia. (Faced with the choice of deportation or servitude, Spurlock chose to remain with Marshall's daughter to the end of his life.)

The relationship between Marshall and Spurlock was remarkable, and it seems likely that Spurlock made a strong impression on Marshall's views about African Americans and slavery. Marshall trusted Spurlock to manage his household during his long absences. When Marshall was home, the two men often shared chores. Contemporary accounts describe Marshall going to the market dressed in wrinkled, oversize clothing, his hair wildly askew, closely followed by the meticulous Spurlock. Spurlock was famous in Richmond for his elegant outfits and spirited attitude. He wore well-fitted, brightly colored silk trousers and matching suits with bright yellow socks, flamboyant hats, and patterned scarves. Sometimes he added feathers or gold braids to his eye-catching costumes. Spurlock was graceful and proud while Marshall appeared gawky and informal. When they returned from the market, Marshall would insist on carrying his own basket of groceries. Townspeople quipped about which one looked more like a famous attorney.[18]

OVER THE COURSE of his practice as a lawyer, Marshall handled a few cases concerning slavery. In three of these cases, he defended the slaves pro bono. Why would a provincial lawyer and politician accept cases without pay that would bring him into conflict with his affluent neighbors and clients? Marshall acted out of principle and against his own economic self-interest. But how did he come to represent enslaved clients? The most likely explanation is that Spurlock, who was a leader in the Richmond slave community, sought Marshall's help on behalf of these slaves. For a slave to ask his master to defend another slave must have seemed odd, but if this is what happened, it is some measure of Spurlock's relationship with Marshall.[19]

Three of these slave cases related to mixed-race children born to an Indian woman and a slave father. Both Virginia law and Indian tribal law regarded these offspring as full-blooded Indians and therefore free. But some slaveowners continued to enslave these children. Marshall sponsored a law in the General Assembly to punish anyone trying to sell such mixed-race offspring as slaves.

The status of a mixed-race child was a particularly sensitive subject for white slaveholders, who often fathered children with slaves. The three cases Marshall brought established judicial precedents for defending the liberty of these mixed-race children.[20]

Marshall also defended an African American woman, Angelica Barnett, who was wrongly accused of murder. In 1793, Barnett was a free black woman living in Richmond. One night a white man, Peter Franklin, broke into her home to look for his runaway slave while she was asleep. Franklin assaulted her and threatened to bludgeon her in front of her terrified children. She grabbed an ax and struck him in the head, killing him. Barnett was quickly tried, convicted, and sentenced to death. White and black women of Richmond, including Marshall's wife, Polly, vigorously protested. Marshall, perhaps urged by Polly and Spurlock, agreed to organize the leading attorneys in Richmond to petition Governor Henry Lee for a pardon. Marshall's efforts succeeded, and Barnett was freed a day before she was scheduled to hang.[21]

In another case that began in 1799, Marshall fought for the manumission of four hundred slaves. John Pleasants, a Quaker slaveholder who died in 1771, wanted to free his slaves when they reached the age of thirty, but Virginia law at that time would not permit it. So in his will Pleasants left his slaves to his heirs with the condition that if manumission ever became legal his slaves should be set free. After Virginia legalized private manumission in 1782, Pleasants's son and executor, Robert Pleasants, freed his slaves in deference to his father's intentions. John Pleasants's other heirs—in particular, his daughter Mary, who had inherited three hundred of her father's slaves—refused to comply with the manumission clause. Robert Pleasants retained Marshall to file suit in the Virginia High Court of Chancery to force the other heirs to honor Pleasants's will and manumit their slaves. It was an uphill challenge. The chief obstacle Marshall faced was that the will violated the notorious "rule against perpetuities," which limits a person's ability to tie up a future interest in property beyond the length of a particular individual's life plus twenty-one years. Since John Pleasants died not knowing if, or when, the Virginia legislature might permit manumission, the provision clearly violated the rule. The case came before Marshall's former law professor, Chancellor George Wythe.

Marshall made a novel argument that the rule against perpetuities should not apply because the slaves were not "property" for purposes of this case; they were, in fact, the beneficiaries of Pleasants's will. Chancellor Wythe concurred and ordered that all four hundred slaves be freed. This was a stunning but short-lived victory. Pleasants's heirs appealed, and Wythe's ruling was reversed by the Virginia Supreme Court of Appeals. The slaves remained in bondage.[22]

However, Marshall did profit, albeit indirectly, from transactions involving slaves. One of Marshall's most significant cases concerned Martha Wayles Jefferson, the wife of Thomas Jefferson. It began when Richard Randolph, one of Marshall's cousins, and John Wayles, Jefferson's father-in-law, contracted in 1772 for a consignment of 280 slaves. The slaves would be shipped from Africa aboard the *Prince of Wales*, a British slaver. The consignment was arranged and financed by a British trading company, Farell & Jones.

Before Randolph died, he was facing financial ruin. Seeking to protect his estate from his creditors, he transferred whatever property he had left to his heirs. After Randolph's death in 1795, Farell & Jones sued Randolph's estate for the nearly ten thousand pounds owed for the slaves (about two million dollars today). Marshall successfully defended Randolph's bankrupt estate from the British creditor.[23]

Unable to collect from Randolph's estate, Farell & Jones next sought a judgment against Wayles's estate for the debt owed by Randolph. In response, the executors of Wayles's estate, Martha Wayles Jefferson and her brother-in-law, sued Randolph's estate, asking the court to set aside the transfers of Randolph's property to his heirs so that this amount could be used to indemnify Wayles's estate for the debt owed to Farell & Jones. The case pitted Marshall and the Randolph estate against Jefferson, and it dragged through state and federal courts for many years.[24]

Marshall eventually lost the argument on behalf of Randolph's estate in the High Court of Chancery, and he appealed to the Virginia Supreme Court of Appeals. There he crafted a winning argument that Randolph's heirs should not be burdened by the debt owed to Farell & Jones based on British common law.[25] Marshall's legal victory left the Wayles estate—and by extension, Jefferson—indebted to British slavers for millions of dollars.[26] Jefferson bitterly complained that the British merchants had enslaved Virginia planters with "debts that had become hereditary from father to son for many generations so that the planters were a species of property annexed to certain mercantile houses in London."[27] But Jefferson's bondage to his family's debt was only a metaphor; his family's profit from the sale of 280 souls was a harsh reality.

Marshall's role in depleting Martha Jefferson's inheritance may be seen as rough justice when one considers that Jefferson's father took control of the Randolph estate at Tuckahoe, where Marshall's grandmother was raised. From Jefferson's perspective, Marshall's victory was just another wound in his long struggle with Marshall. The earliest wound may have come when Marshall married Polly, who was the daughter of Jefferson's first love, Rebecca Lewis Burwell. Burwell's marriage to Jaquelin Ambler was a crushing blow to the young Jefferson.[28] From Jefferson's point of view, Marshall seemed to be continually encroaching on both his personal life and his political projects. The outcome of the Wayles litigation added more toxin to the already poisoned relations between cousins.

Neither Marshall nor Jefferson was innocent of profiting from slavery, but while Marshall engaged his slaves as members of his own household, Jefferson averted his gaze from the cruel source of his own wealth. At Monticello, for instance, he designed his house and arranged his household to minimize encounters with his own slaves. When dining at home, Jefferson preferred to serve himself from a dumbwaiter rather than allow slaves in his presence.[29] He closed his eyes to the egregious contradictions in his own slaveholding. Jefferson withdrew from people and found comfort in elegant abstractions; Marshall, by contrast, leaned in to embrace the muddle of humanity.

Marshall, like Jefferson, was guilty of hypocrisy—fighting for liberty in the Revolutionary War while denying it to others. But Marshall engaged with real people in real-life situations. If Jefferson lived his life in poetry, Marshall lived his in prose. For him, the struggle for human dignity was experienced in the cases he won, in his support for African colonization, in his defense of the federal power to end slavery, and in the humanity and respect he showed to the least among us in his quotidian routines.

CHAPTER FIVE

INNOCENCE LOST

alf a world away from the serenity of Marshall's Virginia, events in France were taking place that would change the trajectory of his life and bring him to national prominence. To understand how Marshall became the lion of the Supreme Court, it is necessary to understand how the French Revolution polarized the United States and defined our political parties. These events would also set Marshall on a collision course with his cousin Jefferson.

In July 1789, a little more than two months after President-elect Washington took the oath of office for the first time in the temporary national capital, New York City, the long-simmering French Revolution erupted. Most Americans welcomed news of the fall of the Bastille and the establishment of a republic, smug in the confidence that their French cousins were following in their footsteps. Americans assumed that France would establish a liberal republic modeled after the United States. "We were all strongly attached to France," Marshall recalled, "scarcely any man more strongly than myself. I sincerely believed human liberty to depend in a great measure on the success of the French Revolution."[1]

No man better exemplified the connection between the American and French revolutions than General Lafayette, whose leadership in the Continental Army had been critical to the success of the American Revolution. Lafayette had returned to France after the American Revolution. He became the leader of his own party of moderate reformers known as the Fayettistes. The morning after the fall of the Bastille, the French National Assembly appointed Lafayette commander of the National Guard to maintain order. As a tribute to his former commander in chief, Lafayette sent Washington the key to the fallen Bastille, which Washington proudly hung on the wall of the presidential mansion in New York City. Americans celebrated the French Revolution with parades, toasts, and fireworks. Gentlemen demonstrated their support by singing "La Marseillaise" and wearing cockades with the French tricolors. They wore long trousers in place of their conventional silk knee breeches to emulate the radical French working class.[2]

Even before the Bastille was overrun, Jefferson, who became the U.S. minister to France in 1784, disregarded diplomatic protocol to support the Fayettistes. He encouraged them to remove Louis XVI, the United States' principal ally, and seize power. Jefferson was either disingenuous or uninformed in his reports back to Congress. In 1786, as the rumblings of revolution in France were already audible, Jefferson blithely reassured Abigail Adams in a letter that "here we have singing, dancing, laughter, and merriment. No assassination, no treasons, rebellions nor other dark deeds." Jefferson acknowledged that there were "some little bickerings between the king and his parliament," but he did not foresee any rebellion.[3] To Washington, he predicted in 1788 that "the present disquiet will end well."[4] Even after the fall of the Bastille and the increasing disorder of the Paris mob, Jefferson maintained a sanguine view of the revolution's prospects. He reported to Secretary of State John Jay that stories of mass executions and tumult were wildly exaggerated. He dismissed rumors that the French royal family and the aristocracy were in danger. According to Jefferson, only three people were killed in all the rioting that followed the fall of the Bastille. (In fact, at least one hundred people were killed, and more than seventy were injured.[5]) "Tranquility is now restored to the capital," Jefferson wrote. "[T]he shops are again opened; the people resuming their labors, and if the want of bread does not disturb the peace, we may hope a continuance of it."[6]

Jefferson was beguiled, as he often was, by his ideology. His rose-colored reports to Congress kept American policymakers ignorant of the extremism of the French revolutionaries.[7] Only a month after the fall of the Bastille, Jefferson returned to the states still bubbling with enthusiasm for the revolution. In his last letter from Paris, he wrote to Thomas Paine that order had been established throughout France: "I think there is no possibility now of any thing's hindering their final establishment of a good constitution, which will in its principles and merit be about a middle term between that of England and the United States."[8] Jefferson did not anticipate danger and therefore was not prepared for the tumultuous events that engulfed Europe any more than he had prepared Virginia for attack by the British when he was governor. Later, as secretary of state, he continued to misjudge the character of the French Revolution with dire consequences for the United States.

BY OCTOBER 1789, events began to spin out of control in France. A bad drought that summer had produced a poor harvest. Bread prices soared from eight to more than fourteen sous a loaf in a few months. Bread was the main source of calories in the diet of most working families, and a typical French laborer consumed about three pounds of bread daily. A loaf of bread now cost a worker more than half the average daily wage of about twenty or thirty sous.[9] As a consequence, families starved, hungry mobs rioted across France, and neither the police nor the army could keep order. Farmers and landholders suspected of hoarding food were attacked, and homes were looted and burned. Local governments were displaced by citizen councils. People in authority were attacked and sometimes brutally murdered. A mob tortured and killed one of the king's highest official agents, Joseph Foullon de Doué. They beheaded him after failing to hang him, stuck his head on a pike, and gleefully paraded their bloody trophy through Paris. When the ugly crowd surged past the home of the newly arrived U.S. minister, Gouverneur Morris, he gasped, "Gracious God, what a people!"[10]

In the months that followed, Louis XVI agreed to reign as a "citizen king" in a new constitutional monarchy. Over the next couple of years, an uneasy peace returned to Paris as Louis consented to a wide range of reforms.[11] The royal family regained popularity, and the aristocracy was largely unaffected. When a commoner at the Comédie-Française threw an apple at Lafayette's sister-in-law, she blithely joked that it was "the first fruit of the Revolution that has so far come into my hands."[12]

There was no sense of the impending cataclysm until June 1791, when the royal family was arrested trying to escape France and was forcibly brought back to Paris on the order of General Lafayette. A new assembly convened that was dominated by a faction known as the Girondists, which wanted to liberate all of Europe from monarchy. The previous summer, the Holy Roman emperor and the Prussian king had issued a joint declaration at Pillnitz calling on France to restore the freedom of the French royal family and warning that their fate was a "common concern" to Austria and Prussia. Even though the Girondists supported the monarchy, they saw the Declaration of Pillnitz as a military threat, and in April the National Assembly, in a spasm of bravado, declared war on Austria and Prussia.

Preoccupied as it was with internal strife, France was unprepared for war. The army lacked arms and uniforms. Officers deserted rather than swear an oath that omitted any mention of the king. Soldiers mutinied. French defenses disintegrated as Austrian and Prussian forces easily pushed across the border and marched toward Paris. The capital panicked. Austria and Prussia threatened to destroy Paris if it resisted invasion or if members of the royal family were harmed. Violent demonstrations erupted, and a more radical faction known as the Commune seized power. The National Assembly voted to imprison the king and remove him from power. He was stripped of his title and would be known only as Louis Capet. In response, other European powers withdrew their diplomats from France and shuttered their embassies. Aristocrats, already stripped of their titles and lands, now fled, but many were captured and arrested along with members of the clergy who refused to swear allegiance to the new regime. Persistent rumors of royalist plots stoked the public's fear and anger. On September 2, a mob broke into the Prison de l'Abbaye and brutally massacred twelve hundred aristocrats and priests whose crimes were either their titles or their clerical robes.[13] Despite all this bloodshed, Jefferson continued to defend the revolutionaries and minimize the loss of human life in his dispatches to Washington.

On January 21, 1793, at the Place de la Révolution, the king was guillotined before tens of thousands of his former subjects. This began a reign of repression and terror unlike anything Europe had seen before. Tens of thousands of people, mostly without privilege, title, or priestly collars, were drowned, shot, or guillotined on unsubstantiated charges of betraying the nation.

NEWS THAT THE KING of France had been executed reached Philadelphia just as President Washington was preparing for his second inaugural in March 1793. Most Americans were shocked by the execution. Unlike George III, who was despised as a corrupt tyrant, Louis XVI was beloved in the United States as an indispensable ally of the American Revolution. Louis' birthday was even celebrated as a national holiday.[14]

As Washington had predicted, Louis's decision to aid the American Revolution had contributed to France's insolvency, and the consequent tax increases helped fuel the French Revolution. Washington, unlike Jefferson, recognized that the French Revolution had unleashed terrible and uncontrollable forces.[15] On the day of his second inauguration, these events were not far from his mind. The president, dressed in a new black velvet suit, silk stockings, and diamond knee buckles, took his seat at the front of the Senate chamber in Philadelphia. Behind him hung twin portraits of Louis XVI and Marie Antoinette, which someone had discreetly covered with a cloth.[16]

After a short ceremony and an inaugural address consisting of four sentences, President Washington returned to his home in Mount Vernon for a much-needed break. He was exhausted from four frustrating years in office. At sixty-one, he was in continual pain from bone loss in his jaw and rheumatism. He had grown fat and old in office and suffered from poor hearing and a failing memory. He doubted the wisdom of seeking a second term, but the leaders of both parties begged him to stay on to consolidate the new government.[17] Soon after arriving at Mount Vernon in 1793, he received word from Secretary of State Jefferson that following Louis' execution, Britain had expelled the French ambassador, and France had responded by declaring war against England and the Netherlands.

Washington was stunned. France, England, and the Netherlands were all important trading partners for the United States. But the United States owed a moral and financial debt to France. Washington knew that without the arms, talent, and fleet that France had provided, his army would have been crushed. France expected to be paid for the ammunition, guns, uniforms, and cannons they had provided, but Congress did not have sufficient funds to discharge the debt of $5.6 million (more than $130 million today).[18] Legally, the United States had bound itself by the Treaty of Alliance to defend France. It would be a matter of principle to a man like Washington to honor his debts.

But the United States had signed a peace treaty with Britain and now depended on Britain for three-quarters of its total world trade. It had no cause to go to war against its largest trading partner.[19] Moreover, the United States could not possibly defend itself against Britain. The United States might be bound to defend France from an armed attack, but in this instance, France had declared war first. And there was also the question of whether the United States was bound by the Treaty of Alliance to defend the present government of France or the ancien régime of Louis XVI, whose head his former subjects had severed.

Washington concluded that the United States must remain neutral.[20] Contemporary international law gave neutral states the right to trade with belligerent states so long as they did not ship contraband goods such as arms and munitions.[21] Washington wrote to Secretary of State Jefferson that the United States must "use every means in its power" to prevent its citizens from "embroiling us with either of those powers by endeavoring to maintain a strict neutrality."[22] But the question remained what "strict neutrality" would look like. Washington rushed back to Philadelphia to meet with his cabinet.

The cabinet was divided between Jefferson, the leading republican, and Treasury Secretary Alexander Hamilton, the leading federalist. In the absence of any formal political parties, these terms referred to loosely defined networks of like-minded people. Jefferson and Madison, for example, shared many republican principles, just as Hamilton and Marshall agreed on most federalist principles. Rather than speak of a "Republican Party," Jefferson might refer to "republican interests" as being distinct from those of the federalists, whom he excoriated as either "Tories," "monocrats," or even "monarchists."[23]

After the execution of Louis XVI and the bloody events that followed, most federalists were shocked. Hamilton doubted the French had anything in common with the American Revolution. In his view, liberty had given way to "licentiousness."[24] Other federalist leaders, such as John Adams, expressed the fear that the violence of the mob could set an example that would endanger the fledgling American Republic.[25]

By contrast, most republicans leaned toward the revolutionaries as champions of liberty. Jefferson, for instance, shrugged off the arrest and

execution of the king, whom he thought should be treated "like other crim-
inals."[26] He hoped that the revolution would "bring at length kings, nobles,
and priests to the scaffolds which they have been so long deluging with
human blood." Even when the Reign of Terror turned on his friend Lafayette, Jefferson was unmoved.[27] Rather than see the revolution fail, he would
prefer to "have seen half the earth desolated. Were there but an Adam and
an Eve left in every country, and left free, it would be better than as it is
now."[28] Jefferson thought the revolution was progressing "at a steady pace."
He dismissed the bloodshed as a minor detail. France could not expect "to
be translated from despotism to liberty in a feather-bed."[29] Even three decades later, Jefferson would persist in arguing to John Adams that the
French Revolution was "worth rivers of blood, and years of desolation."[30]
Ignoring all evidence to the contrary, Jefferson held to the naïve belief
that the revolution would lead to a democratic republic on the American
model—even after Napoleon Bonaparte established a ruthless dictatorship
and declared himself emperor.[31]

Other republicans shared Jefferson's enthusiasm for the bloodletting in
France. Madison thought that the revolution was "wonderful in its progress
and . . . stupendous in its consequences."[32] And Monroe thought that the
French king's execution, though regrettable, was justifiable for the greater
end of the revolution.[33]

The republican romance for the French Revolution was partly rooted in
their loathing of Britain. Jefferson viewed the British as "our natural enemies . . . who wished us ill from the bottom of their souls."[34] England, he
charged, tried to "exterminate us in war, insulted us in all her councils in
peace, shut her doors to us in every port where her interests would admit it,
libeled us in foreign nations, endeavored to poison them against the reception of our most precious commodities."[35] Jefferson believed that the United
States should allow French military ships and privateers to operate out of
U.S. ports. He looked forward to celebrating France's conquest with the
victorious French generals in London.[36]

Republicans displayed their affinity for the French in their taste for French furnishings, wine, and even fashion. They avoided any ostentation in their dress and their homes. They went wigless with short-cropped hair in the manner of the French revolutionaries. Silver-buckled shoes and knee britches disappeared into republican closets. Republicans toasted the success of the revolution, and they amused guests by setting their tables with toy guillotines as centerpieces.[37] In all their giddy excitement, the republicans had no sense of the suffering inflicted by the revolution not just on the aristocracy but on the poor and the bourgeois as well. When news of the king's execution reached Philadelphia, a leading republican journal, the *National Gazette*, sneered, "Louis Capet has lost his caput."[38]

The French Revolution became the serpent in the garden tempting Americans like Jefferson on the one hand and Hamilton and Marshall on the other to taste the bitter fruit of partisanship. American democracy had lost its innocence.

BACK IN RICHMOND, Marshall had little time to speculate about American debt to France. He was preoccupied with a different debt. By the 1790s, Americans owed British and Scottish creditors as much as five million pounds sterling (around seven hundred million dollars today) for imports delivered before the American Revolution, and half of that was owed by Virginians.[39] Despite Marshall's personal interest in vindicating Lord Fairfax's title to his Virginia property, Marshall had earned a reputation as a champion of Virginia debtors against claims brought by British and Scottish creditors on pre–Revolutionary War debts. Prior to the Constitution's adoption, these cases were generally dismissed by Virginia courts. But after the Constitution was ratified in 1787, the federal courts were open to British and Scottish creditors, who expected that federal judges would enforce the provisions of the Treaty of Paris that promised to honor their debts. Marshall defended as many as one hundred Virginia debtors, including men as prominent as Edmund Randolph and Thomas Jefferson, from claims worth about fifteen million dollars (around three hundred million dollars today).[40]

One such case was filed in federal court against Daniel L. Hylton and Co., a successful merchant in Richmond. In 1774, Hylton owed fifteen hundred pounds sterling to the British mercantile house of Farell & Jones, the same company that had sued Randolph's estate for the consignment of 280 slaves. In 1777, Virginia passed the Sequestration Act, which appropriated all the debts owed to British creditors and required debtors to pay the state rather than the original creditors. Debtors could now discharge their debts in Virginia currency, which was worth appreciably less than the original debt in British pounds sterling. Hylton, for example, paid the Commonwealth of Virginia a stack of Virginia bills with a face value of fifteen hundred pounds, but which were actually worth a mere fifteen pounds. William Jones sued Hylton, and in 1791, Marshall defended Hylton before the federal circuit court.[41]

As it evolved, the case assumed national importance. The question of whether British debts could be discharged by state law had enormous economic significance. Marshall was joined by three of the most prominent lawyers of the day—Patrick Henry, Alexander Campbell, and James Innes. Marshall argued that after independence Virginians were no longer answerable for their obligations owed to British creditors under the old regime. Virginia had barred British creditors from recovering on these debts, and Hylton's debt had been properly paid to the commonwealth in compliance with the Sequestration Act.[42]

Jones's lawyers argued that the United States had promised to enforce these debts in accordance with Article Four of the 1783 Treaty of Paris. They insisted that the Treaty of Paris trumped state law and bound Virginia. If there was any doubt about that, they pointed out that under Article VI of the Constitution, known as "the supremacy clause," treaties were the "supreme law of the land," superseding state law.[43]

Marshall responded that the treaty did not retroactively preserve rights that were previously taken by the state. Even if the court found that the treaty had been intended to restore the rights of British creditors, Marshall argued that since Britain had violated the treaty—by maintaining a military presence south of the Canadian border and by refusing to pay slaveholders for the slaves freed by British forces during the Revolution—the peace treaty was void.[44]

Claiming that the treaty was void went too far. It raised troubling questions about the appropriate role of federal courts. Did a federal court have the power to void a treaty? Should a federal court interfere in the conduct of foreign affairs by risking war with Britain? Marshall buttressed his position with scholarly citations to international authorities such as Hugo Grotius, Emer de Vattel, and Samuel von Pufendorf, but his client was in an unenviable position. The equities of the situation, as well as the treaty, were against Hylton. After all, he had paid fifteen pounds to Virginia in order to erase a debt of fifteen hundred pounds to his British creditors, and he was now claiming that state law could override a federal treaty and that a federal court could void a peace treaty.

At this point, Marshall shifted his argument to reframe the question in terms of the federal Constitution. He knew it was unlikely that the circuit court would risk plunging the nation into war by voiding the peace treaty, and so he changed tactics. He argued that the president had no authority to make a treaty that superseded the legal rights of a private citizen under state law. In effect, Marshall was asking the circuit court to strike down a federal treaty as a violation of state rights under the Constitution. No court had ever before struck down federal or state law in conflict with the federal Constitution. It was not until Marshall's most famous Supreme Court decision, *Marbury v. Madison*, that the Supreme Court first asserted the power to void federal law.

Marshall had one more arrow in his quiver. He argued that the treaty imposed only a moral obligation on states to adopt legislation that would restore debts owed to British creditors. States were not legally bound, and the treaty had no force of its own. In other words, Marshall contended that the treaty's provision to provide creditors with a remedy in state courts was not intended to be directly enforceable in state courts unless the state legislators agreed to make it enforceable. Since Virginia had never enacted such a law, Hylton was not bound to pay his creditors. The significance of this point is that Marshall was proposing that at least some treaties might be nothing more than a promise to enact legislation in the future. There was nothing in the law of nations suggesting a distinction like this among treaties. It was a completely novel idea—one that Marshall found convenient to introduce into U.S. law later on the Supreme Court.[45]

The circuit court was unable to reach a decision, and the judges ordered the case for retrial two years later in May 1793. Jones had died by then, and the executor of his estate continued the action. Hence, the case was subsequently renamed *Ware v. Hylton*.[46] Marshall appeared again with his co-counsel before a three-judge U.S. circuit court of appeal composed of Chief Justice John Jay, Associate Supreme Court Justice James Iredell, and District Judge Cyrus Griffin. Marshall's arguments against the Treaty of Paris were hardly convincing to Chief Justice Jay, who was one of the treaty's principal negotiators and who was well aware that the treaty intended to preserve the rights of British creditors. The three judges unanimously held that the court could not declare the Treaty of Paris void and that the supremacy clause in Article VI of the Constitution meant that the treaty preserved the rights of British creditors to file claims. However, the court split on the question of whether the Treaty of Paris overrode Virginia's Sequestration Act of 1777. Chief Justice Jay agreed with Marshall's argument that the Sequestration Act survived, but he thought that the debt also survived under the treaty and the customary law of nations. In his view, state law could not interfere with international law. Justice Iredell and Judge Griffin agreed that, to the extent that some debtors had already paid the state to discharge their debts, the state was now liable for paying the

British creditors all the money they were owed. Thus the circuit held by a vote of two to one that Hylton had paid his debt and that the creditor's only recourse was against the State of Virginia. The case was subsequently appealed to the Supreme Court.[47]

WARE V. HYLTON reached the Supreme Court in February 1796. That was the same month that Marshall was prepared to argue the case on behalf of Lord Fairfax's property rights before the Supreme Court. The action he had first filed more than a decade earlier was now called *Hunter v. Fairfax*. This case would determine whether Fairfax's heir had good title to the land. Marshall had a personal stake in that question as he was hoping to purchase a portion of the property for himself. David Hunter's lawyer died just days before the case was to be argued, and the Court postponed the argument to give Hunter time to hire new counsel.[48] Eventually, Hunter abandoned his appeal, and the Supreme Court dropped the case from its docket.[49] Marshall never had the chance to argue the Fairfax case before the Supreme Court. Almost twenty years would pass before the question of whether Fairfax owned good title to the property finally reached the Supreme Court in *Martin v. Hunter's Lessee*. By then, of course, Marshall was chief justice.

Marshall traveled from Richmond to Philadelphia to face the Supreme Court for the first and only time he appeared before them as counsel. Anxious to arrive, he described the long journey as "beyond measure tedious" as he bumped along rutted roads through empty woods stripped bare and deep in shadows. The silver hush of winter was broken only by the rumble of carriage wheels over rocks and gravel. He yearned to get out and stretch his long legs. There was nothing for miles but an occasional flock of crows cawing across an ashen sky.

Marshall had not seen Philadelphia in more than fifteen years. The last time he visited during the war he had walked there in boots worn through to rejoin General Steuben's army. He had arrived looking like a vagrant with a dirty beard, messy hair, and torn uniform. Innkeepers shut their doors to him. Fifteen years earlier, Philadelphia hardly looked like a capital city. It still bore the scars from the British occupation. Now the city sparkled as Marshall arrived by carriage in his finest suit. Philadelphia in 1796 was the second largest city in the English-speaking world after London, with a population of more than forty thousand, paved streets, clean sidewalks, and the finest architecture in eighteenth-century America. He was dazzled by the transformation from a war-battered town to a gleaming metropolis.

While he waited several days for his co-counsel, Alexander Campbell, to arrive from Richmond, Marshall explored the capital. He loved the theater as much as he loved politics and law, and he saw two performances in Philadelphia, *The Bank Note* and *Hop in the Well*. Marshall enjoyed both of these comedies, but he thought that the shows' leading lady was not quite up to the standards of Richmond's own Virginia Company.[50]

Philadelphia was preparing to celebrate Washington's sixty-fifth birthday as if he were a reigning monarch. There were already rumors that Washington intended to retire at the end of his term. In seeming anticipation of the grand event, the weather had turned uncommonly balmy and dry. Though December had been especially cold, the snow had disappeared by February. "We have weather as mild as April, streets as dirty as March," John Adams wrote to his wife.[51] Even a false spring was welcomed in the capital.

Ware v. Hylton was probably the most important case to reach the Supreme Court at that time. Most of the country's debt was owed by Virginians, and the courts of Virginia were the least sympathetic to British creditors. Millions of dollars—and possibly peace with Britain—hung in the balance. Justice Iredell, whose dour countenance belied his penchant for hyperbole, exclaimed that *Ware* was "the greatest Cause which ever came before a Judicial Court in the World!"[52]

The Supreme Court convened in the musty east wing of the old city hall across from where Congress sat. The Court's docket was so bare—averaging fewer than ten cases a year—that the Court generously allocated three days for oral argument. (By contrast, the modern Supreme Court receives approximately ten thousand petitions in a typical year, hears roughly eighty cases, and allows each party only thirty minutes for oral argument.) The Supreme Court in 1796 did not possess the kind of influence or respect that it commands today, and consequently, it had a high turnover.

The Court in 1796 included Chief Justice Oliver Ellsworth and Associate Justices James Wilson, William Cushing, James Iredell, William Paterson, and the newly appointed Samuel Chase. Chase had been named to replace Justice John Blair, who resigned because of a mental illness that was politely termed a "strange disorder." Chase was considered an unbridled High Federalist, irascible, abrasive, and crafty. John Adams described Chase as being surrounded by a cloud of "suspicion and Impurity."[53] Chase was unapologetically blunt and as fiery as Patrick Henry. He did not keep his political views to himself. Of the six justices, the chief justice did not participate.

Marshall pared down his argument before the Court to two points that had the appeal of simplicity: First, Marshall argued that an individual's "property is the creature of civil society, and subject, in all respects, to the disposition and control of civil institutions." That was a surprisingly modern idea of property rights. Rather than rely on natural law as the source of all property rights, Marshall asserted that those rights originated from the state. As a sovereign state, Virginia had the right under international law to confiscate the property of enemy aliens in wartime. The act sequestering British property provided that British creditors could sue Virginia but not the debtor. In other words, Virginia had not expropriated property, but rather it had assumed responsibility for the debts of its citizens.[54]

Second, Marshall pointed out that the treaty did not expressly state an intention to restore rights that were already confiscated even though Congress surely knew that some states had confiscated British debts. The treaty's silence meant that the treaty had tacitly approved Virginia's action. Even if the treaty intended to restore rights to the debtor, the Constitution surely would forbid Congress from compelling debtors to pay the same debt twice.[55]

Marshall's argument presaged some of his later views on the Court. First, Marshall acknowledged that Congress was constrained by the Constitution and that it was up to the courts to determine the limits of congressional power. "The judicial authority can have no right to question the validity of a law, unless such jurisdiction is expressly given by the constitution."[56] Here, in a single sentence, Marshall distilled the principle that he would later enshrine as judicial review. Second, Marshall acknowledged that a treaty could override state law if it was clear that this was the intent of the parties to the treaty. Third, Marshall applied the norms of customary international law to interpret the meaning of the treaty based on its plain language. All of these principles would reappear later in Marshall's decisions and become foundational to American law.

Despite the brilliance and originality of his argument, Marshall lost. Each of the justices issued opinions unanimously siding with the British creditors. Only Justice Wilson agreed with Marshall's argument that as a sovereign state Virginia had the right to expropriate enemy alien property. But Justice Wilson insisted that international law did not permit states to confiscate private debts and that when the states became independent they were "bound to receive law of Nations in its most pure & modern State."[57] Justice Chase agreed in principle with Marshall that Virginia could discharge the debtor, but that as the supreme law of the land "a treaty can totally annihilate any part of the constitution of any of the individual states, that is contrary to a treaty." Chase concluded that the treaty had, in fact, trumped the laws of Virginia.[58] The justices voted to reverse the decision of the circuit court and ordered Hylton to pay the full amount of his debt in pounds sterling.[59] The Supreme Court's decision in *Ware* affirmed that the United States could not shirk its obligations to Britain. The private debt owed to British and Scottish exporters would have to be paid. This was the only case Marshall ever argued before the Supreme Court, and it was only one of two Supreme Court cases in which Marshall found himself on the losing side.

At the same time, President Washington's policy of neutrality meant that the United States would not discharge the debt that the French felt was owed to them for their aid during the Revolutionary War. Washington's neutrality policy was an exercise in pragmatism, and it certainly seemed like the wiser course to navigate between Britain and France. But in the end, neutrality would fail to keep America out of the conflict between these two belligerents, and it would ultimately fall to John Marshall to steer the ship of state between these two great powers.

CHAPTER SIX

CITIZEN GENET

O n April 8, 1793, the French Revolution arrived in America in the person of Edmond Charles Genet, better known as Citizen Genet, the newly appointed French minister to the United States. Charismatic and combative with lapis eyes, auburn hair, and a rosy complexion, he was a fervent revolutionary.

Despite a volatile temperament, Genet was bred for the diplomatic service. His father, Edmé Jacques Genet, was the Foreign Ministry's chief interpreter with expertise on American affairs during the reign of Louis XVI. When his father died, Genet was appointed to replace him as the American specialist.[1] But the young Genet was too restless for the civil service. He cultivated relationships with the French revolutionaries, particularly the relatively moderate Girondists. When the Girondists took power, they decided that the imprisoned king should be exiled to America. Louis would certainly be accorded great respect in the United States, where he was regarded as a patron of the American Revolution. The leadership agreed in November 1792 that Genet, with his perfect English, would be the ideal candidate to convey the royal family into exile. For that purpose, the

Girondists appointed Genet as minister to the United States. Happy to be freed from the stuffy confines of the Foreign Ministry, Genet joked that he would teach the French king to be a good American farmer.[2]

The Girondists, whose idea of diplomacy consisted of spreading universal brotherhood by using the bayonet, charged Genet with a mission that was destined to fail. He was instructed to expand the "Empire of liberty" by persuading the United States to help France liberate Canada, Louisiana, and Florida from rule by Britain and Spain. If the Americans refused to help, Genet was instructed to act on his own to "germinate the spirit of liberty" by presumably instigating a popular uprising in these colonies.[3] Second, Genet was to demand that the United States honor its obligation to support France under the Treaty of Alliance. Specifically, the French expected the Americans to allow Genet to commission volunteers to fight in Florida, Louisiana, and Canada and issue letters of marque authorizing American privateers to attack British ships. Additionally, France wanted American courts to libel British ships seized as prizes of war even though the Americans had a peace treaty with Britain. And the Girondists wanted the Americans to grant French imports preferential treatment. Finally, France wanted the United States to advance payment of three million dollars (about seventy million dollars today) on its outstanding debt owed to France for military supplies during the Revolutionary War.[4] This was an amount roughly equal to the federal government's annual tax revenues.[5] It was an impossible mission.

Four weeks before Genet departed Rochefort, his mission took an unexpected turn when Louis XVI was executed in Paris. Genet was no longer needed to carry the king into exile. Even though it now made little sense to send an unseasoned thirty-year-old to a foreign post to carry out an impossible assignment, Genet left for America anyway. Soon after he departed, the Girondists lost power to the more radical Jacobins. The Jacobin leader, Maximilien de Robespierre, a man who never shied away from the sight of blood, denounced the Girondists for their foreign aggression: "No one loves armed missionaries," declared the not-so-lovable leader of the Reign of Terror.[6] The Jacobins had no use for Genet either, but it would be months before that message reached him. Thus, Genet arrived in Charleston, South Carolina, on April 8 on the frigate *Embuscade* with two personal secretaries, two servants, and tons of luggage that included a carriage and a bidet, but without a mandate from the new Jacobin government.[7]

Genet had intended to land in Philadelphia, but contrary winds forced the ship to change course.[8] It was a fortuitous accident. No city in America was more fiercely anti-British than Charleston, which had suffered a terrible defeat at the hands of British forces during the American Revolution.[9] From the moment Genet stepped off the ship, he was mobbed by well-wishers. Recalling past outrages, Charleston's residents enthusiastically embraced the representative of Britain's most determined enemy. Genet's youth, vitality, and eloquent English captured the attention of Americans who yearned nostalgically for the passion of their own revolution. While most republicans preferred plain clothes and natural hair, Genet dressed with flair. He embodied the spirit of republicanism—but with better grooming.[10]

Genet immediately launched his campaign to push America into war against Britain and Spain. He embraced his instruction to "germinate the spirit of liberty" by sowing the field of American politics with the seeds of partisanship. In ten short days in Charleston, he issued letters of marque authorizing four privateers—American ships manned by Americans—to capture British merchant ships. He made no effort to hide his responsibility: One of the privateers was even christened *Citizen Genet*. He instructed the French consul in Charleston, Michel Ange Bernard de Mangourit, to establish a French court on American soil for the purpose of libeling British ships as prizes of war. This was an astounding breach of diplomatic protocol and international law. Even more incredible, he recruited Americans for a volunteer army under his own direction to invade Spanish Florida.[11]

Rather than sail to Philadelphia, which might have taken him five or six days, Genet decided to send the *Embuscade* ahead while he proceeded overland. It was a cunning bit of theater. Genet traveled for nearly a month over seven hundred miles of rough roads as he inched northward toward Philadelphia in an elaborate carriage drawn by four horses. Cannon fire, church bells, and adoring crowds greeted him in every city. A wave of anticipation and popular acclaim swept before him. He was toasted and feted at elaborate banquets. Only President Washington had received this kind of popular acclaim.[12] All of this public adulation generated momentum that he hoped would shake the pillars of federalist power. By the time he arrived in Philadelphia, Genet was drunk on his own grandiosity.

BACK IN RICHMOND, the papers were full of stories about Genet, but Marshall was not paying much attention to his arrival. Marshall was preoccupied with one of the most lurid criminal cases to rock Virginia in the eighteenth century. It involved Marshall's distant cousin Richard Randolph, who inherited the family plantation, aptly named Bizarre.

Richard had married a cousin, Judith Randolph. In the winter of 1791–1792, Nancy Randolph, Judith's sister, came to live with Richard and Judith at Bizarre. Nancy intended to marry Richard's younger brother, Theodorick, but before they could marry, Theodorick died. That September, Richard, Judith, and Nancy were visiting the home of Randolph Harrison, another Randolph cousin. Nancy was not feeling well and went upstairs to lie down. Richard went to help his sister-in-law in her bedroom. He locked the door, and the guests downstairs heard Nancy screaming. The next day, Mrs. Harrison noticed bloodstains on a back staircase and on Nancy's pillowcase. Oddly enough, the sheets and quilt had disappeared from Nancy's bed. One of Harrison's slaves reported that she had witnessed Nancy giving birth. Another slave discovered a bloodstain on a pile of old shingles. Tongues began wagging, and word quickly spread that Nancy had given birth to an illegitimate child fathered by her brother-in-law and that he had brutally murdered the infant.[13]

Since slaves could not testify and there was no physical evidence of a crime, Richard Randolph could not be charged. But Randolph felt that his reputation had been damaged, and he wanted the opportunity to clear his name. Randolph sought Marshall's legal advice.

Marshall concocted a daring legal strategy: He called for a judicial inquiry to determine the facts. Marshall prepared the case and persuaded his colleague Patrick Henry to appear on behalf of Randolph. Although seventeen witnesses came forward to testify against Randolph, none had direct evidence of a crime, and under Henry's withering cross-examination, the case against Randolph collapsed. The court dismissed all charges in April 1793, though rumors persisted for years after.[14]

With the inquest over, Marshall's attention turned back to the national scene. In May, Marshall received a commission from Virginia's governor as the commander of a newly formed Richmond regiment. The swelling support for Genet and the French revolutionaries threatened to drag the country into another war with Britain. The European war was becoming a domestic concern, and the bitter partisanship that Genet had brought to America would soon compel Marshall to take a leading role.

LIKE A GATHERING STORM, Genet slowly advanced toward Philadelphia. Washington anxiously called his cabinet together in April 1793 to discuss how to respond to the outbreak of war between France and Britain. The cabinet was locked in a bitter debate for two days over what would prove to be the most fateful decision in Washington's presidency. Over Jefferson's objections, the cabinet agreed that the United States should remain neutral, but the cabinet could not agree on what neutrality meant in practice. Treasury Secretary Alexander Hamilton and Attorney General Edmund Randolph favored Washington's signing a proclamation of neutrality. Secretary of State Jefferson argued that the president did not have authority to issue a declaration of neutrality any more than he could issue a declaration of war; only Congress had that authority. Hamilton countered that there was a distinction between sending soldiers into battle and preserving the peace. After much wrangling, Washington ordered the attorney general—rather than Jefferson as secretary of state—to draft a neutrality proclamation for his signature.[15]

Jefferson admonished his colleagues that despite the country's neutrality, the Treaty of Alliance required the United States to provide arms to France. Hamilton replied that since the treaty was made with Louis XVI and no legitimate government had succeeded him, the treaty was suspended for the time being. The other cabinet members agreed that neutrality meant the rules would apply equally to France and Britain. But it would fall on Jefferson as secretary of state to enforce the neutrality he so fiercely opposed.[16]

Finally, the cabinet debated whether the president should receive Citizen Genet as the proper representative of France. Hamilton advised Washington to receive Genet politely without acknowledging him as the official representative of a legitimate government. President Washington concurred that he would accord Genet the same honors as any other foreign diplomat but "not with too much warmth or cordiality."[17]

Relations between Jefferson and Hamilton were irreparably damaged over the question of how to deal with France, and their mutual disdain disintegrated into childish name-calling: Hamilton accused Jefferson of a "womanish attachment to France,"[18] and Jefferson told Monroe that "Hamilton is panic-struck if we refuse our breech to every kick which Great Britain may choose to give it."[19] Jefferson felt disillusioned and betrayed by Washington and his cabinet. His frustration had reached a breaking point. "The motion of my blood no longer keeps time with the tumult of the world," he confessed to Madison. He was worn down from a "desperate & eternal contest against a host who are systematically undermining the public liberty & prosperity . . . in short, giving everything I love, in exchange for everything I hate."[20]

Three days after the cabinet meeting, Washington, in his customary terse language, issued the one-page Proclamation of Neutrality. In it, Washington warned citizens not to engage in any conduct that would compromise the nation's neutrality. He declared that the United States would not protect any citizen who was found guilty by another country of "abetting hostilities" in violation of the law of nations and that the United States would prosecute any citizen who attacked the vessels of either France or Britain.[21]

As the commander of Richmond's newly formed regiment, Marshall had a duty to enforce the Proclamation of Neutrality at the Port of Richmond. The small port on the James River was the least likely spot for French privateers to appear, but Marshall could not ignore the popular support for Genet and the French revolutionaries.[22] Though Marshall remained sympathetic to the cause of the French Revolution, he read the newspapers with growing anxiety as Genet appeared to challenge the leadership of General Washington. He had no reason to suspect that the Genet affair would soon drag him into national politics.

The Proclamation of Neutrality ignited a firestorm of protest. This was the first time that a president asserted primary authority in foreign affairs. Until then, it was widely assumed that all the power over foreign affairs was vested in Congress by Article I of the Constitution. Republicans reproached the president for acting without authority from Congress. Jefferson remained silent in public while stealthily prodding his lieutenant Madison to attack. Madison, writing under the nom de plume Helvidius, denounced Washington's action as an unconstitutional violation of the separation of powers and America's treaty obligations. When Washington questioned Jefferson over what Madison thought of his policy, Jefferson replied that Madison wrote to him only about farming and crop rotation.[23] Washington may have suspected that Jefferson and Madison were undermining his neutrality policy, but he could not have anticipated what would happen next.

AFTER A MONTH of fevered anticipation, Citizen Genet reached Philadelphia on Thursday, May 16, 1793. He crossed the Schuylkill on the floating bridge at Gray's Ferry, where he was greeted by a crowd of dignitaries and reporters who proceeded with him into the city center. Streets were lined with French flags. Jubilant crowds wearing floppy red "liberty caps," popular among the French revolutionaries, burst into the Marseillaise, the rousing military anthem written the previous year after the declaration of war against Austria. Cannons thundered in tribute. A committee of Philadelphia's most distinguished citizens signed a pledge opposing the Proclamation of Neutrality.[24] Receptions celebrated Genet and the French revolutionaries with rhapsodies and toasts to Jean Paul Marat and Robespierre, whose cold-blooded vengeance surpassed the malevolence of any French monarch. Washington's former aide-de-camp, Pennsylvania Governor Thomas Mifflin, called for war against England.[25] Philip Freneau, a republican journalist working for Jefferson at the State Department, composed a song to the tune of "God Save the King," which he sang at a dinner in Genet's honor. The song concluded: "May France ne'er want a Washington." Even to Francophiles, these lyrics must have sounded shockingly inappropriate coming from the mouth of a State Department employee.[26] All this fuss was made to honor a thirty-year-old who had accomplished precisely nothing.

Genet's comely looks and rhetoric stirred revolutionary passions that had been dormant for at least a decade among Americans. In the wake of his procession up the coast, he left a trail of eleven republican societies that became the seedlings for a still unformed and unnamed political party. Some of these societies, as in Pennsylvania, were called democratic societies, but they were all inspired by French republicanism. Twenty-four more societies sprang up the following year.[27] Federalists suspected that these societies would become breeding grounds for revolutionaries. As frenzied mobs of supporters paraded the narrow streets of Philadelphia, Vice President John Adams barricaded himself in his home with guns loaded, ready to defend his family. Perhaps exaggerating the danger, Adams later recounted how "ten thousand people in the streets of Philadelphia, day after day, threatened to drag Washington out of his house and effect a revolution in the government or compel it to declare war in favor of the French Revolution and against England."[28]

On the afternoon of May 18, Washington waited impatiently in the President's House to receive the French diplomat. It was a flagrant breach of diplomatic protocol for a foreign diplomat to spend six weeks parading around the country, making public appearances, and issuing commissions and letters of marque without first presenting his credentials to the head of state. Genet's conduct no doubt offended Washington, who was fastidious about etiquette. Gouverneur Morris, the U.S. minister to France, had warned the president that Genet was an opportunist with "the manner and look of an upstart."[29] Jefferson, as secretary of state, accompanied Genet to the president, who received him on the second floor of his spacious mansion. Portraits of the late Louis XVI and Marie Antoinette hung prominently on either side of the fireplace. Genet presented his credentials and tried to romance the president. "We see in you the only person on earth who can love us sincerely & merit to be so loved," he told Washington.[30] The president responded to Genet with such formality and coldness that even Genet, a man dazzled by his own celebrity, could not have mistaken the president's intention.[31]

By contrast, Jefferson was enchanted by this Frenchman. Just a few weeks earlier, Genet's ship, the *Embuscade,* had sailed into the port of Philadelphia on May 2 with a captured British merchant vessel, the *Grange.* The *Embuscade* had captured the *Grange* while it was anchored in Delaware Bay and now claimed it as a prize. This was almost certainly in violation of international law, but popular opinion was on the side of France. Jefferson rushed to the wharf to see thousands of Philadelphians cheering as they watched the *Grange* dock flying the British flag upside down beneath the French tricolor. The sight thrilled Jefferson as well.[32] But his joy would be short-lived. Blinded by the cataracts of his ideology, Jefferson did not foresee the diplomatic crisis unfolding.

OVER THE COURSE of a few weeks, Jefferson and Genet met frequently at the comfortable house that Jefferson leased for the princely sum of thirty pounds (around four thousand dollars today) on the bend in the Schuylkill close to Gray's Ferry. They dined outside in the thick shade of towering sycamores along the riverbank.[33] Plants shriveled in the fierce stillness of summer, and the magnificent lawn was the color of burnt caramel after months of drought. While Jefferson and Genet talked, slaves would have ferried cool refreshments and plates from the kitchen. Though Pennsylvania had adopted a gradual abolition law in 1780, it permitted slaveholders from other states to bring slaves into the state if the slaveholder registered them with a county clerk. Jefferson evaded the registration requirement by cycling slaves back and forth to Monticello every few weeks.[34]

Genet flattered Jefferson as a champion of liberty and equality. The Frenchman seemed indifferent to the apparent contradiction between Jefferson's fine rhetoric and his ownership of so many Africans. He exceeded even his diplomatic instructions suggesting that "we ought in some sort to form one people." Genet suggested that the alliance between America and France would be something like a republican version of the Family Compact that had united the Bourbon powers of France and Spain.[35] Jefferson, who opposed centralized power and favored local government, was nonetheless fascinated by the possibility. Jefferson gushed later to Madison that Genet "offered everything and asks nothing . . . It is impossible for anything to be more affectionate, more magnanimous than the purport of his mission."[36] In fact, it soon emerged that Genet would ask a great deal.

Jefferson and Genet forged a marriage of convenience over many hours. Jefferson wanted Genet's help to elect a republican majority in Congress that would support an alliance with France. Jefferson shared confidential details of cabinet meetings with the French envoy. Jefferson made clear that *his* enemies—the federalists, particularly Adams and Hamilton—were *France's* enemies.[37] Only the republicans in France and the United States could save democracy from the federalist monocrats, he argued. From these conversations, Genet formed the misimpression that the president was irrelevant and that an appeal to Congress, or to the people directly, would be more effective.

Genet wanted Jefferson to agree to remove tariffs on French imports and advance repayment of the entire U.S. war debt to France—an amount equivalent to more than one hundred million dollars today. Both would be impossible to deliver.[38] High tariff rates had been levied to finance public projects, pay off the national debt, and protect America's infant industries from European competition. Moreover, any tariff preference for French imports would violate the U.S. treaty with Britain. The United States simply could not afford to repay France, and a large payment to help France's military would risk antagonizing Britain.[39]

At the same time, Genet pursued plans to liberate Spanish Florida and Louisiana. Jefferson was privately sympathetic to France's aim to start a war with Spain. Spain controlled the mouth of the Mississippi at New Orleans, and Jefferson thought that the ability to navigate the river would open up the interior of the continent. As secretary of state, Jefferson had tried to persuade Spain to cede Louisiana to the United States, and when Spain refused, Jefferson suggested that the United States should declare war on Spain.[40]

Genet confided in Jefferson his plans to arm regiments in South Carolina and Kentucky to attack Spanish Florida and Louisiana, respectively. Jefferson proposed that Genet send André Michaux, a French explorer and botanist, as his agent in Kentucky to organize the military expedition. Without considering the consequences of plotting war against a friendly government, Jefferson drafted a letter of introduction for Michaux to the Kentucky governor, Isaac Shelby, explaining that Michaux was acting on behalf of the French minister. Jefferson also put Genet in touch with several Kentucky congressmen who could facilitate his plans. While Jefferson cautioned Genet that what he was doing would violate the Proclamation of Neutrality, he did nothing to warn the president of impending war with Spain.[41] Jefferson was knee-deep in a foreign conspiracy to attack Spanish territory—the very crime he later accused Aaron Burr of committing.

Jefferson's relationship with the French envoy was ill-advised, probably illegal, and certainly disloyal to Washington. But it was politically expedient. Jefferson accused the proponents of neutrality of siding with the British: "The old Tories, joined by our merchants who trade on British capital, paper dealers, and the idle rich of the great commercial towns are with the kings." He was confident that the rest of the country would support France and that the growing polarization would benefit republicans. He happily added, "The war has kindled & brought forward the two [political] parties with an ardour which our interests merely, could never excite."[42] Jefferson predicted that the division over Genet's mission would sweep his party into power.

While Jefferson shared Genet's criticism of neutrality, he worried about the activities of privateers in U.S. ports. Genet continued to recruit numerous American privateers to attack British ships. Jefferson gently reminded Genet that the United States did not approve of privateering in its territorial waters, but he still winked at some French violations of neutrality.[43] By late June, Jefferson began to worry that Genet "will enlarge the circle of those disaffected to his country." Jefferson was less concerned about the harm Genet might do to the United States than the harm to republicans. Jefferson claimed that he was "doing everything in my power to moderate the impetuosity of his movements," but that remained to be seen.[44]

More trouble was brewing. In early July, Jefferson learned that the *Embuscade* had captured another British merchant vessel, the *Little Sarah*. The vessel was brought into Philadelphia where the ship was renamed the *Petite Démocrate*, recommissioned as a French privateer, and outfitted with fourteen guns. The president ordered that the ship remain docked in Philadelphia, but Genet defied the president and instructed the *Petite Démocrate* to set sail with a crew of 120 Americans and French into the open Atlantic.[45]

Genet's defiance of the president literally cast his fate upon the water. Jefferson felt humiliated knowing that the cabinet would blame him. Genet arrogantly informed Jefferson that if the executive did not honor its treaty commitments to France, he would go directly to Congress or the people.[46] But the Frenchman had dangerously misjudged American politics.

In the public's mind, Genet personified the republican cause, and Jefferson feared that if Genet continued to defy Washington, the public would side with Washington against the republicans. In private, Jefferson had growing doubts about Genet's fitness. "Never in my opinion was so calamitous an appointment made as that of the present Minister of F. here," he wrote to Madison. "Hot headed, all imagination, no judgment, passionate, disrespectful & even indecent toward the [President] in his written as well as verbal communications, talking of appeals from him to Congress, from them to the people, urging the most unreasonable & groundless propositions, & in the most dictatorial style . . . He renders my position immensely difficult."[47] Jefferson bristled at the young man's "ignorance" of the law of nations and predicted that Genet would "sink the republican interest if they do not abandon him."[48]

Marshall, like most Americans, continued to support the ideals of the French Revolution. "If there be among us men who are enemies to the French revolution, or who are friends to monarchy, I know them not." But

Marshall was offended that Genet publicly criticized the president's Proclamation of Neutrality and should "dare to pursue measures calculated to
raise a party to oppose our government under his banners." Marshall believed both in the soundness of neutrality as a principle of American foreign relations and in the authority of President Washington to pursue
neutrality. Marshall applauded the "gallant people" of France "contending
for the rights of human nature" against her enemies. But the United States
also had treaties with France's enemies that were "no less obligatory on us,
than those with France." Unless Congress declared war, it was the president's duty, Marshall felt, to execute those treaties and preserve good relations with all the belligerent powers. Marshall was especially angered by the
"most malicious charges" raised by Genet and the republican clubs against
Washington. Marshall concluded that "however devoted we may be to
France, we cannot permit her to interfere in our internal government."[49]

THE GENET AFFAIR came to a head at a series of cabinet meetings at the
President's House beginning on July 23. The president and the cabinet
agreed to request Genet's recall. Secretary Hamilton seized the moment to
accuse Jefferson and the republicans of threatening to overthrow the
American government.[50] Washington ordered Jefferson to produce any
correspondence he had with the Frenchman, and Hamilton proposed they
publish it to expose Genet's scheming. (Of course, it would also have the
convenient effect of embarrassing Jefferson.) Jefferson warned that this
would damage relations with France. "Friendly nations always negotiate
little differences in private," he pleaded.[51] At one point, Secretary of War
Henry Knox waved a pamphlet lampooning the president in Washington's
face. It featured a drawing of Washington on a guillotine—proof, he asserted, that the republicans threatened his government.

Washington lost his self-control. He had had enough "personal abuse" heaped on him. He angrily "defied any man on earth to produce one single act of his since he had been in the government which was not done on the purest motives." Washington's rage was uncharacteristic. Months of arguing over neutrality and Genet had taken a toll. Washington swore that "by god he had rather be in his grave than in his present situation. That he had rather be on his farm than to be made emperor of the world and yet they were charging him with wanting to be a king."[52]

The Genet affair would have enormous consequences for the president, his cabinet, the nation, and Marshall. Jefferson tendered his resignation to the president effective at the end of September 1793. He wished "to retire to scenes of greater tranquility, from those which I am every day more and more convinced that neither my talents, tone of mind, nor time of life fit me."[53] The toxic partisanship that Jefferson and his republican colleagues had cultivated had driven him from office. Perhaps Jefferson would have remained in office if he had known that Hamilton had reached the same conclusion about retiring.

Washington, too, was exhausted by the unpleasantness that Jefferson and Genet had sown. The president feared that the republican societies inspired by Genet were fomenting a second revolution.[54] Washington had been routinely savaged by the leading republican newspaper in Philadelphia, the *National Gazette*, established by Jefferson and Monroe and run by Philip Freneau, Jefferson's employee in the State Department.[55] Washington felt betrayed by his fellow Virginians, and his once robust health deteriorated. He, too, resolved to retire from public life at the end of his term.[56]

Meanwhile, the battle over Genet and the Proclamation of Neutrality widened. Republicans in Congress continued to denounce the proclamation as exceeding the president's constitutional powers. Under the pseudonym Pacificus, Hamilton wrote a series of essays arguing that the president had broad implied authority to function as the chief organ of foreign relations and that empowered him to issue the Proclamation of Neutrality.[57] "If the Legislature have a right to make war on the one hand—it is on the other the duty of the Executive to preserve Peace till war is declared," he asserted.[58]

Jefferson instructed Madison to go after Hamilton: "For God's sake, my dear Sir, take up your pen, select the most striking heresies, and cut him to pieces in the face of the public."[59] Writing under his nom de plume, Madison blasted the idea that the executive possessed any authority beyond the literal text of the Constitution or whatever additional powers Congress assigned to him. Madison insisted that since treaties are the "supreme law of the land" under the Constitution, Washington was legally obligated to enforce the Treaty of Alliance with France.[60]

In his reply to Madison, Hamilton warned his countrymen not to "rashly mingle our destiny in the consequences of the errors and extravagances of another nation."[61] Hamilton worried that the Republic would be irreparably damaged if it allowed itself to be entangled in foreign alliances. These were the same sentiments echoed in Washington's famous Farewell Address two years later. Hamilton, who largely wrote Washington's speech, could be excused for repeating himself.[62]

The partisan sniping over Genet and the French Republic drove Washington, Hamilton, and Jefferson out of the federal government. And it spawned two competing political parties. In Virginia and much of the South, Jefferson's party dominated. The opposition to this emerging Republican Party called themselves Federalists. Southern Federalists needed a leader who could match the intellectual firepower of Jefferson and Madison. They found that leader in John Marshall.

CHAPTER SEVEN

ENTANGLING ALLIANCES

ugust 1793 was a cruel month in Philadelphia. The unusually dry warm weather combined with the lack of sanitary conditions in the densely populated capital had triggered an outbreak of yellow fever. Every morning carts stacked with jaundiced corpses prowled the streets looking for more bodies. In the space of two months, about five thousand souls perished out of a population of about forty thousand.[1] Half of the remaining population fled, including nearly all the nation's leaders. Those inhabitants who remained covered their noses with cloths dipped in vinegar to avoid the stench of rotting flesh. People were too fearful to shake hands as they passed one another on the street. Physicians had no effective treatments, and many patients died after being treated with bloodletting. Both Hamilton and his wife fell gravely ill. They retreated to their estate outside the city, where they suffered tense days of violent fevers, chills, and vomiting before recovering. Jefferson callously accused Hamilton of faking his illness to win sympathy.[2] Yellow fever continued its killing spree until the first chill of October.

The epidemic brought a quick end to the debate over neutrality. The specter of so much death had, for the moment, eclipsed partisan politics as the chief preoccupation of the capital. But beyond the capital, Genet began a speaking tour to drum up opposition to the president's neutrality policy. Genet made increasingly aggressive public statements denouncing Washington during the autumn of that year. When Jefferson tried to dissuade him, Genet felt betrayed by Jefferson. He was unaware that the cabinet had requested his recall and that his speeches were triggering a powerful backlash among federalists. Federalist clubs now sprung up to compete with the republican societies.

Hamilton, though still recovering, began to orchestrate rallies around the country to show support for Washington and neutrality. Hamilton and Chief Justice John Jay leaked some of Genet's correspondence to Jefferson that criticized Washington. Hamilton also persuaded Jay and New York Senator Rufus King to publish an article in a New York newspaper attacking Genet for interfering in the country's domestic politics.[3] Genet and his republican supporters launched a ferocious counterattack in the press and called on the U.S. attorney general to prosecute the chief justice for defaming Genet in public.[4]

Dozens of public rallies in support of Washington's Proclamation of Neutrality were held throughout New England, New York, New Jersey, Delaware, and Maryland. The most significant rally was held in Virginia, the heart of republican territory. To organize that critical event, Hamilton reached out to the man who was the effective leader of the federalists in Virginia: John Marshall.

Madison was visiting Monroe at his farmhouse in Charlottesville when he learned that Marshall was organizing a rally in Richmond in support of the Proclamation of Neutrality. Madison and Monroe appreciated how persuasive Marshall could be as a legislator and an advocate. Monroe wrote to Jefferson that Marshall "threatened the most furious attack on the French minister [Genet]."[5]

They were right. Marshall staged the Richmond rally with finesse. He won support from Governor Henry Lee, the last federalist governor of the commonwealth, and in a brilliant stroke, he invited his former law professor, George Wythe, Virginia's leading legal authority and an associate of Jefferson's, to preside over the meeting. Marshall knew that Wythe agreed with Hamilton's analysis of presidential power. Wythe's reputation added credence to the federalist argument while creating a veneer of nonpartisanship to attract Virginians who were not federalists. Marshall cleverly framed the meeting as a call to support Virginia's own colossus, George Washington, but it was much more than that: It was the beginning of a resistance movement against the republicans. Marshall published a public notice in the capital's newspaper—the *Virginia Gazette, and General Advertiser*—inviting all citizens to attend on Saturday, August 17, 1793. He drew the largest crowd of any rally in the nation. People flooded into the capital to demonstrate support for Virginia's native son and president.[6]

Marshall drafted six resolutions to put before his fellow Virginians. All six were adopted unanimously by the hundreds in attendance. The resolutions began by endorsing "strict neutrality towards the belligerent powers of Europe" and praising "our illustrious fellow citizen, GEORGE WASHINGTON, to whose eminent services, great talents, and exalted virtues, all America pays so just a tribute" for the Proclamation of Neutrality. Marshall condemned Washington's critics as "wicked" for daring "to gratify [their] paltry passions at the risk of [their] country's welfare, perhaps its existence." And he blasted Genet's "extravagant pretensions" and "indiscreet arrogance." Marshall's resolutions warned the republicans that "any interference of a foreign minister with our internal government or administration; any intriguing of a foreign minister with the political parties of this country; would violate the laws and usages of nations, would be a high indignity to the government and people of America, and would be a great and just cause of alarm."[7] Marshall had bested Jefferson and Madison in their own backyard.

The rally also adopted an address crafted by Marshall to President Washington to be published in the Richmond newspaper. The address was an unqualified endorsement of the president. In a rebuke to the republicans, Marshall wrote that "[a]s genuine Americans, with no other interest at heart but that of our country, unbiased by foreign influence, [we concur with the] propriety, justice, and wisdom" of the Proclamation of Neutrality.[8]

By implicitly questioning the motives and loyalty of republicans, Marshall became the target of republican attacks in pamphlets and newspapers around the state. Madison spread a false rumor that the National Bank that Hamilton had created had loaned Marshall the money to buy the Fairfax property. This was taken as evidence that Marshall was under the control of "monied interests."[9] Republicans charged that Marshall, like Hamilton, was a closet monarchist. They claimed that Marshall was a drunk—a false allegation that plagued his career. (Marshall's sister-in-law swore that "he was, of all men, the most temperate.") Marshall mused that "there appears to me every day to be more folly, envy, malice, and damn rascality in the world than there was the day before and I do verily begin to think that plain downright honesty and unintriguing integrity will be kicked out of doors."[10]

In response to the Richmond meeting, Monroe wrote an essay under the pen name Agricola that was published in the *Virginia Gazette, and General Advertiser* in September. In it, Monroe charged that the organizers of the Richmond meeting, by which he meant his old school friend Marshall, were monarchists and enemies of France. He accused federalists of being "more attached to the Constitution of England, than to that of their own country." Monroe alleged that federalists were determined to impose a constitutional monarchy "upon the ruin of our own [government]."[11] He also attacked Chief Justice Jay for leaking Genet's diplomatic correspondence.[12] Jay was guilty of the leak, but Monroe accused Jay and Marshall of embarrassing the executive in the conduct of foreign relations, which was quite the contrary. This was the first instance in American politics—certainly not the last—in which a political party falsely alleged that leaked state department documents risked damaging our foreign relations.

Republicans were not troubled by the inconsistency of their position: on the one hand, attacking President Washington for exceeding his authority in foreign relations, and on the other hand, criticizing the federalists for compromising the secrecy of the secretary of state's diplomatic correspondence. Though republicans extolled the virtues of popular democracy in theory, they now denounced federalist rallies as interfering with federal foreign policy.

Monroe's letter initiated a round of responses and counterresponses with Marshall that ran in the *Virginia Gazette, and General Advertiser* from September through November 1793. This exchange crystallized two opposing views of America's role in the world and clarified the positions of the two emerging political parties.

Marshall felt that these attacks were personal. He later commented that "[t]he resentments" of republicans "had been directed towards me for some time," and he was "attacked with great virulence" by Monroe, who accused Marshall of being a tool of Hamilton's.[13] Marshall responded to Monroe under the pseudonym Aristides—after Aristides the Just, an Athenian reformer. Marshall certainly knew that the source of Agricola's letter was either Jefferson, Madison, or Monroe, and since he was familiar with their writing styles, he probably suspected Monroe. It would be equally obvious to Monroe that the only man who could write so persuasively in defense of the Richmond resolution was Marshall. The use of pen names allowed these two old friends to attack each other in the strongest terms without risking a lawsuit or a duel.[14]

Marshall questioned Agricola's (Monroe's) loyalty for burying "the love of country under a zeal for party or affection for a foreign nation." He skewered Monroe for opposing the right of citizens to voice their views by adopting resolutions. The citizens of Richmond, Marshall asserted, were not enemies of France or the French Revolution, but they were "every day offended by the most malignant charges against their beloved Chief Magistrate." For Marshall, the issue was not how well we love France but rather how well we love our own country.[15]

Monroe, as Agricola, replied that Washington's policies—tariffs on French imports, the appointment of Morris as envoy to France, and the Proclamation of Neutrality—all threatened America's single alliance.[16] He charged that there was a cabal within the government plotting against France and threatening to destroy universal "Liberty and Equality."[17] To suggest that Marshall and Hamilton were not committed to the values of the Revolutionary War in which they had risked their lives and served with distinction was infuriating.

Marshall, as Aristides, responded that any defense of Genet's "extreme impropriety" would only "impair the affection of America" for France. By distinguishing support for the ideals of the French Revolution from support for Genet, Marshall undercut Monroe's principal argument. Marshall railed against republicans for defending a foreign envoy who had meddled in U.S. politics and warned that if republicans aligned themselves with a foreign power it would threaten democracy.[18]

The Richmond meeting and the exchange with Monroe confirmed Marshall as the leading federalist in the nation's largest state. There was no more effective advocate for federalist ideas south of Philadelphia. Marshall's views on the president's role in foreign relations had won a wide audience. President Washington and the federalist leaders knew they could rely on Marshall as a powerful ally in Jefferson's base. The Genet affair and the debate over the Proclamation of Neutrality accelerated the formation of political parties in America. Americans often say that "politics stops at the water's edge." In fact, our party politics started at the water's edge with the battle between the friends and foes of the French Revolution.

AS A CONSEQUENCE of this debate, supporters of neutrality coalesced into the Federalist Party, and critics of the administration formed the Republican Party, led by Jefferson. The congressional election in 1794 was the first time that representatives ran and were elected on party tickets. The House of Representatives in 1795 had fifty-nine Republican and forty-seven Federalist representatives; the Senate had twenty-one Federalists and eleven Republicans. The bitter disagreement over the French Revolution had produced a familiar result—a divided government with a Senate friendly to the president and a House governed by a hostile Republican majority.

It would be a mistake to superimpose the longitudes of our liberal-conservative politics onto the political landscape of the early Republic. Both Republicans and Federalists were conservatives in the sense that they sought to protect the existing institutions and elites in their respective regions. Though Republicans were more likely to deploy terms such as "liberty," "democracy," and "equality" in challenging Washington and his allies, they were the party that fought to protect state power, slavery, and an agrarian economy from the reach of federal power and opposed the transformative influence of industry, finance, and cities. And though Federalists feared populism and revolution, they embraced a strong federal government as an instrument for modernization, industrialization, and urbanization. Marshall considered himself a conservative in the sense that he wanted to protect property rights and resisted following the path of the French republicans. But his conservatism was like that of the British statesman Edmund Burke. Marshall was forward-looking, progressive, and reformist. By defending federal power and aligning himself with financial and urban interests, he favored a more modern national economy. In so doing, he challenged the power elite in Virginia and implicitly the slave plantation system from which that elite derived its wealth.

Marshall, like other Federalists, supported a standing military and a strong executive to safeguard the liberty won in the American Revolution against foreign adversaries. Federalists favored a policy of neutrality to keep a safe distance from foreign wars and high tariffs to protect infant manufacturing industries from European competition. By contrast, Republicans saw the French Revolution as a continuation of the American Revolution, and they embraced the revolutionary idea of liberating all the peoples of the earth from monarchy. Republicans had a missionary impulse to transform the world by force if necessary, but conversely they opposed a standing army as a threat to liberty. Southern Republicans opposed tariffs that drove up import prices because they had no manufacturing to protect.

What makes this all more confusing is that Jefferson's Republicans (also known as Democratic-Republicans) eventually morphed from the Jacksonian Democratic Party into the contemporary Democratic Party with its support for a strong national government and the rights of minorities. By contrast, Hamilton's Federalists, after a long period wandering in the wilderness as Whigs, eventually formed the core of the contemporary Republican Party, representing what Madison denounced as the "monied interests." For these reasons, it would be a mistake to tag eighteenth-century Federalists and Republicans with contemporary labels.

What eighteenth-century Republicans and Federalists shared was a sense of American exceptionalism: For Republicans that meant remaking the world in the United States' image. Federalists had a more modest and perhaps realistic goal: to preserve the Republic from the corrupting influences of European power politics. These two faces of American exceptionalism— one universalist and moralist, and the other isolationist and pragmatic— endure to the present.

OCTOBER 1793 BROUGHT relief from the saga of Citizen Genet when the Committee of Public Safety recalled him to France. The Jacobins intended to arrest him the moment he set foot in Paris, so Genet preferred to remain in America rather than face the real possibility of being guillotined. But by now he had burned his bridges among Republicans. Jefferson, who might have offered him sanctuary, showed no compassion for the man he had embraced so warmly only months earlier. Ironically, it was Hamilton who intervened on Genet's behalf. Hamilton persuaded Washington to allow Genet to stay in the United States as a private citizen. Genet, the young upstart who a year earlier had joked that he would bring Louis XVI to America to teach him to be a good American farmer, now retired from public life and lived out the remainder of his days on a farm in upstate New York. He eventually married the daughter of New York Governor George Clinton, the leader of the Republican Party and Hamilton's sworn adversary.

Jefferson remained in Washington's cabinet until the end of December 1793. Then he withdrew to his plantation at Monticello. After twenty-four years of public service, he was exhausted.

But Jefferson sought the presidency three years later. His rivalry with John Marshall was just beginning.

CHAPTER EIGHT

JAY'S TREATY

Though President Washington had hoped that neutrality would keep the country from being dragged into the European conflict, the Proclamation of Neutrality actually pushed the United States closer to conflict with both Britain and France. The British navy retaliated against the Americans for selling goods to France by seizing hundreds of U.S. commercial vessels. "We fear & not without reason a war," Marshall advised a friend. "The man does not live who wishes for peace more than I do, but the outrages committed upon us are beyond human bearing . . . pray Heaven we may weather the storm."[1]

Marshall felt a strong sense of duty to the public and his commander in chief. He was now a brigadier general in command of Virginia's second brigade. After Congress adopted the Neutrality Act in June 1794, Marshall was pressed into active service. He was charged with enforcing the statute by preventing Virginians from accepting commissions as French privateers. One of the most famous privateers was Captain John Sinclair, a hero of the Revolutionary War. Captain Sinclair had outfitted a vessel for privateering, and in July, General Marshall and his men were ordered to capture the vessel on the James River. Sinclair, who was heavily armed, and the local Smithfield militiamen initially resisted Marshall's regiment, but they eventually surrendered without firing a shot.[2] A few weeks later, Virginia's Governor Henry Lee sent General Marshall's forces into battle against the Whiskey Rebellion in Pennsylvania. Marshall had to remain behind in Richmond, however. That October, Governor Lee named Marshall acting attorney general for the commonwealth to replace James Innes.[3]

Marshall juggled these public responsibilities while continuing his private law practice to support his growing family. In 1795, Polly gave birth to a daughter, Mary. This was the sixth child born in the decade in which Polly had already lost two children, and Mary was the only daughter who would survive. Plagued by nervous tension and depression, Polly confined herself to the upstairs bedroom, leaving Marshall to manage his large household alone.

Meanwhile, Marshall felt squeezed by his financial obligations. In February 1794, Marshall had purchased from Lord Fairfax's nephew Denny Martin all of the South Branch Manor for six thousand pounds sterling (roughly eight hundred thousand dollars today).[4] The South Branch Manor was a fifty-five-thousand-acre tract in Hampshire and Hardy counties that Marshall bought jointly with his brother, his two brothers-in-law, and Virginia Governor Henry Lee.[5] This was the first of his two major land purchases from the Fairfax estate, and it required a bank loan to finance the deal. Marshall sought a line of credit from the newly formed First Bank of the United States, and when that failed, he sent his brother James to the Netherlands in search of a foreign loan.[6]

ON AUGUST 31, 1795, a letter arrived from President Washington. "The Office of Attorney General of the U States has become vacant by the death of Willm. Bradford esqr.," Washington wrote in his direct and unadorned style. "I take the earliest opportunity of asking if you will accept the appointment?" In addition to the salary, there was the added inducement of "the prospect of a lucrative practice" in Philadelphia.[7] Twenty years earlier, Marshall was an obscure rifleman in Washington's army from the backwoods of Virginia with no formal education and limited prospects. Now the president of the United States was asking him to join his cabinet as the nation's highest-ranking legal officer. Marshall replied graciously to President Washington that his involvement in the legal wrangling over the title to the Fairfax property prevented him from accepting a cabinet appointment.[8]

Marshall's father, whom Marshall had not seen in almost fifteen years, wrote to his son in November from his home in Kentucky. He was replying to the news that Marshall's sister Lucy, who was married to Polly's cousin John Ambler, had died months earlier. Thomas mentioned in passing that "[w]e are informed that you are appointed Attorney General for the United States." Thinking that Marshall had accepted, he continued matter-of-factly complaining that no U.S. attorney had yet been appointed for the new state of Kentucky.[9] Thomas Marshall was not the sort of man to lavish praise—or grief—on his children. Thomas treated his son with the same detached paternal attitude that Marshall displayed toward his own sons.

President Washington clearly thought highly of Marshall's talents. When Marshall's cousin Edmund Randolph resigned from his position as secretary of state in October 1795, Washington discussed with Hamilton whether to appoint Marshall in his place. Since Marshall had already refused the job of attorney general, for which he was certainly better qualified, the president thought he would not be able to persuade Marshall to take the job.[10]

One of Marshall's friends was running for the Virginia House of Delegates that spring, and on election day Marshall went to vote for him. At the polling place, another voter suggested that Marshall's name be added to the ballot. That evening, to his surprise, Marshall learned he had been elected. "I regretted this for the sake of my friend," Marshall later remarked, but he quickly patched up the friendship and was happy to be back among his former colleagues in the General Assembly.[11]

Madison worried that Marshall's return to the legislature would fortify the increasingly vocal Federalist minority. Both Jefferson and Madison viewed Marshall as the most dangerous man in Virginia. Jefferson thought that Marshall's laid-back style, what Jefferson called his "lax lounging manners," and his "pretense" of nonpartisanship had misled voters. He hoped that now that Marshall was back in the House of Delegates, they could expose Marshall as a "monocrat."[12]

THE NEUTRALITY POLICY Marshall had campaigned for did little to assuage the tensions between the belligerents. Both the French and the British felt that America's neutrality policy discriminated against them. The British felt that the Americans did nothing to stop French privateers while they still refused to repay their debts to British creditors in violation of the Treaty of Paris. In the summer of 1793, the British cabinet issued a secret order to naval vessels to seize any neutral vessels bound for French territory. Any merchandise intended for France was a "lawful prize," meaning it could be captured and sold. By the summer of 1794, more than 250 U.S. merchant vessels sailing in the West Indies had been captured, and at least 150 were condemned as lawful prizes. Hundreds of crew members were left stranded in the British West Indies with no way to return home and no means of support. Even worse, British officers forcibly conscripted, or "impressed," hundreds of American seamen into the British navy.[13] Impressment of British subjects was a long-standing prerogative of the Royal Navy whenever they needed more sailors. Given the poor wages and conditions on ships, the British navy was always short-handed. Impressment was a primitive form of the military draft, albeit an irregular and a capricious one. Squads of British seamen known as press gangs would descend on taverns or ships, seize men they presumed were British subjects, and kidnap them for His Majesty's Navy.

Relations with Britain were further strained in 1794 when the Canadian Governor General Lord Dorchester gave an inflammatory speech to Canadians relating to a border dispute with New York. He warned that Britain would soon be at war with the United States for its failure to honor the Treaty of Paris. Canadians were not generally known for being a belligerent people, and President Washington and Congress were alarmed by Dorchester's unusually aggressive language.[14]

In response to the growing tension with Britain, President Washington, on the advice of Treasury Secretary Hamilton, appointed Chief Justice John Jay as a special envoy to Britain in April 1794 to settle the ongoing dispute. As chief justice, Jay was thrust into an awkward position: Was it constitutional or even appropriate for a member of the Court to serve as a diplomatic representative for the president? Jay felt compelled to set these qualms aside. No American had more diplomatic experience. Jay had negotiated the Treaty of Paris, which ended the Revolutionary War, and he had served as the first secretary of foreign affairs prior to the establishment of the State Department. America could not afford another war with Britain. The country had no standing army or navy, and France, convulsed with revolution and tied up in a land war against her European neighbors, could not possibly spare support for the Americans as it had in the Revolutionary War. Besides, Jay found the job of chief justice boring. He had no wish to remain on the Court, which had little authority over few cases. Jay's ambition was to run for governor of New York State, and he may have concluded that making peace with Britain would help to secure him the governorship.[15]

Jay arrived in London in July 1794 and began several months of negotiations with the British foreign secretary, Lord William Wyndham Grenville, the son of the former prime minister. Grenville was superbly well qualified as a diplomat but notoriously prickly. His nickname was Bogy, as in the boogeyman, apparently because he terrified his colleagues. Jay sought compensation for the seizure of ships and U.S. sailors, but Grenville made it clear that this was out of the question. Negotiations stretched on through the summer and fall. Grenville was in no rush. The treaty was of marginal interest to Britain, but Grenville knew that Jay would be eager to return to New York in time for the gubernatorial election. Jay knew that without a navy, the Americans were in a weak position to bargain with the British.[16]

By November the two men reached an agreement on a treaty that to many Americans looked terribly one-sided: The British denied any compensation for the ships, goods, or sailors they had seized, and they would not promise to stop impressment. Their only substantive concessions were to agree to withdraw from forts on U.S. territory by July 1796 and allow U.S. merchant vessels to trade with the British West Indies. In exchange, the United States would establish a joint commission to settle claims of British creditors that were not enforced by state courts. The United States also would compensate British subjects for any British goods or ships captured by French privateers outfitted in U.S. ports, and if British creditors were not able to collect from U.S. debtors, the U.S. government would pay them in gold or silver coins rather than paper bills, which could lose value. Most galling of all, the treaty recognized the ancient right of the British to capture ships belonging to neutral countries and seize goods destined for France. This was a repudiation of the prevailing international custom that neutrals had the right to trade with belligerent parties during wartime and that only a narrowly defined class of "contraband" goods—strictly military supplies—were subject to capture.[17]

By contrast, the U.S. commercial treaty with France recognized the principle that "free ships make free goods." In other words, Americans had consented to allow the British navy to seize goods on U.S. vessels bound for France, but France could not seize goods on U.S. vessels bound for Britain. This asymmetry would obviously not sit well with France or its Republican supporters in the United States. Jay knew the treaty would be unpopular, but in his view it was better than fighting a war the young nation could not win. Besides, he needed to get back to the United States in time for his election as New York's governor.

President Washington, realizing that the treaty would be controversial, asked the Senate to consent in secret. Republicans demanded that the treaty be made public, and someone leaked the document to the Republican press. Republicans immediately pounced. They found it was much easier to oppose a treaty than to negotiate one—or fight a war. They attacked the treaty as a complete surrender to British demands. Republicans disparaged the treaty as "Jay's Treaty" as a way of placing blame on the Federalist governor. Why should Americans compensate British losses suffered at the hands of French privateers, they argued, when there was no compensation offered to Americans whose ships or goods were captured by the British navy? The treaty discriminated against goods bound for French territory. And the treaty failed to address the two most emotionally charged issues: the impressment of U.S. nationals and the "theft" of U.S. slaves by the British during the Revolutionary War. For many southerners, the loss of their slaves was reason enough to reject the treaty and go to war. There were angry public demonstrations against the treaty.[18] Henry Adams, a great-grandson of President John Adams, later wrote that few would deny that Jay's Treaty "was a bad one" and that the United States would not "have hesitated to prefer war to peace on such terms." The historian, like many of his contemporaries, thought that the "palliative" of avoiding war was not worth the surrender of principles.[19]

The public view of Jay's Treaty was summarized in a bit of popular doggerel.

May it please your highness, I, John Jay
Have traveled all this mighty way,
To inquire if you, good Lord, will please,
To suffer me while on my knees,
To show all others I surpass,
In love, by kissing of your _____

As by my 'xtraordinary station,
I represent a certain nation;
I then conclude, and so may you,
They all would wish to kiss it too.[20]

Jay shrugged off the controversy with his characteristic humor. He joked that he could find his way across the entire country by following the light of his burning effigies.[21] In fairness, Jay had a weak hand to play, and the Republicans' insistence that they could negotiate a better treaty was a facile boast. The treaty had implicitly secured two important points that its critics overlooked: First, the British had acknowledged for the first time the territorial integrity of the United States as a sovereign country by committing to withdraw its forces from all U.S. territory, which went beyond the 1783 Treaty of Paris. Second, the United States avoided a war and a disruption in its trade that it might not have survived. About 75 percent of all U.S. imports and exports were traded with Britain. Moreover, Treasury Secretary Hamilton had created high tariffs to protect infant U.S. industries and provide a revenue stream for the federal government to fund its projects. More than 90 percent of all federal revenue came from customs duties, and around 90 percent of all goods subject to tariffs in the 1790s were British. In other words, British imports provided the vast bulk of U.S. tax revenues.[22] Any disruption in trade with Britain would have had devastating and possibly ruinous consequences for the country's finances.

Given that France was unable to help defend the United States again, financing a war against Britain in 1794 would have been even more difficult than it had been in 1776. Jay's Treaty failed to resolve all the underlying problems in U.S. relations with Britain, but by forestalling war until 1812, it bought the United States the time it needed to strengthen its fledgling economy and military. Procrastination is a failing in a tradesman, but it is often a virtue in a statesman.

————

THE DEBATE over Jay's Treaty engaged the entire nation. In Virginia, Republicans seized the opportunity to make political hay as Jefferson looked toward the presidential election the following year. Republicans in the Virginia General Assembly proposed a resolution calling on Virginia's U.S. senators to vote against Jay's Treaty. This was a gratuitous swipe; in fact, no such resolution was necessary, considering that both Virginia senators were solid Republicans appointed by the General Assembly. Nevertheless, the debate became a register of opposition to the treaty and an opportunity to attack the Washington administration. Marshall argued that the Virginia General Assembly had no authority to challenge a federal treaty, but the Republican representatives easily won.[23]

In the spring of 1796, the issue resurfaced in the Virginia General Assembly. Washington had asked Congress to appropriate funds to implement U.S. obligations under Jay's Treaty. Virginia Republicans now argued that since Jay's Treaty pertained to commercial relations, it should have been submitted first to the House of Representatives as legislation—rather than to the Senate as a treaty—since the power to regulate trade is shared by both houses.[24] This argument negated the plain language of Article I of the Constitution, which clearly gave the Senate the power to act alone when consenting to treaties.[25]

Marshall was once again faced with defending the supremacy of federal power over the states. In addition, he had a financial interest in Jay's Treaty. The treaty affirmed the pre–Revolutionary War property rights of British subjects.[26] That meant that any doubt as to the title to Lord Fairfax's land would be resolved in his favor and that Marshall could complete the acquisition of the property.[27]

Friends warned Marshall that if he defended the treaty it would "destroy [him] totally." Marshall replied that "a politician even in times of violent party spirit maintains his respectability by showing his strength; and is

most safe when he encounters prejudice most fearlessly." Marshall neutral-
ized some of the criticism by focusing on the narrow constitutional question. He quoted Jefferson and Madison, who had previously argued that the
Senate alone had the power to approve a commercial treaty like this. Marshall later boasted that when he sat down "[t]here was scarcely an intelligent
man in the house who did not yield on his opinion on the constitutional
question."[28] But partisanship often trumps reason. Republicans in the Virginia General Assembly voted against the treaty anyway.

Marshall thought that questions of foreign policy should be left to the
executive and Congress rather than popular opinion or state legislators.
Nevertheless, he decided the only way to fight the Republicans' opposition
to Jay's Treaty was to appeal directly to the people. As Marshall wrote to
Hamilton, "As Man is a gregarious animal we shall certainly derive much
aid from declarations in support of the constitution & of appropriations if
such can be obtain'd from our sister States."[29] For the second time in three
years, Marshall convened a public rally to support the president's foreign
policies. More than four hundred residents participated in the largest public assembly that Richmond had ever witnessed. And "after a very ardent &
zealous discussion which consum'd the day," Marshall wrote, "a decided
majority declar'd in favor of a resolution that the welfare & honor of the nation requir'd us to give full effect to the treaty."[30]

Once again, Marshall had made himself a target for the Republican
press that violently opposed Jay's Treaty. Marshall's defense of an unpopular treaty may have been motivated in part by his self-interest in the Fairfax
property, but he won respect from Federalists around the country for his
political courage to challenge Republicans in Jefferson's heartland. The experience also taught him a valuable lesson about how viciously national
politics was played. Marshall never expected colleagues such as Madison
and Monroe to manufacture false allegations against him. "Accustomed as
I was to political misrepresentation," he noted, "I could not view without
some surprise the numerous gross misrepresentations which were made on

this occasion; and the virulent asperity, with which the common terms of decency in which nations express their compacts with each other, was assailed."[31]

Marshall's political education was just beginning.

IN HIS LAST full year in office, President Washington again turned to Marshall in July 1796 and asked him to serve as minister to France. Washington had decided to replace the current American envoy, James Monroe. Washington felt that Monroe's loyalty to the Republican Party preceded his loyalty to the president. Washington decided he needed someone who was more politically reliable and astute.

This was the third major post that Washington had offered to Marshall in as many years, but Marshall again replied that it was impossible "in the present crises of my affairs to leave the United States."[32] He was still struggling at the time to make the payments on the purchase of the Fairfax estate. Though the Republicans viewed Marshall as being overly ambitious, there is little evidence that Marshall had any intention of leaving Richmond at this point.

Marshall's political influence as the Federalist leader in Virginia and his reputation as one of the leading attorneys in Virginia were both peaking at the same moment. And Marshall had an interesting new client: Pierre-Augustin Caron de Beaumarchais, the French comic playwright who wrote *The Barber of Seville* and *The Marriage of Figaro*. During the American Revolution, Beaumarchais had formed an arms-smuggling operation with the American envoy at the time, Connecticut merchant Silas Deane. Beaumarchais sold thousands of tons of arms and supplies from France to the Americans and had expected to receive Virginia tobacco in exchange. But Congress never repaid Beaumarchais or France.[33] Marshall agreed to represent Beaumarchais in a suit against Virginia demanding payment for the arms, ammunition, and supplies delivered to the Virginia militia. Even when Virginia agreed to pay a portion of what Beaumarchais was owed in Virginia currency, the currency was so depreciated that the playwright refused it.[34] But the relationship between Marshall and Beaumarchais would prove fateful.

The presidential election of 1796 resulted in a divided executive branch. Vice President John Adams, a Federalist, narrowly defeated Jefferson, a Republican, in the electoral vote. Since the Framers of the Constitution had not foreseen the development of political parties, they had not provided for candidates to run on party tickets. Thus, Jefferson, having received the second largest number of electoral votes, was chosen as Adams's vice president. Adams's election was an especially bitter pill for France to swallow. Practically quoting the Republicans, the French government denounced Adams as an Anglophile and a monarchist. Adams's election felt like a slap in the face to France.

Shortly after Adams's inauguration in March 1797, France registered its disapproval by refusing to accept the credentials of the newly appointed U.S. envoy, Charles Cotesworth Pinckney. France recalled its minister to the United States, Pierre Adet, and then France began seizing U.S. vessels on the high seas for trading with Britain. Over a period of eighteen months, more than three hundred vessels were captured by French ships, millions of dollars of cargo was taken, and hundreds of American seamen and passengers were harassed, detained, jailed, and brutalized.

It was true that Adams had no love for the French Directory. As a former commissioner to Paris with Jefferson during the American Revolution, Adams thought that he understood the French. As president, Adams feared that France was veering dangerously close to anarchy. His judgment was more astute than those of Francophiles like Jefferson. Adams's blunt conclusion was clear: "The French are no more capable of a republican government than a snowball can exist a whole week in the streets of Philadelphia under a burning sun."[35] Nevertheless, President Adams set aside his own prejudices to try to reduce tensions with France.

Just days before he was sworn into office, he met with Vice President–elect Jefferson in his room at the Francis Hotel in Philadelphia. They had not spoken in three years since Jefferson had quit the cabinet, but their meeting was cordial. In the course of their conversation, Adams informed Jefferson that he hoped to make a fresh start with France by sending a peace commission to negotiate with the Directory, and he wanted Jefferson and Madison to serve on the three-man commission. Sending two of the most prominent advocates for France would signal Adams's good intentions. Jefferson accepted Adams's offer graciously, but two days later he reversed himself. Both Jefferson and Madison refused to cross party lines to cooperate with the Federalist administration.[36] Loyalty to their political party trumped any desire for a peaceful resolution of the crisis with France.

In the spring of 1797, as President Adams came into office, the United States was on the brink of war for the first time as an independent nation. President Adams called a joint session of Congress and announced that he would send a peace commission to France. At the same time, he called on Congress to prepare for war. The president wanted Congress to establish an army and a navy, but Republicans resisted raising a military. They denounced Adams as a warmonger while Federalists praised his resolve. Vice President Jefferson concluded that President Adams had joined the extreme wing of the High Federalists in his hostility toward France.[37]

Adams nominated a Republican friend from Massachusetts, Congressman Elbridge Gerry, and Charles Cotesworth Pinckney as co-commissioners to France. Gerry was a controversial choice among Federalists. He was one of the few men at the Constitutional Convention who refused to sign the federal Constitution, and he was outspokenly pro-French. Federalists and most Republicans agreed that Pinckney was a fair choice. He was a moderate southern Federalist whom Washington had appointed ambassador to France. Since the French Directory had refused to accept his credentials as ambassador, Pinckney was already living in The Hague waiting for diplomatic instructions.

For the third man on the commission, Adams wanted another loyal Federalist from the South. Most likely it was Washington or Hamilton who suggested Marshall, whom Adams had never met. Adams nominated Marshall, and despite Republican concerns that he was hostile to France, he was swiftly confirmed by the Senate as "envoy extraordinary and minister plenipotentiary." Marshall learned of his appointment by letter from Secretary of State Timothy Pickering only after the Senate's vote.

When Jefferson learned that the third commissioner would be his meddlesome cousin Marshall, he surely must have grimaced. Jefferson could not have been happy that President Adams would send any staunch Federalist to France—even though Adams had first asked Jefferson and Madison to go—but Marshall was a particularly offensive choice to Jefferson. Marshall, after all, had championed Jay's Treaty, supported Washington's neutrality policy, and opposed Genet. And from Jefferson's perspective, Marshall did not know his proper place in the world. He lacked formal education. He could not speak French and was unfamiliar with European customs. To Jefferson, Marshall seemed uniquely unqualified.[38] Jefferson could comfort himself with the smug assurance that Marshall's certain failure would doom both the Federalist Party and Marshall when he returned.

Why did Marshall accept this commission after refusing Washington's prior appointments as U.S. attorney for Virginia, attorney general, and minister to France? Marshall had no experience overseas—indeed, he had never been on board a ship before and had left Virginia only the few times he had gone to Philadelphia. But he cared about the outcome of the negotiations, and he was familiar with the underlying issues. While it pained him to leave his family and his practice, Marshall assumed that the mission would be a matter of only a few months, and he assumed that he could hold on to his clients during that time.[39]

Marshall had other personal motives for traveling to Europe as well. His brother James had gone to Europe two years earlier to seek funding for the acquisition of Fairfax's estate, but he could raise only about seven thousand pounds from a Dutch banker. Much more was needed to purchase the choicest portion of the Fairfax property, Leeds Manor, which was near Markham in Fauquier County. Marshall needed the financing in place by the spring of 1797, or he risked losing his option to buy Leeds Manor. Now that Jay's Treaty had presumably cleared the title to the property, Marshall was determined to find financial backers in Europe.[40]

But first Marshall would have to explain his absence to Polly. At thirty-one, Polly was frail, anxious, and pregnant again. Even with a household of slaves, she was unable to take care of their three children. Polly did not respond well to Marshall's news. She feared for her husband's safety, as he would be traveling such a long distance between two belligerent powers that were convulsed by war and revolution and willing to seize or sink an American vessel. And she dreaded the thought that he could be gone for many months or even years. Marshall left Robin Spurlock to manage the household in his absence. There was no time for a quiet good-bye. Well-wishers crowded their house day and night as Marshall rushed to pack and hurry to Philadelphia at the earliest opportunity. He and Polly exchanged harsh words before he left. Perhaps Polly said more than she really meant. She remained bitter for some time afterward.[41]

On his way from Richmond to Philadelphia, Marshall stopped at Alexandria to visit Washington. He wrote to Polly that his trip by horseback was uneventful: "All your other fears will be as foundationless as this." He asked her to write to him at Philadelphia and "do tell me & tell me truly that the bitterness of parting is over & your mind at rest—that you think of me only to contemplate the pleasure of our meeting & that you will permit nothing to distress you while I am gone." He was even sad to say good-bye to his slave Dick, whom he sent back to Virginia. Perhaps Marshall felt completely alone for the first time. "[E]very step I take carries me further & further from what is to [me] most valuable in this world but I will suppress such sensation & will be quiet if I can only be certain that you are so." He closed, "I must now give you one positive order. It is, be happy."[42]

Marshall knew that it was unlikely that this order would be obeyed, and Polly did not reply to Marshall for some time, much to his anxiety and annoyance.[43] When she did, he reminded her that "[g]ood health will produce good spirits." Marshall's cheeriness suggests that he had little appreciation of the depths of depression his wife suffered from losing four children. Marshall's buoyancy and resilience helped him survive the hardships of wartime; he viewed his wife's unhappiness as a failure of will rather than as a feature of her personality. Marshall's experience had taught him that reality follows appearance—that if you appeared cheerful and confident, things would turn out. He warned his pregnant wife that her "melancholy may inflict punishment on an innocent for whose sake you ought to preserve a serene & composed mind." It was not what she needed to hear. And then he closed by assuring her that he would hurry home as soon as possible.[44] The French foreign minister, Charles Maurice de Talleyrand-Périgord, however, would have other plans for Marshall.

MARSHALL MET President and Mrs. Adams for the first time over dinner at the President's House in Philadelphia on a muggy Saturday evening, July 1, 1797. The president immediately liked the Virginian. He thought Marshall was "a plain Man, very Sensible, cautious, guarded, learned in the Law of Nations." Abigail, who was a keen observer of human nature, was also impressed by Marshall's character and judged him an "upright honest man." Likewise, Marshall was "much pleasd" with this Yankee lawyer whose certitude and prickliness so often rattled his contemporaries.[45]

While Marshall waited two weeks for a ship, he amused himself in the capital. He dined with Robert Morris, the financier and former senator whose daughter was married to Marshall's brother James. He had hoped that Morris would lend him money to purchase his share of the Fairfax property, but Morris's financial empire was unraveling. Morris was once the wealthiest man in Philadelphia, if not the United States, but he was now facing bankruptcy. Marshall noted to Polly in a letter that despite the threat of insolvency, Morris continued to live lavishly. The only sign of impending doom was the absence of visitors.[46]

Marshall visited old friends and Federalist members of Congress eager to meet the new envoy. He shared ice creams along the banks of the Schuylkill and attended a performance of *Romeo and Juliet* starring the celebrated actress Ann Brunton Merry. Though he liked the play, once again he thought that Mrs. Merry was no better than the leading actress in Richmond's own Virginia Company.[47] He dined with the William Binghams, prominent Philadelphia socialites, at their gracious estate on the Schuylkill. He appreciated their elegant dining table crowned with an enormous gold vase ornamented with cupids, but he took exception to Mrs. Bingham's audacious dress, which exposed her elbows.[48]

After a fortnight in the capital city, Marshall grew restless. He wrote Polly almost daily, perhaps feeling guilty for his sudden departure and anxious for some word from her. "This dissipated life does not long suit my temper," he noted. "I woud give a great deal to dine with you today on a piece of cold meat with our boys beside us & to see little Mary running backwards & forwards over the floor playing the sweet little tricks she [is] full of."[49] Had he known he would be delayed so long, he would have preferred to spend the time at home. He had already grown "sick to death of this place."[50]

Secretary of State Pickering wrote out lengthy negotiating instructions that he delivered to Marshall on July 15. Pickering listed a number of "offensive and injurious measures of the French Republic" for which the ministers should seek redress, including offensive remarks by the president of the Directory, the seizure of U.S. vessels, the taking of cargo, and the imprisonment and torture suffered by American sailors. Second, the negotiations should establish a claims commission to settle all outstanding disputes. France would have to pay compensation for all U.S. property taken. Third, the United States sought a new commercial treaty that ensured a "perfect reciprocity" in respect to all goods and that all goods on board neutral vessels would be free from capture. In other words, the treaty must recognize the principle that "free ships make free goods." Finally, the peace commission should clarify that the United States was not bound by the Treaty of Alliance to aid France against Britain. If France insisted that the United States was bound to fight Britain, then the United States would have to repudiate the treaty.[51]

On Monday, July 17, Marshall set sail from New Castle, Delaware, on the *Grace*, a small, sleek brigantine. The pilot guided the ship into Delaware Bay and then left the *Grace* under the command of a Captain Willis. It was a windless, humid day. The sails barely rippled. A blinding sun bleached everything white such that the slowly disappearing coast hovered like the wisp of a cloud over the silver water. The bay seemed strangely tranquil. The great voyage had commenced, but the *Grace* just rolled languidly on the waves while seagulls mocked its progress.[52]

CHAPTER NINE

TALLEYRAND

The voyage seemed interminable. Good weather meant calm waters and light wind but a longer journey. Marshall's cabin was small but clean, and his berth was just long enough for his six-foot frame. There was plenty of fresh chicken, eggs, wine, and brandy on board. He was already homesick, and occasionally he would sink into melancholy when he realized the enormity of the stakes he was facing and the risk that negotiations could drag on for months.[1] The *Grace* was stopped and searched on three separate occasions by British men-of-war looking for contraband or British subjects to impress into the Royal Navy.[2] The British had no reason to suspect that the *Grace* was carrying a secret envoy to France. Marshall was a man of no particular importance.

After six weeks of sailing, the *Grace* crossed the Zuiderzee to Amsterdam on the evening of August 29, 1797. Ships crowded the docks, and dockworkers carried crates and barrels laden with Virginian tobacco, Venetian glass, Chinese silks and jade, Japanese furnishings, Persian carpets, Turkish spices, and Indian teas. Though the Netherlands was no longer the economic behemoth that had dominated the known world in the seventeenth century, its declining fortune was not evident to an American visitor.

The French Revolution had swept through the Netherlands only two years earlier. The so-called Dutch Patriots drove out the hereditary stadtholder, William V, Prince of Orange, and proclaimed a democratic "Batavian Republic" aligned with France. At first, these Dutch Patriots welcomed French troops as "liberators," but for the privilege of calling France a "sister republic," the Dutch paid dearly. To finance Bonaparte's army, France extorted at least one hundred million florins from the Dutch economy—more than 20 percent of the Dutch gross domestic product.[3] Marshall observed that the Dutch "willingly relinquish national independence for individual safety." And he pointedly added, "What a lesson to those who would admit foreign influence into the United States."[4]

Marshall's first priority in the Netherlands was to seek additional funding for the Fairfax property from Dutch bankers. Despite the loss of its independence, the Netherlands remained a center of finance. After a few days negotiating loans, Marshall rode south to The Hague to meet Charles Cotesworth Pinckney, who was residing there with his wife, Mary; his young daughter, Eliza; and his nephew and personal secretary, Major Henry Rutledge, while he was in diplomatic limbo. But the seeds of France's contempt for Pinckney had been planted before his arrival by his predecessor, James Monroe. Monroe, before returning to the United States as a U.S. senator, had warned the French government that the Federalist Pinckney was pro-British, which had no basis in fact.

Charles Cotesworth Pinckney was a large, broad-shouldered, flabby aristocrat with a slow drawl that belied a swift mind. He was the talented son of Charles Pinckney, who had served as South Carolina's chief justice before statehood. His famous family included two governors and senators. He was married to the daughter of Henry Middleton, whose twenty plantations and eight hundred slaves made him the richest man in South Carolina. Like many southern gentlemen, Pinckney had been educated at Oxford and joined the bar at Middle Temple in London before returning home. He had distinguished himself in the Revolutionary War. At the Constitutional Convention, he was a fervent defender of slavery.[5] Pinckney proposed the clause in Article I that preserved the slave trade for at least twenty years after the Constitution was ratified. Pinckney was just as passionate in his insistence that slaves should count equally to white persons for the purpose of apportioning congressional representatives so as to enlarge the voting power of the slave-holding South in Congress.[6] Pinckney also proposed that senators should not be compensated for their service in order to reserve the Senate for men of wealth.[7] Bucking the Republican sentiments of his state, Pinckney emerged as a leading southern Federalist and later ran as President Adams's vice president in 1800.

Marshall and Pinckney hit it off from the start.[8] They were both Revolutionary War veterans and southern Federalists who supported President Adams. Marshall joined the Pinckneys, who were living in modest accommodations at the Marshal Turenne Tavern.[9] The two men waited in The Hague for a fortnight for Gerry to arrive by ship from Boston.

While in The Hague, Marshall learned of the momentous events taking place in revolutionary France. On September 4, 1797, the radicals who supported General Napoleon Bonaparte had seized power in the Coup of 18 Fructidor. They arrested their opponents, canceled elections, purged moderates from the Assembly, replaced members of the Directory, and closed opposition newspapers to pave the way for military dictatorship. Marshall thought that the radicals manifested a "wanton contempt of rules so essential to the very being of a republic."[10] Marshall hoped that ongoing negotiations between France and Britain might lead to peace, but he was not sanguine. France's course defies "all human calculation," he thought.[11] As Marshall learned more about the brutality of the radicals, he concluded that peace between France and Britain was unlikely.[12]

As the autumn weather arrived, Marshall and Pinckney grew impatient waiting for Gerry and decided to start for Paris without him. Pinckney traveled with his wife and nephew in one carriage, and Marshall traveled in another. They passed through the great polyglot cities of Rotterdam, Antwerp, and Brussels, where Marshall marveled at the mix of cultures and languages. They crossed the border into France and proceeded through the small city of Valenciennes. The flat landscape was crowded with trees turning amber and brown like ripe pears. From the window of his coach, Marshall marveled at the French agriculture. The air was pungent with the aroma of grapes. "The whole earth appears to be in cultivation," he observed.[13] Near Cambrai, Marshall's carriage lost a wheel, and he was delayed for several hours while Henry Rutledge argued in French with the local blacksmith.[14] Meanwhile, Gerry was on his way from Rotterdam.

On September 27, Marshall and Pinckney arrived in Paris. Gerry joined them a week later. All three took rooms at a large apartment building at 1131 rue de Grenelle in Saint Germain des Prés. The Pinckneys chose for themselves the largest suite on the second floor. Gerry and Marshall, appalled by Paris prices, chose two less expensive rooms on the first floor. The total rent for all three apartments was exorbitant—seventy louis d'or (about twenty-five thousand dollars today).[15] Marshall's suite was cramped and filthy. The linens and drapes smelled of smoke. The upholstery was stained, and the windows were cracked. Marshall's fireplace did not work properly, and there was no carpeting, so in the morning he nearly froze from the damp autumn air. Below them was a stable, and all night the noise of people coming and going and horses neighing disturbed their sleep. The street traffic outside the window—drunken parties, brawls, and carriage rides late in the night—was so close it sounded like someone was inside the room. Gerry was so fearful of the noise that he insisted on sleeping with a loaded pistol under his pillow.[16]

Elbridge Gerry had an oversize head and a miniature body. His flashy dress was as unconstrained as his tongue. He was famously contrarian. At the Constitutional Convention, he fought against nearly every power of the federal government. He opposed, for example, the power to raise a stand-ing army, which he famously compared to an erect penis: "An excellent assurance of domestic tranquility, but a dangerous temptation to foreign adventure." Gerry saw the world as a Manichaean struggle, but he often confused good and evil. For example, he was deeply suspicious of his friend President Adams, but he gave the benefit of every doubt to the treacherous French Directory. Gerry spoke frequently and at great length, but he was not persuasive. His fellow delegates thought he was kind and intelligent but "not well acquainted with mankind." In truth, Gerry enjoyed being the odd man out.[17]

Despite all this, Gerry was later elected the first Republican governor of Massachusetts and then vice president under James Madison. His lasting contribution to American politics was the invention of drawing election districts to favor incumbent politicians—a practice still called gerryman-dering.

When new envoys arrived in Paris, the women who worked in the mar-ket stalls customarily welcomed them with a rowdy street celebration. The ministers deputized Rutledge, who was fluent in French, to receive this du-bious honor. Forty or more women shouted greetings and compliments to the young man. The vendeuses formed a long receiving line, and as each one took turns squeezing, pinching, and kissing the astonished young American, he was overpowered by the smell of cheese and fish.[18]

Later that afternoon, still feeling a bit discomposed, Rutledge carried a letter to Talleyrand, who was the minister of foreign affairs, to officially notify him of the arrival of the three envoys and request a meeting to pre-sent their credentials. Of course, this came as no surprise. French spies had already informed Talleyrand about the Americans soon after Marshall had sailed into Amsterdam. No doubt they were being carefully watched.

The foreign minister replied that he would receive them at his home on October 8 at one o'clock sharp. They should not be late.[19]

———

CHARLES MAURICE DE TALLEYRAND-PÉRIGORD was one of the most extraordinary and amoral men in an extraordinary and amoral time. He was born into a noble family, but as an infant, he suffered an accident to his foot that left him lame. Ashamed of his son's limp, his father sent him away at age eight to train for the priesthood. Depressed and isolated from his family, Talleyrand devoted himself to reading. While he was still a student at the seminary, he began an affair with a young actress. He found that despite his twisted limb, he could win the hearts of women with his quick wit and angelic face. Even after his ordination, the louche Talleyrand never permitted his vows of celibacy to encumber his myriad sexual conquests. As the abbé of Périgord, he cultivated intimate relationships with members of the king's court, which begat a string of rapid promotions. By the time Talleyrand reached the age of thirty-five, the church had elevated him to agent-general of the clergy and bishop of Aucun.

Beginning in 1789, the French Revolution turned against the church and the aristocracy, and Talleyrand hastily embraced the democratic reforms. Whether he actually believed in these reforms was hardly relevant; Talleyrand's only lodestar was self-interest. He was elected to the National Assembly, where he proposed to nationalize all church property. In 1790, he was elected president of the assembly. When the National Assembly required all clergy to swear allegiance to a new democratic constitution in defiance of the pope's authority, Talleyrand was one of only four bishops who consented. When the pope excommunicated him, he was relieved to remove his collar.[20]

As the revolution progressed, Talleyrand became one of the leaders of the moderate Feuillants, who opposed the more radical Jacobins. Talleyrand, a closeted Anglophile, favored a diplomatic settlement and an alliance with England to secure the borders of France so that the revolutionary government could focus on internal reforms.[21] After war broke out with Austria in April 1792, Talleyrand was appointed minister to Britain. Later, as the Reign of Terror swept across France, Talleyrand sought refuge in London among the other French émigrés.[22] When Britain declared war on France, Prime Minister William Pitt tossed Talleyrand out of the country. Rather than face an uncertain fate in France, Talleyrand caught the next ship to Philadelphia.[23]

In Philadelphia, Talleyrand hoped to meet with the leaders of the young Republic. But Gouverneur Morris warned President Washington that the former bishop of Aucun was a man of poor character as he had seduced Morris's mistress, Adelaide de Flahaut.[24] Yet Talleyrand formed an improbable friendship with Alexander Hamilton despite the American's fierce hostility toward France. Hamilton and Talleyrand were both pragmatists and intellectuals who shared a weakness for beautiful women and material pleasures.[25] Hamilton left Talleyrand with one lasting impression that later colored his foreign policy: The natural ally of the Americans was Britain, not France. After two years adrift in the United States, Talleyrand received word that the French legislature had invited him to return to France.[26]

Talleyrand returned to Paris in the late spring of 1797 with no money and few prospects. He begged one of his former lovers, Germaine de Staël, to help him find a position or "I shall blow my brains out." Madame de Staël persuaded the president of the Directory, Paul Barras, with whom she also shared her bed, to appoint Talleyrand foreign minister.[27] Talleyrand had opposed French militarism and favored a peaceful resolution to France's external conflicts. On its face, his appointment by Barras, who favored conquest over compromise, made no sense. Perhaps it showed how little Barras cared about the subject of diplomacy. In truth, Barras had few other qualified candidates. The waves of arrests, massacres, and emigration had depleted the diplomatic service.[28] By the time the Americans arrived at his door, Talleyrand had been in office fewer than one hundred days, and he was no doubt still tiptoeing through the deadly minefield of revolutionary politics.

———

TALLEYRAND LIVED in the foreign minister's mansion at 471 rue de Bac, just three blocks from where the Americans were lodging. The afternoon after Rutledge visited the Foreign Ministry, the three Americans arrived precisely at one. They were told that the foreign minister could not see them until three. They returned at three and waited while the minister met with the ambassador from Portugal. They were brought into the audience room where Pinckney, as the senior member, presented their credentials to Talleyrand. Though fluent in English, Talleyrand felt self-conscious speaking it.[29] Polite but succinct, he carefully studied the credentials as if he were trying to find a mistake. Then Talleyrand looked up and responded that the Directory had requested a report from him on relations with the United States and that he could not accept their credentials until he finished his report. That made little sense, but Talleyrand assured them it would be done in a few days. Then he dismissed them. The whole meeting lasted little more than a quarter of an hour, and the Americans were swiftly ushered out into the somber gray light of an autumn afternoon not quite certain what had transpired.[30]

Thomas Paine, the English author of *Common Sense,* who had recently been released from the Directory's prison, had counseled the foreign minister to treat the Americans with "reproach." As a strident propagandist, Paine had successively offended the British, American, and French governments, and now he was trying his hand at diplomacy. He advised Marshall that the Americans should repudiate their treaties with Britain and accept whatever conditions France imposed. Cheeky Paine told Marshall that since Americans had not shown sufficient gratitude to France for its aid during the Revolutionary War they should not expect anything from France except "high toned indignation."[31] Marshall realized that Paine's impertinent proposal would only make war with Britain more likely and that the commissioners should reject it coldly. Gerry, however, thought that

Paine would make the perfect liaison with the Directory, but Marshall correctly suspected that Paine was already acting on instructions from Talleyrand. Marshall countered that they could not appease France by agreeing to terms that President Adams would certainly reject. Caught between Marshall's firmness and Gerry's appeasement, Pinckney proposed crafting a reply to Paine expressing appreciation for his plan without making any commitment.[32]

The American envoys assumed incorrectly that Talleyrand had authority to negotiate on behalf of the Directory. Talleyrand, in fact, had less bargaining room than the American envoys imagined he had. His approach to diplomacy was conciliatory, but the Directory had little use for Talleyrand's moderation. In October 1797, it was too early for the newly appointed foreign minister to judge how much freedom he had to act. Talleyrand needed time to assess.[33]

Talleyrand did think that the Americans had taken France for granted. He felt that Jay's Treaty, which conferred trading rights on Britain that the United States had not offered to France, violated the 1778 Treaty of Amity and Commerce. But Talleyrand had a more nuanced view of American politics than others in the French Directory. He did not view President Adams as inherently hostile to France. In fact, Talleyrand thought that Adams was less hostile to France than Washington was. Talleyrand doubted that the Republican Party was a reliable ally, and he criticized his predecessor for putting too much faith in America's previous envoy, James Monroe.[34]

Talleyrand believed that the rhetoric of Federalists and Republicans was far less important than the United States' underlying national interests. "Let us, therefore, see what utility demands at this moment," he advised the Directory. "The measure of our future conduct must be that of our interest." The United States was naturally more inclined to favor the British as a function of language and culture, but that should not be a cause for war. "War leads to no useful result," he advised the Directory. If France attacked the United States, it would only drive the Americans into the arms of Britain and give the Americans and the British a pretext for attacking Spain in Louisiana. France needed Spain's help in the European war, and if Spain was tied down in a land war in Louisiana, it would be unable to help.[35]

Talleyrand was prepared to end the harassment of American shipping, which he regarded as illegal and unjustified. "The time has come to remove the despotic actions and violence which are carried out against the Americans," he told the Directory. Instead, he thought it was in the best interest of France to negotiate for unrestricted trade with America. He was even willing to entertain paying compensation to the Americans for the seizure of their ships and releasing their crewmen from captivity. It appeared that there was no substantive disagreement between the Americans and the foreign minister.[36]

However, Talleyrand needed time to persuade the Directory. The real problem was the Directory's response to Adams's speech to Congress the previous spring. Adams had declared that Genet's attempts to "sow among us the fatal seed of discord" must be "rejected by a decision which will convince France and the universe that we are a people neither degraded nor humiliated by a feeling of fear or inferiority, nor destined to be the wretched plaything of foreign influence, nor, finally, devoid of respect for the honor, character, and interests of the Nation."[37] Rather than ask the Americans for an outright apology, Talleyrand asked for an "explanation." That was diplomatic hairsplitting to allow the Americans a face-saving way to walk back from the president's incendiary remarks.[38] It hardly seemed unreasonable.

To avoid crossing the Directory, Talleyrand passed this message to the American commissioners through his personal secretary, and the Americans chose to ignore it.[39] Such misjudgment may have doomed the mission from the start.

CHAPTER TEN

NOT A SIXPENCE

I
t was the coldest October Marshall could remember. He strolled through the Tuileries, honey brown in the autumn light, and along the embankment of the pearl-gray Seine. Few Americans had ever experienced a city this size—ten times larger than Philadelphia. No American could have imagined the grandeur of its architecture, the density of its population, the elegant fashions, or the abundance of distractions. Despite all the terror and war that the city had endured, the public places were crowded and lively. Paris "presents one incessant round of amusement and dissipation," he wrote to Polly. "Every day you may see something, new magnificent and beautiful; every night you may see a spectacle which astonishes and inchants the imagination." He thought that "[a]ll you can conceive and a great deal more than you can conceive . . . is to be found in this gay metropolis, but I suspect it would not be easy to find a friend." Despite all of Paris's charms, Marshall yearned for home. "I woud not live in Paris to be among the wealthiest of its citizens," he wrote.[1]

Bonaparte's army was sweeping across Europe in 1797, forging the largest empire since Charlemagne's time. The heady rhetoric of republicanism coexisted with nationalistic ambitions and imperial remnants. Marshall knew that despite all the talk of equality and fraternity there were slaves in Richmond who lived better and healthier lives than many free citizens in Paris did. Nor could Marshall have overlooked the venality of the French aristocracy. Republican France preached liberty and virtue while practicing public corruption and private vice: debauchery, selfishness, and avarice were excused as long as you had the proper breeding.

A week had passed since their brief meeting with Talleyrand, and the American commissioners had heard nothing official from the ministry. While they were kept waiting "in a manner most unusual & contemptuous," French ships continued to plunder American vessels. Marshall pressed his colleagues to send a letter to the foreign minister demanding an immediate stop to privateering. Gerry cautioned that they should not rush Talleyrand at the risk of offending the government. Marshall replied sensibly that if "France is determined to be offended, she may quarrel with our answer to any proposition she may make or even with our silence." Although Pinckney agreed with Marshall, the three were resolved to act only in unanimity. And so they just waited.[2]

When the Americans failed to respond to the overture from his personal secretary, Talleyrand sent Jean Conrad Hottinguer to visit them.[3] Hottinguer was one of the Dutch bankers who had arranged a loan for James Marshall for the purchase of the Fairfax property. It is likely that Talleyrand knew that Hottinguer was in a position to influence Marshall. That night, while the three envoys were dining at Pinckney's flat, Hottinguer knocked at the door.[4] According to Hottinguer, Talleyrand wanted to negotiate a new treaty but that Talleyrand insisted that the United States should "give satisfaction to the honor of France wounded by the speech of the president," pay France's debts owed to American nationals, and compensate American ship owners for any property losses resulting from privateering. On top of that, Talleyrand wanted the United States to "lend" to France thirty-two million Dutch guilders (more than four hundred million dollars today). That was not all. Hottinguer added one other requirement: "[T]here must be something for the pocket." When Pinckney looked quizzical, Hottinguer explained that the Americans should pay a *pot-de-vin*—a bribe to the ministry—of fifty thousand pounds (around six million dollars today).[5] This was more than pocket money.

Marshall reacted angrily. Paying France for attacking American commerce would be equivalent to the "absolute surrender of the independence of the United States." The commissioners had no authority to pay France anything, and there was no possibility of negotiating on these terms. Marshall advised once again that they should issue a strongly worded remonstrance to the ministry protesting the seizure of U.S. vessels and the delay in negotiations. Pinckney concurred. Gerry agreed that they should not reply to terms proposed through informal back channels that could later be denied by the ministry. However, Gerry still opposed any written protest to Talleyrand.[6]

BY NOW MARSHALL began to doubt that Talleyrand would ever receive them. The capture of U.S. vessels continued unabated. The French government had begun leasing naval frigates to privateers. France appeared to be "radically hostile" to American interests. Marshall wished he could draw some other conclusion, "but to do so I must shut my eyes on every object which presents itself to them." He wrote to George Washington "that the Atlantic only can save us, & that no consideration will be sufficiently powerful to check the extremities to which the temper of this government will carry it, but an apprehension that we may be thrown into the arms of Britain." The fear that America would be pushed into an alliance with Britain was precisely what Talleyrand had warned the Directory against. Marshall's analysis was spot-on, and so was his conclusion that Americans needed a strong navy.[7]

The next evening at seven o'clock, Hottinguer returned with another

visitor, Pierre Bellamy. Bellamy was a Genovese agent employed by Talleyrand to "facilitate" negotiations by first collecting a bribe from the relevant
parties. He served this function in negotiations with Portugal and Britain,
among others. Bellamy modestly described himself as "clothed with no authority" even though he was a friend of Talleyrand's. Bellamy removed a
folded paper from his pocket, set it down, and began reading a statement
prepared by Talleyrand accusing the United States of betraying its alliance
with France by favoring their common enemy, Britain. The chief complaint
was President Adams's speech before Congress. The discussion dragged on
for nearly three hours before they retired for the night.[8]

At nine the next morning, Marshall, Gerry, and Pinckney met over
breakfast in Gerry's flat. They disagreed over the proper response. Marshall thought that they should reply that the proposed loan and bribe were
"totally inadmissible" and that they could not negotiate through informal
channels. Once more Gerry disagreed. He proposed to tell Talleyrand they
would weigh his proposal.[9]

Marshall cut him off and angrily declared that under no circumstances
would he even consider paying a bribe or making a loan. There was no
reason to delay a response. If Gerry insisted, Marshall suggested that one of
them return to Philadelphia to ask for instructions. He offered to leave
Paris immediately—he was only too glad to return home—but only on condition that France must first stop seizing American ships.[10] Pinckney
agreed with Marshall that they needed to tell France that this was unac-
ceptable and that they would not negotiate through unofficial channels.
But in a sense, it was too late for that already. By meeting with Hottinguer
they had already acquiesced to Talleyrand's game plan.[11]

THE DAY AFTER this angry exchange between Marshall and Gerry, Marshall joined the Pinckneys for a bit of sightseeing. They traveled nine
kilometers outside the city to the royal château at Saint Cloud. The gardens

were lovely along the Seine, but the autumn leaves were not quite as brilliant as they were in Virginia. While Gerry remained behind in Paris sulking, a third visitor appeared at his door: Lucien Hauteval. Hauteval was a wealthy sugar planter from Santo Domingo who now lived in Boston and knew both Gerry and the president's son, John Quincy. (Talleyrand had clearly done his homework.) Hauteval also had a close business relationship with Talleyrand. Hauteval informed Gerry that Talleyrand genuinely wanted to reconcile with the United States and that he was offended that the Americans had not paid him a personal visit. In light of Talleyrand's firm refusal to meet with the Americans, this was hard to believe.[12]

Hauteval returned the next day to meet with all three commissioners and assured them that Talleyrand would welcome a visit during his private hours at home. Marshall responded that the foreign minister had told them to wait to hear from him. Gerry, who had previously counseled against contacting Talleyrand, now suggested that he might approach Talleyrand personally to try to request a formal meeting. Marshall and Pinckney agreed. Yet, when Gerry went to the ministry, the foreign minister refused to see him.[13] The commissioners had misread Talleyrand again: He was willing to meet only secretly and unofficially in his home where presumably he felt freer to speak.

DAYS LATER, news reached Paris that on October 17, 1797, the Treaty of Campo Formio had been signed, ending the war between France and Austria. Cannons were fired, and joyous crowds celebrated the peace. With peace on the Continent, Bonaparte could turn his attention to conquering Britain. This was no idle threat, and across the Channel, the usually calm British began to panic. Though Britain commanded a superior navy, it did not have an army as large or as well trained as Bonaparte's.[14] If Bonaparte defeated Britain, France would be unquestionably the world's most powerful empire. France would then demand the return of its prior colonies in North America, including Louisiana. Bonaparte would be unstoppable.

At noon on October 27, 1797, Hottinguer returned to the Americans with a tough message from Talleyrand, who was buoyed by Austria's defeat: The American envoys must reply promptly in writing to the French demand for a loan and a bribe. Hottinguer warned that the minister had lost his patience and that France "would take a decided course with regard to America" if the Americans did not bend to their will. America was either with France or against her.[15]

Gerry explained that the Americans had no authority to negotiate for a loan. Hottinguer grew more heated. He could not believe their naïveté: "Didn't your government know that nothing can be obtained here without money?" Any American in Paris could have told them that much. In a menacing tone, Hottinguer warned that it would be more "prudent" to offer a loan to their French allies than to fight them.[16]

Pinckney had had enough. He had already spoken to that point.

"No, you have not," Hottinguer replied. "What is your answer, General Pinckney?"

Pinckney shot back: "No, no, not a sixpence!"[17]

Marshall did not mince words. American independence "was still dearer to us than the friendship of France." America had every right to remain neutral. "[T]o lend this money under the lash & coercion of France was to relinquish the government of ourselves & to submit to a foreign government imposed upon us by force." Marshall declared that Americans would prefer that "we make at least one manly struggle before we thus surrendered our national independence."[18]

When Marshall stopped speaking, Hottinguer quietly reminded the Americans that France had loaned them millions to win their independence from Britain. Yes, Gerry replied, but when America solicited a loan from France, France was free to say no. Aiding the Americans had helped

France to defeat its rival, but there was no benefit to the United States for aiding France in a war against Britain.[19]

Unless France stopped interfering with U.S. ships, the Americans would not respond to Talleyrand's demands. Unless the Americans demonstrated goodwill by walking back President Adams's speech, extending a loan, and paying a bribe, France would continue to seize U.S. ships. Even before negotiations began, they had reached an impasse. The American commissioners peered over the brink of war.

THE FOLLOWING AFTERNOON, Gerry anxiously paid a visit to Talleyrand's home. Talleyrand kept him waiting for an hour, and when he did receive him, he was brusque: The Directory had issued an *arrêté* (an order) requiring the envoys to provide an explanation of the president's speech to Congress. The Directory would also require a loan from the United States, but Talleyrand declined to name a figure. If the United States had not authorized the envoys to negotiate a loan, they should just assume they had the authority. There was no time to wait for permission from Congress. Talleyrand was clear that "the loan was an absolute *sine qua non*." The audience was over in a few minutes.

It is curious that Talleyrand did not ask for a douceur. But Gerry had no doubt that Talleyrand expected a large gratuity. He thought that "a small cargo of Mexican dollars would be more efficient in a negotiation at present than two Cargoes of Ambassadors."[20]

While the commissioners puzzled over how to respond to the *arrêté*, Hottinguer called on them with a new proposal. "[T]he destruction of England was inevitable," and therefore "the wealth and arts of that nation would naturally pass over to America" if the Americans chose wisely. In lieu of a "bribe," the envoys could simply pay a "fee" to remain in Paris and negotiate with Talleyrand while one of the envoys returned to Philadelphia to obtain authority for the loan. However, the French would not cease their attacks on U.S. vessels while the negotiations proceeded.[21]

Marshall erupted: France had captured more than fifteen million dollars in ships and cargo, and now it asked for another 1.2 million livres so that the commissioners might be allowed to spend the winter at the Paris Opéra while these depredations continued.[22] This was too much to swallow.

Gerry invited Bellamy and Hottinguer to join the three commissioners over breakfast the following morning. At this point, it was clear that the Americans had completely abandoned the idea of not negotiating through back channels, and it was becoming clear that at least Gerry was willing to entertain the possibility of paying something to France in exchange for peace.

Bellamy warned them at breakfast that if the United States crossed France, it might share the same fate as Venice, which had been divided between France and Austria. France would smash England with an army of one hundred and fifty thousand soldiers. Bellamy even threatened the American envoys that if the negotiations failed, France would use the "French party in America to throw the blame" on them. Hottinguer added that none of their proposals would even be presented to the Directory until Talleyrand received a fifty-thousand-pound bribe.[23]

It appeared to Marshall that Talleyrand's principal objective was to postpone negotiations until he had sufficient influence with the Directory to push them toward a settlement.[24] Talleyrand knew that the demand for a loan would delay negotiations at least six months while the commissioners waited for authorization from Philadelphia. But Talleyrand also expected to be compensated for his "service" in negotiating a settlement.[25] Talleyrand considered bribes a fringe benefit of holding public office, and he was candid about his desire to profit from his office: "I have to make an immense fortune out of it, a really immense fortune," he once wrote. When Talleyrand lived in the United States, he was surprised that his friend Alexander

Hamilton, as secretary of the treasury, continued practicing law to support himself. Talleyrand thought it was scandalous that a man who "made the fortune of his country" should have to "work all night in order to support his family."[26]

Marshall understood that the negotiations could not advance without a bribe. The men of the Revolutionary generation to which he belonged saw themselves as fighting to rid America of the corrupt influence of European society. Now Marshall found himself once again defending American virtue against European vice. He was prepared to go to war rather than pay tribute, but in so doing, he knew that he was risking the future of the American Republic.

CHAPTER ELEVEN

LOVE AND WAR

C ool, gray fog descended like a veil across the stony face of Notre Dame. Hard rain rattled windows ceaselessly. Marshall would not have seen umbrellas until his arrival in France, and he must have regarded them with curiosity. But umbrellas were of little practical use against the shrieking winds that announced the early arrival of winter. Streets flooded, and it was almost impossible to go anywhere in the city without being splattered by mud.[1] Marshall discovered that it was futile to complain to his French landlord about his fireplace, which sat cold and useless. It was a cruel joke.

As the days shortened, Marshall felt the passage of time more acutely. The American commissioners had waited more than a month to be formally received. He felt that Talleyrand's continued delay was intended "to degrade & humiliate their country." Marshall suspected that France was delaying negotiations until it ended hostilities with Britain on France's terms; then the French would have more leverage over the Americans.[2]

At the beginning of November, Marshall drafted a strongly worded letter to Talleyrand protesting their treatment and presented it to the other two commissioners for their signatures. Pinkney agreed to it, but to persuade Gerry to sign it, Marshall had to tone it down considerably.[3] The letter rhapsodized about the United States' "ardent friendship, [and] affection for the French Republic" and its "confidence in her justice and magnanimity." The loss of France's friendship was "a subject of unfeigned regret." The United States had a "sincere desire" to correct any misunderstanding or amend treaties. After Gerry's amendments, the letter sounded less like a protest than a groveling plea from a spurned lover. But Talleyrand did not reply.[4]

While the Americans tried to wheedle their way into a meeting with Talleyrand, the French newspapers kicked off a campaign—clearly directly by Talleyrand—to embarrass and criticize the American envoys for the lack of progress in their negotiations.[5] In November 1797, Talleyrand sent a new parade of visitors to Marshall's door to charm—or bludgeon—the American envoys into compliance.

Around the same time, Marshall received a note from Beaumarchais, the playwright and arms dealer Marshall was representing in his claim against Virginia. They had not met previously, but Beaumarchais had heard that there was an American by the name of Marshall visiting Paris, and Beaumarchais wondered if this was his attorney. In fact, Beaumarchais was acting at the direction of Talleyrand, which Marshall may have suspected. Beaumarchais was desperate for funds at this time and may have been working for Talleyrand. When Marshall and Beaumarchais met, they hit it off immediately, and Beaumarchais reported back to Talleyrand that the Americans were not inclined to pay the bribe Talleyrand demanded.[6]

The next stranger to appear at Marshall's flat was Joseph Pitcairn, a New York businessman living in Paris. Pitcairn lived next door to Talleyrand and had business dealings with Pinckney. Talleyrand had asked him to help facilitate negotiations with the Americans. Pitcairn suggested an alternative arrangement whereby the United States could purchase Dutch bonds from the French government at a premium. In other words, the United States could disguise a loan to France from both the U.S. public and the

British government by overpaying the French for Dutch securities. Pinckney and Marshall firmly opposed this scheme as well.[7]

"I counted on being at home in March," Marshall wrote to Polly at the end of November. "I now apprehend that it will not be in my power to reach America until April or May." He had not heard from her since his departure from Philadelphia in July, and he knew she would be disappointed by the news that his return might be delayed until the late spring. He wanted her to know that the situation was beyond his control. "Oh God how much time & how much happiness have I thrown away!"[8] But perhaps Marshall was feeling a bit guilty about the fact that he was beginning to enjoy Paris for the first time now that he had changed residences.

In mid-November, Marshall and Gerry moved from their cramped quarters "in the style of a miserable old batchelor without any mixture of female society," to l'hôtel d'Elbeuf, located at 70 rue de Vaugirard (now number 54). Marshall had three elegant rooms on the ground floor across the street from the Luxembourg Palace for five guineas less per month than he had paid for his inferior accommodations.[9] On the rare days when it was not raining, he could cross the street and stroll for hours in the Luxembourg Garden. He wrote to Polly that this was "the house of a very accomplishd a very sensible & I believe a very amiable lady whose temper, very contrary to the general character of her country women, is domestic & who generally sets with us two or three hours in the afternoon." Polly could not have been comforted to read the next line: "This renders my situation less unpleasant than it has been."[10]

THE "VERY AMIABLE LADY" was Reine Philiberte Rouph de Varicourt, the marquise de Villette. Reine was an intelligent, piquant, and attractive widow with thick black curls and dancing dark eyes who looked a decade younger than her forty-two years.

Reine had a storied past. She was the daughter of an impoverished nobleman. Without a dowry, she was consigned by her father to a cloister. When she was nineteen, Reine met the elderly Voltaire, who was a friend of her parents'. Voltaire decided to rescue her from the nunnery. He invited her to live with him in his country home at Ferney as his "adopted" daughter—though it was rumored that she was, in fact, Voltaire's illegitimate daughter.[11]

At Ferney, Reine became a combination nurse, confidante, and assistant to the famous author. Voltaire in his eighties was a mercurial tyrant subject to violent fits of rage. He was also wildly unconventional. He kept a vicious pet monkey named Luc that Voltaire joked was like the Prussian king "because he bites everyone." Reine, who loved animals, impressed Voltaire by taming the beast.[12] Reine became his favorite, and in his writings, he called her *La Belle et Bonne* because her heart was as lovely as her countenance. Reine was constantly by Voltaire's side during his last years. He taught her to dance and prepared her for a life as an aristocrat. She, in turn, bewitched the savage poet with the same charm that she used to domesticate his monkey.[13]

Before he died, Voltaire hoped to marry Reine off to a wealthy nobleman. He found a convenient match in Charles Michel, the marquis de Villette. Charles had a staggering fortune, which he inherited at a young age from his father. His mother was an especially intimate friend of Voltaire's, and it may have been more than a coincidence that Charles bore a salient resemblance to Voltaire.[14] Charles's ambition was to be a great writer like Voltaire. All he lacked was talent. Charles was a vicious drunk, a wild spendthrift, and a mediocre scribbler. True, he had shown some promise as a law student, and he published something that passed as poetry, but he had long since abandoned any serious literary pursuits for carnal pleasures.

In fairness, Charles had distinguished himself in one respect—as the most notorious homosexual of his day. Eighteenth-century French society generally winked at homosexuality as long as a man was merely being unfaithful to his wife. Charles, however, did not have even the pretext of a spouse. For this, he was ostracized as a "degenerate" and a devotee of the

"Italian vice." His homosexual male friends slyly called him Alcibiades, the pretty youth who tried to seduce Socrates.[15] Charles's licentious behavior often led to encounters with the Paris police, who otherwise avoided arresting nobility for soliciting sex in the Tuileries. He was lampooned and libeled as the leader of the "sodomites," but to his credit, he was largely indifferent to society's censure.[16]

None of this deterred Voltaire from wanting Reine to marry Charles. She was a twenty-year-old virgin without a dowry, and he was a wealthy, if profligate, homosexual more than twice her age. Marriage was, after all, a matter of convenience: De Villette needed a wife to produce an heir and stay out of jail, and the beautiful Reine needed a wealthy husband to support her when Voltaire was gone.

The ideal opportunity to introduce the couple presented itself when Charles was challenged to a duel over the honor of a dancer he had insulted at the Paris Opera. Terrified of swordfights, Charles fled to Ferney to hide out at Voltaire's. That night, Voltaire hosted a dinner in honor of Saint Francis, the Italian mystic who had preached to the birds. Reine had raised and trained a pair of doves to perform for this occasion. Things went awry when the doves were "mistakenly" roasted and served on a platter to the horrified Reine. Circumstantial evidence suggests that Voltaire may have orchestrated this calamity as a pretext for bringing together Charles and Reine. Though Saint Francis would not have approved, the plan succeeded. Reine ran off, and Charles chased after her. Voltaire could not have written it better. He had killed two birds with one stone. Reine and Charles were married soon after. To celebrate their unconventional marriage, they ascended in a hot-air balloon, making Madame de Villette perhaps the first woman ever to fly.[17]

Charles may have hoped that marriage would restore his social standing, but, in fact, it nearly destroyed his young wife. Reine knew about Charles's past, but presumably the wise Voltaire had assured the alluring young Reine that she could "fix" Charles. Even after the marriage and the births of their daughter and son, Charles continued to prefer men to his wife. He humiliated and tormented Madame de Villette with his debauchery, arrests, and cruelty. In their palatial château on the rue de Beaune, he kept two of his male lovers, the marquis de Thibouville and the prosecutor Clos, so there was no need for her companionship.[18]

By the time Charles died in 1793, he had squandered most of his fortune, and his estate teetered on insolvency. To make matters worse, Madame de Villette was jailed as a royalist by the Directory shortly after Charles's death. The French government expropriated some of the houses she had inherited from her husband and redistributed them to the working class. When she was released, Madame de Villette was evicted from their lavish home on rue de Beaune. She relocated to their more modest though still-spacious l'hôtel d'Elbeuf. She now lived with her twelve-year-old daughter and her four-year-old son, whom she called Voltaire though his given name was Charles. To supplement her income, she leased rooms to foreign envoys.

For all of Madame de Villette's refinement, her tastes ran from the peculiar to the macabre. She furnished the house as if it were a shrine to Voltaire. In the sitting room, she displayed his marble bust with burning incense and one of his faded robes. Most bizarre of all, she kept Voltaire's heart preserved in a silver case in the center of the drawing room as if it were a saint's reliquary.[19]

Even after her torturous marriage, Madame de Villette remained youthful. She captivated the hearts of many men in the American expatriate community in Paris. Gerry gushed that she was "one of the finest women in Paris: on account of the goodness of her heart, her excellent morals, & the richness of her mind." But he reassured his wife that "she is not handsome, but such a woman as you would like."[20] That line must have aroused Mrs. Gerry's suspicion.[21] Even Mrs. Pinckney noted that she was "an agreeable pleasing woman," whom she thought looked about thirty.[22]

Marshall could not have been happier with his new accommodations. He described to Polly his spending hours sitting with de Villette. Since she spoke only French and he spoke only English, they must have found some other means to communicate. It's likely that de Villette tutored Marshall in French because he developed a rudimentary knowledge of the language over the next few months. In any case, there is no question that Marshall completely trusted de Villette, and when he eventually left Paris, she was the one person he seemed truly sad to leave behind. All of which is to say that Marshall had no reason to suspect that she, too, might be an agent of Talleyrand's.[23]

GERRY CONTINUED TO MEET secretly with Talleyrand's agents, and this had become a source of friction between the commissioners. On December 17, Marshall knocked on Gerry's door and was surprised to see him meeting privately with Bellamy. Reiterating Pitcairn's earlier suggestion, Bellamy proposed that in lieu of giving France a loan outright, the United States should purchase sixteen million Dutch notes from France for about 1.3 million pounds sterling (about $169 million today)—which was double their market value.[24] Bellamy reported that Beaumarchais even offered to pay fifty thousand pounds of "private gratification" to Talleyrand out of whatever he recovered from Virginia in the suit that Marshall was handling.[25]

Marshall was stunned by the audacity of this plan. Bellamy's proposal threatened to compromise Marshall and entangle his professional representation of Beaumarchais with his public duties. But he seemed to equivocate at first. Marshall might be willing to have Beaumarchais pay a gratuity to the foreign minister, but only if France first recognized American claims for captured vessels. That was all Bellamy needed to hear. He left thinking that Marshall had opened the door for further discussion of the bribe.[26]

By speaking with Bellamy, Marshall had unwittingly reengaged the process of informal negotiation. Pinckney reminded his colleagues that they had agreed not to enter into informal negotiations but insist on direct negotiations with the foreign minister. Accordingly, the three prepared another letter to Talleyrand restating their position and requesting that he either open negotiations or grant them their passports to return to America.[27]

Marshall expected Pinckney to drop by his room that evening for dinner. He answered a knock and was surprised to see Madame de Villette dressed to go out. She had reserved a box at the Odeon for a one-night-only performance of Voltaire's controversial tragedy, *Mahomet*. The play was an allegory that attacked organized religion. She invited Marshall join her. It would be hard to refuse an evening alone with de Villette. She was not just another theater enthusiast; she was Voltaire's "adopted" daughter. And Marshall may have had other motives for accompanying her. Five months had passed since he had seen his wife. Marshall appreciated female companionship. De Villette's sudden invitation delighted him, and in his excitement, he completely forgot that Pinckney was coming for dinner. He rushed out the door without sending a note to Pinckney explaining his change of plans. Marshall was chagrined to find Pinckney's card when he returned late that evening, but he was also embarrassed by the implication of his accompanying de Villette alone, her tiny gloved hand in his.[28] We do not know what transpired that evening, but it set in motion events that Marshall could not control.

On Christmas Eve 1797, Marshall faced a dilemma. Marshall and Pinckney agreed that there was no chance of moving forward with negotiations, but Gerry wanted to keep trying. Marshall was convinced that Talleyrand was dragging his feet so that once France conquered Britain, the French could turn their predatory eyes on North America. Marshall wanted to return to Philadelphia and sound the alarm in Congress to prepare for war with France. However, if Marshall and Pinckney left, it would give France a pretext for blaming a rupture in their relations on the two envoys and divide public opinion in the United States. Marshall thought that the nation would unite against France, but he could not be sure. He and Pinckney decided that if no progress was made by January they would leave for England and wait there until the spring when it was safer to travel.[29]

Marshall and Pinckney recognized that they were in personal danger. Talleyrand's agents hinted darkly that if the Americans did not accede to its demands, the Directory might detain them—or worse. The Directory had never accorded them diplomatic recognition, and therefore the commissioners had no immunity from arrest or prosecution. In reality, it would hardly have mattered if France had accepted their credentials, as the Directory had arrested four foreign diplomats that fall. Mrs. Pinckney worried that the envoys could be seized at any time.[30] She did not want to leave her house, fearing "the risk strangers run of being imprisoned without knowing why or wherefore."[31]

Marshall spent the first two weeks of January preparing a memo to Talleyrand arguing that the United States had complied with the 1778 Treaty of Alliance. Marshall's memorandum has been called "one of the ablest state papers ever produced by American diplomacy."[32] It was surely among the most eloquent. "Openly and repeatedly have France & America interchanged unequivocal testimonials of reciprocal regard," he began. "These testimonials were given by the United States with all the ardor and sincerity of Youth."[33] Then the tone darkened.

The United States, Marshall argued, had considered its treaty obligations and concluded that "her engagements by no means bound her to take part in the war, but left her so far the mistress of her own Conduct as to be at perfect liberty to observe a system of real neutrality." Not only was the United States not legally bound to intervene, Marshall argued, it was bound by the "Laws of nature" to refrain. Beyond moral considerations, national interests "forbid the Government of the United States to plunge them unnecessarily into the miseries of the bloody conflict then commencing."[34]

Marshall set out two starkly different views of world politics. First, he described the contemporary state of European politics.

The great nations of Europe, either impelled by ambition, or by existing or supposed political interests peculiar to themselves, have
consumed more than a third of the present century in war. Whatever causes may have produced so afflicting an evil, they cannot be
supposed to have been entirely extinguished, and humanity can
scarcely indulge the hope that the temper or condition of man is so
altered as to exempt the next century from the ills of the past. Strong
fortifications, powerful navies, immense Armies, the accumulated
wealth of ages and a full population enable the nations of Europe to
support those wars in which they are induced to engage by motives
which they deem adequate and by interests exclusively their own.[35]

He contrasted this with the very different circumstances of the United
States.

Possessed of an extensive unsettled territory, on which bountiful
nature has bestowed with a lavish hand all the capacities for future
legitimate greatness, they indulge no thirst for conquest, no ambition for the extension of their limits. Encircled by no dangerous
powers, they neither fear or are jealous of their neighbours, and are
not, on that account, obliged to arm for their own safety. Separated
far from Europe by a vast & friendly ocean, they are but remotely,
if at all, affected by those interests, which agitate & influence this
portion of the world. Thus circumstanced, they have no motives
for voluntary war.[36]

MARSHALL POSITED THAT American geography shaped American exceptionalism since it would have been tactless to assert the superiority of
the American character. Instead, Marshall rested his argument on the

unique geographical circumstances that insulated America from foreign influences. Geography also made the United States dependent on foreign trade and therefore dictated the necessity to avoid war.

> An extensive undefended commerce, peculiarly necessary to a nation, which does not manufacture for itself, which is and for a long time to come will be almost exclusively agricultural, would have been its immediate and certain victim . . . Great as are the means & resources of the United States for self defence, 'tis only in self defence that those resources can be completely displayed. Neither the genius of the nation, or the state of its finances admit of calling its citizens from the plough, but to defend their own liberty and their own firesides.[37]

MARSHALL EXPLAINED THAT as a nation of farmers it was essential for the United States to trade with both France and Britain. The United States could not afford to become entangled in "all the future quarrels of Europe."[38] Marshall also implicitly suggested that to protect American virtue the United States had to keep its distance from European power politics.

France claimed that Jay's Treaty and Washington's Proclamation of Neutrality violated America's treaty obligations to France. In particular, France insisted that the United States had an obligation to defend French cargo on board U.S. merchant ships from seizure by the British navy. The 1778 Treaty of Amity and Commerce between France and the United States recognized the right of all neutral nations' vessels to resist capture by force of arms if necessary. This was known as the "right of armed neutrality." Though a belligerent power had the right to seize military supplies as contraband, France complained that Jay's Treaty gave the British rights to seize supplies and timber that were not, strictly speaking, "contraband."

Marshall pointed out that Jay's Treaty was silent on the right of armed neutrality. The British navy continued to assert its right to seize contraband on U.S. ships, and Jay's Treaty had specifically listed naval provisions and timber as contraband subject to seizure on board neutral vessels.[39] Marshall pointed to precedents from other countries' treaties and foreign states' practices that relied on a wider definition of contraband.[40] He acknowledged that a rule that protected the free navigation of neutral countries was desirable, "[b]ut the wish to establish a principle is essentially different from a determination that it is already established."[41] Marshall was in the awkward position of having to defend a principle at odds with official U.S. policy.[42] He knew that in the past decade most European countries had recognized the right of neutral parties to "free navigation" and armed neutrality. Many continental countries, including France, had endorsed this principle.[43] Marshall's point was that regardless of the views of the French and U.S. governments, Britain had rejected this principle. U.S. vessels had no choice but to accede to search and seizure of French goods.[44] The United States could not defend itself against British naval power.

In this memorandum, Marshall was stating a legal position as if that would be sufficient to settle the question. France saw the issue very differently. The French were not interested in talking about legal rights; they were asserting their own interests. Marshall's insistence on arguing the law rather than negotiate based on national interests was a sign to Talleyrand of American naïveté. Talleyrand concluded that the American commissioners did not understand power politics.

The Directory responded bluntly to Marshall's legal memorandum: Not deigning to craft a legal response, it issued a decree to capture and condemn any neutral vessels carrying any products from Britain or its possessions.

When Marshall heard this news, his heart sank: The United States was caught between two world powers at war.

—————

DECEMBER HAD BEEN relatively mild, but the weather turned sharply colder in January and February of 1798. The sun appeared rarely, and the winds picked up off the Seine. It had snowed only once during January, but in the mornings the streets were often glazed with ice. February was drier but still quite cold, and heavy clouds hung over the city ominously.[45] Revolutionary Paris in the depths of winter was a dark and unsettling place: Even after the Reign of Terror ended, neighbors and police regarded one another with a toxic suspicion. An English-speaking stranger encountered that uncomprehending look that has long greeted tourists in the French capital. Paris did not welcome strangers even then.

On February 4, Gerry returned from a secret meeting with Talleyrand and informed his colleagues that he was "not at liberty" to tell them what the foreign minister had said. Marshall and Pinckney were furious. All Gerry would say was that the foreign minister would respond to him the next day, and upon his answer "depended peace or war."[46] It turned out that Gerry had been meeting secretly with Talleyrand and his agents for weeks.

When Talleyrand replied a few days later, Gerry proposed that the commissioners consider paying the bribe. At that, Marshall exploded. They had already agreed to refuse to pay the bribe. The United States could not accept a "humble state of dependent solicitation whilst [France] preserved a haughty and an angry distance." Marshall warned that Talleyrand was dragging his feet to delay the United States from taking measures to defend itself against France.[47]

Gerry shot back that Marshall "could not judge of the propositions as they were not known to [him]" and that Gerry had a very different opinion of France.[48]

Marshall knew that further argument with Gerry would threaten their ability to continue to work together. It was late, and he was tired. He held his temper the best he could. "I wished very much that the Directory would order us off," he told Gerry.[49] Marshall could not have slept well that night.

Marshall judged—correctly—that Talleyrand had set out to divide the commissioners. He wondered "whether [France] will be content to leave us our Independence if she can cajole or frighten us out of it," but he had no doubt that France intended to "keep and cherish" the Republican Party as her party. Marshall correctly suspected that the American Republicans were advising Talleyrand and that Talleyrand intended to send Marshall and Pinckney home and keep Gerry in Paris.[50] Pinckney concurred.[51] Marshall and Pinckney were convinced that Gerry had unwittingly become another of Talleyrand's agents.

Marshall observed that France was unwilling to make peace with the United States so long as it believed it could defeat Britain, but it was also unwilling to go to war against the United States and so forge an Anglo-American alliance. Could the American commissioners compel Talleyrand to negotiate in good faith if they all threatened to quit France? In fact, the Americans could neither advance negotiations nor leave France so long as Talleyrand held their passports.[52]

They were trapped.

CHAPTER TWELVE

TOSSED INTO THE SEINE

After months of living in her home, Marshall had formed a close bond with Madame de Villette. He spent hours with de Villette every day, accompanied her to the theater, practiced his French with her, and traveled with her at least once. Whether he transgressed the bounds of marital fidelity is unknowable, but it would not be surprising. He had not heard from Polly for months, since he had departed Richmond. At forty-two, he was still a vigorous and attractive man with a tall, lean frame, dark features, and smiling eyes. Marshall loved women, and de Villette was an unattached dark beauty whose worldliness, vitality, and education contrasted with Polly's sheltered experience and infirmities. Marshall had no close male friends other than Pinckney, who had his wife and daughter to amuse him, and he barely tolerated Gerry. It would be only natural that he, like so many other men, fell under the charm of La Belle et Bonne.

Madame de Villette loved to host parties as a way to introduce the American envoys to her French friends. She would typically invite a few French ladies and gentlemen in addition to Marshall, Gerry, Pinckney, and Pinckney's wife, Mary. The evening usually began with a musical performance that included singers and a pianist. Then there might be some dancing before "tea" was served about midnight. The guests would move into the dining room, and de Villette would set out teapots and a large brioche in the middle of a round table surrounded by cups and saucers. There was a second table that would feature a towering pyramid of assorted cakes and flavored ices. On the sideboards were cold turkey, slices of veal with mint jelly, and baskets of oranges and pears. The gentlemen would assist Madame de Villette by serving the ladies and pouring abundant champagne and sweet liqueurs. After all that, she would serve quarters of orange peel filled with sweet orange jelly. Around one a.m., when everyone was loosened up by the alcohol and the late hour, the *petits jeux* would begin.[1]

On one particular evening, one of the French ladies proposed a new game that the Americans were unfamiliar with. She explained that someone would be sent out of the room, and the rest would secretly decide on a mission that this person must perform when he or she returned. The mission might be something like placing a particular pillow at the foot of a lady or moving a chair to another location. Before the person reentered the room, one of the ladies would sit down to play on the piano very loudly, which was the signal for the person to return. When he or she entered the room, the piano would grow softer if the person moved toward the object of the mission and louder if he or she moved away from it. The only clue the person had was the music.[2]

Mrs. Pinckney later described in a letter to her cousin a certain unnamed "lady, & the most beautiful in the room," who was very likely Madame de Villette. When she was sent out of the room, the guests decided that "she was to present her hand to a [particular] gentleman to kiss." Mrs. Pinckney was being discreet in that there were only a few gentlemen present, and the only two men mentioned who were not accompanied by their wives were Marshall and Gerry. While we cannot be sure whom Mrs. Pinckney referred to, we know that Marshall loved games and was naturally genial and outgoing while Gerry was rather stiff and serious. It seems likely that Madame de Villette was intended to offer her hand to Marshall. She went all around the room as the music grew deafening until she stopped in front of the particular gentleman, who was at that moment standing. Then the music quieted a bit. But as she pondered what she was supposed to do with him, the music grew loud again. She was obviously embarrassed by not knowing what was expected of her, and he did nothing to assist her until she reached out and took his hand. She assumed she had to lead him back to his chair. But the gentleman surprised her by lifting her hand to his lips.[3]

Party games then, as now, were often ways of engaging in behavior that might otherwise be presumptuous. In organizing a game among a few single women and two unaccompanied men after everyone had consumed a fair amount of alcohol, one could expect flirtation to follow. If we are correct that Marshall kissed de Villette's hand, then Mrs. Pinckney's reluctance to name them may indicate that she thought that their kiss was more than a game.

THERE WERE MORE THAN one hundred American merchants doing business in Paris at the time, often with close ties to the French government. A large number of these men came to know Jefferson and Monroe during the time they were envoys to France and considered them friends. Many belonged to the Decadi Club, an informal network of American businessmen who would mingle over meals at an upscale restaurant in the Palais Royal. Most were solid Republicans who staunchly supported the French government even to the extent of criticizing their own. Numerous club members wrote or visited one or more of the American commissioners repeatedly to pressure them to accept Talleyrand's demands. They also wrote letters back to Republican leaders in the United States that accused Pinckney and Marshall of trying to provoke a war with America's oldest ally.[4]

One of these expatriates was Nathaniel Cutting, the U.S. consul in Le

Havre, who had his own business interests in the French West Indies. Cutting wrote to the three American commissioners urging them to avoid a costly war by agreeing to finance France's war against Britain and deferring any claims on behalf of captured American ships. Cutting advised them to set aside "the antiquated Face of Diplomatic etiquette" and any moral qualms about paying bribes: Those "who consult only their own liberal ideas of moral Rectitude and take offence to what they call 'National Honor and Dignity,' are doubtless disposed rather to 'hurl back defiance in the teeth of France,'" he wrote. But "once we 'let slip the Dogs of War,' One hundred millions of Dollars would not enable us to enchain them again."[5]

Cutting also wrote to James Monroe, then a U.S. senator from Virginia, that "the cold reception, bordering on contempt" with which Talleyrand received the Americans was "the most striking comment that can be given on the imbecile and supercilious conduct of many conspicuous characters in the government of the United States." Cutting blamed Marshall and Pinckney and expressed sympathy for the difficult situation in which Gerry found himself, unable to negotiate with his colleagues.[6]

In addition, Cutting wrote to various Republican newspapers in the United States attacking Marshall. One letter called Marshall "an unequivocal enemy of France" and excoriated President Adams for appointing him.[7]

Another prominent expatriate businessman was Fulwar Skipwith, the consul general in Paris. Skipwith wrote to his friend Jefferson demanding that the U.S. government should "confess some of our errors" and lay the responsibility "upon the shoulders of a few persons who perpetrated them." There was no doubt he meant the commissioners. He urged the United States to repudiate Jay's Treaty and "lend France as much money, should she ask for it, as she lent us in our hour of distress."[8]

These American expatriates in Paris were working with Talleyrand and the Republicans in the United States to discredit Marshall, Pinckney, and President Adams. The antagonism of his fellow Americans left Marshall isolated. The only person Marshall felt he could rely upon, besides Pinckney, was Madame de Villette.

SOME HISTORIANS HAVE SUGGESTED that de Villette was another agent working for Talleyrand.[9] No one was better situated than she was to observe the American commissioners. She had known Talleyrand socially since Talleyrand first came to visit Voltaire. De Villette and Talleyrand shared a cultlike devotion to the writer's memory.[10] Talleyrand attended dinners in her home with the envoys on at least two occasions, though neither Marshall nor his colleagues kept any record of these informal meetings.[11] The British ambassador had lived with de Villette at one time, and it's inconceivable that she could have escaped the attention of the French government.

And it was not by chance that Marshall and Pinckney came to live with de Villette. Apparently, either Skipwith; James Mountflorence, Skipwith's vice-counsel; Beaumarchais; or Joel Barlow, another expatriate, had arranged for Marshall and Gerry to move into de Villette's home. All four had working relations with Talleyrand and actively tried to persuade the American commissioners to provide the loan that Talleyrand demanded. Skipwith was actively working with Jefferson to embarrass the commissioners. Mountflorence, a French national, introduced Hottinguer to the Americans. Mountflorence, who had earned his fortune selling worthless land in America to unsuspecting Frenchmen, was not the sort of man to be bothered by a conflict of loyalties.[12] We know that Beaumarchais tried to facilitate the payment of a bribe to Talleyrand. Barlow was de Villette's neighbor and a zealous supporter of French republicanism who collaborated with Talleyrand. He disparaged Pinckney and Marshall and thought that if Gerry had "not been shackled with the other two, the Directory would have negotiated with him without any difficulty."[13]

Talleyrand, it seems, left little to chance. It seems more than coincidental that Gerry and Marshall were invited to move to de Villette's home immediately after Pinckney had rebuffed repeated requests for a loan and a bribe on behalf of Talleyrand. It was at this point that Talleyrand realized that Pinckney was no longer useful to him, and he made the strategic decision to try to influence Marshall and Gerry instead. To accomplish this, he wanted to isolate Pinckney. Moving Marshall and Gerry to a more appealing location away from Pinckney where they were under the lovely, watchful eyes of Madame de Villette made sense.[14]

The French had long relied on a well-developed internal security network to glean information especially from foreign envoys. Every move that foreign diplomats made was reported to the Foreign Ministry. The Paris police also engaged in surveillance, which sometimes was inconsistent with the wishes of the ministry. Revolutionary France, and Paris in particular, was crawling with British agents. The British spies in France were far better informed about the activities and opinions of the American commissioners than was the U.S. government.[15] Talleyrand knew all of this, and he himself had ongoing contacts with British agents. (Talleyrand was always careful to keep one foot on either side of the fence.) The British would want to sabotage any talks with the Americans and prevent any loan to finance the French war effort. For these reasons, Talleyrand wanted a spy in the heart of the American operations to ensure he would know in advance of any American plans to aid the British.[16]

The Paris police had informants watching de Villette's house at all times, and the police dossier on her refers to the envoys meeting at her home. These police reports were provided to Talleyrand at his request. One historian has argued that the fact that the Paris police were already spying on her home would have made it unnecessary for Talleyrand to employ her as a spy.[17] However, it was common for the French and the British to have duplicate spies to corroborate intelligence. During the American Revolution, for example, French and British spies were strategically placed inside the American headquarters in the village of Passy, just outside Paris.[18] Although no correspondence was ever recorded between Talleyrand and de Villette, the foreign minister probably destroyed any records of his own surveillance.

Over drinks in the salon or dinner in her large dining room, Madame de Villette encouraged the three envoys to extend credit to France. Pinckney reported discreetly to Secretary of State Pickering that a certain "unnamed lady" made them an offer: "If you were to make us a loan, all matters will be adjusted," she assured them.[19] "M. Talleyrand has mentioned to me (who am surely not in his confidence) the necessity of your making us a loan, and I know that he has mentioned it to two or three others; and that you have been informed of it; and I will assure you that, if you remain here six months longer, you will not advance a single step further in your negotiations without a loan."[20] We can reasonably assume that the lady in question was de Villette. We know that the envoys met at her home numerous times around December 20, 1797. Pinckney and Marshall did not record any meetings with another woman, and it makes sense that Pinckney would have wanted to protect de Villette's identity. Indeed, Marshall made a point of omitting from his journal Beaumarchais' name as well, indicating that he wanted to protect his friends.

Would *La Belle et Bonne*, a woman known for her kindness, purity, and religious devotion, spy for the French government? De Villette had already spent ten terrifying months locked up by the Directory and narrowly escaped the guillotine. She had struggled with poverty as a young woman, endured a painful and humiliating marriage, and now in middle age found herself with two children to support with little income. It seems reasonable that de Villette would do whatever was necessary to protect her family and avoid offending the Directory. Providing her government with information about the activities and opinions of her houseguests would seem only prudent under the circumstances.

Did Marshall realize the danger in becoming involved with a foreign agent?[21] Or did his heart deceive his head? And did Marshall's relationship with de Villette incline him to continue negotiations longer than necessary? Or did the risk of falling in love cause him to leave France sooner than expected?

AFTER FIVE MONTHS of waiting for negotiations to start, Marshall and Pinckney had decided to return to the United States—although the French foreign minister had not returned their passports. It was eight in the evening one night in February, and Marshall was packing when there was a knock at his door. Marshall was not anticipating this visit from Beaumarchais, who was visibly upset to hear about Marshall's imminent departure. Beaumarchais tried to persuade Marshall that a loan would be unlikely to trigger war with Britain because Britain had too many commercial interests in the United States.[22] Beaumarchais, a playwright who traded in irony, once made the same argument to Louis XVI: That if France aided the American Revolution, it would not lead to war with Britain.[23] He was wrong then, and he was wrong now.

As a friend to America, Beaumarchais warned that France would "revolutionize" Britain and reduce it to the status of the Cisalpine Republic, a French satellite in northern Italy, while France would monopolize world commerce. "It behooved us as wise men," he advised Marshall, "to balance these evils well in our minds and to take such measures as would secure the peace of our nation."[24]

Marshall was well aware of the dangers that Beaumarchais mentioned, but compromising American independence was too high a price to pay. The demand for a loan was extortion, Marshall believed, and if the American commissioners succumbed, there would be no end to France's demands.[25] Beaumarchais left dispirited. The two revolutions he had played a role in were now on a collision course, and he could do nothing to stop it.

Marshall drafted one more letter to Talleyrand, repeating all their prior arguments and concluding that since "the demands of France render it entirely impracticable to effect the objects of their mission," they therefore must "retire from France, til the government of the French republic shall be willing to consider and receive them as the representatives of their country." They requested their passports and added one final request to meet with Talleyrand.[26]

It was probably no coincidence that just when the letter was translated and ready for their signature Marshall and Gerry were invited by Madame de Villette to join her and an unnamed Frenchwoman for a long weekend at her country estate thirty miles outside Paris. Gerry cautioned Marshall that if they signed the letter and delivered it to Talleyrand he would order them to leave France immediately, in which case they should send their regrets to Madame de Villette and prepare to leave France at once.[27]

Madame de Villette's invitation offered Gerry a convenient excuse not to send the letter. This was clearly a clever ruse by Gerry and de Villette. Gerry knew that Marshall would rather delay sending the letter than miss a weekend away with Madame de Villette. Indeed, this incident suggests that Marshall's relationship to de Villette was more than a friendship.

It is also curious that Marshall, who took detailed notes of all his engagements and conversations in France, did not record any mention of this weekend in his journal and that neither he nor Gerry wrote about it to anyone. Mrs. Pinckney, who was not present, wrote a detailed description of the weekend to her cousin. Out of discretion, she omitted Madame de Villette's name, which added to the intrigue.

De Villette's château was situated on a wooded estate fronting the Seine. She once described her country house as "charming without being magnificent," according to Mary Pinckney. The pastoral setting was "delicious, & such as no traveller could pass without stopping to admire it, yet not so splendid as to make him hate the posessors." De Villette liked to look out her window as travelers stopped to admire her château and imagine their thoughts: "What a sweet house, what a charming spot—nature has here taken pleasure in lavishing all her beauties. How happy the owners must be. If I had such a place I think sorrow could never approach me." In fact, since her "reversal of fortune," de Villette had suffered more than enough sorrow for a lifetime.[28] Marshall spent three days here with this extraordinary woman. Whatever transpired between them, the moment must have been bittersweet. Marshall knew he would soon be leaving.

THE PARTY RETURNED TO PARIS on February 24, and the next morning Gerry received a visit from Talleyrand's clerk. Talleyrand had been tipped off as to the envoys' intentions. The clerk made a new proposal: France might accept a promise that the United States would provide a loan *after* peace was achieved with Britain. Such a loan would avoid antagonizing Britain. Gerry found this idea appealing, and it gave him an excuse to refuse to sign the letter to Talleyrand demanding their passports.[29]

Marshall could not believe that Gerry was reneging on his promise. Their shared memories from a weekend in a sylvan paradise with Madame de Villette evaporated instantly in the heat of argument. Marshall reminded Gerry that they had no authority to authorize any loan—either before or after peace was declared.[30] He pointed out that a promise to lend money in the future was no different than a loan in the present because France could borrow against it. Whatever funds France received would work to "aid the descent on England, to subjugate our own country and to forge chains with which to manacle ourselves."[31] Marshall was implicitly acknowledging that American independence was bound up with the fate of Britain.

Gerry admitted that Talleyrand's demand was unreasonable, but he insisted that "we ought to consider the Actual state of things and do that which would conduce most to the interest of the nation." War would cost "at least two-hundred million dollars and would inflict miseries and dangers which were incalculable." What Gerry called "true wisdom" would be to "stand in the gap between our Country and France and prevent a war by the stipulation to lend 8 or 10,000,000."

Gerry had a valid point, of course. Paying extortion would be cheaper than going to war. As a compromise, Gerry suggested that if there was any doubt that they were authorized to lend this amount one of them should return posthaste to Philadelphia and secure Congress's approval. Gerry offered to return home to obtain fresh instructions for this purpose.[32] Of course, this would only serve Talleyrand's purpose of delaying negotiations until after the conquest of Britain.

Marshall retorted that a loan in any amount would be a surrender of national independence and would not spare America from being dragged into the European war. "France had made an unprovoked war upon our commerce as a mean by which to force our Government into measures it disapproved of and deemed highly injurious," Marshall charged. If the United States "under the leash" acceded to France's demands, "we no longer acted for ourselves." Three times the foreign ministry had threatened to expel them, and nothing had happened. "This demonstrated the object of the Government to be to keep us here in our present abject state while every species of hostility should be practiced on our country, until France should be in a situation to strike us effectually." Marshall argued that the envoys should return home at once to warn their countrymen to prepare for war.[33]

Marshall and Pinckney felt that Gerry had betrayed them. As their voices rose in anger, Marshall could barely contain himself. Pinckney, nodding in agreement with Marshall, sat in stony silence, shocked by Gerry's behavior. Gerry accused Marshall of being overly suspicious of France. He warned "that it was extremely unwise for a man to deliver himself up entirely to suspicion" and that for a statesman it endangered the whole nation. Marshall shot back that to assume France would honor its promises was no more justifiable than to suppose France would cheat them. "The best guide we could take for the future was the past," Marshall reasoned, and France's behavior had certainly given them no reason for confidence. Marshall doubted the French really cared about the loan. France was now making this proposition "merely to amuse us."[34] Marshall correctly assessed that Talleyrand's real purpose was to delay negotiations as long as possible.[35] Further discussion was pointless. Marshall went to bed, but he had another restless night. The rift between Gerry and his colleagues was irreparable.[36]

The following morning at ten o'clock, Marshall met again with Beau-marchais. By now Marshall must have realized that Beaumarchais was working for Talleyrand. Marshall had scolded Gerry numerous times for continuing private discussions with Talleyrand's agents, but since Beau-marchais was also Marshall's client in his claim against Virginia, Marshall could not refuse to meet with him.[37]

Beaumarchais' message was stark: Switzerland, Spain, and Portugal were all compelled to help finance France's war effort. "[T]he United States must also advance them money or take the consequences."[38] It was a dis-turbing warning from a man who counted himself a friend of America's.

The three U.S. envoys continued to argue over the proposed loan for the next several days. Gerry warned his colleagues that if they failed to pur-chase peace with France, Americans might revolt against their own gov-ernment rather than risk war with France.[39] Marshall proposed that the envoys ask one last time for an interview with Talleyrand to see if there was any chance for negotiation without first promising to pay France or the foreign minister. Gerry, however, would not agree to any language that pre-cluded the possibility of a loan to France. The envoys agreed not to raise the issue of a possible loan, but that if Talleyrand suggested it they would reply that they would "consider" it.[40] This was a completely disingenuous com-promise. Marshall and Pinckney had already made clear they would never consider lending France money.

To their surprise, Talleyrand promptly agreed to see them. This would be their first and only official negotiation with the foreign minister—after five months of delay.

The day before the scheduled meeting, Gerry was called to a private meeting with Talleyrand before the minister met with the other Americans.[41] Gerry returned and informed his colleagues that Talleyrand had reaffirmed that he would not trouble the Directory with any American proposal until they agreed to a loan. Moreover, Gerry bluntly told them, Talleyrand preferred to conclude a treaty with Gerry on his own.[42]

At three in the afternoon on March 2, 1798, Talleyrand welcomed the three Americans in his office. Sunlight poured through the windows, and for the first time in months, it was warm enough to leave them open. The bright spring weather seemed at odds with the dark mood of the envoys.[43] Pinckney, as the senior negotiator, began by saying that the United States was eager to remove any differences between the two countries and that they had received many informal proposals through various channels that they did not find practical to negotiate through.[44]

Talleyrand replied that the Directory was "extremely wounded" by President Washington's Farewell Address eighteen months earlier and by President Adams's speeches to Congress in May and November of the prior year. Incredibly, Talleyrand complained that the Americans had "not once waited on him," which was manifestly false.[45] The Directory needed some proof of a "friendly disposition" before they would agree to a treaty with the United States. He alluded to a loan as one way of demonstrating this. When Pinckney interjected that they had no authority to negotiate a loan, Talleyrand cut him off quickly. Talleyrand insisted that any diplomat at such a distance from his government would have such authority. Since their instructions were silent as to whether they could advance a loan, then nothing prohibited it. If the commissioners sincerely wanted to settle their differences with France, they would find a way to grant the loan. Otherwise France was not negotiating with "persons of a temper hostile to it."[46]

At this point, Gerry, ignoring his promise not to raise the subject, suggested that a loan could be made payable after the war in supplies to Santo

Domingo, in what is now the Dominican Republic. Talleyrand coyly sig-naled that this might be a solution. Gerry and Talleyrand had obviously discussed this idea in advance.[47]

Marshall ignored Gerry's proposal and responded to the foreign minister that the United States was committed to maintaining its neutrality and there-fore could never furnish money to France. However, the United States could perhaps negotiate a loan when the war was over.[48] Marshall was willing to consider a future loan without putting it down on paper to prevent France from using a pledge of a future loan to obtain credit from another country.

Talleyrand insisted that there must be some "immediate aid" to prove America's friendship. Alluding to France's aid during the Revolutionary War, he added that "the principles of reciprocity would require it." At the end of the hour, Talleyrand abruptly stood up. He coldly informed the en-voys that since the Directory would not recognize them as diplomats they could see him in the future only as private individuals to discuss these mat-ters further.[49] After more than five months in Paris, the Americans had not advanced a single step.

Marshall felt crushed. He wrote in his journal that day, "I have cursed a thousand times the moment when a sense of duty inducd me to undertake this painful embassy."[50]

LATER THAT DAY, Gerry came to Marshall's room at Madame de Villette's thinking he might persuade his colleague to agree to a loan after the war. Marshall replied that he was no less sure "that I stood on my feet and not my head, than that our instructions would not permit us to make the loan required." Marshall suggested that he and Gerry should return to Philadel-phia at once and lay out the case to President Adams for and against a loan. That would leave Pinckney in Paris as the permanent envoy. Marshall feared that if Gerry was left in Paris on his own he would succumb to the influence of Talleyrand and his agents. To his surprise, Gerry agreed.[51]

But the matter was still not settled. The envoys arranged one last visit to Talleyrand on the morning of March 6. First, Gerry stopped by Marshall's room with a new proposal: Since the Directory was offended by the speeches of Washington and Adams, the envoys should offer to insert into a new treaty a clause declaring that the presidents' statements were "founded in mistake." Marshall thought it would be presumptuous for three envoys, acting on their own, to tell a foreign government that their presidents were mistaken—and it would be "an absolute lie."[52]

Gerry exploded. He "wished to God" that Marshall would suggest something "accommodating." Marshall was shocked by Gerry's tone, but rather than lash out at him, he chose not to reply.[53]

At their final meeting with Talleyrand, Pinckney reiterated that they had no authority to proceed with a loan. Talleyrand tried to persuade the commissioners that the loan could be "cloathed" in secrecy. If France acknowledged that it owed compensation to American citizens, would the United States not extend credit for two years before France paid them? Of course, the envoys agreed. Well, then, Talleyrand replied with a sly grin, that was "precisely the same thing" as giving France a loan.[54]

Marshall responded that the two cases were not at all alike: The former relied on the commissioners authorizing an action without permission; the latter depended on France recognizing their debt and then postponing the payment. The first case required the United States to act affirmatively to transfer money; the second case consisted of the French government denying restitution to Americans.[55] The value of a commercial treaty to France would be much greater than the face value of the loan proposed, Marshall pointed out. When he informed Talleyrand that he and Gerry would be returning to Philadelphia for further instructions, Talleyrand said nothing.[56] The foreign minister already knew their intentions.

Late that night, Beaumarchais again visited Marshall. He had learned that the Directory would return passports to Pinckney and Marshall but would insist that Gerry remain to represent the United States. In effect,

Talleyrand had chosen Gerry as the permanent U.S. commissioner to re-place Pinckney. Since Marshall knew that Beaumarchais would report what-ever he said to Talleyrand, he replied indifferently that he "did not wish to stay another day in France, and would as cheerfully depart the next day."[57]

Beaumarchais offered to accompany Marshall back to the United States to provide testimony that Marshall had served the country well and dispute whatever libels the French government and their Republican allies might spread that would blame Marshall for bringing the two countries to the brink of war. Marshall appreciated the offer, but he thought he could de-fend himself against any lies. He "felt no sort of apprehension for conse-quences, as they regarded me personally: that in public life considerations of that sort never had and never would in any degree influence me." Before they parted, Marshall assured Beaumarchais that even if their countries went to war, their personal "conduct would always manifest the firmness of men who were determined, and never the violence of passionate men."[58]

In truth, Marshall was filled with anxiety about the future relations be-tween Europe and the United States. France was gathering an enormous army of fifty thousand men to invade Britain. Marshall wrote to George Washington, who had retired to Mount Vernon, that "no force in England will be able to resist them." Once England fell, France would harness Brit-ain's economic and military might to conquer North America. The United States had no standing army or navy. The whole War Department had fewer than a dozen employees. All the federal government could do was to ask the state militias for volunteers—hardly a match for the military jug-gernaut that Bonaparte commanded. The only obstacle between France's march toward world conquest was France's chronic lack of funds.[59]

Washington was incensed by Marshall's letter. France, his wartime ally, now threatened the independence that Washington and Lafayette had fought for. Washington agreed that yielding to France's demands for a loan was unthinkable. "Submission is vile," Washington spat. "[R]ather than hav-ing her freedom and independence trodden under foot, America, every

American, I though old, will pour out the last drop of blood which is yet in my veins."[60]

On March 19, a letter arrived just before dinner from Talleyrand ordering Marshall and Pinckney to go home and leave behind the one minister "presumed to be more impartial." Gerry's initial response was that he had told Talleyrand he would not negotiate on his own and that he would "sooner be thrown into the Seine than consent to stay under the actual circumstances."[61]

The weather, which had appeared so promising the week before, now turned bleak and cold. Rain clouds darkened the sky. Winter was back with a vengeance.[62] At two that afternoon, Gerry returned from another secret meeting with Talleyrand or his agents and advised Marshall and Pinckney that they must request their passports at once or face expulsion. Gerry had changed his mind and decided to remain behind to prevent war with France. Marshall was aghast. It was less than twenty-four hours since Gerry had said he would sooner plunge into the Seine. But this time Marshall held his tongue. There was no point in arguing.[63]

Pinckney's daughter Eliza was very ill, and her doctor had prescribed that she go to the South of France to recover before the Pinckneys crossed the Atlantic. Marshall would have to travel alone, but he hesitated to leave without a letter of safe passage from the Directory. He had learned, possibly from Madame de Villette, that the Directory had issued secret orders to French privateers to capture Marshall and Pinckney on their return passage to the States and take them to the West Indies as prisoners. If the envoys were forced to leave France without a letter of safe passage, their best chance to avoid capture would be to dash across the channel to Britain. Marshall asked Beaumarchais to request letters of safe passage from Talleyrand for Pinckney and himself. Beaumarchais promised to try, but he cautioned Marshall against fleeing to England; it would offend the French government and lend credence to the charge that Marshall was a British agent.[64]

Talleyrand was in no mood to accommodate the Americans. He refused to give them a letter of safe passage, and out of sheer cruelty, he would not permit Pinckney's daughter to remain in France long enough to recuperate.[65] Gerry, who portrayed himself as selflessly remaining in Paris "to prevent a rupture," made no effort to use his influence with Talleyrand to help. Gerry sniveled that "their conduct to me has not been of that frank & friendly description which I expected."[66] Given Gerry's secret meetings with Talleyrand and his agents, this sounded like the height of hypocrisy.

Marshall drafted one final memorandum to Talleyrand defending American sovereignty. As to the claim that French consuls had the right to exercise jurisdiction over captured British vessels in U.S. waters, Marshall argued that one sovereign may not exercise an official governmental function in the territory of another. "Every nation has of natural right, entirely and exclusively all the jurisdiction which may be rightfully exercised in the territory it occupies. If it cedes any portion of that jurisdiction to judges appointed by another nation, the limits of their power must depend on the instrument of cession." Marshall went on to point out that no state had ever conceded the power to protect vessels within their territory, which was a necessary incident to state sovereignty.[67]

Marshall also rejected the French claim that the U.S. government was using the American press to spread "invectives & a calumnies against the Republic." As a delegate to the Virginia Ratifying Convention, Marshall had helped to draft the language that became the First Amendment. The French did not understand a free press: No principle was more "sacred" in America "which the Government contemplates with awful reverence; and would approach only with the most cautious circumspection" than the freedom of the press. Though "this liberty is often carried to excess, that it has sometimes degenerated into licentiousness," this was "an evil inseparable from the good to which it is allied." Though some newspapers might criticize France unfairly, criticism "has been still more profusely lavished on [France's] enemies, and has even been bestowed with an unsparing hand on the federal government itself." Marshall acknowledged that false accusations are "a calamity incident to the nature of liberty."[68] It was a cogent argument that demonstrated how Marshall had grown as a diplomat in a few short months. But it fell on deaf ears.

That evening, as the three envoys were polishing Marshall's memorandum, Gerry was feeling defensive. He felt that he had been misunderstood by his two colleagues and unfairly criticized. They were "embittered" and conspired against him, he thought. Marshall, who was tired of fighting, sat quietly and watched as Pinckney, who had always kept calm, grew red in the face and finally lost his temper.[69]

In his thick drawl, Pinckney accused Gerry of embarrassing the American government and risking war with Britain. Pinckney charged that Gerry had secretly negotiated with Talleyrand without his colleagues. Gerry had betrayed Marshall and him by deciding to remain behind to negotiate on his own. Now Pinckney, in Marshall's presence, had caught Gerry admitting that he had conspired with Talleyrand against his nation's representatives.[70]

Gerry replied that Talleyrand had warned him that if he left France it would result in war. Gerry gave them a patronizing look and told them that he was not surprised at their attitude. After all, they must have felt "wounded" after being dismissed by the Directory and jealous of the respect Talleyrand extended toward him. Gerry insisted that the situation was entirely a consequence of their own actions and the respect he had accorded Minister Talleyrand.[71] With that, the last thread of civility between them had snapped.

Having threatened Marshall with expulsion, the French foreign minister now kept him waiting more than a week to receive his passport. Marshall and Pinckney were packed and ready to leave at a moment's notice. Expecting to leave at any hour, Marshall did not buy more wine or send his linen to be washed. There were vessels sailing from Bordeaux and Nantes in a few days, but he had no passport or letter of safe conduct. This was urgent because in a few days there would be no vessel ready to take him to the United States. Whatever Madame de Villette felt, the anticipation was killing him.[72]

The next morning, Beaumarchais returned with news that their departure was imminent. Talleyrand, however, insisted that since he had never accepted their diplomatic credentials, Marshall and Pinckney would have to obtain their passports through the American counsel general like any other private citizens. Talleyrand added that no letter of safe conduct was necessary and that he expected Marshall to travel through England, which would, of course, bolster Talleyrand's claim that Marshall "belonged to the English faction [in the United States]." Beaumarchais complained that Talleyrand had behaved toward the American commissioners like a bronze statue with "a foot in the air, with out moving a step."[73]

Two days later, on April 13, 1798, the French Foreign Ministry returned passports to Marshall and Pinckney. Pinckney was allowed to accompany his wife and daughter to the South of France while Eliza recuperated. As a parting gift, Beaumarchais gave Marshall a letter written by Voltaire to Louis XV. Beaumarchais was the editor of a large volume of Voltaire's correspondence. (Apparently, editors in the eighteenth century enjoyed prerogatives that no modern editor would contemplate, and Beaumarchais filched a few letters as mementos.) Marshall was touched and responded with a note he drafted himself in French. It was a thoughtful gesture, but Marshall's poor grammar suggested that his time with Madame de Villette was not spent entirely studying the language.[74]

There is no record of Marshall's parting words to Madame de Villette, but words could not have expressed the anguish he felt. Though he had long since tired of France, Gerry, and Talleyrand, it must have pained him to leave her. He still loved Polly with all his heart, but her life was confined. De Villette was a spirited, soulful woman whose life was the stuff of theater. For a brief moment, he had been permitted to glimpse a rarified and exotic life, but the curtain had come down. It was simply not possible to live more than one life at a time. Though he had lost four children and been wounded in war, he had never before had to confront his own mortal constraints. He would spend the rest of his life half a world apart from Madame de Villette.

His last letter before he left France was sent to Consul General Skipwith. He asked him to "have the goodness to say to Madam Villette in my name & in the handsomest manner, everything which respectful friendship can dictate." And then, after a moment's reflection, he added wistfully, "When you have done that You will have renderd not quite half justice to my sentiments."[75]

The road south from Paris to Bordeaux was no easier for Marshall than the rest of his time in France. His carriage broke down, and his luggage was delayed. He finally reached Bordeaux on April 21. He was happy to "bid I believe an eternal adieu to Europe . . . for its crimes." He had booked a voyage to New York on a ship named for his friend Alexander Hamilton, and he joked to Pinckney that it was "a very excellent vessel but for the sin of the name." He clarified that he was referring only to Hamilton's "political crimes, for those of a private nature are really some of them so lovely that it requires men of as much virtue & less good temper than you & myself to hate them." Marshall was referring to the scandal involving Hamilton's extramarital affair with Maria Reynolds that had exploded in the Republican press the previous year. Was he also hinting at his own infidelity?[76]

Though Marshall's mission to France failed to secure peace, it would soon enough launch his career as a national figure. Moreover, his experience in Paris shaped his conservative ideas about both law and politics. In France, Marshall witnessed the breakdown of a revolutionary society in which ideological extremists showed little respect for life, liberty, property, or the rule of law. Marshall wrote to Washington that he "observd the storm which has been long gathering in Paris. The thunder bolt has at length been launched at the heads of the leading members of the legislature & has, it is greatly to be feard, involved in one common ruin with them the constitution & the liberties of their country."[77]

The French revolutionaries had collapsed the separation of powers between the executive, legislative, and judicial branches, and thus jeopardized the rule of law and civil liberties. Marshall thought that the "wound inflicted on the [French] constitution" by the French radicals was "mortal." Though the radicals claimed that national security justified their actions, Marshall concluded that "[n]ecessity, the never to be worn out apology for violence," could never justify the "slavery of the press" or other violations of civil liberty.[78]

Marshall's experience in Paris convinced him of the fragility of society and the need to diffuse power among the branches of government to safeguard the rule of law. It also made him suspicious of ideologues. Unlike Jefferson, who came away from France with a romantic idea of revolutionary ideology, Marshall's natural inclination toward moderation and pragmatism was reaffirmed by his Paris mission. So, too, was his sense of American exceptionalism reinforced by his exposure to the venality of the French elite. Finally, Marshall's dealings with Talleyrand taught him a valuable lesson about the limits of law and the paramount importance of national interest.

These lessons would shape Marshall's future role as both a statesman and a judge.

CHAPTER THIRTEEN

THE XYZ PAPERS

B ack in Philadelphia, Secretary of State Pickering received three dispatches from the envoys at ten in the evening of March 4, 1798.
The letters, dated from October 22 to mid-November 1797, were
the first to arrive in eight months since the American commissioners set
out on their peace mission. The oldest letter was drafted just a few weeks
after Marshall had arrived in Paris and shortly after his first meeting with
Talleyrand. It had taken more than four months to reach Philadelphia due
to the winter weather and the British blockade, both of which impeded
traffic from France to the United States. Within the next three days, two
more dispatches arrived that brought Pickering up-to-date on the negotiations through mid-January.[1]

Two of the first three dispatches were written in cipher. Marshall wrote
the dispatches in various sets of complex codes that could be easily changed.
Each code consisted of columns of numbers that corresponded to more
than sixteen hundred words.[2] It would take days to decipher these two dispatches, and Pickering would have to wait to read them. The third dispatch,
dated January 8, was a quickly scribbled uncoded note from the envoys

enclosing the order of the French Directory authorizing the capture of all neutral ships carrying goods to or from Britain and shutting the ports of France to neutral ships that docked in Britain. Pickering received it later that night. It closed, "We can only repeat that there exists no hope of our being officially received by this Government, or that the objects of our Mission will be in any way accomplished."[3] Pickering was dumbstruck to learn that the negotiations were a complete failure. Pulling on his coat, the secretary of state hurried in the darkness from his office on Fifth Street in Philadelphia to the President's House a few blocks away. Pickering felt that the news was too important to wait until morning, and if he had to wake the president, he would.

As President Adams read the letter, he could barely contain his anger. All this time French ships continued to assault U.S. merchant vessels while no progress had been made on resolving the dispute. Now, to add insult to injury, France threatened to close its ports to American ships.

In a fit of pique, the president sent a message to Congress the following morning informing them that the diplomatic mission to France had failed and that Congress should appropriate funds for the navy and improved defenses. The president also enclosed the short uncoded letter.[4] Over the next few days, the other dispatches were decoded and they supplied more details of Talleyrand's demands for a bribe and a loan, but the president decided not to disclose this to Congress.

President Adams called the cabinet together to discuss how to respond. Adams wavered over whether to declare war on France outright or increase military preparedness first. The cabinet was split between Secretary Pickering and Attorney General Charles Lee, who favored a declaration of war, and Treasury Secretary Oliver Wolcott Jr. and Secretary of War James McHenry, who opposed it.[5] The president felt torn between the war hawks and the Hamiltonians, who doubted the country's preparedness to defend itself against France. On March 19, the president sent Congress a carefully worded message calling for a naval buildup and measures short of war, which he hoped would avoid escalating the conflict while assuaging the war hawks in his own party.

The president's message failed to quiet his critics. Vice President Jefferson called the president's message to Congress "insane." Jefferson proposed that Congress adjourn "in order to go home & consult their constituents on the great crisis of American affairs now existing." This was purely a subterfuge to prevent a declaration of war. Jefferson hoped that the Republicans would gain "time enough by this to allow [France's] descent on England to have its effect here as well as there." Jefferson thought that once Britain was defeated, the United States would realize the futility of opposing France.[6] It was hard to say whether Jefferson was more concerned about the fate of American merchant ships captured by France or the outcome of the French Revolutionary Wars.

Instead of adopting the measures that Adams requested to build up the navy, Republicans in Congress accused the president of fanning the flames of war and demanded the release of all the dispatches in a mistaken belief that the dispatches would show that Marshall and Pinckney had sabotaged the negotiations with America's oldest ally. Adams was reluctant to release them, fearing it would embolden the hard-line Federalists and drive the country into war. But as the Republicans' insistence grew louder, Adams realized that publishing the correspondence would actually embarrass Republicans and help to make the case against France. He shrewdly waited to disclose them until the right moment when the dispatches would have their maximum effect.

The more extreme Republicans in the House proposed a resolution "that under existing circumstances it is not expedient for the United States to resort to war against the French Republic." Though it may have been true, such a declaration of no war would have the effect of raising a flag of surrender to the French attacks on U.S. shipping. Congressman Albert Gallatin of Pennsylvania, the Republican leader in the House, tried to steer toward a moderate course. Gallatin recognized the need to distance his

party from the French Directory: "I am convinced that at the commence-
ment of her revolution there was a great enthusiasm amongst our citizens
in favor of her cause," he told the House. However, he warned the members,
"I believe these feelings have been greatly diminished by her late conduct
towards this country." He assured his Federalist colleagues that French attacks on U.S. shipping had ended whatever influence France had once exercised over Republicans. His comments were remarkably candid for a
leader of a political party. Gallatin acknowledged that France's depredations "would be justifiable cause for war for this country," but the real question was whether it was in "our interest to go to war."[7]

Gallatin hoped to avoid war if at all possible.[8] Instead of appropriating
money for the navy or adopting the declaration of no war, Gallatin supported a resolution demanding that President Adams turn over all the
correspondence sent by the envoys to the secretary of state. The House
overwhelmingly adopted the resolution on April 2. It was an unprecedented
demand on the executive's privilege that threatened to expose secret diplomatic communications. Federalists joined in demanding the president release the letters.[9]

Gallatin must have felt conflicted about his role. As a young immigrant
from Geneva arriving in Richmond in 1783, he was befriended by Marshall. It was, in fact, Marshall who first recognized Gallatin's potential and
trained him in the practice of law.[10] Now Gallatin was repaying Marshall's
generosity by demanding his secret correspondence with the secretary of
state and putting Marshall's life in jeopardy by possibly offending the
French Directory.

Of course, Gallatin did not know what the correspondence contained or
that President Adams was delighted to comply with the Republicans' demand. The president lost no time responding to the House the following
day. Before releasing the envoys' dispatches, Secretary Pickering replaced
the names of Talleyrand's agents—Jean Conrad Hottinguer, Pierre Bellamy, and Lucien Hauteval—with the letters "X," "Y," and "Z," respectively,

to protect their identities. Henceforth, the whole diplomatic fiasco would be known as the XYZ Affair.[11]

The House met in an extraordinary closed session with doors bolted and guarded while it read the dispatches. Federalists and Republicans alike were stunned at the insulting and grotesque behavior of the French foreign minister. Republicans could no longer pretend that the Federalists were culpable for the collapse of the talks. Moderate Republicans, fearing that they would be tarred with being "French partisans," expressed support for the Federalists and opposition to France. Vice President Jefferson blamed President Adams's speech critical of the French the previous May as the "only obstacle to accommodation, and the real cause of war, if war takes place." Despite all the evidence to the contrary, the papers, in Jefferson's view, did not "offer one motive more for our going to war." However, even Jefferson admitted that the XYZ papers "produced such a shock on the republican mind as has never been seen since our independence."[12]

James Madison later confessed that setting aside Talleyrand's "depravity," he could not believe the foreign minister's "unparalleled stupidity."[13] Gallatin, having argued that the dispatches were of vital national interest, now had nothing to say about their contents. Instead, he spoke passionately of the need to avoid war at all costs, even at the cost of the nation's honor, as he believed that the "present situation" was still "better than war."[14] Privately, he acknowledged that he was appalled by the way France had treated the American envoys: "They behave still worse than I was afraid from their haughtiness they would." And he now feared the worst. "God Save us from War!"[15]

Republicans worried that if the correspondence was made public the tide for war would be irresistible. Jefferson insisted that the revelations in the dispatches had changed nothing, but he was swimming against an irresistible tide.[16] It was impossible to keep the documents secret, especially since the Senate, controlled by Federalists, now demanded copies of the reports as well. The press and the public were hungry to learn what

Congress knew, and both houses agreed to publish the complete contents of the XYZ dispatches.[17]

Marshall's journal recorded every detail of their contacts with Talleyrand and his agents. It exploded any myth of France's benign attitude or of the American commissioners' culpability. As Washington had confidently predicted months earlier in a letter to Marshall, now "the eyes of all in this country, who are not willfully blind, and resolved to remain so (some from one motive, and some from another) will be fully opened." Washington assured Marshall that the Directory "greatly deceive themselves" if they imagined the United States would be polarized by partisanship. But Washington could not help but express his disappointment with Jefferson's party for attacking Adams "in the severest terms, and sounding the Tocsin upon every occasion that a wild imagination could torture into a stretch of power, or unconstitutionality, in the Executive," and yet the same Republican leaders were "the warm advocates of those high handed measures of the French Directory."[18]

Vice President Jefferson plotted in any way possible to undermine President Adams's policies and the momentum toward going to war. Just as Pickering was distributing the XYZ papers, Jefferson and his lieutenants were scrambling to counter the Federalists' arguments. Jefferson went so far as to send copies of Marshall's secret diplomatic instructions to his agents, hoping that this would demonstrate that the Federalists had sabotaged negotiations from the outset. This was an extraordinary breach of government secrecy that substantially undermined U.S. diplomacy with France.[19]

In a matter of days, Republicans sheepishly retired the red, white, and blue cockades they had pinned to their hats as a symbol of Gallic solidarity. After the publication of the XYZ papers, a person wearing a tricolor cockade in the streets of Philadelphia would have been assaulted. Anti-Republican riots broke out in the capital in May. Opponents of France, both men and women, now wore black ribbons in their hats without feeling self-conscious about the fact that black was also the color of the English cockade. Republicans in Congress distanced themselves from France, fearing retribution by the American electorate, and many Republican newspapers lost circulation and advertising. Benjamin Franklin's grandson and the country's most virulent Republican editor, Benjamin Franklin Bache, was physically attacked for his pro-French writings in the Philadelphia *Aurora*. Hard-line Federalists talked about the need to root out their internal enemies even at the risk of civil war, and vigilante groups ominously trailed Republican leaders, who were afraid to speak out against the surging popularity of the president's party. President Adams could now move forward with almost the entire country galvanized behind his efforts to protect commerce from French aggression.[20]

Throughout April, the president easily pushed through Congress nearly two dozen measures to fight the French. Congress agreed to establish an enlarged army and the first U.S. Department of the Navy under the leadership of Benjamin Stoddert, a wealthy Georgetown merchant. The new navy would be separate from the War Department because Adams had so little faith in his secretary of war, James McHenry. Congress appropriated funds for purchasing a dozen ships with up to twenty-two guns each and provided money for substantial increases in arms and ammunition.

In July, Congress approved a trade embargo against France that prohibited any French ships from entering U.S. waters, rescinded all treaties with France, and authorized the navy to seize any French vessels near the coastline and any U.S. vessels going to French ports. This was the beginning of what eventually became known as the Quasi-War against France. Though Adams did not ask for a formal declaration of war, there was no doubt that the United States was engaged in a full-scale naval war with France. The president named Washington as commander in chief of the new army and Hamilton as second-in-command. The Quasi-War, the first undeclared war in American history, lasted for the next two years.

AMID ALL THIS WAR PREPARATION Marshall quietly slipped into New York Harbor on Sunday, June 17, 1798, on the *Alexander Hamilton*. Nearly two months had passed since he had left Bordeaux, and he had no idea of the impact of his dispatches on national politics. His arrival was announced a few days later in a special edition of the *New York Commercial Advertiser*. In the frenzy of the moment, Marshall was hailed as a national hero for standing up to French demands. Just by virtue of being the first of the three envoys to return, Marshall became a symbol of resistance to French aggression. Had Pinckney not been delayed in France by his daughter's illness, Marshall might never have received national attention. Not since Citizen Genet's arrival at Charleston had the nation experienced anything quite so electric. Federalist and Republican leaders alike in New York sought an audience with Marshall. New Yorkers planned a gala celebrating Marshall, but he preferred to leave as soon as possible for Philadelphia.[21]

As Marshall's carriage approached Philadelphia on the evening of Tuesday, June 19, he was greeted by Secretary of State Pickering and the capital city's cavalry. Marshall could not have anticipated this fuss, and as the parade marched down Philadelphia's Market Street, church bells rang for hours, cannons roared, and crowds lined the streets and rooftops waving handkerchiefs and cheering him as they had once cheered Citizen Genet. Marshall was amazed and overcome by the reception. Members of Congress hosted a grand banquet in his honor at Oeller's Hotel for more than one hundred distinguished guests that included foreign diplomats, members of the Supreme Court, and the cabinet. There were sixteen toasts to Marshall, Pinckney, and the United States, but one toast by a South Carolina representative was particularly memorable: "Millions for defense, but not one cent for tribute." That slogan, later mistakenly attributed to Pinckney, became a rallying cry against French aggression. The one person notably omitted from the toasts was Elbridge Gerry, who was still in Paris negotiating.[22]

Marshall had serious business in Philadelphia. President Adams had been traveling around the country making bellicose speeches that sounded more and more like he was preparing the country for war. On June 20, Marshall met with the president and Secretary of State Pickering to lay out his view that France did not intend to go to war. Adams appreciated Marshall's service, and he was impressed and grateful for Marshall's insights.[23] Secretary Pickering asked Marshall to leave his Paris journal with him to be copied. Though much of the journal had already appeared in the published dispatches, some of it had not. Pickering was particularly interested in learning more about Gerry's role and his relationship to Talleyrand. "The President ought to be acquainted with Mr. Gerry's whole conduct," Pickering explained. Pickering detested Gerry and went so far as to express his hope that the French would guillotine Gerry.[24]

As the capital buzzed with excitement over Marshall's presence, Jefferson was obsessed with Marshall's celebrity. Having previously insisted on the disclosure of the XYZ papers, Jefferson now accused Marshall of writing the XYZ papers "with a view to their being made public" to aid the Federalists. Marshall's journal, Jefferson wrote to Gerry, "was truly a God-send to them, & they made the most of it, many thousands of copies were printed & dispersed gratis at the public expence," which "excited a general & high indignation among the people unexperienced in such maneuvers." The vice president maintained that in gratitude "[t]he Federalists (self-called)" had "beamed on your colleagues [Marshall and Pinckney] meridian splendor."[25]

Jefferson had already concluded that war with France was inevitable.[26] He blamed Marshall for the sharp turn in public opinion against France and worried that the Republican Party would be forever tainted by its Gallic association. He was relieved to hear that Marshall preferred to give negotiations more time before lobbying Congress to declare war. Jefferson decided to set aside their bitter rivalry for the moment and pay Marshall a visit.

Marshall was no doubt surprised to see Jefferson's calling card when he returned to his hotel. Jefferson wrote on the card that he was "so lucky" to find Marshall out. Then realizing his error, he changed the word to "UN-lucky." Marshall later joked that it was the only time Jefferson had come close to telling the truth. The two cousins had missed an opportunity to meet and possibly reconcile.[27]

Marshall left Philadelphia hurriedly the next day for Winchester, Virginia, where Polly was recuperating from depression after the birth of their son John.

Throughout Marshall's travels from Pennsylvania to Virginia, he was welcomed as a national hero by uniformed militia, cheering crowds, and artillery salutes. His appearance gave people hope that America would stand strong and united.

When he reached Winchester several days later, he was in for another shock: Polly was far worse than he could have imagined. She was confined to bed and chronically depressed. She had barely written to her husband for most of the twelve months he had been away. He had left her with three children to raise on her own, still grieving the loss of four other children who had died in infancy, and pregnant with one more. It was more than she could manage, and her mind had snapped. The humid weather seemed to aggravate her mental condition. For Marshall, the contrast between the tributes and applause he received from strangers and the sullen reception from his own spouse after a year's absence must have been profoundly disappointing.

Polly never recovered. For most of the rest of her life, she preferred to remain a recluse largely confined to her bedroom. She was so sensitive to noise that Marshall avoided socializing in their home, and the few guests who did visit were encouraged to remove their shoes and speak in a whisper lest they upset her fragile nerves.[28]

As the Quasi-War with France unfolded, Marshall was generally pleased with the defensive measures approved by Congress, but he drew the line at the Alien and Sedition Acts. These were four separate measures breathlessly rushed through a war-crazed Congress in June and July by the hard-line Federalists and supported by President Adams. Though they were justified as internal security measures, they were, in fact, aimed at critics of the president's policies. Congress, it soon became clear, had sacrificed liberty in defense of freedom.

The Naturalization Act made it more difficult for resident aliens to become naturalized citizens, required aliens to register with the federal government, and subjected aliens to government surveillance. The Federalists worried that the recent surge of Irish immigrants, who naturally opposed the English, were inclined therefore to be sympathetic to France and join the Republican Party. The Naturalization Act intended to discourage these immigrants from becoming naturalized citizens—or, to be more specific, naturalized Republicans.

To prove they were sufficiently patriotic, Republicans responded by proposing the Alien Enemies Act. This act provided that in the event of a declaration of war, the president could deport enemy aliens. Since Congress was not about to declare war, the act had no practical effect other than to counter any suspicion that the Republicans were French puppets. However, it may have had the unintended effect of discouraging immigrants from engaging in politics.

The Alien Friends Act gave the president the authority to deport any alien he judged "dangerous to the peace and safety of the United States." It was an extraordinary delegation of power to one man, which President Adams wisely never invoked.

Most important, Congress passed the infamous Sedition Act, which prohibited any statement or writing critical of the U.S. government, Congress, or the president. The maximum penalties included a fine of five thousand dollars and five years in prison for those caught merely conspiring to speak out against the government and two thousand dollars and two years in prison for actually making "seditious" statements. It was plainly intended to silence the Republican press and the president's critics. It is ironic that President Adams signed the law on Bastille Day 1798. The Federalists wrote the statute to lapse the same day that President Adams left office so that it could never be used by a Republican president against Federalists. Though the definition of sedition was purposefully vague, one Federalist paper put it bluntly: "It is patriotism to write in favor of our government—it is sedition to write against it."[29]

The Federalists lost no time in invoking the act to prosecute Republicans. The first person indicted was Vermont Congressman Matthew Lyon, who accused President Adams of a "continual grasp for power, in an unbounded thirst for ridiculous pomp, foolish adulation, and selfish avarice."[30] For his statement, Lyon was convicted and sentenced to four months in prison and fined one thousand dollars. The imprisonment of Representative Lyon sent a chilling message to all opponents of the Federalist administration. Vice President Jefferson, among others, became increasingly paranoid. He suspected that he was being followed by Federalist agents and that his mail was being read.[31] Jefferson worried that the president had trumped up the threat of foreign agents as a pretext to spy on American citizens.

Marshall did not approve of these acts. He thought that the First Amendment had abolished the ancient British crime of "seditious libel," which punished anyone who criticized the king. If the government could punish Americans for dissenting, it was no better than the French Directory. Marshall also foresaw that it was likely that the Federalists' heavy-handed tactics used against Republican newspapers was likely to backfire in the next election. He privately voiced his concerns to Secretary Pickering, but only later did he object publicly.[32] Marshall published a letter in the *Virginia Herald* stating that if he had been in Congress when the Alien and Sedition Acts were adopted, he "certainly [would] have opposed them." Rather than suggest that such laws threaten civil liberties, Marshall toned down his public rhetoric to avoid offending his own party—and risking a possible jail sentence. He merely thought that such laws were "useless" and were likely "to create, unnecessarily, discontents and jealousies at a time when our very existence as a nation, may depend on our union."[33] It was a faint-sounding defense of the First Amendment, but it was no ordinary time, and not one of his fellow Federalists went any further to oppose these laws.

Years later, after the Quasi-War had ended, Jefferson asked Gerry whether peace with France might not have been preserved if either Marshall or Pinckney had agreed to buy off France. Gerry replied, "I have no hesitation to answer in the affirmative."[34] Jefferson felt vindicated that it was, after all, his meddlesome cousin Marshall who was to blame for triggering the Quasi-War with France.

CHAPTER FOURTEEN

THE JONATHAN ROBBINS
AFFAIR

At the beginning of September 1798, Marshall paid a visit to his old commander in chief at Mount Vernon. Washington was aging rapidly, but he had invited Marshall to discuss politics. Marshall rode on horseback through a torrential downpour with his friend Bushrod Washington, the president's nephew. They arrived soaked to the bone and had to change clothes. Only then did they realize that they had mistakenly exchanged saddlebags with another traveler at an inn. They had no clothing of their own. Marshall and Bushrod had to borrow dry clothes from the president, who was about the same height but considerably wider than either man. Dressed in Washington's clownishly oversize suits, Marshall and Bushrod were formally received by the president, who laughed so hard when he saw them that he could barely breathe.[1]

Washington, who had tried to remain nonpartisan after he left office, was finally taking off his gloves. He felt it was critical to prevent the Republicans from gaining a majority in the House. Too much was at stake. Washington asked Marshall to run for Congress from Richmond, and Bushrod to run from Westmoreland County. Washington was confident that his nephew and the hero of the XYZ Affair were two of the few Federalists who could still win election in Virginia. Bushrod dutifully accepted, but Marshall declined. He had lost interest in political life. He was consumed by his family obligations and legal practice. Interest payments were coming due on the Fairfax property. To pay them, he had to rebuild his law practice after his long absence in France.

But Washington would not accept Marshall's answer. Over the next three days, his former commander in chief pressed Marshall to run. Washington even arranged a banquet in Alexandria to honor Marshall. Though Marshall was moved by this tribute, he continued to resist Washington's entreaties. To avoid further argument, Marshall decided he would slip out early the next morning before the president awoke. The next day, when he walked out to the stable, he found himself confronted at daybreak by his old commander. Washington told Marshall that "there were crises in national affairs which made it the duty of a citizen to forgo his private for the public interest." If Washington could accept the necessity of abandoning his retirement to resume command of the armed forces during the Quasi-War, surely no less could be expected of Marshall. Marshall later described this as "a very earnest conversation, one of the most interesting I was ever engaged in." Reluctantly, Marshall yielded and agreed to stand for election to the next Congress.[2]

Winning the election would not be easy. Marshall faced a popular Republican incumbent, John Clopton, who came from an old distinguished Virginia family. The Thirteenth District of Virginia was solidly Republican with a small base of Federalists in Richmond. The Federalist minority in Virginia consisted of middle-class farmers and merchants scattered around the state. They would support Marshall, but Marshall's prominence made him a target for Republicans. Madison and Jefferson did not want Marshall gaining a toehold in Congress, and they were determined to defeat him.[3]

The election of 1798 was unusually heated. The contest centered on the candidates' views of France and the Alien and Sedition Acts. Marshall campaigned by sponsoring barbecues and inviting voters to drinks. His sense of humor and personal warmth were most effective in these social settings. But the Republicans fought back hard. By late fall, the campaign turned ugly. Marshall was vilified in the Republican newspapers for being a "British agent," "a monarchist," and an "enemy of free speech" who was "ridiculously awkward in the arts of dissimulation and hypocrisy."[4]

Patrick Henry, who had opposed Marshall at the Virginia Ratifying Convention, now rushed to Marshall's defense. He praised Marshall's service in France and remarked that Marshall "ever stood high in my esteem as a private citizen. His temper and disposition were always pleasant, his talents and integrity unquestioned," which, Henry added, were "sufficient to place that gentleman far above any competitor in the district for Congress."[5]

In September, President Adams unexpectedly offered Marshall, in the midst of the campaign, a seat on the Supreme Court. Justice James Wilson, one of the original members of the Supreme Court, had just died, and a seat was open. Perhaps remembering what Washington had told him, Marshall promptly declined. He had no interest in the Supreme Court. He was committed to running for Congress, he told Adams, and if he failed to win election, he was content to remain in Richmond with Polly and his children. Adams offered the seat to Bushrod Washington instead. Bushrod happily abandoned his own congressional campaign for a safe seat on the Court with lifetime tenure, and Washington's family friend Henry Lee resumed the race for the Federalists.[6]

In October, Vice President Jefferson secretly drafted his famous Kentucky and Virginia Resolutions against the Alien and Sedition Acts, and forwarded them to John Breckinridge, the Republican speaker of the Kentucky House. The resolutions condemned the Alien and Sedition Acts as being unconstitutional and legally void. More important, they asserted that the Constitution was nothing more than a mere "compact" among states, and as a consequence, each state had the right to nullify any federal law with which it disagreed. (Fifty years later, the Confederate states would in-voke Jefferson's doctrine of nullification to justify secession.) Once the resolutions were adopted by Kentucky, Jefferson forwarded them to Madi-son, who pushed them through the Virginia legislature. For a vice president to challenge the supremacy of federal law and propose the theory of nulli-fication could be seen at the very least as disloyalty if not treason.[7]

Jefferson did not support secession himself, but he may have used the implied threat of secession to temper the hard-line Federalists. "[I]f to rid ourselves of the present rule of Massachusetts & Connecticut, we break the union, will the evil stop there?" he wrote. That was a question no one could answer. Factions were a natural condition of politics, and if the Union was reduced to just Virginia and Kentucky, "they will end by breaking into their simple units." Jefferson would prefer to keep New England in the Union and hope that "we shall see the reign of witches pass over, their spells dissolve, and the people recovering their true sight, restore their govern-ment to its true principles."[8]

Though the Republicans hoped that other states would follow the leads of Kentucky and Virginia, none did. Instead, the Kentucky and Virginia Resolutions sent a shiver down the backs of unionists of both parties and probably hurt the Republicans in some districts, including Marshall's.

As the congressional elections loomed, "the fate of my election is ex-tremely uncertain," Marshall wrote to his brother James. "The means used to defeat it are despicable in the extreme & yet they succeed." His view of political campaigns was that nothing "more debases or pollutes the human mind."[9] Even after he was endorsed by Patrick Henry, Marshall's election looked too close to call.[10]

In the early days of the Republic, each state set its own date for congres-sional elections. Virginia's election day, April 24, 1799, was a rowdy affair. Federalists and Republicans offered barrels of whiskey to their supporters at the polling places. Only white males with at least one hundred acres of undeveloped property (or twenty-five acres with a house) were eligible to vote. Typically, fewer than 10 percent of the total adult population cast ballots. There were no secret ballots in eighteenth-century Virginia. Each man stood up, possibly a bit tipsy, in front of the candidates and his neighbors, and declared his preference to either a sheriff or judge seated at a table to record the vote. The crowd would applaud or boo each vote depending on their preferences. As the drinking increased, the crowd became more boisterous. Fistfights were common.[11] Though the Federalists fared poorly throughout the South, Marshall squeaked out victory by 114 votes out of more than 2,000 cast.[12]

That July, Marshall took a long-delayed trip west to visit his parents at their home in what is now Versailles, Kentucky. Thomas Marshall was sixty-nine and in poor health. Marshall had not seen his parents in fifteen years, and this was his last trip to see them before they died. In the last few years, as Thomas was nearing the end of his life, he expressed his affection more openly. "The thoughts of seeing you once more I really believe is a principal means of keeping me alive," he wrote to his son. For the first time, he acknowledged pride in Marshall's achievements: "The good of my country & our worthy president is nearest my heart," he wrote to Marshall. "And the part you take in the present Storm gives me much pleasure, indeed you never seriously disobliged me in your life."[13] For Marshall, who kept his father on a pedestal, winning his father's approval must have been profoundly satisfying.

THE SIXTH CONGRESS, having less business than the modern one, did not meet until December 2, 1799. For his swearing-in, Marshall brought Polly with him to Philadelphia. She was then pregnant with what would be their fifth surviving child, James. Polly, who rarely left the house and had never traveled outside Virginia, was excited to visit the capital city. Philadelphia bustled with prosperity. Streets were broad and neat. Sidewalks were scrubbed, and polished brass nameplates on freshly painted doors gleamed in the sunlight. There were no homes in Richmond that could rival these handsome brick town houses with their marble stairs. Shops were full of the latest French fashions, and women brazenly wore rouge and fitted dresses that showed the natural lines of their bodies. Most surprising of all was the scarcity of slaves and the number of white servants who cheerfully dusted, swept, and served.[14]

Marshall entered Congress a national celebrity and quickly assumed the leadership of the moderate Federalists. His independence and fair-mindedness won him admirers from both parties, and his popularity annoyed his cousin Jefferson, who as vice president presided over the Senate. Marshall's old friend Albert Gallatin led the Republican majority in the House. Though they differed on nearly every issue, they remained close.[15] In Marshall's time, political differences did not preclude mutual respect.

After little more than two weeks in Congress, Marshall was pulled aside by a colleague on December 18 with the news that President Washington had died of tonsillitis four days earlier. Marshall rose on the floor and in a trembling voice announced the passing of his former commander to his stunned colleagues. "The House of Representatives can be but ill-fitted for public business after receiving information of this national calamity," he said. Then he moved for immediate adjournment until the following day.[16] Washington had held the nation together by his unimpeachable integrity and the universal respect he commanded. His towering influence was a measure of his character—not charisma, intellect, or wealth. There were no other founding fathers whom everyone could trust to do what was right as confidently as the nation trusted Washington. Without him, could the Union survive? Facing the threat of war with France and a looming bitter presidential election that divided the sitting president and vice president, the nation's future seemed clouded.

Since Marshall had moved for the adjournment, he still held the floor according to rules when the House reconvened the following day in a joint session to memorialize President Washington. In this delicate situation, it fell to Marshall to deliver a eulogy.

"Our Washington is no more!" he began. "The hero, the sage, and the patriot of America—the man on whom in times of danger every eye was turned and all hopes were placed, lives now, only in his own great actions, and in the hearts of an affectionate and afflicted people." Marshall praised his former commander not merely for leading the revolution but as "the chief of those patriots who formed for us a constitution, which, by preserving the union, will, I trust, substantiate and perpetuate those blessings our revolution had promised to bestow."[17] Though Marshall attributed the Constitution to Washington, the former president had little to do with the actual drafting.

As Marshall stood before both houses and surveyed the packed chamber, one man was noticeably absent from the official memorial: the Senate's president, Thomas Jefferson. Rather than mourn Washington, Jefferson stayed home. He feared that the wave of grief for the former president would only strengthen the appeal of the Federalist Party.[18]

Washington's friend Henry Lee drafted a resolution expressing the nation's grief, but he preferred that Marshall introduce it. Thus, it was the freshman congressman who spoke before a hushed chamber the immortal line "First in war, first in peace, first in the hearts of his countrymen."[19] For that moment, the country spoke with one voice, neither Federalist nor Republican, unified in its grief.

That sense of unity soon dissolved, and the partisan divide returned to Philadelphia in the form of a historic debate over the case of Jonathan Robbins.

IN 1799, JONATHAN ROBBINS, a British seaman, was arrested in Charleston, South Carolina, for the brutal murder two years earlier of nearly a dozen British officers and enlisted men at sea on board the *Hermione*, a thirty-two-gun British warship. Robbins had allegedly participated in a mutiny, seized control of the ship, and later sold the *Hermione* in a Spanish port. He was arrested in Charleston at the request of the British consul.

Under Article 27 of Jay's Treaty, the United States was obligated to extradite any person charged with murder in Britain. Robbins admitted that he was a member of the crew on the *Hermione*, and the evidence against Robbins sufficed to make out a prima facie case. However, Robbins claimed that he was an American born in Danbury, Connecticut, who had been kidnapped by British seamen and impressed into the British navy. The British consul claimed that Robbins's real name was Thomas Nash and that he was born in Britain.

Since the evidence of his guilt was convincing, and since Jay's Treaty required the president to honor the request for extradition, President Adams requested that the district court judge release Robbins to the custody of the British consul. Robbins was promptly sent back to Britain, tried, found guilty of mutiny and murder, and hanged.[20]

For Republicans, the Robbins case presented the perfect opportunity to reverse the political tide toward the Federalists and undo the damage they had suffered as a result of the XYZ Affair. Robbins was painted as an innocent American Everyman unjustifiably seized and executed by a foreign power with the obeisance of a servile President Adams, who kowtowed to British demands. Vice President Jefferson gleefully reported, "I think no circumstance since the establishment of our government has affected the popular mind more."[21] The Republican press fanned the flames of public outrage. The editors of the *Aurora* wrote, "Look at what has been done in the case of *Jonathan Robbins* . . . A British lieutenant who never saw him until he was prisoner at Charleston swears his name is Thomas Nash . . . The man is hanged!" The journalists thought that Jay's Treaty had given the British license "to pervert the law of nations and to degrade national honor and character." Even the controversy over the Alien and Sedition Acts and the mass arrests of Republican editors did not spark the same degree of popular outrage.[22]

Republicans proposed resolutions to limit extradition under Jay's Treaty and requested that the State Department release documents concerning the extradition. Both resolutions were adopted. Republicans hoped to lay blame squarely on President Adams, but when the State Department complied, the documents proved conclusively that Jonathan Robbins was Thomas Nash, as the British consul had claimed. The documents included a letter from the Danbury town selectmen stating that no one named Jonathan Robbins had ever lived there.[23]

But Congressional Republicans never let objective facts obscure their political convictions. They continued to repeat the false charge that Robbins was an American enslaved by the British navy and that he had acted in defense of liberty.[24] They denounced the president as an English sycophant. New York Congressman Edward Livingston moved to censure President Adams for sacrificing an American to British justice.[25]

The debate in the House over the censure motion was long and heated. On March 7, 1800, Marshall rose to speak. Polly had given birth to their fifth child, James Keith, only three weeks earlier and was still suffering from anxiety and depression. But she sensed that this was a historic moment, so she left their home in Philadelphia to watch her husband from the visitors' gallery. The air was frosty, but brilliant sunlight streamed through the tall windows into Congress Hall as the congressmen filed into the chamber.[26] More than one hundred representatives sat in rows of long mahogany desks that formed a semicircle around the speaker's platform.

In the debate, Marshall approached the issue with a lawyer's attention to detail. He moved carefully and deliberately from one piece of evidence to the next, building to an irrefutable conclusion. Marshall showed that under international law Britain had criminal jurisdiction over a British vessel in international waters, and therefore Robbins, regardless of his nationality, must answer to British law for crimes allegedly committed on the

Hermione. To drive home this point, Marshall reminded his Republican colleagues that Vice President Jefferson as secretary of state had issued an opinion that American privateers who committed acts against British vessels could be charged under British law. If an American could be punished only under British law for crimes on a British ship, a fortiori, the British national Robbins could be punished under British law.[27]

At this point, Marshall tackled the Republican argument that the president had no constitutional power to intervene in the case. Jay's Treaty, Marshall told the chamber, required the United States to extradite on the demand of Britain, and therefore some government official must perform this act. U.S. courts could not extradite a prisoner without a request from the president. This raised the question of whether the Constitution entrusted this power to the president.

Now Marshall was ready for his masterful counterpunch: "The case was in its nature a national demand made upon the nation," he said. Who can answer this demand? "The President is the sole organ of the nation in its external relations, and its sole representative with foreign nations. Of consequence the demand of a foreign nation can only be made on him." Marshall argued that it is not a discretionary act by the president but one he is *required* to perform in accordance with a treaty, which the Constitution states is "the supreme law of the land." Marshall concluded that the president "is charged to execute the laws. A treaty is declared to be a law. He must then execute a treaty, where he and he alone possesses the means of executing it."[28]

In an instant, Marshall stood the Republicans' argument on its head. Rather than asserting the president's power, he was asserting the president's *duty.* Under the Constitution, the president had no right to refuse to execute a treaty that the Senate had ordained. "The treaty stipulating that a murderer shall be delivered up to justice is as obligatory as an act of Congress making the same declaration." Since only the president can communicate with foreign governments and negotiate treaties, it is proper to entrust him with carrying out obligations owed to foreign sovereigns. The president had no inherent power to extradite absent a treaty, but he had no right to refuse to enforce the treaty either. In other words, the president, as the "sole organ" of foreign relations, acts as Congress's *agent*.

Marshall won the argument with a strategic retreat by conceding the Republicans' point that the president's power was subordinate to congressional power. But by identifying the president as the sole organ of Congress's foreign relations power, Marshall demonstrated that Adams had no option but to extradite the prisoner.

It was a stunning display of Marshall's brilliance as an advocate. He had turned the Republicans' argument against them and triumphed. When Marshall sat down, there was a long silence in the chamber. No one knew how to reply to Marshall's carefully reasoned argument. House Republicans gathered around Majority Leader Gallatin, urging him to respond. Gallatin shook his head. From the back of the chamber, Polly overheard Gallatin say: "Answer it yourself. I think it unanswerable." The resolution criticizing President Adams was soundly defeated sixty-one to thirty-five with both Federalists and Republicans voting against it.[29]

Marshall's address would be remembered as among the greatest orations ever given in Congress, and his statement that the president is the "sole organ" of foreign relations powers has become enshrined in constitutional law.

PHILADELPHIA'S SWAMPY SUMMER CLIMATE posed the risk of another outbreak of yellow fever. Even before Congress adjourned, Marshall had returned to Virginia to attend to some legal matters. He continued to practice law to supplement his congressional salary of six dollars per day while Congress was in session (about $120 today).[30] On his way out of Philadelphia, he stopped at the War Department to make some inquiries on behalf of some of his friends. He ran into Secretary of War James McHenry, who greeted him coldly. Marshall was puzzled. He had done nothing to deserve such rudeness. A short time later, he ran into the chief clerk of the War Department, who congratulated Marshall on his appointment as secretary of war. Marshall was flabbergasted. He soon learned that Adams had fired McHenry, accusing him of secretly plotting to bring down his presidency.[31] Adams had not bothered to tell Marshall that he was about to be nominated to the cabinet.

Marshall did not consider himself qualified for the job, and he wanted to return to the practice of law. He promptly wrote the president requesting that he withdraw his name from consideration, but before Adams could withdraw the nomination, Marshall's confirmation sailed through the Senate. Despite the ease with which he was elevated to the position, Marshall refused to accept the commission.[32]

Only days after receiving Marshall's refusal, President Adams fired Secretary of State Pickering, accusing him of acting as Hamilton's handmaiden to undermine him. Adams loathed Hamilton, whom he disparaged as that "bastard son of a Scotch peddler." And the sentiment was mutual. Hamilton, who worried that Adams could not win reelection, was quietly maneuvering to find another candidate to run on the Federalist ticket in lieu of Adams. Hamilton and the other war hawks in the Federalist Party wanted Adams to declare war on France, and they vehemently opposed the appointment of another diplomatic mission to France. Adams blamed Hamilton for Pickering's belligerent attitude toward France and his opposition to sending a second peace mission to France.[33] When Adams appointed a peace mission over his and most of the cabinet's objections, Pickering went so far as to disclose to the British ambassador, Robert Liston, the secret diplomatic instructions given to the peace mission. These efforts to undermine the mission triggered Pickering's firing.[34]

After firing Pickering, Adams nominated Marshall as secretary of state. By now, Marshall had already left town for Richmond and knew nothing about any of these machinations. President Adams once again sent

Marshall's nomination to the Senate without his consent, and the Senate unanimously confirmed him the following day, May 13, 1800. Marshall's friend Charles Lee, the acting secretary of state, notified him by mail of his appointment.

Back in Richmond, Marshall felt deeply torn by this appointment. Unlike the positions he had been previously appointed to, the secretary of state was in effect the head of the cabinet with broad authority over the federal government. For a fortnight Marshall wrestled with the decision to accept his appointment. The job paid $3,500 (nearly $70,000 today), which would be enough to support his family and service his loans on the Fairfax property.[35] Ever since Washington had persuaded him to run for Congress, Marshall had felt trapped: "I was given up as a lawyer, and considered generally as entirely a political man. I lost my business altogether, and perceived very clearly that I could not recover any portion of it without retiring from Congress. Even then I could not hope to regain the ground I had lost." In addition to the loss of income, "the press teemed with so much falsehood, with such continued and irritating abuse of me" that he felt he must fight on. "I could not conquer a stubbornness of temper which determines a man to make head against and struggle with injustice." He was prepared to run again for Congress if only to respond to his critics.[36] On the other hand, joining the cabinet gave him a graceful exit from electoral politics, and since it was likely that Adams would lose the next election, he could return to Richmond in nine months anyway. He must have felt a certain twinge of satisfaction knowing how Jefferson would receive the news that his lowborn cousin had been appointed to his former cabinet post. He later admitted, "[T]he office was precisely that which I wished, and for which I had vanity enough to think myself fitted."[37]

So, with equal parts vanity and ambivalence, Marshall set out not for Philadelphia but for the new capital still under construction. This time, he assured Polly, he would be gone for only nine months.

CHAPTER FIFTEEN

PRIVATEERS AND PIRATES

The coach took three days to travel from Richmond to the new capital of Washington City. The trip was hot and dusty along badly marked roads that cut through thick forests and swamps. Marshall happened to share the coach with Supreme Court Justice Samuel Chase, who had been in Richmond to preside over the trial of James Callender for seditious libel. Callender, who was in the employ of Vice President Jefferson, had been found guilty of violating the Sedition Act for criticizing President Adams in his pamphlet *The Prospect Before Us*. Chase was a tough High Federalist judge with a reputation for speaking his mind even when it was inopportune.[1]

When the coach reached the capital on June 8, 1800, there was little to see: a few hills surrounded by a mosquito-infested swamp, dirt roads lined by drainage ditches, and some scattered buildings still under construction, including the President's House and the north side of the Capitol. Fields were dotted with tree stumps, brick kilns, outhouses, and trash. Pigs and cows wandered about, seemingly indifferent to the metropolis rising around them. Capitol Hill was bare except for a few shabby boardinghouses, a tailor shop, and a grocery. Washington City had a sprinkling of wood-framed houses that needed repairs, two taverns for travelers, and a cluster of slave quarters. There were no churches, theaters, or industry. When the wind shifted, a terrible smell like death rose from the canal: You had to hold your handkerchief to your nose. It was a conceit to call it a city.[2]

Marshall checked into Tunnicliff's, a modest tavern where President Adams and the new secretary of war, Samuel Dexter, were also staying. None of these men had seen the capital before, and they had to disguise their disappointment. Across from the tavern, they could see an army of slaves straining to complete the Senate's half of the Capitol before Congress convened in November. (They had not yet begun construction of the House of Representatives.) Everything was delayed, over budget, and underfunded. What began with a grand classical design by the French architect Pierre L'Enfant was emerging from this fetid swamp as Washington's folly.[3]

President Adams sat down with Marshall in the tavern and laid out his principal areas of concern for the coming months. First, there was the continuing Quasi-War with France. Months earlier, Adams had appointed William Vans Murray, the U.S. envoy to The Hague, as the new ambassador to France. Murray's appointment was fiercely opposed by the war hawks in the Federalist Party, including Hamilton, who regarded him as soft on France.[4] Adams hoped that Murray's appointment would assuage the French and bring an end to the Quasi-War. The president had appointed two other envoys to France in November 1799—Chief Justice Oliver Ellsworth and North Carolina Governor William Davie—to join Murray's negotiations. Since their arrival, Napoleon Bonaparte had seized power in France as first consul. No one could be sure what Bonaparte intended. Adams feared that time for negotiation was running out, and he faced increased pressure to declare war on France if a settlement was not reached quickly.

Second, the president wanted to resolve outstanding issues with Britain. The British were still angry with the Americans for not honoring their debts to British creditors. Jay's Treaty had guaranteed the rights of British creditors to receive full payment, but U.S. courts had refused to enforce these debts. As a result, the British continued to seize U.S. vessels. Adams wanted a settlement.[5]

Third, the president was worried about the Barbary powers—Morocco, Algiers, Tunis, and Tripoli. The Barbary States and their privateers were constantly threatening U.S. ships in the Mediterranean by demanding tribute for the right to navigate in their sea. Some means had to be found to accommodate these states and allow Americans to trade freely in the region.[6]

Relations with Spain were also tense. In violation of a 1790 treaty with the United States, the Spanish permitted French warships to operate in their ports against U.S. ships and French tribunals in Spanish territory to issue prize awards against U.S. flagged vessels. France, Britain, Spain, and the Barbary powers were all threatening U.S. commerce. The president was relying on Marshall to resolve these threats without plunging the country into a larger war.

The president informed Marshall that he was leaving Washington at once to return to his home in Quincy, Massachusetts. The first lady had no desire to spend a blistering summer in an unfinished house adjoining an infectious swamp. Therefore, Marshall would be responsible for overseeing the federal government and the completion of the capital city before Congress arrived in November 1800.[7]

John Marshall took the administrative reins of government at an extraordinary time. Only three men had held the office of secretary of state before him, and by coincidence, two of them were his second cousins, Edmund Randolph and Thomas Jefferson. None of these men held as much authority as Marshall now exercised; none had greater support from their chief executive; and none faced greater challenges. At least for the moment, Marshall's authority was more like a Roman consul's than an untested cabinet secretary's.

The State Department was the executive branch's largest and most important department. It was not merely responsible for overseeing the diplomatic corps, which consisted of five ambassadors and sixteen part-time unpaid consuls. Virtually everything that the federal government did domestically and overseas, other than collecting taxes and supervising the small army and navy, was performed by the State Department. In addition to passports, State issued patents, copyrights, and land patents. State even oversaw the justice system. (At the time, the attorney general was merely a legal adviser to the president.) The department managed the census, ran the mint in Philadelphia, supervised U.S. territories, delivered commissions of federal appointments, and published government documents. All this was accomplished on a budget of $15,000 (around $300,000 today)—just enough to cover salaries, firewood, and stationery.[8]

The district commissioners responsible for constructing the capital would report daily to Marshall with details about street construction and the progress on government buildings. Marshall was charged with overseeing the completion of the President's House before Mrs. Adams arrived in November of 1800.[9] In the original city plan, L'Enfant had imagined a vast presidential palace on the scale of European royalty. But President Washington instructed the architect, James Hoban, to reduce the size of the house to one-fifth of L'Enfant's original plan. Now the presidential palace looked like nothing more than a large plantation house surrounded by a plain rail fence.

In addition to his official duties running the State Department, the executive branch, and the completion of the city, Marshall was the de facto leader of the Federalist Party in Adams's absence. Facing a strong challenge from Jefferson, the Federalists were badly splintered between High Federalists, who refused to compromise with the Republicans, and moderate Federalists like Marshall.

Marshall moved into a temporary office for the summer in the Treasury Building, a two-story Federal-style brick building next door to the

President's House. Treasury was the only completed government building, and it housed the entire executive branch—126 officials and staff. The State Department included a chief clerk, seven assistants, and one messenger, and all nine of them plus Marshall squeezed into two small offices. Between the sultry weather and the pervasive odor of fresh paint, they had to leave the windows open all summer. While that may have helped with the occasional breeze, the malevolent swamp air filled their lungs while fat flies buzzed maddeningly around their heads. They could also hear the constant pounding of nails from the President's House that reminded them that their capital was a work in progress. In September 1800, the State Department moved into a newly completed three-story brick row house on the north side of Pennsylvania Avenue between Twenty-First and Twenty-Second Streets, a few blocks west of the President's House. It took forty-two cartloads to move all the department's furniture, records, books, and paraphernalia.[10]

On his first day as secretary of state, the most pressing issue on Marshall's desk was a note from Rufus King, the U.S. ambassador to London, concerning the debt owed to Britain. Article 6 of Jay's Treaty provided that in the event that U.S. courts refused to enforce debts owed to British creditors, the creditors could file claims against the U.S. government with a joint arbitral commission. The commission, however, was unable to agree on a procedure for judging claims. As long as British creditors' rights were denied, the British government threatened to continue its attacks on U.S. ships and its occupation of forts along the Canadian border.

Marshall instructed King to inform Lord Grenville, the British foreign secretary, that British creditors "meet with no obstructions either of law or fact which are not common to every description of creditors." Marshall cannot have believed that. He himself had spent much of his career successfully defending U.S. debtors from British creditors. He knew better than anyone that Virginia courts disfavored British claimants. Yet, he continued, "[o]ur Judges are even liberal in their construction of the 4th Article of the treaty of Peace, and are believed . . . to have manifested no sort of partiality for the debtors."[11] The United States was already engaged in the Quasi-War with France; it could hardly afford a second war. Almost any resolution would be preferable.[12] Marshall told King to reach an agreement with Lord Grenville to amend the commission's procedures and appoint a new commission.[13]

Lord Grenville wanted the U.S. government to make a lump-sum payment to Britain for all the outstanding debts.[14] Marshall worried how that might look to France. A lump-sum payment was precisely the kind of foreign assistance the French Directory had sought and that Marshall had opposed in his negotiations with Talleyrand.[15] Would it now appear hypocritical for Marshall to agree to pay Britain to stop harassing U.S. ships? He wrote to President Adams for instructions. Adams thought that the two situations were distinguishable: France wanted a loan to make war on Britain; Britain needed to settle the legitimate claims of private creditors. The United States had already committed itself in Article 6 of Jay's Treaty to pay legitimate creditors, and it was only a question of how. The real problem was agreeing on the amount due.[16]

Marshall agreed that the United States would be better off negotiating a lump-sum settlement than leaving it to the commission to decide. If the British creditors were unhappy with the amount of their award from the U.S. government, they could still go after individual debtors for the difference.[17] President Adams hoped that the British would settle for something less than one million pounds sterling (roughly one hundred million dollars today).[18]

Marshall cautioned Ambassador King that reaching agreement on an appropriate number may be complicated by the "notoriously unfounded" and "extravagant claims" filed by some British creditors.[19] He instructed King that the United States was willing to go as high as $2.5 million (nearly $50 million today)—considerably less than Marshall or Adams thought the British claims were actually worth.[20] In fact, it took another eighteen months of negotiation for the parties to agree to a lump-sum payment of six hundred thousand pounds sterling (about seventy-five million dollars today)—far less than the president expected to pay.[21]

Marshall's negotiating tactics had paid off. The final settlement was delayed when President Jefferson replaced Adams after the 1800 election. Jefferson gave Marshall no credit for this diplomatic resolution, but it was probably fortunate that Jefferson rather than Adams had to ask Congress for approval. Congressional Republicans would have squealed like stuck pigs before they would have consented to a request from the Federalist Adams to reward British monarchists with American tax dollars.

As British debt negotiations progressed in the waning months of the Adams presidency, Marshall focused his attention on a more urgent concern: British frigates continued to harass and seize U.S. ships with increasing regularity. And over a nine-year period, the British had impressed about two thousand U.S. sailors into the British navy.[22] No single act by any foreign sovereign was more outrageous to American sensitivities.[23] On September 20, Marshall sat down at his desk in the new State Department building and began drafting a lengthy letter to Ambassador King that addressed British harassment on the high seas. Marshall's letter would become another classic State Department document as it set forth a robust neutrality principle that would form the foundation of American foreign policy for the next hundred years.

Marshall insisted that any negotiation over the capture of U.S. vessels and impressment of U.S. sailors must proceed on a separate track from the debt issue. Under Article 7 of Jay's Treaty, the British had agreed to compensate Americans for losses to any vessel suffered as a result of capture, and a commission was created in Philadelphia for this purpose. Jay's Treaty had also established a commission in London to settle claims owed to British creditors. Both commissions were deadlocked. The British suspected that the United States was delaying settlement in the hope that if France

defeated Britain it would be unnecessary to offer anything to British creditors. And the British hoped that once their troops crushed Bonaparte's
army, the Americans would be more pliable.[24]

Marshall made clear to Ambassador King that it was the consistent policy of the United States to preserve "exact neutrality" between belligerent
powers. The United States had no interest "to mingle in their quarrels."
Therefore, the United States would continue to avoid "any political connec-
tions which might engage us further than is compatible with the neutrality
we profess." The United States stood ready to defend itself—which was, of
course, highly doubtful. But, Marshall added, force would be used only as
a last resort.[25]

At the same time, Marshall asserted that America was not a fair-weather
friend. When France seemed threatened by all her neighbors in 1793, he
reminded King that "when, if ever, it was dangerous to acknowledge her
new government, & to preserve with it the relations of amity . . . the American government openly declard its determination to adhere to that state
of impartial neutrality, which it has ever since sought to maintain." Similarly, when French armies were sweeping triumphantly across Europe and
threatening to invade Britain, "America, pursuing, with undeviating step,
the same steady course, negotiated with his Britannic majesty, a treaty of
amity, commerce & navigation," and recalling his own role in the fight over
Jay's Treaty, he added "[n]or coud either threats or artifices prevent its
ratification."[26]

Marshall objected to Britain's seizure of contraband, its blockade of European ports, its impressment of U.S. sailors, and the capture of U.S. vessels. Under international law, a ship carrying contraband was subject to
capture and condemnation, but Marshall insisted that only certain military goods were contraband. British admiralty courts took the view that
anything that could be used to equip vessels, such as timber or naval supplies, could be considered contraband. Marshall argued that timber and
naval supplies intended for civilian use were not contraband.[27] However,

Marshall had argued the converse to Talleyrand when he justified allowing British warships to seize timber and naval supplies on board U.S. ships bound for France.[28]

Britain claimed the right to confiscate neutral vessels bound for a blockaded port. Marshall protested that the law of nations did not require neutral vessels to honor a blockade unless it was "effective." An effective blockade meant that the British had completely surrounded a town, not merely stationed some warships off the coast. If there was no requirement that a blockade be completely effective, then "every port of all the belligerent powers, may, at all times, be declard in that state, & the commerce of neutrals be, thereby, subjected to universal capture."[29]

Marshall questioned the impartiality of the British admiralty courts. British privateers were enriching themselves at the expense of U.S. commerce, and the courts had failed to impose any reasonable restraint. British admiralty courts rarely acquitted U.S. vessels and never awarded damages to American ship owners. The British courts "tarnish, alike, the seat of justice & the honor of their country, by converting themselves from Judges, into the mere instruments of plunder."[30]

Finally, Marshall took on the highly emotional issue of impressment, "an injury of very serious magnitude, which deeply affects the feelings & the honor of the nation."[31] Marshall charged that U.S. citizens were "dragd on board british ships of war with the evidence of citizenship in their hands, & forcd by violence there to serve, until conclusive testimonials of their birth can be obtaind."[32] Marshall had the names of fifty-two American seamen who were impressed because they could not prove U.S. citizenship.[33]

Of course, the Crown saw impressment in entirely different terms. For at least two centuries, British law gave its naval captains the right to impress any able-bodied male subject of the British Crown into the Royal Navy. The French Revolutionary Wars had created an insatiable need for more seamen. Though the British did not claim the right to impress U.S. citizens as such, they believed in "indefeasible allegiance"; that is, once an Englishman, always an Englishman. Any British subject who became a naturalized U.S. citizen would still be regarded as British for purposes of service in the Royal Navy. Conflict with the Americans arose because of the practical difficulty of determining a man's nationality at sea. Though Congress has issued U.S. citizenship certificates to U.S. sailors, the British routinely ignored such documents.[34] Press gangs kidnapped anyone they regarded as a British subject and forced them into navy service. They were not particularly fastidious about who was a British subject; any man who spoke English was fair game. Marshall asserted that the United States had the right to determine for itself whether an Englishman was a naturalized U.S. citizen. This dispute raised a fundamental question about the nature of citizenship: For Americans, an American was free from foreign allegiances once he was granted citizenship; for the British, nationality was permanent and inalienable.

Marshall believed that the British had a duty to respect the rights of neutrals. Marshall was asserting the sovereign's right to protect its citizens from injury by a foreign state. This principle, known as "diplomatic protection," was already well established under customary international law, but this was the first instance of the United States asserting this right on behalf of its own nationals, and it remains a precedent for protecting Americans and their property worldwide. But Marshall went further. He also thought that the British did not have the right to impress British subjects either. For this reason, the United States could protect even a British national on a U.S. merchant vessel from impressment.[35] This was a radical new notion. It was generally assumed in the eighteenth century that a state could do whatever it wished to its own subjects. Here was a novel instance in which Marshall asserted the right of one country to protect foreign nationals from their own sovereign. And he insisted that the British government could be held accountable under international law for the actions of its naval officers and privateers on the high seas. In so doing, Marshall anticipated the formulation of universal human rights in the twentieth century.

Marshall set forth a new legal standard to protect neutral nations and individuals on the high seas. Marshall's strong rebuke to Britain won a brief respite in the harassment of American shipping, but sporadic impressment continued. Over the next twelve years, between five and ten thousand Americans were impressed, and Britain's disregard for American sensitivities ultimately sparked the War of 1812. Impressment did not end until the British no longer needed American seamen—after Emperor Napoleon's defeat at Waterloo in 1815.[36]

Marshall had a natural talent for reading people and situations. He knew how far he could go without alienating his negotiating partners. With Britain, Marshall fought hard to resolve the twin issues of the debt and the capture of U.S. ships and seamen. With France, Marshall took the opposite tack.

AFTER TWO YEARS of the Quasi-War with France, American merchants were weary of the interruption of their commerce, and the national economy was suffering because of it. High Federalists in Congress continued to call for a declaration of war against France. Yet President Adams resisted.

But much had changed in Paris in the two years since Marshall's hasty exit. Napoleon Bonaparte had completed his conquest of most of Italy, the Holy Roman Empire, and Egypt. After Bonaparte's triumphant return to Paris in October 1799, he managed in the space of a few weeks, with the help of the wily Talleyrand, to depose the government, draft a new constitution, name himself first consul, and declare the revolution finished. From Marshall's point of view, Napoleon seemed like an unlikely figure to be cast as a popular French hero: a Corsican with a sallow complexion and no discernible political principles apart from his own naked self-interest. But as sometimes happens in times of uncertainty, people are drawn to authoritarian outsiders whose only moral compass is narcissism.

Talleyrand, disgraced after the publication of the XYZ papers, had returned to office as Bonaparte's foreign secretary. Marshall's correspondence exposing Talleyrand's venality had catapulted Marshall to national attention in the United States and landed him in the State Department. Now Talleyrand and Marshall were compelled to negotiate an end to the Quasi-War. This time Talleyrand did not ask for a bribe.

Marshall hoped that a settlement could be reached. Despite the naval war, the United States remained popular with the French public. Talleyrand found it convenient to blame the collapse of prior negotiations on the corrupt behavior of the deposed Directory rather than on his own avarice. France relied on neutral trading countries to carry French commerce. To win support from other neutral powers, Bonaparte believed he must end the Quasi-War with the Americans. He also feared that the United States might ally with Britain against France. Though the Americans could not threaten French territory themselves, they might be tempted to seize Spain's colonies in Florida and Louisiana. This concerned France as Spain was France's principal ally, and without the support of Spanish forces, the French Caribbean islands would be vulnerable to attack by Britain.[37]

When news of Washington's death reached Bonaparte, he seized the opportunity to improve relations. The French consulate in Philadelphia proclaimed ten days of mourning in honor of Washington. Washington was honored as an ally and an inspiration for the French Revolution. A bust of Washington was erected in the Tuileries, and a memorial service was held in the imposing medieval fortress known as the Temple of Mars. The French government compared the character and achievements of Washington and Bonaparte. No one mentioned that the Directory had criticized Washington for his Proclamation of Neutrality.[38]

The American peace commissioners, Oliver Ellsworth and William Davie, arrived in Paris in March 1799 to join William Vans Murray in the negotiations. Talleyrand and Bonaparte warmly welcomed them. Over the next six months, the peace commissioners met regularly with French negotiators. Marshall instructed the Americans that they could concede neutrality rights and restitution for the seizure of U.S. ships but that an alliance with France was out of the question. Talleyrand reversed his position from two years earlier and accepted the same terms that Marshall and Pinckney had originally put forth. He proposed that both parties pay restitution for the seizure of ships and cargo, and that all privateering cease. He now accepted the principle that neutral nations had a right to trade freely with belligerents. But Talleyrand insisted that the United States must reaffirm the treaties of commerce and alliance that Congress had abrogated in July 1798 after the publication of the XYZ papers. France wanted to resume its special relationship with the United States as if the Quasi-War had never happened.[39] In addition, France wanted the Americans to grant the French navy the same right to U.S. ports as Americans gave to the British navy under Jay's Treaty. Bonaparte thought it was a question of equity as much as it was a matter of countering British naval power.[40]

Negotiations proceeded almost comically, with the French offering to restore treaties the Americans no longer wanted, and the Americans conceding principles that the French no longer contested. While the Americans insisted that either party had a right to repudiate the treaty, the French stuck to the pretense that there was no war—merely a disagreement among friends. Talleyrand even denied that the United States could terminate its alliance without France's permission. A minor spat was no grounds for divorce.

In the summer of 1800, Bonaparte won a string of military victories, and the coalition against France (Austria, Russia, and Britain) collapsed. For a moment, an uneasy peace descended on Europe.[41] Bonaparte felt confident that France could vanquish Britain without American support. As a result, the negotiations on ending the Quasi-War reached an impasse.

By late summer, Marshall had no encouraging news from the peace mission to report to the cabinet. Based on the envoys' first report dated May 17 and received in late August, Marshall wrote to President Adams that "[w]e ought not to be surprizd if we see our envoys in the course of the next month without a treaty."[42] Their second report, dated August 15, arrived on Marshall's desk on November 1. In it the envoys recommended that "the negotiations must be abandoned or our instructions deviated from."[43]

In the meantime, the High Federalists in Congress demanded that Adams either declare war or quit seeking reelection. Hamilton and his Federalist allies talked openly of dumping Adams and running Charles Cotesworth Pinckney instead. Even Adams's friend Treasury Secretary Oliver Wolcott openly criticized the president and supported General Pinckney. The Federalist caucus endorsed Adams and Pinckney without specifying which one would be their presidential candidate. President Adams had few friends left. He opposed a declaration of war because he had no confidence of winning. As Adams's circle of trusted allies contracted, he came to rely almost exclusively on Marshall as secretary of state.[44]

In the face of all this gloom, Marshall stood resolute against the war hawks. He played France off against Britain just as Bonaparte had hoped to play America off against Britain. Marshall had firsthand knowledge of the French secret police and could be confident that French agents were closely following negotiations between Ambassador King and the British foreign minister. He thought that France might be more willing to end the Quasi-War if an entente between Britain and the United States was imminent. (This was the same tactic used by Benjamin Franklin during the American Revolution when he encouraged the French government to believe that a settlement between Britain and the United States was forthcoming in order to pressure France to form an alliance with the United States.) Marshall coolly advised Adams to remain patient. "I am greatly disposd to think that the present government is much inclind to correct, at least in part, the follies of the past," he assured Adams.[45] Marshall could not know how negotiations were proceeding in London or Paris, but he calculated that both France and Britain would prefer reconciliation with the United States. Marshall's steady hand avoided a costly and unnecessary war that might have depleted the nation.

In October, the peace mission reached an agreement to end the Quasi-War, reestablish commercial relations, and guarantee neutrality rights.[46] The agreement postponed the question of compensation for past losses.[47] It was signed at an elaborate ceremony in the Château de Mortefontaine, with cannons, fireworks, and a glittering ball for two hundred guests. In Washington, the Senate swiftly approved the treaty, ending America's first undeclared war. By giving the peace mission time to complete its negotiations and resisting the temptation to declare war, Marshall and Adams demonstrated that wise statecraft sometimes demands bold inaction.

Unfortunately for President Adams, news of his diplomatic success reached Washington only after his crushing defeat in the 1800 presidential election.

WHILE THE QUASI-WAR still raged, Marshall faced a delicate balancing act with Spain. In July 1800, the USS *Constitution*, known as *Old Ironsides*, captured a French privateer, the *Sandwich*, at Puerto Plata in what is now the Dominican Republic. *Old Ironsides* was commanded by one of the U.S. Navy's legendary figures, Captain Silas Talbot, who had distinguished himself in the Revolutionary War as a privateer. He was a brilliant commander if overly aggressive. There was some question as to whether Puerto Plata was Spanish territory, as Spain insisted, or whether it had been transferred to France by a recent treaty between France and Spain. The Spanish ambassador to Washington, Carlos Martínez, the marqués de Yrujo, insisted that the port had not yet been ceded to France. It still flew a Spanish flag and was protected by a Spanish garrison. Spain's ambassador accused Talbot of violating Spanish sovereignty and demanded restitution of the French vessel with her cargo.[48] Without waiting to hear from President Adams, Marshall accepted responsibility for the violation of Spanish sovereignty and ordered the federal marshal in New York, where the ship was docked, to restore the *Sandwich* to Spain.[49]

The federal marshal, however, contended that he had no right to seize Talbot's property. This posed the interesting question as to whether Talbot could possess a property interest in a stolen French vessel. Marshall obtained an order from the federal district court directing Talbot to return the vessel and then asked Talbot to return the ship *voluntarily*. The captain grudgingly obliged.[50] It would not be the last time Marshall tangled with Talbot.

Problems with Spain were further exacerbated by the activities of William Bowles, an adventurer who tried to instigate a revolt of Muscogee Nation (Creek) Indians in Florida against Spain. Bowles raised a small army in the Bahamas to attack Florida. He succeeded in capturing a Spanish fort on the Gulf Coast in West Florida and stirring up the Muscogee against Spanish authorities. This violated Pinckney's Treaty with Spain, which promised to maintain peace with the Indian nations and respect Spanish territory.[51] Spain's ambassador suspected that the British were supporting Bowles to undercut Spain. Lord Grenville, the British foreign secretary, reassured Marshall that Britain had nothing to do with Bowles. Marshall sent Colonel Benjamin Hawkins, the General Superintendent of Indians, to "restrain the Mischief makers" and suppress Bowles' army.[52]

At the same time, the United States complained that Spain had interfered with U.S. vessels. As France's ally in the war against Britain, Spain permitted Spanish privateers to capture U.S. vessels and bring them into Spanish ports to be libeled as prizes of war. Spanish privateers often used violence against unarmed merchant seamen.[53] This, too, violated Pinckney's Treaty, which required each party to respect the other's vessels.[54] The issue reached a head when two U.S. vessels, the *Nancy* and the *Franklin,* were captured by the *Bonaparte,* a Spanish privateer, at the Bay of Campeche off the east coast of Mexico. Since the *Bonaparte* was partly owned by Spanish officers, Spain could not deny responsibility.

In early September 1800, Marshall instructed the U.S. ambassador to Madrid, David Humphreys, to protest Spain's complicity in the seizure of

U.S. vessels captured by Spanish and French privateers. The letter closely mirrored the argument that Marshall penned to Ambassador King in London protesting British interference with U.S. ships. Marshall warned that "[t]he aggressions committed by the subjects of His Catholic Majesty" against U.S. vessels "are totally incompatible with real peace."[55] Marshall insisted that Spain had a legal duty not merely to prevent its own privateers but also to prevent French privateers from attacking U.S. ships.[56] Marshall accused Spain of violating international law by permitting French courts of admiralty to condemn U.S. ships in Spanish territory. The United States would retaliate against Florida and Louisiana if Spain did not end this practice.[57]

Marshall instructed Ambassador Humphreys to speak plainly but with assurances of America's "amicable temper" and insist on assurances that Spain would cease equipping privateers and condemning U.S. vessels in Spanish ports. In addition, Marshall demanded that Spain restore captured vessels or pay full compensation to the American owners.[58] Marshall's tough stance toward Spain combined with the success of the peace mission in Paris ultimately resolved both crises without resort to war.

IN ADDITION TO CONFLICTS with Britain, France, and Spain, the other threat that the United States faced during Marshall's nine months in office was the risk of war posed by the Barbary pirates. The Barbary—or Berber— Coast was named for the indigenous people of North Africa who lived in what is now known as the Maghreb. Almost the entire southern coast of the Mediterranean—from Morocco east across Algeria, Tunisia, and Libya— was governed by Berber monarchs that included the bey of Tunis and the pasha of Algiers.[59] Since at least the sixteenth century, the Barbary pirates roamed the Mediterranean at will, plundering European ships and capturing crews. The popular notion of outlaw Barbary pirates is misleading. The so-called Barbary pirates were agents sent to collect tribute for their monarchs from ships passing through the Mediterranean, which they claimed as their territory. In one sense, the Barbary pirates were overzealous customs agents sailing lightning-fast corsairs, but their aggression and brutality threatened commerce throughout southern Europe. They not only seized ships and cargo but they also often imprisoned, enslaved, ransomed, or murdered Americans and Europeans. By the 1790s, the problem was becoming a serious obstacle to the expansion of U.S. trade. Algiers alone captured at least eleven U.S. ships and more than a hundred sailors in a single year.[60]

Congress approved the creation of a navy in part to defend U.S. vessels from Barbary corsairs, but the demand for protecting U.S. ships from French and British attacks took priority. Unable to provide enough protection for all U.S. commerce worldwide, President Washington chose to take a more pragmatic approach that followed the practice of the European powers. Since the late seventeenth century, Britain, Holland, France, and Venice found it more expedient to pay tribute to the Barbary States than to fight them.

Washington agreed to pay ransom for the release of American prisoners and signed treaties with the Barbary States agreeing to pay more than one million dollars annually in today's money for protection. Payments were made in cash and military supplies and personal gifts to the ruling dynasties. Washington signed a treaty with the bey of Tripoli in 1796, which, in addition to promising to pay tribute to the bey, also guaranteed religious tolerance by the United States. President Washington reassured the bey that "the government of the United States of America is not in any sense founded on the Christian Religion, as it has in itself no character of enmity against the laws, religion or tranquility of Musselmen."[61] The founding fathers were clear that commerce, not Christianity, guided our foreign policy.

During the Adams administration, the incidence of attacks on U.S. commerce escalated, and many in Congress demanded military action against the Barbary States. Once again, Marshall opposed military action for practical reasons. He recognized that the payment of tribute saved the United States millions in military spending. Perhaps he also understood that from the perspective of the Barbary States it was no less reasonable to charge Americans for the privilege of navigating their waters than it was for the United States to impose tariffs.

Just days after Marshall arrived at the State Department, he received a communication concerning the Barbary pirates from the president's son, John Quincy Adams, who was then ambassador to Prussia. John Quincy forwarded a proposal from the Swedish foreign minister that would establish a joint naval force in the Mediterranean for the neutral states of Denmark, Sweden, and the United States. The force would police the sea to protect commerce from the Barbary corsairs. John Quincy strongly endorsed the proposal, but Marshall saw at once that it would be "a hazard, to which our infant Navy ought not perhaps be exposed."[62]

Ironically, though Marshall rose to prominence by refusing to pay a bribe to Talleyrand, he now felt compelled to honor the commitments of Washington and Adams. Marshall estimated that the tribute paid to the Barbary States cost about $288,886 annually (more than $5.5 million today). But Marshall's one concern was that the government should properly account for all funds expended on the ruling families of the Barbary States. The beys of Tunis or Algeria would frequently request payment in the form of some specific items that were often difficult to obtain or value. Marshall thought it was improper to provide personal gifts and preferred to pay cash.[63] Nevertheless, Marshall thought it was more prudent to comply with the demands of the Berber monarchs than risk another naval war. As a result, the secretary of state spent countless hours arranging the purchase of certain jewels or yards of fabric for various monarchs. It seemed an absurd drain on his time while he was managing the entire federal government, but he viewed it as the "the less evil."[64]

Jefferson later proved the wisdom of Marshall's pragmatic approach to dealing with the threat posed by the Barbary corsairs. As president,

Jefferson, who had rejected traditional Christianity himself, considered Islam uncivilized. Unlike the European powers that had agreed to pay what he regarded as blackmail to these pirates, Jefferson refused to pay tribute. Tripoli responded by cutting down a flagpole at the American consulate and declaring war. The Tripolitan War stretched from 1801 to 1805 at an enormous cost. Jefferson escalated the conflict to the point that it crippled the U.S. Navy, and in the end, he accomplished nothing. Jefferson's approach to "civilizing" the Berbers included bombarding the capital city of Tripoli. After a series of disastrous naval adventures, Jefferson finally acceded to the Berber demands for tribute and paid ransom for the return of American soldiers held captive. In the end, Jefferson's rigid adherence to "principle" cost the United States much more in lives and treasure than the payment of tribute ever had, and the result was that the United States was required to increase its payments to the Barbary States in the future.[65]

IN NINE MONTHS as secretary of state, Marshall completed the construction of Washington City in time for the arrival of the president and the Congress in November. He managed the federal government in the absence of President Adams, and he successfully navigated negotiations with France, Spain, Britain, and the Barbary States. Untold American lives and treasure were spared, and the nation was kept secure. While Republicans and Federalists dueled over their ideological absolutes, Marshall's patient pragmatism and tactical restraint carried the day.

CHAPTER SIXTEEN

THE NEW ORDER
OF THINGS

A bigail Adams could hardly contain her fury. She had no patience for the vicious lies directed at her husband. She was "disgusted with the world, and the chief of its inhabitants do not appear worth the trouble and pains they cost to save them from destruction."[1] The Republicans had showered her husband with calumnies while he was president. The Republican libelist James Callender had charged Adams with every manner of corruption and called him "twice a traitor." All this "abuse and scandal," Abigail regretted, was "enough to ruin and corrupt the minds and morals of the best people in the world."[2]

Even worse, and far more damaging, were the attacks launched by Hamilton. Adams blamed Hamilton for splintering the Federalists and thought he was the "greatest intriguant in the world—a man devoid of every moral principle."[3] In a letter written and published as a pamphlet addressed to Federalist leaders in New York, Hamilton feverishly and foolishly savaged Adams. Hamilton's letter was a desperate last-gasp effort to replace Adams with Pinckney, and it proved fatal to both the president's reelection and Hamilton's future. In it, Hamilton betrayed private communications between the president and members of the cabinet and described the "disgusting egotism, the distempered jealousy and the ungovernable indiscretion of Mr. Adams' temper."[4] The Republican press got hold of Hamilton's letter and republished it widely. Abigail could dismiss Hamilton as "the little cock sparrow general," but the damage was done.[5] The Federalist Party was now at war with itself.

President Adams rode up to the President's House on Pennsylvania Avenue on November 1, 1800. He traveled alone by carriage. Abigail made the long trek from Quincy on her own so she could stop off in New York to see their son Charles, who was estranged from his father. Charles, a troubled young man, was dying from alcoholism.[6] The President's House was still under construction, and the lawn was rutted and muddy. There was no one to welcome the president except for a few workers and some city commissioners who happened to be inspecting progress on the building on a Saturday afternoon. The workmen set up a temporary office for the president next to his bedroom on the second floor. They had not yet gotten around to hanging doors, and the rooms were sparsely furnished. Throughout the mansion, the walls were bare except for a lonely portrait of Washington soberly surveying the scene.

Marshall was called to meet with Adams as his first visitor.[7] It was a dispiriting sight: the aging president alone in his cold, unfinished mansion, estranged from his party, anxiously awaiting the outcome of the upcoming election in the shadowy gloom of an autumnal day.

Abigail arrived in Washington City unprepared for the provincial character of the capital. There was nothing but woods from Baltimore to the city, "which is only so in name." Georgetown, she sniffed, was "the very dirtiest hole I ever saw," and the surrounding countryside was "wild." She found the President's House barely habitable—cold, damp, and woefully understaffed. There were no water closets—only a privy out back. The grand East Room, still unpainted, was suitable only to hang laundry.[8] Her one consolation was knowing that she probably would not have to reside there for long.

The selection of presidential electors had already begun. The process varied widely according to state law. In some states, state legislators chose electors without voting. Voting occurred in different states on different days throughout the month, but the actual "election day," on which the electors cast their ballots, did not occur until December 3. Throughout the month, as reports of the voting in the various states drifted into the capital, the president's hopes rose and fell. The Republicans swept the House of Representatives, sixty-eight to thirty-eight, and won a narrow majority in the Senate, seventeen to fifteen. Federalists hoped that Pinckney would deliver South Carolina and that Rhode Island would follow the rest of New England.[9] But Republicans had a majority in the South Carolina legislature, and they chose electors for Jefferson. Rhode Island remained loyal to the Federalists, as did all of New England. In New Jersey, Maryland, and North Carolina, electors were divided between Federalists and Republicans. The real surprise was New York City, where Federalists had assumed the electors would support Adams but instead narrowly voted for Jefferson. Adams lost New York State by a painfully thin margin of 250 votes, and with it, the election. The Republican who extolled the virtues of the yeoman farmer and decried the vices of cities and finance snared the presidency by a whisker in the urban capital of bankers and merchants.[10]

President Adams was bitterly disappointed. Fairly or not, Adams blamed Hamilton for his defeat in New York. But he consoled himself that Hamilton had lost more than he had: Hamilton had destroyed his political career and elected the two men he most feared, Thomas Jefferson and Aaron Burr. "Mr. Hamilton has carried his eggs to a fine market," Adams quipped.[11]

Abigail, however, was relieved. "For myself and my family," Abigail wrote, "I have few regrets." She knew she would be "happier at Quincy" than struggling to survive in an uncultured and inhospitable southern swamp. In any case, the First Family had no time to grieve over the election returns. In a tragic coincidence, the president received news on the day that the electors cast their ballots that his son Charles was dead from alcoholism.[12]

On November 7, Marshall brought the president good news: France had agreed to a peace treaty ending the Quasi-War. News of the treaty came too late to affect the outcome of the election, however. The election of 1800 was the first American election in which foreign policy played a major role. The long-running battle over Franco-American relations had bitterly fractured the Federalist Party, and Adams's policies were prematurely judged as failures. If the treaty had arrived a month sooner, Adams might have won in a landslide. Or if Adams had refused to negotiate with France and declared war as the war hawks demanded, he might have held his party together— but at what cost to the nation? Throughout their time working together, Marshall and Adams insisted on negotiating first. Their success represented the triumph of patience and reason over belligerence. But voters rarely reward patience or reason.

ON DECEMBER 28, 1800, Vice President Jefferson, as president of the Senate, officially informed Secretary of State Marshall of the returns from the Electoral College.[13] Marshall, of course, already knew the tally: President Adams had received sixty-five votes, his nominee for vice president, Charles Cotesworth Pinckney, had received sixty-four, and Jefferson and his running mate, Aaron Burr, had each received seventy-three votes. The Federalists had lost the presidency. But who had won it? Burr, who had run for the office of vice president, refused to say that he would not accept the office of president if it was offered to him.

Under the Constitution, a tie in the electoral vote between Burr and Jefferson meant that the House of Representatives would have to decide which of the Republican candidates would be president. Each of the sixteen states' congressional delegations had one vote, which would be cast according to the votes of the members of each delegation. The candidate with a majority—at least nine out of sixteen votes—would be elected president, and the candidate having the second greatest number of votes would be elected vice president. The state congressional delegations were closely divided between Federalists and Republicans, and no one could be sure whether the Federalists would vote for Jefferson, Burr, or someone else.

Republicans worried that the uncertainty would create an opportunity for the Federalists to undo the election results. Jefferson warned Madison that the Federalists were determined to prevent his election and would choose either New York Governor John Jay or Secretary of State Marshall as president.[14] Rumors that the Federalists would contrive to elect Marshall interim president circulated throughout the South.[15] One can only imagine how Jefferson felt contemplating the possibility of his upstart cousin usurping his presidency.

If the Federalists were planning to select Marshall, he had no knowledge of it. Nevertheless, in the aftermath of Adams's defeat, Marshall emerged as the one man who could hold together the warring factions of the Federalist Party.

Marshall was disappointed with the election outcome, but he avoided intervening in the House vote. He was already tired of Washington and looked forward to returning to his law practice on the day the new president was inaugurated.[16] After nine intense months running the government, he missed his family, who had remained in Richmond. Polly wrote him only sporadically, and he fretted over her fragile emotional health. When his son Tom wrote to him without mentioning his mother, Marshall wrote to Polly, "This was a cruel disappointment to me because I cannot flatter myself with respect to you that silence is an evidence of good health."[17]

Federalists in Congress feared Jefferson. Many conspired to throw the election in the hope that they could strike a deal with the unctuous Burr. But Hamilton wrote to Marshall, who had greater influence with moderate Federalists, asking for his help to stop Burr from becoming president.

Hamilton, who had fought Jefferson vigorously in the cabinet and done everything in his power to save the country from what he called "the fangs of Jefferson," regarded Burr, for good reason, as his private bête noir.[18] He thought on balance the country would be better served by Jefferson.

Marshall knew little about Burr, but Marshall had "almost insuperable objections" to Jefferson. For Marshall's whole life, from the poverty of his boyhood to his service in the Continental Army to his political fights in Virginia, he had been locked in a bitter rivalry with the cousin who was born with all the advantages that Marshall's family had been denied. He had witnessed Jefferson at his worst: leaving his state undefended as its governor while fleeing the British invasion of Richmond; defending the slave trade in Virginia while hypocritically declaring "all men equal"; denying support for the Constitution during the ratification debates; undercutting President Washington by opposing Jay's Treaty and the Proclamation of Neutrality as secretary of state; supporting the French revolutionaries and aligning himself with Citizen Genet against his own government; and repeatedly betraying President Adams as vice president. Jefferson was a radical ideologue, and Marshall had witnessed how French ideologues had undermined the rule of law. Jefferson lacked genuine empathy and embodied precisely the kind of elitism that he attacked in theory. He could never be trusted to act in the interests of the nation. "His foreign prejudices seem to me totally to unfit him for the chief magistracy of a nation which cannot indulge those prejudices without sustaining deep & permanent injury," Marshall wrote to Hamilton. Jefferson would weaken the presidency, "diminish his responsibility, sap the fundamental principles of the government," and put party and personal power ahead of national well-being. "The Morals of the Author of the letter to Mazzei cannot be pure," Marshall warned. This was a reference to Jefferson's inflammatory letter to Philip Mazzei, which was published in an Italian newspaper in 1796, that attacked President Washington and the Federalists as a pro-British "Anglican monarchical, & aristocratical party" whose secret agenda was to impose monarchy on the United States. Marshall respected Hamilton's opinion that Burr was a dangerous man, but "I cannot bring myself to aid Mr. Jefferson." Given all this, Marshall preferred to remain neutral.[19]

The House did not begin the process of voting until February 11. In the meantime, Jefferson moved into Conrad and McMunn's boardinghouse on the corner of New Jersey Avenue and C Street. His daily routine began at sunrise. He breakfasted with his fellow boarders, all members of Congress, and then strolled the short distance to the Capitol to preside over the Senate. He pretended to remain aloof from the contest, depending on surrogates to move votes his way. Around him, the capital city buzzed with rumors about whether the Federalists in the House would line up to support Burr and deny Jefferson the presidency or whether the Federalists intended to cancel the election altogether and transfer power to either Marshall or Jay.[20]

Monroe alerted Jefferson that the Virginia General Assembly was considering what actions to take to prevent the Federalists from canceling the election results. Monroe feared that "[i]f the union cod. be broken, that wod. do it." He continued that if the Federalists denied the House a chance to vote for the president, it would "be sure to expose the usurpers to exemplary punishment." In a starkly candid moment, Monroe advised Jefferson that the "[e]astern people have no thoughts of breaking the union, & giving up the hold they have on the valuable productions of the south." Rather, "they only mean to bully us, thereby preserve their ascendancy, and improve their profits." Monroe concluded that the Republicans must remain firm and "shew themselves equal to the crisis."[21] There could be no compromise, no backing down. The future of the Republic was on the line.

MARSHALL AND ADAMS began the transition even before the House chose the new president. Adams had little more than a month to name a successor for Chief Justice Ellsworth, who had resigned for health reasons.

In late December, Adams nominated New York Governor John Jay to serve again as chief justice. He did not wait to ask Jay before sending his name to the lame-duck Senate. Jay had been the first chief justice appointed by Washington, and he had resigned to run for governor. Marshall wrote to Jay informing him of the nomination.[22] Jay had quit the Supreme Court because he was bored and frustrated by the Court's impotence. It made little sense for him to accept the nomination now with a hostile Republican executive and Congress. Besides, Jay had already decided to retire from politics. He wrote back to Marshall declining the appointment on the grounds that the federal judiciary lacked the resources and stature it deserved and that "the efforts repeatedly made to place the judiciary department on a proper footing have proved fruitless." If he accepted the position of chief justice, "it would give some countenance to the neglect and indifference with which the opinions and remonstrances of the judges on this important subject have been treated." But just in case Marshall would try to convince him otherwise, he added that his age and health made it impossible for him to accept the office.[23]

On January 19, 1801, Marshall met with Adams at the President's House to discuss a number of matters, including the Supreme Court nomination. "Who shall I nominate now?" the president asked. Marshall suggested Associate Justice William Paterson. Adams did not think it wise to appoint a sitting justice as chief because it would likely create jealousy among the other sitting justices if one of their colleagues was elevated. After a moment's hesitation, the president responded, "I believe I must nominate you."

Marshall had never heard his name mentioned for that post, and he later claimed that he had never considered it. Too stunned to reply, Marshall simply bowed his head in silent acquiescence. The next day, the president nominated Marshall as the fourth chief justice of the United States.[24]

It is more surprising that Marshall accepted this appointment than it is that Adams offered it. The position of chief justice at that time was not the august position we now assume it to be. The Supreme Court in 1800 was insignificant, and few men worthy enough to be nominated were interested in serving. After John Jay quit to become the governor of New York, President Washington asked Hamilton, who declined, preferring to return to his lucrative New York City law practice. Then Washington named John Rutledge as a recess appointment pending the Senate's confirmation. Rutledge had previously served on the Supreme Court as an associate justice and had quit to become chief justice of the Supreme Court of South Carolina, which was regarded as a promotion. The Senate, however, rejected Rutledge because he was an outspoken critic of Jay's Treaty and, some alleged, insane, which may or may not have been true. (Rumors of Rutledge's mental condition were later corroborated when he attempted suicide by diving into Charleston Harbor.) Next, Washington offered the job to Patrick Henry, the lion of Virginia, who demurred. Then he appointed Associate Justice William Cushing, who also declined. In frustration, Washington turned to Oliver Ellsworth, a Connecticut senator. Ellsworth lasted only four years, during which time he spent almost twelve months away on the peace mission to Paris. Only Associate Justices Paterson and Cushing had remained on the Court longer than five years.

The reasons no one was interested in this job were clear. First, the Supreme Court had a small and unimportant docket of cases. In its first decade, the Court had issued only sixty-three decisions, and only a handful of those had any significance. The Supreme Court's jurisdiction was limited to a few classes of cases that mostly concerned admiralty law. There were occasional questions of federal law, but there were so few federal laws that interesting questions rarely arose. Most legal disputes were governed by state statutes and decided almost exclusively by state courts. Moreover, the Supreme Court had little authority, and it had never struck down a federal or state law. The Supreme Court did not even have its own courthouse.

Worst of all, since there were no lower courts of appeal, the job required the justices to spend most of their term "riding circuit." This meant that the justices were expected to ride around the country on horseback and listen to arguments by poorly trained lawyers. They had to eat and stay in rough taverns and often had to share beds with strangers when there was no other room available. It was not a glamorous life. Compared to Marshall's tenure as secretary of state, the Supreme Court was undeniably a step down. For a man of Marshall's demonstrated talents and ambition, there were higher offices to seek.

Marshall's political career in Virginia was finished. By now, Virginia was solidly Republican. He could return to practicing law, but many of his clients had moved on, and his law practice seldom earned as much as the chief justice's salary.[25] Money, however, was not the deciding consideration. Something else led Marshall to accept this challenge.

Marshall saw himself as defending the Constitution against the onslaught of the Jeffersonians. Jefferson's populism profoundly troubled Marshall. He believed that the Court's function was to uphold the foundational principles that the national government depended on against the political whims of the moment.

Destiny had preordained that Marshall would struggle with Jefferson for the soul of the Union. He accepted President Adams's nomination out of a sense of duty. Marshall was committed to stand vigil over the principle of federalism, keep the country on the path of moderation, and resist ideology with pragmatism.

Predictably, there were some Republican critics of Marshall's nomination, but most Republicans and certainly all Federalists thought Marshall's moderation and intellect made him an obvious candidate. The fact that he was also a Virginian did not hurt. Even Republicans did not question the authority of a lame-duck president to name a Supreme Court justice in his last month in office.

On January 27, 1801, the Senate confirmed Marshall's nomination, and his commission was issued on January 31 with the Great Seal of the United States affixed by Treasury Secretary Samuel Dexter, who was acting in lieu of Secretary of State Marshall.[26] The very day that Marshall's nomination was approved, Jefferson was presiding over the Senate. No doubt he flinched slightly when he announced the vote. Though Jefferson's own election was still in doubt, Marshall's confirmation would deny Jefferson the opportunity to appoint a member of his own party as chief justice. Now his contentious cousin had a lifetime appointment to spar with him.

President Adams decided that for his remaining month in office it made no sense to appoint an acting secretary of state, so he asked Marshall to hold both positions simultaneously. Most legal scholars today would agree that for one man to simultaneously serve in the executive and judicial branches violates the separation of powers. But given the size of the American government and the improbability that anything Marshall did as secretary of state could end up before the Supreme Court, it seemed prudent enough. History would laugh at that presumption.

In the closing days of the Adams administration, Federalists manned the barricades against the revolution that they feared Jefferson would bring. President Adams had long before proposed legislation to expand the judiciary. Now faced with the prospect of a Republican takeover, Federalists swiftly approved the Judiciary Act of 1801, better known as the Circuit Court Act, which established six new circuit courts in place of the four existing ones and reorganized the federal judiciary.[27] The act created sixteen new circuit judges to hear cases on appeal and eliminated the need for Supreme Court justices to ride circuit. Second, the act reduced the size of the Supreme Court from six to five justices whenever the next vacancy should occur. While nominally this could be justified by the fact that the justices no longer had to ride circuit, it was a transparent effort by Federalists to deny Republicans the opportunity to appoint one of their own to the Court. Third, it reorganized the federal district judges into ten districts and expanded their jurisdiction to hear cases. In particular, the act opened up the federal courts to hear a broader range of claims by individual property owners and creditors, which gave Federalists some assurance that their property rights would be protected by the federal judiciary.

In addition to the Circuit Court Act, Congress adopted an act concerning the government of the District of Columbia on February 27.[28] The District of Columbia Organic Act provided for the establishment of a D.C. circuit court with three judges, and it empowered the president, with the Senate's advice and consent, to appoint as many justices of the peace for the district as he thought necessary. The justices of the peace would serve for five years without salary, but they could collect court fees. Three days later, President Adams nominated forty-two justices of the peace. All the nominees were hastily confirmed by a breathless Senate the following day. There was no justification for the sudden urgency apart from the fear that Federalists were about to lose power. It was a naked exercise in political patronage for friends of the Federalist Party.

As Republicans hollered about the so-called midnight judges being rammed through the Senate by Federalists in the waning hours of the Adams administration, Marshall was busy both recruiting candidates for the new judgeships and issuing and delivering their commissions. As the crush of work in the closing days proved too much for Marshall, he ran out of time to deliver the commissions to the justices of the peace. Marshall's negligence in delivering the commissions would prove to be the triggering event of the single most famous decision ever issued by the Supreme Court—*Marbury v. Madison*.

As CONGRESS MOVED toward voting on the presidency in February, the whole country simmered with rumors that the Federalists would cancel the election and find some means to hold on to power. Monroe warned Jefferson that Marshall had issued an opinion that Congress could appoint someone other than Jefferson or Burr as president, and Monroe claimed that "intrigues are carrying on to place us in that situation."[29] In fact, there was no evidence Marshall thought that, but the rumors proliferated.

From Massachusetts, Elbridge Gerry, still licking his wounds after the

XYZ Affair, sought to ingratiate himself to Jefferson. Though Gerry was a personal friend of President Adams, he expressed his outrage at "the insidious plan" of Federalists to elect Burr. Gerry frankly acknowledged that the "measure does not proceed from any respect or attachment to him, whom they abhor as well as yourself . . . but from a desire to promote that division among the people, which they have excited & nourished as the germ of a civil war."[30]

Anxious about the outcome of the backroom deals that were being struck, Jefferson wrote to his would-be vice president, Aaron Burr. "It was to be expected that the enemy would endeavor to sow tares between us," Jefferson began, "that they might divide us and our friends. Every consideration satisfies me that you will be on your guard against this, as I assure you I am strongly."[31] In truth, Jefferson was deeply embittered that Burr had refused to withdraw his name from consideration for the presidency. Meanwhile, Jefferson, no less than Burr, was prepared to strike almost any deal to assure his election. Jefferson wrote to his daughter that he was "worn down here with pursuits in which I take no delight, surrounded by enemies & spies & perverting every word which falls from my lips or flows from my pen, and inventing where facts fail them."[32]

ON FEBRUARY 11, 1801, the two houses of Congress met in a joint session as Vice President Jefferson formally read and recorded each of the ballots of the Electoral College. As soon as the ballots were recorded, the senators were excused from the chamber and the House locked its doors to begin voting on which of the top two candidates—Jefferson or Burr—should be president. The outcome was not a foregone conclusion. The first balloting by the House of Representatives had eight states voting for Jefferson and six for Burr, with two states equally divided and therefore abstaining. The voting continued in the House for six days while Jefferson sat anxiously in the other chamber, pretending to preside over a Senate that pretended to conduct business. Crowds gathered outside Congress to express support for each of the candidates. The press also fired volleys for and against Burr and Jefferson. There were threats of armed force from various extreme factions and rumors of an impending civil war. No one was sure what might happen if the deadlock was not decided by Inauguration Day, March 4.

On the thirty-sixth ballot cast on the sixth day, the single representative from Delaware, James A. Bayard, changed his vote from Burr to Jefferson, giving Jefferson a bare majority of nine states. Though Bayard claimed that he had switched his vote when Jefferson agreed to meet certain Federalist demands, Jefferson later denied that.[33] Burr was elected vice president. The drawn-out drama that Burr had staged by refusing to concede to Jefferson as the leader of his party now assured that the coming four years would be stormy between them. Jefferson had little reason to hope that Burr would be any less treacherous a vice president than Jefferson had been.

ON MARCH 4, 1801, Marshall wrote to General Pinckney. "To day the new political year commences—The new order of things begins." Marshall expressed the hope that the nation would survive and prosper under the Republicans, but he feared that they "are divided into speculative theorists & absolute terrorists." If Jefferson chose to align himself with the terrorists, "much calamity is in store for our country," and if he opposed them, "they will soon become his enemies & calumniators." In sum, Marshall's assessment was bleak.[34]

Jefferson woke early that morning in his rooming house to rework his inaugural address. He had had less than two weeks to draft it since the House vote. He slowly rehearsed his lines: "Every difference of opinion is not a difference of principle. We have called by different names brethren of the same principle. We are all Republicans, we are all Federalists." He took a breath. He wished to set a tone of reconciliation after a divisive election. Having fathered the first political party and having led the bitter debates over America's relations with France, Jefferson now wanted to put all that controversy behind him. "If there be any among us who would wish to dissolve this Union or to change its republican form, let them stand undisturbed as monuments of the safety with which error of opinion may be tolerated where reason is left free to combat it."[35] As the author of the Kentucky and Virginia Resolutions, Jefferson had claimed that the Constitution was a mere pact among the states and that the states were free to nullify federal law or decisions of the Supreme Court. He could hardly blame others if they challenged the Union.

Jefferson left his rooming house just before noon, accompanied by a contingent of state militia. Presidents Washington and Adams had ridden in fine carriages to their inaugurations, but Jefferson insisted on walking in his plain dark suit the quarter mile to the Capitol. He expected to be greeted at the Capitol by the outgoing president, but John Adams was already on his way home to Massachusetts. He had no wish to remain where he was not welcome. The ornate Senate chamber was full of distinguished visitors when Jefferson rose to give his inaugural address in his soft girlish voice. He pledged that "though the will of the majority is in all cases to prevail, that will, to be rightful, must be reasonable." He sought to reassure the Federalists that "the minority possess their equal rights, which equal laws must protect, and to violate would be oppression."[36]

After Jefferson finished speaking, he stood with one hand on a Masonic Bible and the other hand raised to take the oath of office. Standing opposite him to administer the oath of office was a familiar face: John Marshall, the chief justice of the United States and the man who administers the presidential oath of office. History had predetermined their fateful collision. Two cousins who had stood on opposite sides of every public issue for a generation now led two branches of the federal government. Jefferson coldly stared past Marshall, and Marshall turned his back to the president in what many thought was a slight.

Marshall commented magnanimously that he thought Jefferson's address was "well judgd & conciliatory . . . giving the lie to the violent party decla-mation which has elected him." Then Marshall added that there was still reason to worry, for it was still "strongly characteristic of the general cast of his political theory."[37] Though they always displayed civility in public, there was little doubt that each man was determined to stop the other at any price.

CHAPTER SEVENTEEN

SHOWDOWN

W ashington in 1801 was what Congressman and Treasury Secretary Albert Gallatin called a "hateful place," devoid of any real society or culture. There were scarcely three thousand inhabitants, including at least six hundred slaves. Clustered around the Capitol were six boardinghouses packed with members of Congress, a grocer, a tailor, a dry goods store, a shoemaker, and a laundry. The rest of the city still consisted largely of swampland, forest, and brush. Miles of unpaved and unmarked roads separated houses so that an invitation to dine often entailed an expedition of several hours with an uncertain outcome. Since most members of Congress left their families at home in their districts, there was a notable shortage of women. In this social desert, men resorted to whomever was available for companionship and conjugation. As often happens, government provided an appealing market for prostitution.[1]

Jefferson settled into the still-unfinished President's House, and much as he had done as governor of Virginia, he immediately set out designing new architectural features. He was accustomed to living in a work in progress: After all, his beloved Monticello took him fifteen years to complete. He soon began sketching out changes to the President's House. Jefferson transformed the south lawn, which at the time was nothing more than a muddy field sloping toward a creek, into an elaborate flower garden with a serpentine design like he had seen at the Louvre in Paris. He erected a sturdy post-and-rail fence around the property, and around the southern border he ordered an eight-foot ha-ha—a ditch usually dug in front of a wall—to keep wayward animals off the grounds.[2] The ha-ha was another idea Jefferson borrowed from French aristocrats who used it to keep angry peasants from storming their estates.

The Supreme Court under Chief Justice Marshall convened for the first time on February 2, 1801, in a vacant committee room of the Capitol. The great gray eminence, Justice William Cushing, sat in solitary splendor hunched and bewigged in a majestic black-and-crimson robe before an empty chamber. The other justices, delayed by bad weather, poor roads, or casual neglect, failed to appear. Court adjourned and resumed two days later when Justices Samuel Chase, Bushrod Washington, and Marshall joined him. Justices Alfred Moore and William Paterson still had not arrived. Since there was nothing of consequence on the court's docket, Moore and Paterson did not bother to appear until the Court's summer session.[3]

The Supreme Court met in a dark, nondescript ground-floor room in the north wing of the unfinished Capitol, down the hall from the grand Senate chamber with its elegant scalloped ceiling. The planners for the capital city had neglected to build a federal courthouse, so only a few days prior, Congress had grudgingly agreed to allow the Supreme Court to share committee room number two with the federal district court and the D.C. Court of Appeals. The room was the size of a small classroom and unadorned except for the crimson robes edged in ermine that hung on pegs in one corner. There were two windows facing west that overlooked a swamp, a line of tulip poplars, and a muddy creek some wit had named the Tiber after the river in ancient Rome. There was no formal bar or bench. The justices sat behind a table facing the lawyers and a few rows of chairs for the few spectators. The public had little interest in the Court's languid calendar with an average of six cases a year. This prosaic scene and the physical location of the Court underscored the lowly status of the nation's highest court.

Chief Justice Marshall sat wedged between his more rotund colleagues. They were all men of far greater experience and learning than Marshall. On the far end was the aged Justice William Cushing. He was the first associate justice appointed by Washington and probably the last American judge to still wear a horsehair wig. Cushing was a crusty Boston Yankee who rarely spoke and authored few opinions in his long tenure on the court. While he was still a judge in Massachusetts, Cushing once stared down an angry mob during Shays's Rebellion armed with nothing but his considerable gravitas. He was the only justice to bring his wife with him to Washington and everywhere he rode on circuit. His shoe buckles and his three-cornered hat branded him as old-fashioned, and he wore that brand with dignity.[4]

Then there was an empty seat for Justice William Paterson of New Jersey, a boisterous Irishman with a lively intellect and shrewd political instincts. As one of the Framers of the Constitution, he had proposed the New Jersey Plan that would have given each state one vote in Congress. Paterson's instinct for political compromise helped Marshall forge a consensus on the Court.

Justice Samuel Chase of Maryland resembled a bear with his bulky mass and fierce demeanor. His rough complexion earned him the nickname Old Baconface Chase. He was the most outspoken Federalist in the judiciary. Though some people found him prickly and obnoxious, he was beloved and admired by his colleagues on the Court. Before Marshall arrived, Chase was the Court's intellectual leader. Chase's views and fiery personality led to a controversy that would ultimately threaten the Court's independence and test Marshall's political instincts.

Next came Justice Bushrod Washington, who was among Marshall's closest compatriots—they had been friends since Marshall attended classes at William & Mary. During his long service on the Supreme Court, Washington was Marshall's most reliable ally.

Finally, there was the puckish Justice Alfred Moore from North Carolina, who, like Marshall, had just been appointed. At slightly more than four feet tall, Justice Moore peered from behind the table like a hand puppet. Despite Moore's sharp wit and youthful energy, he was frail and had to resign from the Court after only three years due to ill health. Cushing was nearing seventy, and Paterson and Chase were almost sixty. Moore and Marshall were both forty-five, and Washington was a boyish thirty-eight.

Powerful forces outside the court were massing to challenge the judiciary. Both political branches were now dominated by Republicans stewing over the appointment of Adams's "midnight judges." The range of ages, backgrounds, and personalities on the Supreme Court suggested that they had little in common, and their philosophical differences made them an easy target for the Jeffersonians. To withstand the political attacks of Republicans, Marshall knew that he needed to blend these disparate voices into one voice that spoke with authority.

Unlike the other justices, who dressed in the elegant gowns favored by the British High Court judges, Marshall wore a plain black robe that hung loosely on his tall, narrow frame. Marshall's robe was a symbolic gesture. He toned down the judiciary's pomp to conform to the classical simplicity favored by Republicans.

But it wasn't merely for show. Marshall's manner and dress were always plain and simple. Even when his innate intelligence and personality thrust him into the public eye, he never forgot who he was. Unlike many of his colleagues, Marshall's Federalism did not stem from a sense of entitlement, a desire to mimic the affectations of the aristocracy, or a fear of the lower orders of society. His manner was entirely ordinary. He was not a philosopher like Jefferson. Marshall's Federalism sprung not from theory but from his practical experience as a frontiersman, a soldier, and an attorney. Marshall believed in the practical necessity for collective action against the dangers facing his community at home and abroad. He was in all things a pragmatist.

The contrast with the Republican Jefferson was striking. Jefferson lived life on a grand scale. He extravagantly squandered his family's fortune to perfect his classical home at Monticello. (In Jefferson's last years, he had to be rescued from insolvency by a public fund-raising effort.) He reigned over hundreds of slaves with a sense of privilege that most English lords would have envied. He much preferred scholarly pursuits and practicing his violin to indulging in the sweaty give-and-take of politics. Jefferson may have loved humankind, but he was not especially fond of most people, and he had few close friends. Though Marshall belonged to the party of elites, he practiced republicanism in his everyday life. By contrast, Jefferson preached democracy but lived more like the European aristocrats he despised.

Since Jefferson had vacated his room at Conrad and McMunn's boarding-house, there would be space there for the justices. Marshall arranged for the justices to live together as boarders for a charge of fifteen dollars per week, which covered candles, firewood, and wine.[5] Conrad and McMunn's was already filled with members of Congress, some sleeping two or three in a single room and sharing beds; in Washington, economy made strange bedfellows. Since there was no life in Washington for wives or children, the justices lived like bachelors in an elite—albeit ascetic—fraternity. They ate, drank, and played cards together, reading briefs and discussing cases late into the night. In the same way that Marshall corralled his younger siblings out on the frontier and took charge of his ragtag regiment during the Revolution, Marshall, despite being one of the youngest justices, became a father figure for all of them. He served them his prized Madeira, but "only" when it rained—somewhere. When it came time for a drink in their room, he would ask one of the other justices to look out of the window to check the weather. If the justice reported back that the sky was clear, Marshall would respond, "All the better, for our jurisdiction extends over so large a territory that the doctrine of chances makes it certain that it must be raining somewhere."[6]

Marshall also took an interest in the other justices' personal lives, and he assumed the role of matchmaker for his widowed colleagues.[7] For the next three decades, while Marshall presided over the Court, the justices lived together as a family, always sharing the same hotel. They built a close web of relationships that yielded an astonishing degree of consensus.

Marshall served on the Court for thirty-four years—longer than any other chief justice. By contrast, from 1981 to 2015, there were three chief justices. And his influence over the court was enormous. Prior to Marshall's tenure, there was no such thing as a majority decision. Each justice issued his own individual opinion *seriatim*, as was the tradition in English courts. Marshall thought that the Court's authority would be enlarged if he could forge a single decision on behalf of the entire Court. During his thirty-four years as chief justice, Marshall personally wrote 547 opinions. Of these, 511 were unanimous. In his first two years on the court, there were forty-two unanimous decisions, and Marshall authored every one of them. In his first decade on the court, there were 227 published opinions, and all but 13 were unanimous. Marshall wrote at least 152 opinions in that time period and probably many more that were unsigned. This is a staggering output compared to any modern justice, who typically writes fewer than ten majority opinions annually in a vastly more crowded docket. Even more remarkable, Marshall shepherded the court toward unanimity in nearly every decision rendered. In his long tenure on the Court, there were 1,129 decisions, and all but 87 were unanimous. By contrast, fewer than half of the Court's decisions from 1995 to 2015 were unanimous. The issues of Marshall's time were no less contentious than our own. What made it possible to reach consensus was Marshall's extraordinary personality and pragmatism.

In 1879, looking back on Jefferson's presidency, Henry Adams observed that Republicans were blinded by their rigid idealism. Jeffersonians inhabited a world of absolute good and evil. The complexity of human motives and relations did not register with them. In reaction against the violence and corruption of the Old World, they clung to an impossible ideal of human society free from all the evils of human nature. What divided Republicans and Federalists often came down to a question of the size and scope of government. Jefferson, who lived much of his adult life in debt, wanted to extinguish the public debt and shrink the already modest federal government. Federalists, by contrast, believed in the importance of a strong military and central government to safeguard the nation's security from foreign adversaries. Jeffersonians loathed standing armies and saw no reason to arm the country in defense of its liberty.

As Henry Adams aptly put it, "The interests of the United States were too serious to put to the hazard of war; government must be ruled by principles; to which the Federalists answered that government must be ruled by circumstances."[8] George Cabot, a Massachusetts senator, lamented, "We are doomed to suffer all the evils of excessive democracy through the United States . . . Maratists and Robespierrians everywhere raise their heads . . . There will be neither justice nor stability in any system, if some material parts of it are not independent of popular control."[9] Another Federalist wrote that Jeffersonians "love liberty . . . and, like other lovers, they try their utmost to debauch . . . their mistress."[10]

With Adams and Hamilton gone from Washington, Marshall was the de facto leader of the Federalist Party, but he was never comfortable with partisanship. His friendships, like that with Gallatin, bridged the political divide. He later regretted "those distinct and visible parties, which, in their long and dubious competition for power, have since shaken the United States to their centre." In his view, political parties bred a "tendency to abolish all distinction between virtue and vice; and to prostrate those barriers which the wise and good have erected for the protection of morals."[11] Marshall had no patience for ideology. In his jurisprudence, abstract concepts never eclipsed the facts on the ground. He was firmly committed to a strong national defense and a vibrant national economy, and he recognized that leading the Court effectively in a Republican era would require both flexibility and compromise. He also needed to forge a strong cohesive judiciary to strengthen the court's legitimacy and its public profile. Marshall's natural talent for compromise and his genius for invention would be tested.

THE FIRST TEST for Marshall's court came in a case that arose out of the Quasi-War with France. Chapeau Rouge was a trading company owned by a Hamburg businessman, Hans Seeman. In April 1799, the company's merchant ship *Amelia* sailed from Calcutta to Hamburg loaded with a valuable cargo of cotton, sugar, and textiles. On September 6, the ship was stopped in the Atlantic by the *Diligente*, a French corsair. Although Hamburg was a neutral city-state, the ship was carrying goods from a British port, and under French law, any goods originating from British territory were subject to capture even if they were owned by a neutral party. The Hamburg crew was forced onto the *Diligente*, and a French crew took the *Amelia* as a prize and raised the French flag. The French intended to sail the *Amelia* to the French territory of Saint-Domingue to be condemned there by a French court as a prize of war.[12]

On September 15, Captain Silas Talbot on board the USS *Constitution* spotted the *Amelia* sailing nearby. It was clear that the ship was an armed vessel—with eight-mounted iron cannons and eight wooden guns—flying a French flag. According to the secretary of the navy's explicit orders, all armed French vessels were subject to capture. After a quick pursuit, Talbot captured the *Amelia* and brought the ship to New York to be condemned as a prize. At some point Talbot learned that the original owner was from Hamburg, a neutral city. Under federal statutes, a ship owned by a neutral party should be returned to the original owner. Talbot insisted that he was still entitled to receive half the value of the recaptured vessel and its cargo for the service he had performed in rescuing the vessel from the French. Seeman contested the proceedings. He argued that neither France nor the

United States had the right under international law to seize a neutral vessel and that therefore no valuable service had been performed and Talbot was not entitled to compensation.

Captain Talbot was a heroic figure in the U.S. Navy. At age twelve, he left home in Dighton, Massachusetts, to be a cabin boy, and from that day forward, he grew up at sea. During the American Revolution, he served in both the Continental Army and Navy, capturing more British ships than any other U.S. captain and earning a fortune in prizes. His swashbuckling exploits were celebrated in a popular song of the time:

> *So heave away for Talbot, for Talbot, for Talbot,*
> *So heave away for Talbot, an' let th' Capting steer,*
> *For he's the boy to smack them, to crack them, to whack them,*
> *For he's th' boy to ship with, if you want to privateer.*[13]

In 1793, Talbot was elected to Congress from New York. A few months later, President Washington plucked him out of Congress and appointed him as one of the first captains in the newly formed U.S. Navy. Talbot oversaw the construction of the USS *Constitution* and served as its captain through the Quasi-War.

Many disputes over prizes grew out of the Quasi-War, but the value of this prize, both the ship and its cargo, was estimated at $180,000 (around $3.5 million today).[14] Given the amount at stake and the fame of Captain Talbot, the case received wide attention. Republicans hoped that a victory for Seeman would call into question the validity of the Quasi-War. Federalists, supporting the war, took the opposite view. The case attracted two of the most prominent attorneys of the day: Alexander Hamilton on behalf of Captain Talbot, and Aaron Burr on behalf of Seeman. The district court ruled for Captain Talbot based on the clear language of the federal statutes, and the case was appealed to the circuit court of appeals. Presiding over the circuit court of appeals, Justice Bushrod Washington held in favor of

Seeman. Justice Washington ruled that under the laws of war neither France nor the United States had the right to interfere with a neutral ship. Captain Talbot appealed to the Supreme Court.

Before the Supreme Court, Talbot's new lawyers, Federalist Congressman James Bayard and famed Philadelphia lawyer Jared Ingersoll, argued that under federal law, the *Amelia*, as an armed merchant ship flying a French flag, was clearly liable to capture. In the alternative, they argued that even if the ship had to be returned to Seeman, Captain Talbot was entitled under federal statutes to salvage in the amount of half the value of the ship and its contents for rescuing the ship from the French.

Seeman's attorneys now included Alexander Dallas, a prominent Republican who served both as the first Supreme Court reporter and would later serve as treasury secretary and acting secretary of war in James Madison's cabinet. Dallas responded that since neutral states have a right to trade freely, the initial seizure by France was illegal and the ship could not have been legally condemned in any event by a French court. As a consquence, Talbot had not earned salvage because the USS *Constitution* did not, in fact, rescue the ship or provide any service to the owner; if the vessel had been adjudicated in a French tribunal, it would have gone free in any case.[15]

The Supreme Court heard four days of oral argument in stifling July humidity before a courtroom packed with onlookers tormented by mosquitos. The justices quietly took notes as the attorneys spoke. Justices at the time rarely interrupted the argument. After a week of deliberation, the court issued its opinion.

In his first substantive opinion as chief justice, Marshall delivered for the first time in the Court's history a single opinion for a unanimous court. By agreeing to issue a unified opinion, the justices both clarified the law and conveyed greater weight to their decision. By forging consensus, Marshall had invented a new and more effective form for issuing decisions.

Marshall's opinion in *Talbot v. Seeman* set forth a number of important principles. First, Congress possessed the whole power of war, including the exclusive power to authorize a limited or undeclared war. The corollary of that principle was that the president had no authority to initiate military action without Congress. In this case, Congress had expressly authorized the seizure of "any armed French vessel found on the high seas." Second, since the *Amelia* met that description, there was "probable cause" to believe that she was liable to capture at the time that Talbot acted. Talbot had no reason to know that she was, in fact, a neutral vessel, so he acted properly. Third, Talbot had performed a valuable service in rescuing the vessel from condemnation by France and was therefore entitled to some amount of salvage.[16]

An outright victory for Talbot could be read as a signal of Marshall's partisanship. Yet Marshall tempered his decision in a way that would allow both Federalists and Republicans to declare victory. Federal law provided that a captain who captured an enemy ship was entitled to receive half the value of the ship and its contents as salvage. However, since the *Amelia* was not an enemy vessel but a neutral vessel, Talbot's capture violated international law. Marshall opined that a law of the United States ought never to be construed in a way that violated international law. This was a new principle of statutory interpretation. Applying this principle, Marshall held that the statute could not be read to entitle Talbot to half the ship's value.[17]

But surely it would have seemed unjust to deny Talbot any compensation and leave him paying court costs. After all, Talbot had provided a valuable service by rescuing Seaman's ship from its French captors. Marshall found that there was an implied contract between Talbot and Seeman, and therefore Talbot was entitled to some compensation for his services. Marshall thought that Talbot's compensation should be less than half the value of the ship and its contents. Weighing all the circumstances, he and his brethren agreed that an award of one-sixth the value of the ship and its contents less court costs would fairly compensate Talbot for his service to the ship's owner.[18]

It was a Solomonic decision to split the proceeds this way. It was also a sign of Marshall's political acumen that he struck a compromise he thought would placate partisans in both political parties.

MARSHALL'S FIRST DECISION signaled that his tenure would be characterized by moderation. But Republicans were not placated. Despite Jefferson's inaugural message of reconciliation, the new Republican Congress, egged on by President Jefferson, was gearing up to repeal the Circuit Court Act of 1801, which had created the new circuit courts and reduced the Supreme Court from six justices to five. Jefferson grumbled that the Federalists "have retired into the judiciary as a stronghold," and he predicted that "from that battery all the works of republicanism are to be beaten down & erased, by a fraudulent use of the constitution which has made judges irremoveable, they have multiplied useless judges merely to strengthen their phalanx."[19]

The federal judiciary was widely viewed as an ally of financial interests. Merchants, banks, and landholders all expected that the federal courts would be more sympathetic than state courts, which were often elected positions and tilted in favor of tradesmen, debtors, and farmers. By expanding the size and authority of federal courts, the 1801 act created a firewall against the populism of the Jeffersonians. It was precisely for that reason that the Republicans found the act intolerable. One of the leading Republicans of the time, Virginia Congressman William Branch Giles, called for the removal of all Federalist judges "indiscriminately." So long as the Federalists remained in office, he warned his fellow Republicans, "[T]he strong fortress is in [the] possession of the enemy."[20]

For Marshall, Giles's comments must have felt like a stinging rebuke. Marshall had befriended Giles years earlier, and when Giles first arrived in Congress, Marshall introduced him to Madison with a warm letter of reference.[21] Giles now made no secret of the Republicans' intentions. Addressing the federal judiciary, Giles crowed, "We want your offices for the purpose of giving them to men who will fill them better."[22]

Marshall had confronted the French, the British, the Spanish, and the Barbary pirates. Now he faced a more personal menace.

CHAPTER EIGHTEEN

A STRATEGIC RETREAT

I n 1801, the Supreme Court had few cases on its docket and did not resume deliberation until December of that year as prescribed by Congress. One of the first petitions presented was from William Marbury, whose name was embarrassingly familiar to Marshall. Marbury was one of the forty-two justices of the peace for the District of Columbia rushed through the Senate confirmation process in the final hours of the Adams administration. On March 3, 1801, Adams's last day in office as president, Marshall had applied the Great Seal of the United States to Marbury's commission. Marshall was frantically packing up his papers, processing commissions, and arranging to deliver the commissions for sixteen new circuit judges as well as the justices of the peace. By noon the next day, the sixteen circuit judges had received their commissions, and Thomas Jefferson had been sworn in as president. On his first full day in office, Jefferson was surprised to find forty-two commissions for justices of the peace neatly stacked on Marshall's desk at the State Department. It's not certain why the commissions were never delivered. Some historians attribute the failure to Marshall's inattention to details.[1] Whatever the reason, this clerical oversight set off the most famous case in the history of the Supreme Court, *Marbury v. Madison.*

Jefferson instructed Levi Lincoln, who was serving as interim secretary of state before James Madison arrived to take the post, not to deliver the commissions. Jefferson considered that the commissions did not vest until they were delivered, and he thought that forty-two judges for the district was excessive given the fact that the total population of the district was barely three thousand free persons and slaves. Jefferson eventually told Madison to deliver twenty-five of the commissions plus another five nominated by Jefferson. Among the seventeen commissions that Jefferson refused to deliver was Marbury's.

William Marbury came from a formerly wealthy Maryland plantation family. He began his career at nineteen as a clerk to the Maryland state auditor and eventually rose to become agent for the state of Maryland. In this capacity, Marbury helped to refinance the state's Revolutionary War debt. Marbury learned he could score an easy fortune selling worthless state bonds in exchange for valuable federal securities. By 1793, Marbury had founded the Bank of Columbia with Benjamin Stoddert. In 1798, President Adams appointed Stoddert the first secretary of the navy. At the time, Stoddert had suffered an embarrassing financial setback, and Marbury stepped in to rescue him. He was rewarded in 1799 with an appointment as the agent for a new naval yard to be built at Anacostia in Washington. Marbury moved to Georgetown, which was then little more than a small port on the Potomac. There he built a fashionable redbrick town house on M Street.[2]

Marbury was working in the Department of the Navy when President Adams nominated him to be a justice of the peace. It is unclear whether Marbury accepted out of political ambition or loyalty to Adams. The real mystery is why he would go to court to fight to keep his commission. The position of a justice of the peace was a vestige of the colonial era that had lost nearly all its significance. By 1800, a justice of the peace was a lowly local magistrate who performed ministerial functions such as notarizing land documents and arresting drunks, prostitutes, and runaway slaves. A justice of the peace could also decide claims for fewer than twenty dollars.[3] There was no compensation apart from nominal filing fees, and as a successful financier, Marbury hardly needed the income or the aggravation.[4]

Of the seventeen men nominated as justices of the peace who were denied their commissions, only three others—William Harper, Robert Townsend Hooe, and Dennis Ramsay—cared enough to join Marbury in seeking redress. It's likely that all four plaintiffs were motivated more by a partisan desire to embarrass Jefferson than a genuine interest in the office. They wanted a judgment holding Secretary of State Madison—and, by implication, President Jefferson—liable for violating the law.

Marbury's attorney, Charles Lee, the former attorney general and a close friend of Marshall's, filed suit in the Supreme Court asking for an order known as a writ of mandamus that would command the secretary of state to deliver Marbury's commission. The Supreme Court agreed to hear Marbury's petition during its June 1803 term.

Marbury's lawsuit was filed against the backdrop of an ominous constitutional crisis. When the Court agreed to hear Marbury's case, Republican Senator John Breckinridge from Kentucky rose on the Senate floor to accuse the Supreme Court of launching "the most daring attack" against the president.[5] Breckinridge called for repealing the Circuit Court Act. Though Jefferson had already hinted at the need to change the act, Marbury's challenge emboldened the Republicans to act swiftly.[6] Proposing to abolish federal courts was equivalent to a declaration of war against the Federalist judiciary. Federalists, including New York Senator Gouverneur Morris, warned that the Repeal Act was a threat to the rule of law itself: "What will be the effect of the desired repeal? Will it not be a declaration to the remaining judges that they hold their offices subject to your will and pleasure?" Morris, one of the Constitution's Framers, feared that if the repeal succeeded, it would destroy the independence of the judiciary.[7]

The Repeal Act was narrowly approved by a single vote in the Senate, but it sailed through the House on a party-line vote. The Repeal Act, also known as the Judiciary Act of 1802, eliminated the sixteen new circuit judges, restored the Supreme Court to six justices, and canceled the Supreme Court's term for 1802 to prevent Marshall's court from responding. (The Supreme Court did not resume hearing cases until February 1803.)

The circuit court judges who had lost their jobs argued that the 1802 act was unconstitutional. Under Article III of the Constitution, federal judges have lifetime tenure during "good behavior" and can be removed only by impeachment and conviction for treason, bribery, or other high crimes and misdemeanors. It seemed clear that Congress could not dismiss circuit court judges by legislation. Marshall was sympathetic to those who lost their jobs, including his brother James, who in the last hours of the Adams administration had been appointed to the D.C. Circuit Court.

The Repeal Act placed Marshall and his brethren in an awkward position. If the circuit court judges were no longer hearing cases, then the Supreme Court justices themselves needed to resume the arduous and unappealing work of riding circuit. The justices considered whether they should refuse to ride circuit until Congress relented. That would bring the federal judiciary to a crashing halt and provoke a confrontation with the Republican Congress. But if the justices simply resumed riding circuit and acquiesced to an unconstitutional act of Congress, then the independence of the judiciary would be compromised.

Marshall, Chase, and Paterson agreed that they should not ride circuit. Marshall thought that the Constitution gave Supreme Court justices limited power to hear only certain trials; therefore Congress could not give the justices additional power to hear other trials as circuit court judges when they were obligated to hear the same cases on appeal.[8] In effect, these three justices were prepared to go on strike. Justices Cushing and Washington, however, disagreed with their colleagues. They thought that the precedent for Supreme Court justices riding circuit had already been well established since the beginning of the federal government. They felt they had to accept the 1802 act.[9] Marshall worried that if the justices did not act unanimously, the strike would be fatal to the Court's legitimacy. Marshall was prepared to compromise to preserve the Court's effectiveness. With the Court split and unable to meet until 1803, Marshall could see no practical way to refuse riding circuit until a case challenging the Repeal Act reached the Supreme Court.[10] Thus Marshall and his brethren saddled up for another arduous term riding circuit.

Around the country, cases were filed challenging the constitutionality of the 1802 act. The first case was heard by Justice Bushrod Washington on circuit in Hartford, Connecticut. Washington dismissed the suit knowing that more such challenges were headed to the Supreme Court. One of the circuit judges, Richard Bassett, petitioned the Supreme Court directly. Bassett warned that if Congress could fire judges, all the constitutional limits on government and the protections of individual liberty "would become nugatory." Bassett asserted that when Congress acted contrary to the Constitution, the Supreme Court had authority to declare the Repeal Act unconstitutional.[11]

SINCE THE COURT would not be meeting for the year and Marshall had no law practice to resume, he planned to work on a new project, a five-volume biography of Washington. Marshall had been approached by Bushrod Washington, who had inherited all his uncle's public and private papers. Bushrod had hoped to write the biography with Washington's personal secretary, Tobias Lear, but Bushrod changed his mind and turned to Marshall instead. Marshall was not sure he was the right man for the job of biographer. Bushrod persuaded Marshall that he was uniquely well suited given his close relationship with Washington from Valley Forge through his presidency. Moreover, Marshall was closely associated with Washington in the public's mind. He had spoken movingly at Washington's memorial in Congress, and in 1802, he was overseeing plans authorized by the Federalist

Congress to construct a monument to Washington.[12] (Congressional Republicans opposed the monument and incongruously denounced Washington as a counterrevolutionary hero. Instead, a private society was formed in 1848 to raise funds for the Washington Monument, but it went bankrupt before the monument could be completed. Congress did not appropriate funds to complete the monument until 1876, nearly three-quarters of a century after Marshall began that effort.) Marshall agreed to write Washington's biography both out of devotion to his former commander in chief and his urgent need to raise cash to pay off the balance owed for Lord Fairfax's estate.[13] Thus the first presidential biography was launched largely to finance a real estate venture.

Marshall's *The Life of George Washington* was the first of many presidential biographies to flop. His five glutinous volumes totaled nearly one thousand pages. Sold in advance by subscription, the first volume appeared two years late, by which time hundreds of angry subscribers had demanded refunds. It opened with an interminable and wholly tangential history of pre-Columbian America through the French and Indian Wars. Washington was hardly mentioned. With little early biographical detail, Washington sprang full-grown in volume two and plunged immediately into the Revolutionary War.

Marshall's flat descriptions of the war left readers disappointed. Even his account of the cruel winter at Valley Forge lacked grit: "The winter had set in with great severity, and the sufferings of the army were extreme. In a few days, however, these sufferings were considerably diminished by the erection of logged huts, filled up with mortar, which, after being dried, formed comfortable habitations, and gave content to men long unused to the conveniences of life."[14]

The whole biography revealed more about Marshall than it did about Washington. Marshall implicitly contrasted Washington, who avoided partisanship, with Republicans who were threatening to dismantle the national government. Marshall praised Washington for pursuing the "real interests" of the Republic and resisting the "gusts of passion." Washington, Marshall said, stood firm in pursuit of the nation's true interests "in opposition to a torrent." Washington was a "real republican." For Washington, "[r]eal liberty" depended on "preserving the authority of the laws, and maintaining the energy of government." He attributed to Washington the thought that a demagogue was the opposite of a patriot, but whether Washington actually said that, it seems likely that Marshall was referring to the Republican president.[15]

When the first two volumes were published in the summer of 1803, the reviewers were not kind. Marshall admitted he was "mortified beyond measure to find that it [had] been so carelessly written."[16] Even before it was published, he begged his publisher to remove his name from the volumes, but the publisher refused.[17] Marshall had assumed that as chief justice he would not have to ride circuit, but after the Repeal Act, he had far less time to write. And he was not a biographer by temperament. Marshall was an extrovert; he had no patience for self-reflection, let alone the quiet observation of another's life. If Marshall had hoped to write a hagiographic triumph that would resuscitate the Federalist Party, he was sadly disappointed. It was too late to pull together the dispirited Federalists into a unified political organization, and Marshall's judicial responsibilities made that impractical as well as ill advised. *The Life of George Washington* was the single public failure of Marshall's career.

Even before the book's appearance, Jefferson had launched a preemptive attack. Republicans were warned that Marshall's book would be a thinly veiled assault on the Republican Party. When Marshall's publisher wrote to twelve hundred local postmasters asking them to advertise the book, Jefferson ordered the postmasters to refuse. Marshall hoped to sell as many as thirty thousand five-volume sets at the price of three dollars for each volume. By 1806, the publisher had sold only seven thousand sets. While the book was a failure, Marshall's royalties netted nearly $20,000 (slightly more than $400,000 today), which was just enough for Marshall to purchase the Fairfax property.[18]

Jefferson feared that the biography would seize control of the narrative of the American Revolution from the Republicans. Jefferson criticized Marshall's "cold indifference" to the struggle for liberty. Jefferson wrote that "[n]o act of heroism ever kindles in the mind of this writer a single aspiration in favor of the holy cause which inspired the bosom, & nerved the arm of the patriot warrior." Jefferson felt that Marshall had misused Washington's papers "for the suicide of the cause, for which he had lived."[19] For Jefferson, who had shirked military service, to question Marshall's patriotism revealed more about Jefferson than it did about Marshall.

WHILE CONGRESS KEPT the Supreme Court shut down in 1802, Marshall rode circuit in Virginia and North Carolina. This was the busiest circuit in the nation. One of the most significant suits filed before the circuit court involved a case brought by Marylander John Laird against Virginia resident Hugh Stuart. Laird sued on behalf of a firm of Scottish merchants, Laird and Robertson of Glasgow, to collect a debt owed by Stuart. In 1801, the newly established Fourth Circuit in the eastern district of Virginia issued a verdict for Laird. When Stuart failed to pay, Laird went back to the circuit court to enforce the debt. By now, the Repeal Act had dissolved the Fourth Circuit, so Laird came before Marshall on the Virginia circuit to request an order executing the prior judgment of the now defunct circuit court.

Stuart happened to be represented by the same attorney as Marbury, Charles Lee. Lee argued that the Repeal Act was unconstitutional and that the chief justice had no authority to hear cases on circuit.[20] Lee's argument mirrored Marshall's own view, but Marshall nevertheless ordered Stuart to pay. Marshall preferred to reserve the question of the law's constitutionality for the Supreme Court to decide. At this point, no federal court had ever struck down an act of Congress as unconstitutional. Stuart appealed to the Supreme Court, which scheduled arguments the following February.

JUST ONE WEEK before the court heard Marbury's case, Republicans sent a warning shot across the bow of the federal judiciary: Jefferson called on the House to impeach New Hampshire District Judge John Pickering. Pickering was a leading Federalist in New England. He had served in the New Hampshire state government in numerous roles, including as chief justice of the state supreme court. He was one of the principal advocates for ratification of the federal Constitution at the New Hampshire ratification convention and was nominated by Washington as the second federal district court judge in New Hampshire. Pickering had served the public with distinction and had generously offered pro bono legal services to the indigent, but he was an easy target for Republicans. He had struggled with hypochondria, depression, and alcoholism throughout his life. He once admitted from the bench that he was too intoxicated to hear the case. Republicans also accused him of favoring Federalists. That was enough for Jefferson and his party to make an example of Pickering. With flimsy evidence, Republicans accused him of smuggling, corruption, drunkenness, and insanity. The House impeached him by a party-line vote on March 2, and the Senate, without hearing any testimony from him, convicted him one year later by another vote along party lines.[21]

No one doubted that the Republicans' real intention was to intimidate the Supreme Court as it began deliberations in *Marbury* and *Stuart*. New Hampshire Federalist Senator William Plumer warned his colleagues that Republicans were planning to rid both the federal and state courts of Federalist judges: "The removal of the Judges, & the destruction of the independence of the judicial department, has been an object on which Mr. Jefferson has been long resolved."[22] Even before Pickering's impeachment,

Pennsylvania Republicans had impeached and convicted a state judge, Alexander Addison. Judge Addison was a partisan Federalist who made no effort to moderate his views after the national Republican victory. But so far as Republicans were concerned, Addison and Pickering were just target practice for their real enemy: the Marshall Court.

As THE JUDICIAL CRISIS DEEPENED, the Supreme Court convened on Thursday morning, February 10, 1803, to hear Charles Lee present Marbury's argument. The Potomac had frozen the previous night, and the courtroom's single fireplace was not enough to warm the chamber.[23] Committee room number two was unusually packed, but the defendant, Secretary of State James Madison, refused to appear and did not even bother to retain a lawyer to represent him. Madison disdained the Court's proceedings. The trial, which lasted four days, was one of the very few trials ever held before the Supreme Court, which usually hears only appeals from lower courts.

The trial posed a challenging evidentiary hurdle for Lee. Everyone in the courtroom—indeed, nearly everyone in the country—knew that the Senate had confirmed Marbury as one of the forty-two justices of the peace but that his commission had not been delivered. Nevertheless, every fact in a trial must be proved unless both sides stipulate to the facts. Lee had asked Madison to provide the commissions to the court or at least to confirm their existence, but Madison would not even acknowledge the Supreme Court's jurisdiction over him. Lee asked the Senate to provide a written record that Marbury and his co-plaintiffs had been confirmed. The Republican-controlled Senate refused. Then Lee called the State Department's chief clerk, Jacob Wagner, and an assistant, Daniel Brent, to testify. Marshall knew that both clerks had personally handled the commissions, but under oath, they had a convenient lapse of memory. Lee even called Attorney General Levi Lincoln to testify. Lincoln had served as the acting secretary of state for the first few weeks of the Jefferson administration before Madison arrived in Washington. But Lincoln refused to respond to any questions. Rather than claim executive privilege, Lincoln asserted the Fifth Amendment privilege against self-incrimination, which implied that he thought his failure to deliver the commissions was illegal. The next day Lincoln reluctantly agreed to respond to a few questions in writing. He admitted seeing a stack of commissions sitting on his desk on March 4, 1801, but he could not recall whether Marbury's commission was in the stack, and he refused to say what might have happened to the commissions, which presumably President Jefferson had ordered him to destroy.[24]

The one person who was uniquely situated to testify that the plaintiffs were confirmed as justices of the peace and that the commissions were properly signed and sealed was John Marshall. But as he was the sitting chief justice, that was impossible. Instead, Lee read an affidavit signed by James Marshall, the chief justice's brother and business partner, who was himself one of the midnight judges appointed to the D.C. Circuit Court and now out of a job. James averred that on March 4 he was called to the State Department and asked to deliver the commissions of the justices of the peace in Alexandria. He believed that there were twelve such commissions, which he picked up and gave a receipt for. "[F]inding that he could not conveniently carry the whole, he returned several of them, and struck a pen through the names of those, in the receipt, which he returned." He recalled leaving commissions for Robert Townsend Hooe and William Harper, two of the co-plaintiffs.[25] James's testimony was the only evidence that the commissions were issued—and it was most likely a complete fabrication.

Historians have long accepted James's story, but it made no sense.[26] Just a fortnight after Jefferson was sworn in as president, long before Marbury's suit was filed, the chief justice heard from James that Jefferson had refused to deliver the commissions to some of the justices of the peace. He replied to James "with infinite chagrin" that he assumed that since the commissions had been signed and sealed, Madison would deliver them. Now he blamed himself: "I shoud however have sent out the commissions which had been signd & seald but for the extreme hurry of the time & the absence of Mr. Wagner who had been calld on by the President to act as his private Secretary."[27] If James was responsible for delivering the commissions, then Marshall's explanation to James would have been superfluous. It is apparent that James Marshall perjured himself in the Supreme Court and that the chief justice not only knew this but probably asked him to lie.

For most of us today, it is unthinkable that a chief justice would suborn perjury in his own court or that he would sit in judgment on a case in which he was the principal witness. But the time and circumstances were extraordinary. Facing a constitutional crisis—Republicans were threatening the independence of the judiciary—Marshall thought that the ends justified the means. Jefferson and the Republicans had left Marshall no choice by refusing to respect the court's orders to provide proof that the commissions were signed and sealed. The lie bridged an evidentiary gap by establishing in court the existence of the commissions, which the whole world knew was true.

In court Lee argued convincingly that Marbury's right to receive his commission had vested and that the executive was bound to deliver the commission by the legislative act that created the justices of the peace. Lee's oration went on for four days. No one representing Madison was present to cross-examine witnesses or defend Madison. At the end of the trial, Chief Justice Marshall looked around the courtroom and asked if there was anyone present who wished to speak on behalf of Madison. He was greeted with silence. Jefferson made it unmistakably clear that if the court held for Marbury he would refuse to comply. Marshall faced the unappealing prospect of either acceding to the president's will or defending principle and proving the court ineffectual. In either case, the court's legitimacy would suffer, and it would lose any semblance of authority as a coequal branch of government. The court appeared trapped.

As Justice Chase was ill and confined to his room at Stelle's Hotel, the whole court met there to discuss the case. The decision was announced in the crowded lobby of the hotel on February 24. Washington had warmed a bit by then, and the frozen Potomac had cracked open and began to flow again.[28] The room fell silent as the chief justice read the Court's unanimous decision. The decision, which ran more than forty pages, or eleven thousand words, took four hours to read. It would be remembered as the single most significant constitutional decision issued by any court in American history.

First, Marshall posed the question of whether Marbury had a right to receive the commission. The Court found that once the commission was signed, the president had no right to deny a judge his commission or remove him from office. This was an unmistakable reference to the repeal of the circuit courts as much as it referred to the justices of the peace. The Great Seal affixed to the commission attested to the fact that the right to the commission had vested. In effect, Marshall was saying that Madison's failure to deliver the commission was unlawful.[29]

Second, Marshall asked if Marbury had a right to a remedy. What he meant was whether a court could examine the official actions of an executive officer, such as the secretary of state. "The government of the United States has been emphatically termed a government of laws, and not of men," Marshall wrote. "It will certainly cease to deserve this high appellation, if the laws furnish no remedy for the violation of a vested legal right." The real issue here was of monumental importance, perhaps more than any other aspect of the opinion. Marshall conceded that some acts were assigned by the Constitution to the president's discretion—and by extension to the secretary of state—and courts should not question the exercise of discretionary power. But this action was examinable by the Court since Congress had approved the appointment and the secretary of state had a legal obligation to deliver the commission that Marbury was entitled to receive.[30] In so holding, Marshall affirmed the ancient principle of

Anglo-American law that even the king is not above the law. Thus Marshall established that private citizens have the right to sue federal officials for denying them benefits to which they are entitled.

Finally, Marshall addressed the issue of whether the Court could provide the remedy Marbury was seeking. Marbury's attorney petitioned the Court to issue a writ of mandamus commanding the secretary of state to deliver his commission. Marshall broke down this issue into two independent questions: First, did the court have authority over the secretary of state? And second, did the court have authority to grant this writ of mandamus?

As to the former question, Marshall, a former secretary of state and close adviser to President Adams, acknowledged that "[t]he intimate political relation" between the president and his cabinet officers renders any judicial order addressed to "one of those high officers peculiarly irksome, as well as delicate," and a court should proceed cautiously. Marshall acknowledged that courts cannot judge political questions. But in this case the president was not exercising any discretionary power. The secretary of state was "directed by law to do a certain act affecting the absolute rights of individuals," and therefore Madison was not immune from the Court's jurisdiction.[31]

At this point, after almost three hours of listening to the chief justice read in his soft, deliberate drawl, the tension in the hotel lobby must have felt combustible. Marshall was poised to order the secretary of state to do something that everyone understood Jefferson would not allow. Was the Court willing to bet its authority against the president's? Marshall at last came to the final question: Did the Supreme Court have the power to issue a writ of mandamus? The room held its breath in anticipation.

The Judiciary Act of 1789, which established the federal courts, was one of the landmark bills adopted by the first Congress. Section 13 expressly gave the Supreme Court the power to issue writs of mandamus. That would seem to settle the question, but Marshall now took a surprising turn. Article III of the Constitution gave the Supreme Court jurisdiction to hear trials—or what the Constitution calls "original jurisdiction"—in certain specific types of cases involving ambassadors, public ministers, and states. Since Article III did not expressly grant the Supreme Court original jurisdiction over writs of mandamus, Marshall held that Congress could not expand the Court's original jurisdiction to include a writ of mandamus.[32]

Marshall found that by granting the Supreme Court the power to issue writs of mandamus, Section 13 of the Judiciary Act violated Article III of the Constitution. Should Section 13 of the statute trump the Constitution, or should the Constitution trump the statute? If the answer appears obvious to us today, it's only because of Marshall's opinion in *Marbury*. Before 1803, it was not clear whether the Constitution was enforceable by courts, or whether it was merely an expression of principles, like the Declaration of Independence. After all, why should unelected judges be empowered to strike down the acts of a democratically elected Congress?

Marshall asserted that the Constitution was a higher form of law established by "We the People" rather than by a mere legislature. The supreme will of the people inscribed in the founding document trumped the transient preferences of Congress.[33] And it was up to the Supreme Court to decide the meaning of the Constitution because "[i]t is emphatically the province and duty of the judicial department to say what the law is."[34] Marshall struck down Section 13 of the Judiciary Act as unconstitutional. The Supreme Court had no authority to issue a writ of mandamus as a trial court. Marbury would have to go back to the circuit court and start his case over.

MOST PEOPLE BELIEVE, incorrectly, that Marshall invented the power of judicial review in *Marbury v. Madison*. True, it was the first time a federal court had struck down a federal law as unconstitutional. (The Supreme Court did not invalidate another federal statute until its infamous decision to uphold slavery in *Dred Scott*, fifty-four years later.[35]) However, well before *Marbury*, state courts, legal authorities, and even the Framers of the

Constitution had asserted that courts could strike down statutes that were contrary to the Constitution.[36] Indeed, it was a young John Marshall at the Virginia Ratifying Convention who declared that if Congress "were to make a law not warranted by any of their powers enumerated [in the Constitution], it would be considered by the Judges an infringement of the Constitution which they are to guard . . . They would declare it void."[37] Even Jefferson did not object to the principle of judicial review. Far more controversial was Marshall's holding that the Court had jurisdiction over executive officials in the exercise of their official duties.

Marbury v. Madison demonstrated Marshall's political genius. He struck a pragmatic compromise that avoided a direct conflict with the president while he asserted the Court's authority to hold both Congress and the executive accountable to the Constitution. Marshall wove together his decision so artfully that few people noticed the flaws in the stitching: The first question a court should always ask is whether it has jurisdiction to decide a case. Since Marshall concluded there was no jurisdiction, the Supreme Court had no business deciding that Marbury was entitled to his commission in the first place. The Court's holding that Madison had violated Marbury's rights under the law was merely gratuitous and arguably improper.

The second flaw in Marshall's opinion was that there was nothing in Article III of the Constitution that explicitly prohibited Congress from giving the Supreme Court original jurisdiction over writs of mandamus. Marshall inferred something that was not stated. (Indeed, in another case thirteen years later, the Marshall Court held that Congress could grant the Supreme Court additional appellate jurisdiction beyond the terms of Article III.[38]) Many of the Constitution's Framers, including Madison, served in the first Congress that wrote the Judiciary Act. Surely they understood better than the Supreme Court what their original intention was in writing the Constitution, and one might assume that they would not have adopted a statute that contravened the Constitution they drafted.

Marshall invented a conflict between the Constitution and the Judiciary

Act in order to create the opportunity to assert the power of judicial review. In fact, Section 13 of the Judiciary Act did not grant the Supreme Court original jurisdiction over writs of mandamus. The act listed all the cases in which the court had original jurisdiction without mentioning writs of mandamus. Then it went on to list all the cases in which the Supreme Court had appellate jurisdiction from the circuit courts, which included writs of mandamus.[39] In other words, the Judiciary Act gave the Supreme Court *appellate* jurisdiction over writs of mandamus; it did not give the Court original jurisdiction to hear trials like Marbury's for a writ of mandamus. Marshall ignored the plain meaning of the statute in order to manufacture a conflict with the Constitution that did not exist.

Why would Marshall create a constitutional conflict unnecessarily? If Marshall had not invented this conflict and if the Court had ordered Madison to deliver the commission, there's little doubt that Madison would have refused to comply, and the Court's authority would have been undermined. Instead, by conveniently inventing a constitutional conflict, Marshall made a strategic retreat from a direct confrontation with Jefferson while asserting the power of judicial review.

This leads to a question that has long puzzled historians: Why did Charles Lee, one of the smartest lawyers of his generation, misread the statute and file the writ of mandamus in the wrong court? The proper court having jurisdiction over the writ of mandamus would have been the circuit court for the District of Columbia. He could easily have filed his lawsuit there. The circuit court was appointed by President Adams in the last days of his administration, and it included Lee's friend James Marshall, the brother of the chief justice.[40] If the case had been filed with James Marshall, the only available witness to prove the existence of the commission would have been the chief justice. But if the chief justice had testified, then he would almost certainly have had to recuse himself when the case was inevitably appealed to the Supreme Court. Instead, the case was purposely filed in the wrong court so that James Marshall could testify to the existence of the commissions. The case created the perfect opportunity for holding that federal judges could not be denied their commissions and for affirming the power of judicial review without risking a head-on collision with President Jefferson. Most likely, John and James Marshall sat down with their friend Charles Lee—perhaps over a glass of Marshall's favorite Madeira—and constructed this case from start to finish.

Public reaction to Marshall's decision was generally positive.[41] Leading Republican newspapers, such as the *National Intelligencer* in Washington, the *Aurora* in Philadelphia, and the *Independent Chronicle* in Boston, found little to quarrel about in *Marbury*. Even the *Virginia Argus,* an aggressively Republican publication, did not question the power of judicial review or the principle that executive officers could be held accountable by the courts. Even prominent Republicans publicly endorsed the doctrine of judicial review.[42] Neither Jefferson nor Madison publicly criticized the decision, and both had previously acknowledged the power of judicial review.[43] Privately, however, Jefferson fumed that Marshall had the audacity to suggest that Madison had violated the law by refusing to deliver those commissions.[44]

One week after Marshall's historic decision in *Marbury,* the court issued its opinion in *Stuart v. Laird.* Everyone in Washington now expected the Supreme Court to declare the Repeal Act unconstitutional. To Republicans, the court's assertion of judicial review in *Marbury* had set the stage for an all-out war with Congress. Once again, Marshall's court surprised everyone. Rather than striking down the Repeal Act and reinstating the Federalist circuit court judges, Justice Paterson issued a curt unanimous opinion that since it had been the practice of the Supreme Court to ride circuit years before the 1801 Circuit Court Act, this practice "affords an irresistible answer" against any claim that Supreme Court justices cannot constitutionally sit on two courts.[45] The court dismissed Stuart's suit challenging the Repeal Act. Another confrontation between the Court and the Jeffersonians was averted.

The chief justice, having decided the case on circuit, had recused himself from participating in the decision. Yet there's no doubt that he had a great influence on his colleagues and their decision, and that the bold stroke of *Marbury* bought the court some breathing room. It was no longer urgent for the court to assert itself in this manner in this case.

Marbury and *Stuart* demonstrated Marshall's moderation and his pragmatism in forging consensus on the Court to find common ground between political partisans. Marshall relied on the tactical skill he had learned from General Steuben and the diplomatic experience he had gained in Paris. In one bold stroke he had avoided a constitutional crisis and enlarged the Court's authority.

The crisis between the Court and the president was averted or at least postponed. But one thing was sure: In Chief Justice Marshall, President Jefferson had met his match.

CHAPTER NINETEEN

PRIZES OF WAR

F rom the moment that Marshall joined the Court, his tenure was dominated by international cases. Though Marshall's eloquent decisions on constitutional law may be better known today, he authored more than twice as many decisions on international law as he did on constitutional law.[1] Whereas Justice Joseph Story, who joined the Court in 1811, was a recognized authority on constitutional law, his contemporaries regarded Marshall as the leading authority on international law. International cases dominated the Court's caseload for much of the first fifty years of the Court's proceedings, and most of these cases concerned the rights and obligations of merchant ships, naval vessels, and privateers. The U.S. economy in 1800 was significantly more reliant on international trade than it is today. In 1800, around 40 percent of the country's gross domestic product was represented by imports and exports; by contrast, in 2015 that number was around 25 percent of the U.S. GDP.[2] Given the importance of trade at the time, it's hardly surprising that admiralty law dominated the Court's docket.

Several of the most important cases to come before the Marshall Court concerned the Quasi-War with France. One of these arose out of the capture of the schooner *Peggy*, a French merchant ship, by the USS *Trumbull* near Haiti. The *Peggy* was condemned by the circuit court in Connecticut on September 23, 1800, the same day that President Jefferson ratified the peace treaty with France ending the Quasi-War. The treaty provided that any ships captured but not yet "definitively condemned" after the treaty's ratification should be restored to their owners. The Court faced the question of whether the condemnation of the ship was "final" before all appeals to the Supreme Court had been exhausted. In December 1801, Chief Justice Marshall held that the condemnation was not final and that the vessel should be restored. Though Marshall conceded that normally "[e]very condemnation is final," here the Court must be mindful of a treaty, which under the Constitution has the same effect as any act of Congress. Though courts should not ordinarily apply rules retrospectively to alter property rights, a peace treaty was exceptional. "[W]here individual rights, acquired by war, are sacrificed for national purposes, the [treaty] making the sacrifice ought always to receive a construction conforming to its manifest import." In other words, if the U.S. government waived the rights of its citizens to collect a prize, it is up to the government, not the Court, to provide compensation.[3] Marshall's opinion demonstrated his deference to treaties and his respect for the property rights of aliens.

MARSHALL KEPT A JUDICIOUS silence as political events were unfolding in Washington. In 1802, Jefferson quietly invited the rabble-rouser Thomas Paine to return to America from France on a navy frigate—presumably because Paine was too impoverished to pay his own fare. When Paine published the fact that he had returned at Jefferson's invitation, the incident embarrassed Jefferson. Federalist newspapers blasted Paine as an "obscene old sinner," a "notorious drunkard," and the "living opprobrium of humanity" for his defaming Washington, his support for the French Revolution, and his opposition to religion. Though Jefferson said nothing publicly to defend Paine, he entertained him at the President's House and privately expressed his "high esteem" for his service to the Revolution.[4]

Marshall took some satisfaction at Jefferson's expense. The chief justice had nothing kind to say about Paine, who had acted as Talleyrand's stooge during the XYZ Affair by lobbying Marshall to pay the bribe. Marshall wrote to Pinckney: "It is whisperd among those who affect to know a great deal that a certain eminent personage [Jefferson] is already fatigued almost beyond bearing with a great democratic & religious writer whose useful labors were of sufficient magnitude to entitle him to an invitation to cross the Atlantic in a national frigate." Marshall was delighted that the newspapers were hurling criticism at Jefferson for welcoming Paine home. "I wish such deeds woud always bring their own reward. It woud induce infidels to believe there was a possibility of there being a superintending providence."[5]

ANOTHER IMPORTANT CASE arising out of the Quasi-War concerned the capture of the *Jane*, an American-owned vessel. On the morning of April 10, 1800, toward the end of the Quasi-War with France, the *Jane* set sail from Baltimore with a cargo of flour bound for the French West Indies. The *Jane* was a sleek schooner low to the water with its masts raked back for speed and balance. The cargo was sold to a merchant on St. Barts, and from there the schooner proceeded to St. Thomas, then a Danish possession, where it was sold to Jared Shattuck, a successful merchant originally from Connecticut who now lived on the island. Since Denmark was neutral, the two acts banning commerce between the U.S. and France did not apply to trade with the island. Shattuck rechristened the vessel the *Charming Betsy*.

On June 26, the *Charming Betsy* set sail loaded with wine, fish, and meat for Guadeloupe, a French island. Days later, the ship was captured by several dozen French privateers on board the *Rosiette* under the command of a Captain Bonnival. Bonnival concluded that the ship was clearly American and therefore could be claimed as a prize according to a decree of the French government. Captain Bonnival removed all but three of the original crew and put seven hands on board to sail the *Charming Betsy* toward Guadeloupe with the intention of libeling the ship there as a prize of war.[6]

The U.S. Navy had several ships in the vicinity that were patrolling the Caribbean for French warships or U.S. merchant vessels sailing to French territory in violation of the 1798 act that prohibited vessels owned by Americans from entering French ports. One of these naval vessels was the USS *Constellation*, a massive thirty-eight-gun frigate—one of the six original frigates that constituted the U.S. Navy. Around midnight on July 2, a crew member on board the *Constellation* spotted the *Charming Betsy* and fired a single shot over the bow. The French privateers had helped themselves to much of the wine on board and were startled from their drunken stupor by the appearance of this hulking warship. The *Constellation*'s captain, Alexander Murray, ordered the *Charming Betsy* to stop and submit to inspection. Lieutenant Miles King and a small group of sailors climbed aboard the *Charming Betsy* to search for evidence of contraband or evidence that this ship, a Danish-registered vessel, could be either American or French. An American vessel sailing toward French territory would be violating the ban on trading with France and subject to seizure, and a French warship could be seized as a prize of war. King asked to review the ship's logbook and found there was none. Had someone tossed the logbook overboard? His suspicions were further aroused when he found the bill of sale for the purchase of the ship dated only two weeks prior. The name Jared Shattuck hardly sounded Scandinavian. There was no evidence of Danish ownership or even a Danish flag. King could not have missed the captain's Scottish brogue. And the French privateers who had seized the ship clearly did not think it was a neutral vessel.

The French captain told King that he thought the ship was American. This was confirmed by one of the hands from Baltimore. It was widely known that Americans registered ships as Danish in order to escape seizure while being free to trade with all parties. Under these circumstances, Captain Murray reasonably concluded that there was probable cause to seize the ship.[7]

Captain Murray's men sailed the *Charming Betsy* to Philadelphia, where it was libeled under the 1798 act. The Danish consul in Philadelphia asserted that the ship and the cargo were the property of a Danish subject and could not be seized. The district court judge found that although Jared Shattuck was born a U.S. citizen, he had married and resided in Danish territory and had taken an oath of allegiance to the Danish Crown in 1797. Accordingly, the property belonged to the subject of a neutral country and had been illegally seized. The district court ordered Captain Murray to pay costs and damages to Shattuck in the amount of $20,594.61 (nearly $400,000 today)—more than twenty times his annual salary.[8] For a naval officer acting in good faith that seemed like a staggering injustice. On appeal the circuit court affirmed the judgment but reduced the amount of the award. Both Murray and Shattuck then appealed to the Supreme Court in 1804.

The case turned on the question of Shattuck's nationality. Murray's attorney argued that Shattuck had moved abroad only in the past decade to avoid the ban on commerce with France and that he had no documentary proof of naturalization nor had he ever formally renounced his U.S. citizenship. The argument might seem obscure, but it drew national attention. The case posed a fundamental question about the nature of citizenship that divided Federalists and Republicans. Jefferson and his party believed that a person had the right to change his citizenship. Republicans cast this right to expatriate as a fundamental liberty.[9] Federalists thought that a person's nationality was immutable and that only the government could alter the nationality of its citizens.[10]

This was more than a philosophical disagreement. Republicans generally welcomed European immigrants, especially from Ireland and France, who just happened to vote Republican.[11] Federalists wanted to discourage immigrants from these countries for the same reason. Federalists found it convenient to frame their opposition in terms of national security: Republican extremists might slip into the United States and threaten the nation's security. In fact, claims about immigrants threatening security were no more justified then than they are today.

Lurking just below the surface of the expatriation dispute was the persistent debate over relations with France. Federalists wanted the acts banning commerce enforced rigorously, and therefore they sided with Murray against Shattuck. Republicans were less inclined to punish France—even though Jefferson later proposed his own embargo against France and England. Disagreements over U.S. policy toward France fueled interest in this Supreme Court argument.

Marshall personally accepted the legal principle, well established in British common law, that a person owed "perpetual allegiance" to his sovereign and could not expatriate himself.[12] Yet he once again sidestepped a direct challenge to Jefferson and steered the court away from a broad pronouncement on the right to expatriate. Speaking for a unanimous Court, Marshall wrote that the question of whether a U.S. national "can divest himself absolutely of that character otherwise than in such manner as may be prescribed by law, is a question which it is not necessary at present to decide."[13] Instead, Marshall asserted that a merchant such as Shattuck who is a permanent resident of a foreign country assumed the "character" of a foreign national even if he had not technically surrendered his U.S. citizenship. In effect, Marshall invented a new category of nationality for commercial purposes. U.S. merchants residing abroad could avoid the reach of U.S. laws, but they could be subject to any restrictions imposed on foreign nationals.[14] Assuming then that Shattuck should be treated like a Danish national, Marshall turned his attention to whether Captain Murray had exceeded the ban on trade with France by capturing a neutral vessel.

In one of his most important decisions on international law, Marshall wrote that "an act of Congress ought never to be construed to violate the law of nations if any other possible construction remains."[15] This was the same principle that Marshall had introduced in his first opinion, *Talbot v. Seeman*. In other words, courts should interpret statutes consistent with customary international law unless Congress clearly stated its intention to act contrary to international law. This principle of statutory interpretation implied that customary international law is part of U.S. law. Since courts interpret customary international law, the principle of *Charming Betsy* expanded the power of courts to interpret acts of Congress.[16]

What customary international law governed the interpretation of acts imposing a trade embargo on France? Drawing on his diplomatic experience, Marshall asserted that the acts should be read in light of the rights of neutral nations to trade. That was the very principle Marshall had defended in France. Marshall reasoned that Congress did not intend to apply the law in a way that violated neutral rights. A U.S. national who had assumed the character of a Danish resident for commercial purposes was therefore exempt from the 1798 act. The chief justice reserved the possibility that U.S. criminal laws might still apply to him as a U.S. citizen, but "while within the territory of the sovereign to whom he has sworn allegiance," Shattuck was beyond the reach of the United States.[17] Marshall concluded that since the *Charming Betsy* was a neutral vessel, Captain Murray had no legal right to seize it. The Court ordered Murray to return the vessel to Shattuck and pay damages for the loss of cargo and the interruption in the voyage.

Was Murray entitled to compensation from Shattuck for recapturing the vessel from French privateers? Under U.S. statutory law, a U.S. naval captain and his crew who recaptured a ship from the French were entitled to half the value of the ship and its contents as salvage. Marshall found that since *Talbot* was decided, France had recognized the right of free navigation. Marshall held that the *Charming Betsy* was not at risk of being condemned by a French court, and therefore Captain Murray was not entitled to a reward.[18]

Marshall's decision rested on shaky ground. It was true that the French government had repealed a decree authorizing the seizure of neutral vessels

in March 1800 and that a French tribunal had issued two decisions returning a neutral vessel in May. However, Captain Murray could not have known
that at the time he captured the *Charming Betsy*, and there was no authoritative source on French law introduced into evidence. The only proof that
Shattuck could produce that showed a change in the French government's
policy was a poorly translated summary by an anonymous Englishman of a
French tribunal's decision.[19] Under the circumstances, it was far from clear
whether a French tribunal would have freed the *Charming Betsy*.

Why then did Marshall rely on such thin evidence in deciding that Captain Murray had not performed a valuable service to the ship's owner? Marshall gave France the benefit of the doubt despite his own experience
negotiating with Talleyrand's government. Marshall held out the hope that
even if the French court's decision was not authoritative, France might be
induced to comply with the law of neutrality in the future. Marshall was
acting according to the principle of international comity: He thought that
U.S. courts should defer to the laws of other states based on the expectation
that other states would accord reciprocal treatment to U.S. law.[20]

At the dawn of the nineteenth century, Marshall's respect for the law of
nations was widely shared by enlightened Americans. The principle that
customary international law applied in U.S. courts was well established
even before the adoption of the Constitution.[21] The Constitution expressly
acknowledged the authority of the customary law of nations and granted
Congress the power to punish violations.[22] Marshall's decision in *Charming Betsy* was widely accepted as consistent with the contemporaneous
understanding of the Constitution. By establishing a rule of statutory interpretation, Marshall sought to ensure that U.S. law would limit the power of
the government to infringe on the rights of other states. But international
law was not merely a constraint on what the United States could do; it was
also a tool of statecraft.

To our century, Marshall's faith in the power of international law and
the *Charming Betsy* principle may seem naïve, but Marshall recognized

that a vulnerable nation depended on international law.[23] He hoped that adherence to the law of nations would encourage reciprocity and provide the nation with a shield against the naked ambitions of foreign powers.[24]

It seemed unduly harsh that the Court held Captain Murray personally liable for an honest mistake when he had no way of knowing the true ownership of the *Charming Betsy*. However, it should be borne in mind that Murray stood to profit personally from seizing the ship. Marshall must have felt conflicted about punishing a military officer, but the equities favored Shattuck as the vessel's owner. While the courts could not provide redress for Murray, Marshall thought that Congress should. Indeed, that's precisely what happened: Congress reimbursed Murray for the full amount owed to Shattuck.[25]

THE OTHER MAJOR CASE to reach the Supreme Court in the 1804 term was another prize case. The Non-Intercourse Act of 1799 prohibited a vessel owned by a U.S. person from sailing *to* any French territory on penalty of forfeiture. The statute specifically authorized the president to instruct naval commanders to stop and examine any vessel when there was a "reason to suspect" that it was headed to French territory.[26] President Adams had authorized Secretary of the Navy Stoddert to issue orders pursuant to this act. On December 2, 1799, two U.S. frigates, the *Boston* and the *General Greene,* spotted a Danish brigantine sailing near Hispaniola in the Caribbean. They suspected that the Danish ship, the *Flying Fish*, could be an American vessel coming from French territory. Secretary of the Navy Stoddert instructed the captains in writing "to do all that in you lies to prevent all intercourse, where direct or circuitous, between the port of the United States and those of France and her dependencies, in cases where the vessels or cargoes are apparently, as well as really, American." Moreover, the secretary warned commanders to be especially vigilant that some vessels that were "really American" might be carrying Danish papers to elude the act. The secretary was quite explicit that the captains should ensure that any U.S. ships "bound *to or from* French ports, do not escape you."[27]

As the *Boston* and the *General Greene* approached, the *Flying Fish* attempted to flee. In their pursuit, the Americans observed someone on the *Flying Fish* tossing the logbook and other papers overboard. This raised their suspicion that it could be an American vessel disguised as Danish. Once they captured the *Flying Fish* and inspected it, they found a cargo of dry goods from the French port of Jérémie in what is now Haiti, where the ship had previously docked. They learned that the vessel was owned by Samuel Goodman, who was born in Prussia and spent years in the United States and on board U.S. ships before settling in St. Thomas, which was then a Danish island. It was unclear whether Goodman was American, Prussian, or Danish, but the ship's master spoke English with an American accent, the first mate was a U.S. citizen, and the cargo was undeniably French. The crew acknowledged that the ship had docked in Jérémie, but they claimed they had been forced to do so by French privateers, which was a lie. Taken together, the evidence seemed overwhelming that the crew was hiding something. Convinced that it was indeed a U.S. vessel, Captain George Little of the *Boston* seized the *Flying Fish* and directed it to Boston to be libeled. He expected to receive half the value of the ship and its cargo as his reward for capturing the vessel as provided by the 1799 Act.[28]

In Boston, District Court Judge John Lowell Jr. found that the *Flying Fish* was, in fact, a neutral Danish vessel that should not have been seized. He ordered the ship returned to Samuel Goodman without damages or costs. The district court found that under the law of nations, a belligerent power has the right to stop and examine a neutral vessel and that a neutral vessel must submit to the search. Judge Lowell concluded that the crew's failure to comply and its suspicious conduct meant that the *Flying Fish* was not entitled to damages.[29]

On appeal, the circuit court found that regardless of the nationality of the vessel's owner, Captain Little knew that the *Flying Fish* was coming *from* French territory but that the act prohibited only ships going *to* French territory. Therefore Little was, in any event, operating outside of the law and should pay damages, which were assessed in the amount of $8,504 (around $160,000 today), more than seven times his government salary.[30] The circuit court ignored the clear order of the secretary of the navy to Captain Little to seize all ships going *"to or from"* French territory even though Little had sworn an oath "to observe and obey the orders of the President and the orders of the officers appointed over me."[31] If Little had failed to carry out the secretary's order, he could have been court-martialed. Surely it was not fair to expect Little to parse through a federal statute and reach a conclusion that the secretary's order was improper. Little appealed to the Supreme Court.

In *Little v. Barreme*, Chief Justice Marshall delivered one of his most important decisions on the power of the executive branch. If Marshall wanted to avoid a confrontation with the executive, the case offered him several outs. Marshall might have decided that since the federal act did not *forbid* the seizure of ships coming *from* French territory there was no actual conflict with the executive's order. Alternatively, Marshall could have decided that the act infringed on the president's authority as commander in chief and struck it down as he had struck down part of the Judiciary Act of 1789 in *Marbury*.

Marshall clearly wrestled with the issue of whether to hold a naval commander liable for following orders that contradicted an act of Congress. "It is by no means clear," he acknowledged at the outset, "that the president . . . who is commander in chief of the armies and navies of the United States, might not, without any special authority for that purpose, in the then existing state of things, have empowered the officers commanding the armed vessels of the United Sates, to seize and send into port for adjudication, American vessels which were forfeited by being engaged in this illicit commerce." Marshall might have decided that the president's military authority in wartime extends so far as to order all U.S. vessels seized. Instead, he held that the president's command was voided by Congress' contrary intent.[32]

"I confess," Marshall admitted, "the first bias of my mind was very strong . . . that though the instructions of the executive could not give a right, they might yet excuse from damages." Marshall surely felt that the distinction "between the acts of civil and those of military officers" deserved to be weighed in favor of Captain Little. Also, the circumstances that Little found himself in, having to make a decision on his own at sea without the advice of legal counsel, argued that he should not bear the cost. After all, the claimant here could always apply to Congress for compensation. "But I have been convinced that I was mistaken," Marshall admitted. The chief justice had been persuaded by his colleagues that the executive's "instructions cannot change the nature of the transaction, or legalize an act which without those instructions would have been a plain trespass."[33] Not even the president could order a soldier to do something contrary to an act of Congress. Therefore he concluded that Captain Little must pay damages to the owner.

For a good soldier and an advocate for a strong military, this decision must have been especially hard. Marshall knew the suffering and isolation that soldiers face in the field of battle. A soldier in the field without benefit of counsel clearly cannot be expected to make independent judgments about the legality of the president's order. It seemed particularly unjust to impose a penalty against a distinguished naval officer. But as Marshall had established in *Marbury*, the president must be held accountable: The president's "instructions cannot change the nature of the transaction, or legalize an act which without those instructions would have been a plain trespass."[34] The president, after all, was empowered to execute only the laws that Congress adopted. He was merely the agent of Congress, as Marshall had famously argued in the Jonathan Robbins case.

Little v. Barreme stands as a robust counterargument against the claim that the president, as commander in chief, is supreme in wartime. Though some modern presidents have ignored this principle and initiated military actions without congressional authority, the precedent still endures. If Marshall's opinion strikes us today as antiquated or unfair, it is a measure of how much the imperial presidency has distorted our vision of the Constitution.

In just five years Marshall had so consolidated the Supreme Court's authority as a coequal branch of government that it could declare U.S. military operations abroad illegal. But that is only part of the story. At the same time that Marshall was fortifying the Court's position, Jefferson and his party were laying siege against the federal judiciary.

CHAPTER TWENTY

HIGH CRIMES

After Republicans had canceled the Supreme Court's term in 1802, Chief Justice Marshall rode the circuit from Virginia to North Carolina. He usually traveled on horseback with his slave Peter, leaving Robin Spurlock in Richmond to manage the household. Life on the road was difficult as travelers had to stay overnight in inns that were often dirty, crowded, and inconvenient. While spending the night at a tavern in Raleigh, Marshall discovered that Peter had failed to pack any breeches for him to wear in court. He had nothing but his riding clothes. So he sought out a tailor to sew a new pair of pants as quickly as possible. There was no time to sew a proper pair of dress pants. "I thought I should be a *sans culotte* only one day," he joked, referring to the French revolutionaries who wore working-class trousers. Unfortunately, all the tailors in Raleigh were too busy for the chief justice. "I have the extreme mortification to pass the whole term without that important article of dress," he wrote Polly.[1]

In June 1802, Marshall's father passed away on his farm in Kentucky. Thomas Marshall died with significant landholdings in Virginia and Kentucky, which passed to his sons. John Marshall, as the eldest, inherited more than one thousand acres at Oak Hill in Fauquier County. That summer Marshall moved the family to Oak Hill, near what today is Delaplane, to escape the heat and the noise of Richmond. Marshall's family gathered in the same house that Marshall had left twenty-seven years earlier to join the Virginia militia. Marshall's eldest son, Thomas, had just finished Princeton, and Jaquelin, Marshall's second son, was preparing to leave for Harvard that fall. Polly worried that Jaquelin would fall under the influence of the New England secessionists who were threatening to secede out of growing resentment toward southern Republicans.[2]

IN FEBRUARY 1805, the Senate opened the trial for the removal of Justice Samuel Chase. Old Baconface Chase had done his utmost over the course of several years to antagonize Republicans. He was notoriously abrasive and brazenly partisan. Among other sins, Chase was accused of skewing a series of trials against prominent Republicans. The most vivid example was James Callender's trial for violating the Sedition Act. Chase compelled a juror who was openly hostile to Callender to serve on the jury. He refused to allow Callender's defense counsel to question witnesses except by written questions submitted first to Chase, and he allegedly harassed the defense lawyer throughout the proceedings. Chase sentenced Callender to nine months in prison and a hefty fine of two hundred dollars (about four thousand dollars today). Republicans hurled invectives at Chase, which only inflamed him further. In the spring of 1803, while addressing a grand jury in Baltimore, Chase castigated the Republican Party. He charged that by repealing the federal circuit courts Republicans threatened to "take away all security for property and personal liberty" and that the government would "sink into a mobocracy."[3]

The knives were drawn. Republicans saw Chase as a proxy for Chief Justice Marshall and impeaching him as a chance to intimidate the whole federal judiciary.[4] President Jefferson wrote to one of the Republican congressional leaders: "Ought this seditious and official attack on the principles of our Constitution and on the proceedings of a State to go unpunished?" And he added, "I ask these questions for your consideration; for myself, it is better that I should not interfere."[5] As Henry Adams archly remarked, "Jefferson was somewhat apt to say that it was better he should not interfere in the same breath with which he interfered."[6] Jefferson advised the House leaders what charges to file against Chase and what evidence would be most damning. At Jefferson's suggestion, the House focused its prosecution on Chase's handling of the Callender trial.[7] Leaving little time for deliberation, Republicans quickly concluded their investigation of Justice Chase the same day the Senate voted to convict Judge John Pickering.

The articles of impeachment charged Chase with eight counts of acting "highly arbitrary, Oppressive, and unjust" and with "intent to oppress and procure the conviction of James T. Callender in his sedition trial" and making "an intemperate and inflammatory political harangue" before a grand jury among other procedural irregularities in multiple cases. There was no precedent, but none of these allegations sounded like the "[h]igh crimes and misdemeanors" that the Constitution required to remove a sitting justice.[8]

Though Chase's political diatribes probably offended Marshall, the chief justice respected Justice Chase's integrity and his service during the Revolutionary War. Marshall feared that the impeachment threatened the judiciary and the Constitution, and wrote to his brother James that the articles of impeachment "are sufficient to alarm the friends of a pure & of course an independent judiciary, if among those who rule our land there be any of that description."[9]

Chase's trial opened at 9:45 a.m. on Monday, February 4, 1805, in the Senate chamber. The usually grimy capital glistened under a thick blanket of snow that had fallen the week prior. Icicles hung precariously over the entrance to the Capitol. The trial drew a large and lively audience despite the freezing temperature and a steady northern wind that made the ride to the Capitol seem endless. As the president of the Senate, Aaron Burr, whose fondness for pomp and ceremony belied his republicanism, insisted that the chamber be transformed into a grand courtroom appropriate for the occasion. Burr sat center stage with benches covered in crimson on either side for the thirty-four members of the Senate. In front of him on one side was a box for the prosecuting House managers led by another of Marshall's distant cousins, the fiery John Randolph, and on the opposite side was a box for Justice Chase and his legal team led by Robert Goodloe Harper, an equally fierce Federalist senator from Chase's home state of Maryland. The rest of the Senate's ground floor accommodated members of the House, foreign diplomats, members of the executive branch, and military officers. The visitor's gallery was packed with members of the public. A special gallery was built below that for the curious wives of congressmen and senators to separate them from the unwashed public. Burr, whose promiscuous eye was legendary, would have appreciated the view of so many finely dressed women.[10]

Jefferson and the Republicans tried their utmost to influence the trial by persuading Burr that it was in his own interest to rule against Chase.[11] After ignoring the vice president for two years, suddenly the president and his cabinet warmly welcomed Burr into their inner circle despite his recent indictment for the murder of Alexander Hamilton. Jefferson invited Burr to the President's House with increasing frequency. Treasury Secretary Gallatin spent hours cultivating Burr in his home. Jefferson even considered supporting Burr for New York governor.[12] In a flurry of appointments, Jefferson named Burr's stepson a superior court judge in New Orleans, Burr's brother-in-law the secretary of the Louisiana Territory, and Burr's friend General James Wilkinson governor of the Louisiana Territory. Republican senators called on the New Jersey governor to dismiss the murder charges against Burr, and rumors circulated that Jefferson offered to pardon Burr if he would ensure a guilty verdict against Chase.[13] Despite all these inducements, Burr would be scrupulous in his conduct of the trial, which enraged Jefferson.[14]

Chase was represented by one of Maryland's most prominent lawyers, Luther Martin. He was a somber-faced man who had suffered the loss of several children and wives. Life's cruelties had taught him to stand alone against the current of popular opinion. As a Maryland delegate to the federal Constitutional Convention, Martin walked out in opposition to a strong central government. One of Martin's fellow delegates said that Martin "never speaks without tiring the patience of all who hear him."[15] Martin became an outspoken anti-federalist but later joined the Federalists to oppose Jefferson, whom he distrusted more than a strong central government. Martin was well-respected for his legal acumen, but he was not well-liked. Jefferson once called Martin an "unprincipled and impudent federal bull-dog."[16]

Martin's defense strategy was to show that the articles of impeachment had failed to identify a single crime and had misquoted and mischaracterized Chase throughout. One of the key witnesses for the defense was William Marshall, one of the chief justice's younger brothers, who was the clerk of the court during the Callender trial. William Marshall corroborated Chase's own testimony that the articles of impeachment misrepresented the facts of the case.

Congressman John Randolph, another distant Marshall cousin, assumed the role of the chief prosecutor against Justice Chase. Randolph looked like a tall, skinny child with a piercing, womanly voice.[17] What Randolph lacked in legal knowledge and skill he tried to compensate for in bombast and hyperbole. His intemperate performance during the trial only confirmed in the minds of most observers that the prosecution had no case. But even in the absence of any evidence of criminal conduct, the Republicans had a majority to convict—unless at least three Republican senators switched sides.

Over the course of Chase's trial, the prosecution's case evaporated. Randolph surprised everyone by calling the chief justice as a witness. Marshall was called to testify because as a member of the Richmond bar he had observed Callender's sedition trial. The articles of impeachment charged

Chase with demonstrating "manifest injustice, partiality, and intemperance." Marshall appeared uncharacteristically ill at ease being questioned by Randolph, who had declared his intention to rid the federal judiciary of men like his distant cousin.

"Did you observe anything unusual in the conduct on the part of the counsel towards the court, or in the court towards the counsel," Randolph queried.

"I would probably be better able to answer the question if it were made more determinate," Marshall cautiously replied.[18]

Randolph questioned whether Justice Chase was especially belligerent toward the defendant's counsel during Callender's trial. Marshall testified that Callender's counsel kept arguing that the sedition law was unconstitutional and that Justice Chase kept cutting him off by insisting that the constitutionality of the law was not a proper subject for a jury to decide.

"Was there any misunderstanding between the counsel and the court?" Randolph asked, fishing for answers.

Marshall answered squarely: "On the part of the judge it seemed to be a disgust with regard to the mode adopted by [Callender's] counsel." For a judge to object to the conduct of a defense counsel hardly sounded like an impeachable offense.[19]

Randolph pushed Marshall to admit that there were other procedural irregularities, but Marshall refused to be pinned down, and Randolph was losing patience. "I am aware of the delicacy of the question I am about to put," he acknowledged, but he wondered, "Did it appear to you, sir, that during the course of the trial, the conduct of judge Chase was mild and conciliatory?" The visitors' gallery broke into loud laughter. No one would ever describe gruff Old Baconface as "mild" or "conciliatory."

Marshall paused for a moment to consider his reply. "Perhaps the question you propound to me would be more correct if I were asked what his conduct was during the course of the trial."[20]

At this point Vice President Burr interrupted the prosecution to query

Marshall. "Do you recollect whether the conduct of the judge on this trial was tyrannical, overbearing, and oppressive?" he asked. Burr had tossed the chief justice a softball.

"I will state the facts," Marshall began. "The counsel for [Callender] persisted in arguing the question of the constitutionality of the sedition law, in which they were constantly repressed by judge Chase. Judge Chase checked [defendant's counsel] whenever he came to that point, and after having resisted repeated checks, [counsel] appeared to be determined to abandon the cause." Marshall raised his voice for dramatic effect. "If this is not considered tyrannical, oppressive and overbearing, I know nothing else that was so."[21] It was a wry remark theatrically underplayed. The point was made.

Randolph tried one last effort to wrestle the chief justice into admitting that Chase had acted inappropriately: "Did you hear judge Chase apply any unusual epithets; such as young men, or young gentlemen, to the counsel?" Marshall admitted that Chase may have used such terms to describe Callender's attorney, William Wirt, who was then thirty.[22] That was all that Marshall would concede. The assembled senators could not have been impressed with the argument that calling someone a young man was grounds for impeachment.

The trial ended on March 1 when the senators acquitted Justice Chase on each of the eight counts by a wide margin. The vote was a vote of no confidence in Randolph by his fellow senators.[23] Publicly, Jefferson tried to distance himself from the whole mess. He took no responsibility and, in the words of Henry Adams, "held himself studiously aloof."[24] Privately, Jefferson abandoned any hope of cleaning out the judiciary. He later groused in letters that impeachment was "a mere scarecrow" and a "farce not to be tried again."[25] The Republicans had tried and failed to use impeachment as a partisan weapon. Jefferson blamed Burr for failing to impeach Justice Chase. Henry Adams later wrote that "Chase's impeachment was a blow from which the Republican Party never wholly recovered."[26] But Marshall and an independent judiciary had been spared.

CHAPTER TWENTY-ONE

TREASON

I n March 1805, Marshall swore in Jefferson as president for the second time. In the election of 1804, Jefferson had easily trounced Marshall's friend and co-commissioner to Paris, Charles Cotesworth Pinckney, by 162 electoral votes to 14. The Federalist Party was crushed. A reporter for the *Aurora* wryly observed that at Jefferson's first inauguration the chief justice had turned his back to the president-elect. Whether Marshall had acted out of disrespect or bad manners, this time the chief justice faced Jefferson directly.[1] After years of bitter enmity between the two cousins, it's unclear whether the reason Marshall did not turn his back was out of respect or distrust.

After the Chase impeachment, Republicans were unlikely to launch another assault on the Supreme Court. Congress was preoccupied with a host of more pressing issues arising out of the acquisition of the Louisiana Territory. Jefferson's second term might have been a welcome respite for Marshall had it not been for Jefferson's plan to rid himself and the nation of Aaron Burr.

Jefferson bore a grudge against Burr for challenging him in the 1800 presidential election and for the acquittal of Justice Chase. With Jefferson's blessing, the national Republican Party refused to renominate Burr as vice president in 1804 and did not support Burr when he ran for New York governor. Burr's opponents crudely attacked his character and his well-earned reputation for promiscuity. He was falsely accused of running a bordello out of his home, cross-dressing as a woman, and enjoying sex with young men. Burr was defeated by the Federalist machine candidate, Morgan Lewis, by nearly nine thousand votes.[2]

Burr decided he would head west and make a fresh start. He had a grand albeit vague ambition either to develop western land or liberate Mexico and either annex it to the United States or perhaps create his own independent state. Burr repeatedly met in secret with the commander of the army and governor of the Louisiana Territory, General James Wilkinson.[3] Burr proposed to Wilkinson that he provoke a war with Spain as a pretext for Burr to invade Mexico—or possibly lead a secession of the western territory from the United States. Wilkinson indicated his support for whatever Burr was planning.[4] Recognizing the need for secrecy, Wilkinson invented a cipher to encrypt their secret communications.[5] Wilkinson also gave Burr a letter of introduction to the governor of the Indiana Territory. Burr toured the Louisiana Territory, trying to recruit young men for a private army with the promise of land in exchange for liberating Mexico from Spain. At the time, many westerners despised Spain and wanted access to Mexican land. Kentucky Senator John Adair and the governor of Tennessee, General Andrew Jackson, were among those who expressed support for Burr's campaign.

It was never clear whether Burr actually intended to liberate Mexico in particular or Latin America in general, whether he was acting to enlarge the United States, or whether he just wanted to tear off a piece of the Louisiana Territory for his own empire. Whatever Burr was intending, his activities were inconsistent with any single plot. In Ohio he ordered the construction of fifteen boats to carry up to seven hundred men into battle. He sought support for his expedition from the ambassadors of Britain and its adversary Spain. At the same time, Burr also asked Jefferson if he would appoint him ambassador to Britain. This suggests that Burr was not sure whether he planned to make war against Spain or the United States.

Burr's activities were widely known at the time. As early as 1805, U.S. newspapers published reports that Burr was planning to invade Mexico or start a secessionist movement in the west. During this time, Burr met with Jefferson several times seeking a diplomatic appointment. Jefferson had plenty of opportunity to ask Burr what he was up to, but apparently Jefferson found these stories too incredible to believe and said nothing to Burr. Jefferson had reason to doubt the accuracy of these allegations, which were spread largely by western Federalists with the intention of making Jefferson look ineffectual. (By coincidence, two of Burr's chief accusers were John Marshall's cousin Humphrey Marshall and his brother-in-law Joseph Hamilton Daveiss.) Nevertheless, in October 1806, Jefferson ordered Wilkinson to report on Burr's activities.[6]

If Jefferson genuinely believed that Burr was on the verge of leading a serious rebellion, he would not have relied on General Wilkinson, whom newspapers had already named as one of Burr's co-conspirators.[7] Once alerted by Jefferson, Wilkinson recognized the danger to himself.[8] The general decided it was time to betray Burr and transform an act of treachery into heroism.

That same month, Wilkinson received a letter in cipher from former New Jersey Senator Jonathan Dayton, a Burr acolyte.[9] The letter was hand delivered to General Wilkinson by Burr's friend Samuel Swartwout, and it described Burr's half-baked plot to invade Mexico. The letter falsely boasted that Burr's army was moving ahead. But the general knew that Burr did not pose a serious threat to the status quo. Wilkinson had just concluded an agreement with Spain that settled the outstanding border dispute, which made war with Spain highly unlikely. Burr's plot was already falling apart.

Dayton had also sent a copy of the cipher letter to General Wilkinson through another messenger, Dr. Erick Bollman. To prevent Swartwout and

Bollman from exposing his own role in the plot, Wilkinson arrested both men on charges of treason.[10] He wrote to President Jefferson alleging that Burr was planning an imminent attack on New Orleans with an army of thousands. Wilkinson must have known that this was not true. He enclosed a decoded version of the cipher letter from Senator Dayton, which he altered to make it appear more incriminating. Wilkinson apparently destroyed the original cipher letters so that no one could contradict his version of what Burr intended.[11] Senator Dayton was later arrested but never tried.

President Jefferson knew that General Wilkinson was notoriously unreliable and was a coconspirator.[12] Why else would Burr—or Dayton—have described their plot to the army's commanding general, and why would they be sending the letter in a secret code that only Wilkinson knew? Jefferson also had reason to believe that General Wilkinson was a spy working for Spain—which was true.[13] Since 1797, the Spanish government had kept Wilkinson, known by the inauspicious code name Agent 13, on a two-thousand-dollar annual retainer (roughly forty thousand dollars today).[14]

But despite the evidence that Wilkinson was a traitor, Jefferson valued the general's personal loyalty to him. When, for example, Jefferson told the general that he feared that a large standing army could threaten his presidency, Wilkinson ordered his soldiers to swear allegiance to the president rather than to the United States.[15] Though Jefferson received repeated warnings that Wilkinson was a spy, he promoted him as commander of the army, governor of the Louisiana Territory, and commissioner of Indian affairs. After Burr's trial, Wilkinson faced multiple courts-martial and a congressional investigation, but Jefferson steadfastly defended him.[16]

Jefferson also had good reason to know that Burr did not write the cipher letter. Jefferson knew Burr's florid prose style. The letter did not sound like him, and it referred to Burr in the third person.[17] Rather than questioning Wilkinson's loyalty or investigating further, Jefferson addressed Congress in January of 1807 and declared Burr "guilty of treason" and ordered his arrest. The penalty for treason was hanging.

Wilkinson seized the opportunity to declare martial law in New Orleans, appropriating for himself unlimited military power. He intimidated the local population and tossed his critics into jail. He arrested all of Burr's associates and their lawyers. Jefferson defended Wilkinson's brutal measures as necessary to preserve public order.[18] He reassured Wilkinson that "[o]n great occasions every good officer must be ready to risk himself in going beyond the strict line of law, when the public preservation requires it."[19]

In December 1807, thirty young recruits assembled on Blennerhassett Island in the Ohio River near Parkersburg in what is now West Virginia. Harman Blennerhassett, a wealthy eccentric who was funding Burr's expedition, owned part of the island. But Burr was absent. He was already floating down the Ohio River toward New Orleans to meet Wilkinson on a barge extravagantly equipped for his comfort. On December 10, Blennerhassett heard rumors that the West Virginia militia was about to attack his island. Before the militia arrived, Blennerhassett and the young men fled by boat, and Burr's "army" evaporated.[20] The events on Blennerhassett Island were the critical linchpin in the federal government's charges against Burr.

Before reaching New Orleans, Burr voluntarily submitted to authorities in Mississippi where a grand jury was called in February. The charge of treason was quickly dismissed, and Burr continued on toward New Orleans. Wilkinson ordered his men to capture Burr and bring him to justice. Burr surrendered to Wilkinson's soldiers in Alabama and was brought to Washington to face trial.

The case against Burr would be difficult to prove. While it was true that Burr had talked about fighting Spain—a plan he shared with Andrew Jackson—there was no solid evidence of treason.[21] Levying war against Spain was not treason. At worst, it may have been a misdemeanor in violation of the Neutrality Act of 1794. War against Spain was a popular cause throughout the west. Indeed, Jefferson, when he was secretary of state, had secretly plotted just such a military expedition with Citizen Genet.

Jefferson, however, was not interested in the truth about Burr. He considered Burr "a crooked gun, or other perverted machine, whose aim or stroke you could never be sure of."[22] Jefferson rightly feared that Burr might challenge Jefferson's chosen successor, James Madison. And the president had a score to settle. Jefferson arranged for Burr to be indicted and tried in Richmond where he could be confident of a jury sympathetic to his aim. By moving the trial to Richmond, Jefferson placed Burr's fate in the hands of the U.S. circuit court presided over by John Marshall. If the Republicans had not insisted that Supreme Court justices ride circuit, Marshall would have had nothing to do with Burr's trial. By a strange twist of history, Jefferson's archrival in Virginia would sit in judgment on Jefferson's archrival in the Republican Party.

Was Jefferson's decision to send the trial to Richmond an error of judgment or a carefully calculated ploy? Perhaps Jefferson thought that he could destroy Marshall by dropping an explosive criminal case in his lap. If Marshall dismissed the charges or if the jury acquitted Burr, Marshall would be condemned in the court of public opinion.

Before Burr's trial even began, the two messengers received by General Wilkinson, Swartwout and Bollman, were sent to Washington for trial in January 1807. Jefferson ordered that neither Bollman nor Swartwout should be allowed to see an attorney as guaranteed by the Sixth Amendment to the Constitution.[23] Jefferson and Secretary of State James Madison personally interrogated Bollman in the marine barracks where he was being held. The president tried to coax Bollman into implicating Burr in a war against the United States, but Bollman insisted that Burr was interested only in liberating Mexico. Jefferson persuaded Bollman to write out his account and assured him that no one else would see his statement. Jefferson later broke his promise and had Bollman's written statement introduced against Burr at trial before the D.C. Circuit Court.[24]

Charles Lee, Marshall's friend and Marbury's attorney, intervened on behalf of Bollman and Swartwout and appealed to the U.S. Supreme Court for their release. On February 13, 1807, the Supreme Court heard their appeal. The central issue in the case turned on the question of what constituted treason.

Article III of the Constitution spelled out that "[t]reason against the United States, shall consist only in levying war against them" and that "[n]o person shall be convicted of treason unless on the testimony of two witnesses to the same overt act, or on confession in open court." Since the beginning of the Republic, there had been only five prior convictions for treason. These had resulted from the 1794 Whiskey Rebellion and the 1799 Fries's Rebellion among the Pennsylvania Dutch. All five cases had been tried in the circuit court for Pennsylvania, none reached the Supreme Court, and all the defendants were later pardoned, so these cases did not provide precedents for interpreting the law of treason.[25] The 1790 federal crimes act made it a crime punishable by death to make war against the United States or aid the enemy. Under that act, a person accused of treason was guaranteed legal counsel, which Bollman and Swartwout had been denied.[26]

Charles Lee, joined by attorneys Robert Goodloe Harper and Francis Scott Key, who later composed the national anthem, argued before the Supreme Court that in the absence of an overt act of levying war, the defendants could not be charged with treason. The government's case rested entirely on an affidavit submitted by Wilkinson that was based on his interrogation of Swartwout and his unauthenticated translation of the cipher letter. It was an exceedingly weak case. Attorney General Caesar Augustus Rodney admitted that the affidavit alone was not enough to sustain a conviction and that if Burr's only aim was to foment war against Mexico then that was not treasonable. However, the government argued that since the president had declared that Burr was engaged in war against the United States, that alone was sufficient to convict Bollman and Swartwout of treason.[27]

On February 21, Chief Justice Marshall read out his unanimous opinion to a packed courtroom. The whole country understood that the Court's decision as to the evidence and the definition of treason could affect the outcome of Burr's trial in Richmond. Once again Marshall was in the midst of a heated political battle. In his opinion, the chief justice stuck to the literal language of the Constitution. To prove that the defendants were guilty of treason, the government must show that they actually engaged in war against the United States. It was not sufficient to show that they intended to do so. The government had to produce at least two witnesses to the same overt act, and General Wilkinson's affidavit did not prove that any overt act had occurred. Even assuming the witnesses had intended to commit treason, mere conspiracy was not punishable under the Constitution. So Marshall freed Bollman and Swartwout in what would be a dress rehearsal for Burr's trial two months later.[28]

Back in Richmond that spring, Marshall could not have been looking forward to Burr's trial. He knew he was facing a political trap. Virginians were eager to see Jefferson's nemesis hang. The trial was a public sensation. People from all over the country descended on Richmond to watch the proceedings. Since Burr was staying at the Eagle Tavern, Marshall thought it would be most amenable to conduct the proceedings there. The pretrial proceedings opened in a spare room at the Eagle on March 30 with Marshall presiding as a circuit court judge. The Richmond newspapers complained that given the number of spectators eager to observe the historic trial, the limited seating was reminiscent of the "Spanish Inquisition."[29] Marshall agreed to move the proceedings to the courthouse, but when even the courthouse could not accommodate the press and the public, the proceedings were moved to the Virginia House of Delegates. Over the next several months, as many as six thousand people mobbed Richmond hoping to catch a glimpse of Aaron Burr in the dock, elegantly attired in a new black silk suit with his hair perfectly coiffed and powdered. (If Burr was going to be hanged, he was going to hang fashionably.) Visitors from across the country camped along the James River just to witness this historic event. People packed into taverns and wagered huge sums on Burr's conviction.[30] Among those who crowded into the courtroom was the New York writer Washington Irving, whom Burr had invited to chronicle his trial.

Marshall found that there was probable cause to try Burr for violations of the 1794 Neutrality Act for plotting war against Mexico. However, he was not impressed by the evidence presented by the government on the charge of treason. The prosecution presented affidavits from Generals Wilkinson and William Eaton even though neither general had witnessed any overt act against the United States.

Marshall chastised the government for not providing any evidence of the alleged army of thousands of men. "[T]o constitute his crime, troops must be embodied, they must be actually assembled; and these are facts which cannot remain invisible," Marshall insisted. "Treason may be machinated in secret, but it can be perpetuated only in the open day and in the eye of the world."[31] If Burr had raised an army of thousands, surely there must have been at least two witnesses. "What could veil his troops from human sight?" Marshall asked. "[A]n invisible army is not an instrument of war."[32]

More than five weeks had passed since the Supreme Court had issued its opinion in the Bollman case. The government had more than enough time to find witnesses to prove Burr's guilt.

The chief justice released Burr on ten thousand dollars bail pending a grand jury investigation of the more serious charge of treason. The local newspapers denounced Marshall for not demanding a higher bail. "This act of the Chief Justice has certainly injured him considerably in the opinion of his country," warned the *Virginia Argus*. And if as a result "a traitor should escape by his contrivance, his consolation will be in the applause of that party [the Federalists] to which he is attached in opposition to his country and whose approbation he prefers to that of the rest of mankind in the present and of posterity in future ages."[33]

To make matters worse, in a rare moment of poor judgment, Marshall had attended a party given in his honor by one of Burr's attorneys, and Burr had appeared at the event. "What will the people of Virginia . . . think when they learn, that the chief justice has feasted at the same convivial board with Aaron Burr?" asked one local writer. "We regard such conduct as a willful prostration of the dignity of his own character, and a wanton insult he might have spared his country."[34] The fete was widely reported in the press as a "Feast of Traitors."[35] The trial had not even begun, and the Virginia press was already savaging Marshall's reputation. Jefferson must have been delighted.

The grand jury was impaneled in late May and did not return an indictment on treason until the end of June. Public interest in the outcome was so great that the local press gave a nearly verbatim report on each day's proceedings.[36] Jury selection did not begin until mid-August, and the trial finally opened on August 17, 1807.

Burr's legal team had expanded to include two Framers of the Constitution—Luther Martin and Edmund Randolph, who was also a former attorney general and governor of Virginia. Burr also added two popular local lawyers to appeal to the Virginia jurors—John Wickham and Benjamin Botts. And Burr hired a prominent member of the New York bar, John Baker, just to keep him off the government's legal team. The government's legal team was notably weaker. U.S. Attorney George Hay led the prosecution, repeatedly bumbling the government's case. He relied principally on William Wirt, one of Virginia's best legal minds. The other members of the government's team included Virginia's lieutenant governor, Alexander MacRae, who provided a little star power but mostly bored the assembled public, and Attorney General Rodney, whose performance was so lackluster that he quit in the middle of the trial.[37]

President Jefferson publicly voiced his confidence that Burr was guilty and sent orders from Monticello to the prosecutors about how to conduct the trial. Jefferson even provided prosecutors with a stack of signed presidential pardons with a space for inserting a name so the prosecutors could offer pardons to anyone willing to testify against Burr. Jefferson confided to an ally that the evidence "will satisfy the world, if not the judges of Burr's guilt."[38]

Burr's lawyers demanded that President Jefferson be subpoenaed to testify as to his role. They also demanded that Jefferson be required to turn over original copies of his correspondence with General Wilkinson.

Once again, Marshall faced a confrontation with Jefferson and sought to find a practical compromise. Rather than requiring the president to appear in person, Marshall ruled that Jefferson must turn over his correspondence with Wilkinson. The president claimed that private correspondence within the executive branch was protected by "executive privilege" and could not be subpoenaed. This was the first time that a president refused to comply with a subpoena. (One hundred and seventy years later, President Nixon's lawyers would refer to this case as a precedent for refusing to turn over tape recordings of his conversation during the Watergate investigation.) However, Jefferson, too, wanted to avoid a direct confrontation with the chief justice, so he "voluntarily" released the documents to the court. Burr's attorneys used this correspondence to cast doubt on Wilkinson's credibility.

When General Wilkinson entered the courtroom, all eyes turned to observe Burr's accuser. Washington Irving recorded that Wilkinson "strutted into court . . . swelling like a turkey cock, and bracing himself up for the encounter of Burr's eye." Burr took no notice of the general bedecked in his dress uniform until Wilkinson's name was called. Then "Burr turned his head, looked him full in the face with one of his piercing regards, swept his eye over his whole person from head to foot, as if to scan its dimensions, and then coolly resumed his former position . . . tranquilly as ever." Irving was impressed by Burr's "admirable" composure, "no affectation of disdain or defiance; a slight expression of contempt . . . such as you would show any person to whom you were indifferent, but whom you considered mean and contemptible." Though Irving did not agree with Burr's politics, his grace made him a sympathetic figure in Irving's eyes.[39]

From the outset of the trial, the prosecutors struggled against the paucity of hard evidence. They could show only that Burr had talked about levying war, though it was far from clear it was against the United States. Wilkinson's testimony was contradicted. The prosecutors could not produce a single witness to an overt act of making war against the United States. They tried to fill this gap by arguing that the overt act consisted in Burr's assembling recruits on Blennerhassett Island. In other words, evidence of an intent to commit treason was sufficient to constitute the crime.

Marshall responded that intent cannot substitute for the lack of an overt act; it can be introduced into evidence only as an element of the overt act of levying war.[40] Leaving aside the fact that the purpose of the gathering was not clear, that the prosecution had no witnesses, and that there was no overt act of levying war, it was impossible to connect whatever happened on the island to the defendant. The most glaring obstacle for the prosecutors was that Burr was not even present on the island at the time.[41]

In desperation, U.S. Attorney Hay reached for a novel argument: the ancient British common law doctrine of "constructive treason."[42] Constructive treason gave British courts broad authority to treat a mere statement critical of the king as treason. Constructive treason was a convenient way to stifle dissent. It was precisely the kind of despotic measure that Americans had rebelled against. If the court tolerated constructive treason, the government could censor anyone's speech. Republicans, who had charged that the Alien and Sedition Acts violated First Amendment rights, now found themselves on the flip side of the argument. Marshall firmly rejected constructive treason and demanded that the government meet the stricter standard for treason according to the letter of the Constitution.[43] It was a courageous stand in the face of hostile public opinion.

Burr's attorneys then asked Marshall to rule that the jury could not hear any evidence that did not prove an overt act of levying war. The effect of this ruling would be to exclude virtually all the testimony against Burr as well as the cipher letter, none of which showed an overt act. Marshall ruled that none of the evidence pertaining to Burr's character or any events other than what happened on Blennerhassett Island could be presented to the jury. In effect, Marshall directed the jury to acquit Burr of treason.[44] On September 1, 1807, the jury found Burr not guilty. Burr's life was spared.

The press erupted again with another round of vicious attacks on Marshall's character and motives for acquitting Burr. One critic charged that "[t]o the Federalists Mr. Marshall is indebted for all his influence," and that he had manipulated the law to serve the Federalist cause.[45] The *Virginia Argus* declared that Marshall's conduct of the trial had proved that an independent judiciary "is a very pernicious thing." And it called for an amendment giving the President the power to remove any judge at the request of a majority of both houses of Congress without the need to impeach.[46]

Under pressure from Jefferson for a conviction, Hay now sought to try Burr for the misdemeanor of violating the Neutrality Act by conspiring to wage war against Spain. Since Marshall ruled that the government's evidence was inadmissible, the jury again acquitted Burr. Then the prosecutor tried one more tactic: He asked the court to commit Burr to face trial for treason and violations of the Neutrality Act in either Kentucky or Ohio, where presumably more evidence might be gathered. Marshall listened to another month of testimony and argument before deciding that Burr could be tried in Ohio only on the lesser charge of violating the Neutrality Act. Ultimately, the federal government conceded that they did not have enough evidence to prosecute, and they abandoned their efforts. By then, Jefferson could be confident that Burr would no longer threaten him—either in politics or in the judgment of history.

With Burr's acquittal, enraged Republicans turned against Marshall. Rather than blame the prosecutors for overreaching, they vilified the chief justice. Republicans accused Marshall of playing party politics and taking sides with a traitor against the president. A mob in Baltimore burned Marshall in effigy.[47] The Virginia press was particularly vicious. William Thompson, writing under the pen name Lucius, attacked the chief justice in a series of articles that were widely circulated. He accused Marshall of having "eaten of the same bread, and drank of the same cups" as the trai-tor, "[i]gnorant of the satanic services he was mediating." He continued that Marshall had exhibited conduct "disgraceful to the character of a judge" and that he had "prostrated the dignity of the chief justice of the United States." Marshall had manifested "culpable partiality towards the accused."[48]

Marshall knew the risk to his own reputation and acknowledged as much in his opinion: "That this court dares not usurp power is most true. That this court dares not shrink from its duty is not less true. No man is desirous of placing himself in a disagreeable situation . . . But if he have no choice in the case, if there be no alternative presented to him but a derelic-tion of duty or the opprobrium of those who are denominated the world, he merits the contempt as well as the indignation of his country who can hesi-tate which to embrace."[49]

Marshall's conduct of Burr's trial was the greatest act of political cour-age in his long career. He had no personal interest in sparing Burr's life, but by rejecting the argument for constructive treason, Marshall did more to secure free expression and prevent tyranny than any other court in our history.

Jefferson blamed Marshall for engineering Burr's acquittal. Years later, he still fumed that Marshall's "twistifications" in Burr's trial, as in *Mar-bury*, "show how dexterously he can reconcile law to his personal biases." And he accused Marshall of shrouding his "rancorous hatred" against the government with "cunning and sophistry."[50] It was politically expedient for the president to attack the judiciary rather than admit the weakness in his own legal position. An independent judiciary can be an inconvenience to an ambitious president.

But Jefferson consoled himself that "[t]he nation will judge both the of-fender & judges for themselves." The people "will see that one of the great co-ordinate branches of the government, setting itself in opposition to the other two, and to the common sense of the nation, proclaims impunity to the class of offenders which endeavors to overturn the Constitution, and are themselves protected in it by the Constitution itself." Jefferson urged Congress to amend the Constitution to limit the judiciary in the future and make it possible for the president to remove a judge for any reason with the consent of two-thirds of both houses without the "farce" of an impeachment trial. "If [the court's] protection of Burr produces this amendment," he thought, "it will do more good than his condemnation would have done."[51]

Though Burr's acquittal did not produce the desired constitutional amendment, Jefferson had reason to be grateful for the outcome. At considerable risk to his own political standing, Marshall unwittingly rescued Jefferson's historical reputation. If Jefferson had succeeded in obtaining a guilty verdict and Burr had been hanged, Jefferson's legacy would be tainted. He would be remembered today not as a defender of civil liberties but as a vicious tyrant who squelched dissent, manipulated the justice system, and executed his political rival in cold blood.[52]

CHAPTER TWENTY-TWO

ESTRANGEMENT

After only six years of meeting in the new Capitol, the Senate began to disintegrate, literally. The walls and ceiling cracked and crumbled. The polished wooden floors warped and rotted.[1] Senators dusted plaster off their heads when they rose to speak. In the frantic rush to complete the Capitol before the election of 1800, contractors had used inferior materials and shoddy craftsmen. Faced with the need to restore the Capitol, Republicans desired something more majestic that belied their democratic principles. Congress instructed the Capitol's second architect, Benjamin Henry Latrobe, to redesign the entire Senate wing. Latrobe moved the Senate upstairs to the same level as the House in an enlarged and sumptuously decorated chamber. Latrobe also designed a new chamber underneath the Senate for the Supreme Court. After a decade of meeting in a cramped makeshift committee room, Marshall and his brethren were pleased with their spacious new courtroom.

Latrobe had designed a novel semicircular vaulted ceiling. The engineering of the ceiling was so innovative that no one could be confident it would bear its own weight during the construction. One of the assistant architects, in fact, was crushed to death when a vault collapsed on him. Latrobe designed a long mahogany bar and bench for the Court and a private robing room and space for the justices to mingle after hearing arguments.[2] The formal courtroom signaled that the Supreme Court had assumed a more equal footing with the other branches of government.

When the ailing Justice Moore retired in 1804, Jefferson had his first chance to appoint an associate justice. He named William Johnson, only thirty-two, a staunch Republican on the South Carolina Supreme Court. Johnson had clerked in the law offices of Charles Cotesworth Pinckney, so Marshall knew Johnson by reputation. Johnson could be argumentative and sometimes disagreed with his colleagues; but Marshall's gregarious personality, unfailing wit, and soothing temperament were seductive. Marshall's gentility often masked his searing intellect. When he could not win over someone from the opposing side, Marshall managed to find common ground. Rather than remain a Republican stalwart, Johnson soon fell under Marshall's influence. Johnson became an avid defender of a strong central government.

When Justice Paterson died in 1806 from injuries suffered in a coach accident, Jefferson appointed Henry Brockholst Livingston. Justice Livingston, forty-nine, was a Republican on the New York Supreme Court (and a forebear of both Presidents Bush). Republicans assumed he would be a tough opponent for Marshall, but his warm, open personality mirrored Marshall's own affability. The two got along famously, and over his long tenure, Livingston dissented from Marshall's opinions only eight times out of more than four hundred cases.[3]

Though Jefferson opposed expanding the size of the federal judiciary when Adams did it, he relished the opportunity to name a third justice and persuaded Congress to add a seventh justice to the Supreme Court. In 1807, he named Thomas Todd, forty-two, another reliable Republican, who was chief justice of the highest court in Kentucky. Justice Todd, like Marshall, grew up on the Virginia frontier, and he, too, was quickly seduced by

Marshall's genial manner. In two decades on the court, Todd dissented only once from the chief justice.[4] There were now three Republicans and four Federalists living, eating, and voting together in Marshall's cozy fraternity.

Marshall spent as much time as possible back in Richmond caring for Polly and raising five sons and one daughter, ages four through twenty-five. Polly remained in "wretched health," he reported. "Her nervous system is so affected that she cannot set in a room while a person walks across the floor." In the spring of 1809, the seventeen-year cicadas returned to Virginia. From May through June, Richmond's streets and yards were littered with mounds of dark exoskeletons. After seventeen years of solitary slumber, they emerged with ecstatic and incessant shrieks of liberation that would drive anyone to distraction. For Polly Marshall, the noise and the carnage must have been especially agonizing. At Christmas it was necessary to move Polly out of town to avoid any celebratory noise that might set her off.[5] For a man as naturally gregarious and hearty as Marshall, it was difficult to comprehend his wife's frailty. "I am entirely excluded from society by her situation," Marshall wrote.[6] When he was away from her, Marshall worried incessantly. "The weather has been so very cold as to fill me with apprehensions for you," he wrote Polly. He feared Polly would expose herself "to more cold than is consistent with your health or safety."[7] Her declining health haunted him.

But Polly was not his only concern. After graduating from Princeton, Marshall's eldest, Thomas, decided to abandon his ambition to become a lawyer and chose farming instead. Marshall did not mask his disappointment. Thomas, like his father and grandfather, would later represent Fauquier County in the Virginia General Assembly. The second-oldest son, Jaquelin, quit his studies at Harvard to join his brother as a farmer. Marshall felt he could not raise a girl on his own, so he sent his one daughter, Mary, to be raised by his sister Elizabeth in Berkeley County, more than 150 miles away. Marshall worried most about the three younger boys, John,

James, and Edward. He sent them to Harvard, where they all floundered. John was expelled, and James quit.[8] Only the youngest, Edward, managed to graduate under the watchful eyes of Harvard's President John Thornton Kirkland.[9] When John and James turned sixteen, Marshall arranged through Bushrod Washington to apprentice them to Willing & Francis, a counting house in Philadelphia. Marshall's expectations of his sons were not high. He so doubted James's character that he wrote to his son's future employer and asked the firm to "exercise the authority of a Father, a Guardian & a master" to prevent his son from "sliding into bad company." If his son misbehaved, he urged that James should be "firmly & sternly corrected."[10] Marshall's worst fears about James later proved well-founded.

WHEN THE THIRTEEN ORIGINAL STATES declared their independence from Britain, many of them possessed large claims to western territory. During the decade that followed, Virginia, Connecticut, Massachusetts, and New York ceded their claims to the United States, and these territories formed the new states of Vermont and Kentucky. Georgia, however, was one of the states that refused to cede land. It claimed a vast undeveloped territory known as the Yazoo lands after the Yazoo River that traversed it. The Yazoo lands encompassed all of Alabama and Mississippi. A succession of Georgia's governors arrogated to themselves the power to issue land grants to hordes of foreign and domestic speculators. The governors may have had some personal stake in these deals, for they sometimes issued multiple grants to the same property or nonexistent property. As a practical matter, the land was largely inaccessible and occupied by Cherokee and Creek, who were not moving without a fight.[11]

In 1795, the Georgia legislature approved a bill granting four land companies thirty-five million acres of the Yazoo for five hundred thousand dollars, or approximately one and a half cents per acre. These four companies included many prominent financiers, judges, and politicians from Georgia,

South Carolina, and Pennsylvania, who had bought off a majority of the Georgia state legislature. They offered each legislator six hundred to one thousand dollars or stock in the land companies for their votes. The director of the largest of the four companies was Georgia's U.S. senator, James Gunn, who threatened legislators who opposed the sale. Georgia's governor, George Mathews, at first vetoed the sale and then was "persuaded" to change his mind by Senator Gunn.[12]

When the public learned that nearly 70 percent of Georgia's western territory had been given away for almost nothing to a handful of powerful speculators and that the legislators had been bought off, there was a storm of protest led by Georgia's other U.S. senator, James Jackson. A fresh crop of legislators unsullied by the land deal was swept into office in 1796. One of their first legislative acts was to repeal the land grant of 1795 and offer to refund the original sale price. The sale was voided on the questionable ground that it had violated Georgia's own constitutional requirement that all laws must be "necessary and proper for the good of the state," which this sale plainly was not. By the time the act of 1796 was adopted, many of the original investors had already resold their land. New England speculators were especially hungry for new territory to develop. One group of investors purchased eleven million acres of the Yazoo through another land company, the New England Mississippi Land Company, for a bit more than one million dollars, or about ten cents an acre.[13] The stage was now set for a regional and partisan conflict that risked tearing the country apart.

New Englanders, who were termed New Yazooists, having paid nearly ten times the original price for their investment, were not satisfied with Georgia's offer to repay the original sales price. Anti-Yazooists, who predominated among southern Republicans, blamed moneyed interests for tainting the land sale in the first place. They saw no reason to reward wealthy northern speculators. Federalists, who were concentrated in the North, generally sided with the New Yazooists in defense of property rights against the claim of sovereignty by the southern states. Moreover, the Yazoo

debacle gave Federalists a chance to embarrass Republicans. Alexander
Hamilton, who had retired to a lucrative law practice in New York, argued
that the repeal act not only violated the "first principles of natural justice
and social policy" but also the federal Constitution. Hamilton pointed out
an overlooked provision of Article I of the Constitution that prohibited
states from passing any "law impairing the obligation of contracts." In
Hamilton's view, the 1795 land grant was analogous to a contract between
two private parties and could not be revoked by the act of a subsequent
legislature.[14] Federalists in Congress, including then Congressman John
Marshall, favored the federal government stepping in to purchase all the
Yazoo lands and distribute it to the claimants, but Republicans in the
House defeated their efforts. The growing disaffection among New En-
glanders threatened secession over the issue.

The conflict had become so contentious that by 1801 President Jefferson
tasked three of his cabinet officials—Secretary of State Madison, Treasury
Secretary Gallatin, and Attorney General Levi Lincoln—to negotiate with
Georgia for the purchase of the Yazoo. Though the original sin of the Yazoo
purchase could not be cleansed, Republicans reluctantly sought a compromise to preserve the Union. Georgia agreed to sell all the Yazoo to the federal government for $1.25 million. The difficulty remained that a bill to
compensate the New Yazooists had to pass the House Ways and Means
Committee, and its powerful chairman, John Randolph, bucked his party
leadership and opposed the compensation bill. Randolph's opposition to
the Yazoo compromise was as extreme as his prosecution of Justice Chase,
but this time he succeeded in killing the bill. Jefferson was so antagonized
by his cousin Randolph that he arranged for the House Republicans to eject
him as chairman. As a result, Randolph spent the rest of his political career
fighting Jefferson and his own party.[15]

Congress's inability to pass the Yazoo compromise bill meant that the
New Yazooists had little choice but to resort to the federal courts. However,
the Eleventh Amendment prohibited a lawsuit by citizens of one state

against another state. Thus, New Englanders could not directly sue Georgia. It would require a bit of creative lawyering to put the issue before the Supreme Court.

In 1803, John Peck of Newton, Massachusetts, sold fifteen thousand acres of Yazoo land to Robert Fletcher of Amherst, New Hampshire. Peck was a director of the New England Mississippi Land Company, and Fletcher was another friendly land speculator. The transaction was prearranged to clarify title to the property, and Peck specifically represented to Fletcher that Georgia had acted legally in granting Peck complete title to the property. Fletcher sued Peck in the U.S. Circuit Court for Massachusetts, claiming that Peck had misrepresented the facts, but the suit was contrived. Both Peck and Fletcher had a common interest in a judicial determination that Georgia had granted title to the property and that the repeal act was invalid. The circuit court unanimously held in favor of Peck, affirming that Peck had good title to the land and that the repeal act was a nullity.

The case did not reach the Supreme Court until February 1809. Peck was represented by John Quincy Adams, a U.S. senator from Massachusetts and the future president. Adams's co-counsel was Robert Goodloe Harper, who in addition to being Justice Chase's lead attorney in his impeachment trial was a former South Carolina congressman and one of the original investors in the land company. Fletcher was represented by Luther Martin, who had successfully defended Chase and Burr. Peck was asking the Supreme Court to strike down a state statute as invalid for the first time in history and, by doing so, to validate a land purchase that everyone understood had been obtained by bribery. With the nation watching closely, the Supreme Court chose to duck the case. The justices sent it back to the circuit court on a legal technicality concerning the form of the pleadings.

The case did not bounce back to the Supreme Court until the winter of 1810. Nearly fifteen years had passed since the repeal of the Yazoo grant. President Madison had appointed John Quincy Adams as ambassador to Russia, so Peck had added to his legal team Joseph Story, a Massachusetts congressman and future Supreme Court justice. Story had represented the New England Mississippi Land Company for a number of years, and his father-in-law was an original shareholder in the company. Luther Martin argued Fletcher's case. Despite a fabled legal career, Martin made a feigned effort on behalf of Fletcher. After all, his client intended to lose the case. Martin, for example, dropped the argument that the original 1795 grant was properly invalidated because it had been obtained fraudulently. One explanation for Martin's poor performance may have been alcohol. Martin was a notoriously heavy drinker, and at one point he was so intoxicated that the chief justice adjourned the Supreme Court to give him time to sober up.[16]

There was no doubt as to the outcome of the case. As a young congressman, Marshall had voted in favor of the Yazoo compromise, and his natural inclination as a land speculator would be to side with the New Yazooists. Moreover, Marshall was keenly aware of the risk to the Union if the Supreme Court failed to provide the New Englanders with a remedy.

On March 16, 1810, Marshall announced the Court's unanimous opinion in *Fletcher v. Peck*. He began cautiously: "The question, whether a law be void for its repugnancy to the constitution, is, at all times, a question of much delicacy, which ought seldom, if ever, to be decided in the affirmative."[17] Marshall acknowledged that Georgia's land grant in 1795 may have been obtained fraudulently. "That corruption should find its way into the governments of our infant republics, and contaminate the very source of legislation . . . are circumstances most deeply to be deplored"; however, the courts could not examine the motives of a state legislature. "It would be indecent, in the extreme," in a private lawsuit over a contract for the sale of property for a court to "enter into an inquiry respecting the corruption of the sovereign power of a state."[18] Under the cloak of judicial restraint and respect for state sovereignty, Marshall found a way to uphold the original land grant to the New Yazooists.

Then Marshall turned to the key issue: whether the subsequent repeal

act of 1796 was valid. The chief justice wrote that even if the original purchase was "infected with fraud," Peck and Fletcher were innocent purchasers who had no notice of it. The traditional rule of contract would have
voided a transaction that was deemed corrupt. Marshall implicitly rejected
the traditional rule and insisted instead that Georgia was bound to the
terms it had agreed to without regard for its motives. The contractual rights
of the purchasers could not be disregarded.[19]

Marshall treated the original legislative land grant of 1795 as if it were a
contract between the State of Georgia and the original purchasers. This was
a radical reconceptualization of legislative grants. Up to this point, courts
had regarded land grants as a privilege that sovereigns could convey or
withdraw at will. Now Marshall was positing that Georgia's land grant was
no different from any other private transaction. Just as Marshall had treated
Marbury's commission as a justice of the peace as if it were his property,
Marshall transformed a privilege into a contract right in this case. "When,
then, a law is in its nature a contract when absolute rights have vested under
that contract, a repeal of the law cannot devest those rights," he wrote.[20]

Marshall relied not only on general principles of contract law or equity.
Like Hamilton's famous legal argument, Marshall cited Article I of the federal Constitution that prohibits states from passing any laws "impairing
the obligations of contracts." He concluded that Georgia's repeal of the land
grant was invalid.[21] For the first time the Supreme Court had treated a legislative enactment as if it were a contract between two private parties and
applied the contract clause to invalidate a subsequent enactment.

Marshall's opinion in *Fletcher* enraged southern Republicans even as it
delighted northern Federalists. The Supreme Court had carved out a way to
provide redress to the New Yazooists in the face of congressional deadlock.
Marshall would not be a prisoner of regional loyalties. His decision in
Fletcher signaled both his defense of contract rights and his growing estrangement from the provincial politics of Virginia. His fellow southerners
would not forget, or forgive, this betrayal.

CHAPTER TWENTY-THREE

THE MEANING
OF SOVEREIGNTY

I n March 1809, Marshall swore in James Madison as the newly elected president. Madison, an awkward, gloomy intellectual, was peculiarly unsuited for electoral politics. Madison appeared uncomfortable in public, pinched and cold to the point of being churlish.[1] Washington Irving once described President Madison as "a withered little apple-John." Even at his inauguration, he spoke in a barely audible whisper. Despite Madison's lugubrious personality, Marshall thought he possessed "superior talents."[2] Madison's charming wife, Dolley Payne Todd Madison, brought gaiety and elegance to the President's House after the dour years of the bachelor Jefferson. To the public, Dolley was the "presidentess." Her popularity eclipsed her dyspeptic husband's, and her portrait by Gilbert Stuart was engraved and sold to her admirers for five dollars.[3] Dolley's festive Wednesday parties drew officials, diplomats, and their wives to what was then known as the Executive Mansion for punch, cookies, and strawberry ice cream. She graciously entertained her guests in sumptuously decorated rooms while a military band serenaded them. Dolley's extravagant socializing made Washington a more hospitable place for congressional families. As more wives and children flocked to the capital, the city morphed from a congressional stag party into a family-friendly community.[4]

Justice Cushing died in late 1810, creating an opening on the court for Madison to fill. Jefferson wrote to Madison to offer "congratulation[s]" on Cushing's passing. He recommended Attorney General Levi Lincoln—with reservations: "I do not consider him as a correct common lawyer, yet as much so as any one which ever came, or ever can come from one of the Eastern states. Their system of Jurisprudence made up from the Jewish law, a little dash of common law, & a great mass of original notions of their own, is a thing sui generis, and one educated in that system can never so far eradicate early impressions as to imbibe thoroughly the principles of another system."[5]

Madison dutifully followed Jefferson's suggestion, but Lincoln declined the position. In his place, Madison named Joseph Story, who at thirty-two was the youngest man ever appointed to the Supreme Court. Story was the Republican speaker of the Massachusetts House and a member of Congress. Madison was hoping he could be relied on to be a strong opponent of Marshall's court. Yet Story would prove to be Marshall's strongest ally on the court and the leading advocate for a strong national government. In time, Story would emerge as one of the great intellectuals in Supreme Court history. His multiple-volume *Commentaries on the Law* became the standard treatises in American law for generations, and he has been compared to the great British jurist William Blackstone. Story was also instrumental in the founding of Harvard Law School.

Shortly before Justice Story joined the Court in 1811, Justice Chase died. Now Madison had the opportunity to fill a fifth Republican seat, leaving Marshall and Bushrod Washington as the lone Federalists. Madison chose Gabriel Duvall, fifty-nine, who had served as chief justice of Maryland's Supreme Court. He was a close friend of the president's. But even Duvall would fall under the spell of Marshall's charm and intellect.

Though Marshall felt that the Court was more secure after the tumultuous first decade, he worried about the direction of the nation, especially in foreign affairs. Napoleon Bonaparte was gobbling up the Continent and had turned on Spain, France's former ally. Events in Europe threatened America's security and prosperity. Marshall worried that Republicans, including Madison, were eager to push the nation into war against Britain.[6] The chief justice regretted that "many of our leading men with professions of liberty in their mouths do in their hearts devoutly pray for the subjugation of that gallant & injured country." Privately, he accused the Republicans of supporting Bonaparte's aggression at the risk of American independence: "[T]hey would see national independence & consequently human liberty banished from Europe although the loss of our self government would be the infallible consequence."[7]

In 1806, Bonaparte had issued a decree in Berlin prohibiting any country, including the United States, from trading with Britain. The British retaliated by issuing an order that no ships would be allowed to dock at any European port without first docking at a British port and paying customs duties on its cargo. Not to be outdone, Bonaparte issued a decree in Milan that asserted the right of the French navy to seize any ship that paid duties to Britain.

The Napoleonic Wars had created both opportunities and risks for American ships. The war sidelined many European merchant ships that were impressed into military service or subject to blockades. While the war raged, most European countries depended on U.S. vessels to carry goods to and from their colonies. And U.S. merchant vessels carried more exports from India and China than from all of Europe combined.[8] But the belligerents harassed and seized U.S. ships without regard for American neutrality. From 1803 to 1812, nearly fifteen hundred U.S. vessels—almost one-fifth of all U.S. merchant ships—were captured by France or Britain.[9] Congressional Republicans thought that by cutting off all foreign trade the United States could compel France and Britain to respect American neutrality.[10] They were woefully mistaken. The embargo weakened the U.S. economy far more than it affected either of the belligerent parties.

Congress adopted the first of a series of embargo acts beginning in December 1807. Collectively, these laws made it a crime for U.S. ships to sail to any foreign port or for any U.S. company to export anything without the explicit permission of the president or his agents. Violators were fined up to twenty thousand dollars, and informers were promised a bounty of half of the fine collected. To make matters worse, the embargo was not limited to the belligerent parties but included friendly countries throughout Europe, Latin America, and Asia. By leaving it up to the executive's discretion as to what ships could leave port, the law opened the opportunity for arbitrary judgments and political corruption.

The embargo proved nearly impossible to enforce uniformly despite the bounty for informers. It required an administrative bureaucracy that did not yet exist. The president called on state governors to help implement the embargo by deploying state militia to enforce it at gunpoint. When the Massachusetts governor sought to comply with the president's request, the state legislature threatened to impeach him.[11] The specter of armed troops enforcing a trade blockade in Boston Harbor was all too familiar to the Revolutionary generation. The embargo was a betrayal of republican ideology.[12]

Prior to the embargo, approximately 40 percent of the total U.S. economy depended on foreign trade.[13] Without it, the U.S. economy collapsed. The loss of tariff revenues plunged the national government toward insolvency. The ironic consequence was that the government could no longer afford to arm itself. Republicans lusted for war, but they were unwilling to raise taxes to pay for it. Marshall quipped that "[t]here would be a great majority for war if it could certainly [be] carried on without money."[14] Faced with a looming government deficit, congressional Republicans proposed to cut military spending. So long as the Republican fiscal hawks barred tax increases, the Republican war hawks were stopped—at least for the moment. The stage was set for one of Marshall's most far-reaching decisions on international law.

IN DECEMBER 1810, the schooner *Exchange* set out from Baltimore loaded with cargo bound for San Sebastián in Spain. The ship was seized by French privateers acting pursuant to Emperor Napoleon's Berlin and Milan decrees. The French condemned the ship and refitted it as a warship with the name *Balaou*. In July 1811, the *Balaou* was en route to the West Indies when it encountered bad weather and was forced to dock at the port of Philadelphia. The original Maryland owners of the *Exchange*, John McFaddon and William Greetham, learned that their ship had docked there, and they filed a libel in federal district court demanding the return of their property. The French government did not appear.

The district court dismissed the libel on the ground that a foreign sovereign's naval vessel was immune from the court's jurisdiction. On appeal, the circuit court held that since the French vessel voluntarily entered the U.S. territorial waters, it had submitted to U.S. jurisdiction. President Madison did not want to offend France on the eve of war with Britain and decided that the U.S. government would defend the vessel on behalf of France. At the president's request, the U.S. attorney for Pennsylvania, Alexander Dallas, filed an appeal on behalf of France to the Supreme Court, which agreed to hear the case in late February 1812.

When the Supreme Court convened to hear the case, the one party missing was Napoleon's government. France's absence meant that it was up to the U.S. government to defend France's interest. It was a strange spectacle: U.S. Attorney General Pinckney and U.S. Attorney Dallas defending the seizure of an American vessel by a belligerent European emperor whose ships trolled the waters capturing U.S. merchant ships. They argued that the French warships represented the exercise of sovereign power and were entitled to immunity under the law of nations. France had never consented to U.S. jurisdiction; it was merely an accident that had forced the vessel to land in Philadelphia.[15]

Attorneys Charles Hare and Robert Harper on behalf of the schooner's owners rejected the argument that a foreign sovereign's property was immune from the court's jurisdiction. Whatever immunities the Emperor Napoleon's property enjoyed inside France surely were not applicable inside U.S. territory. The schooner had voluntarily entered U.S. waters and, by doing so, waived any claim to immunity.[16] The leading international legal authorities, such as Cornelius van Bynkershoek and Samuel Rutherford, supported their argument that foreign property in another state's territory is subject to the law of the territorial sovereign.[17] Moreover, the *Exchange* was stolen property, and denying the original owners their property would be unduly harsh. What could be more plainly unjust, Hare argued: "Your own citizens plundered. Your national rights violated. Your courts deaf to the complaints of the injured. Your own government not redressing their wrongs, but giving sanction to their spoliators."[18]

To this argument, Attorney General Pinkney replied, "When wrongs are inflicted by one nation upon another, in tempestuous times, they cannot be redressed by the judicial department." The attorney general dismissed the libellant's reliance on foreign authorities. He insisted that only the executive branch could demand redress from a foreign sovereign; courts should not interfere in the conduct of foreign relations.[19]

Five days after the close of arguments in February 1812, Marshall delivered the Court's unanimous opinion. Marshall began by acknowledging that this was a case of first impression and that "[i]n exploring an unbeaten path, with few, if any, aids from precedent or written law, the court has found it necessary to rely much on general principles, and on a train of reasoning." The Court would have to invent a new doctrine to address the exigencies of the situation and that would guide the nation in the future.[20]

In what has become the classic statement on territorial sovereignty, Marshall wrote, "The jurisdiction of the nation within its own territory is necessarily exclusive and absolute. It is susceptive of no limitation not imposed by itself." Only a sovereign could grant an exception to its territorial jurisdiction.[21] Marshall was echoing his famous memorandum to Talleyrand, in which he wrote, "Every nation has, of natural right, entirely and exclusively, all the jurisdiction which may rightfully be exercised in the territory it occupies." Marshall had cited the same principle in his famous speech in the House defending President Adams's decision to extradite Jonathan Robbins to Britain for mutiny and murder.[22]

That sounded like support for the American ship owners. But on the next page Marshall declared that according to customary international law "every sovereign is understood to wave [sic] the exercise of a part of that complete exclusive territorial jurisdiction, which has been stated to be the attribute of every nation."[23] Unless foreign warships are expressly excluded, "the ports of a friendly nation are considered as open to the public ships of all powers with whom it is at peace."[24]

To describe the Emperor Napoleon's government as "friendly" was a stretch. Indeed, Marshall's whole argument was entirely fabricated. Marshall knew there was no common practice of granting immunity to foreign warships.[25] There were a handful of British cases and a single related decision by the U.S. Supreme Court in 1795 that was not quite on point, but these hardly counted as evidence of customary international law.[26] Marshall's view was not supported by other legal authorities.[27] Marshall analogized sovereign immunity over foreign warships to diplomatic immunity, but one has little to do with the other.[28] Marshall acknowledged that the U.S. government could exercise jurisdiction over foreign warships, but only if it had explicitly declared its intention to do so in advance.[29] Marshall concluded that because the *Exchange* had entered U.S. waters with an expectation that she would be exempt from U.S. jurisdiction, the Court could not libel the ship.[30]

Marshall suggested that the ship's owners should seek redress from the political branches rather than from the courts. "[T]he sovereign power of the nation is alone competent to avenge wrongs committed by a [foreign] sovereign, that the questions to which such wrongs give birth are rather questions of policy than of law, that they are for diplomatic, rather than legal discussion." The president, for example, could negotiate with France to provide a remedy for the ship's owners, or Congress could appropriate funds.[31] In other words, because the case implicated sensitive foreign relations, the court should not interfere. Marshall fashioned his doctrine of foreign sovereign immunity not based on customary international law but in order to preserve the Constitution's separation of powers.

The *Schooner Exchange v. McFaddon* case is one of the most important opinions in the development of international law in the United States. Yet it is at odds with Marshall's own convictions about the rights of U.S. vessels and the character of the French Empire. Throughout his judicial career, Marshall had upheld the property rights of ship owners against capture, but here Marshall was siding with the French government against a Maryland ship owner. The case was decided against a backdrop of growing tensions with Great Britain over impressments. Republicans were spoiling for a fight with Britain, and France was the country's only apparent ally. Though France claimed that it had repealed the Milan and Berlin decrees against U.S. vessels in 1810, Marshall doubted their sincerity.[32] When President Madison insisted that the French had repealed these decrees, Marshall dismissed it as "a bold experiment in deception" and "one of the most astonishing instances of national credulity." The chief justice complained privately that if the so-called friends of peace and those who cared about "the real honor & real independence of our country" were honest, "I can scarcely think the opinion could have become general that Britain was the sole aggressor on neutral rights." When the Republicans defended France, he thought they were acting against the "national honor or national interest to engage in the confederacy for [our own] destruction." Marshall prayed that war with Britain could be avoided and that the United States would recognize the true nature of the French emperor before it was too late.[33] As he wrote these words to a friend on June 18, 1812, from his home in Richmond, he was unaware that on that very day President Madison had signed a declaration of war against Great Britain.

After Congress declared war on Britain, Marshall feared the country's "ruin." Yet writing to a fellow critic of the war, he advised that "the lines of subdivision between parties, if not absolutely effaced, should at least be covered for a time . . . all who wish peace ought to unite in the means which may facilitate its attainment, whatever may have been their differences of opinion on other points."[34]

Like a good soldier, Marshall remained loyal to his commander in chief. Once war was declared, Marshall fell silent: Politics stopped at the water's edge.

CHAPTER TWENTY-FOUR

WASHINGTON BURNING

T he strangest war in American history" is how the historian Gordon Wood described the War of 1812.[1] Republicans plunged the nation into an unnecessary war for reasons that no one was quite sure of then and that remain obscure today.

From 1803 to 1812, the British navy had captured 917 U.S. vessels. Between 1806 and 1807, the British navy had seized one out of every eight U.S. ships. That might have justified going to war except that France had captured 558 U.S. ships, and in the past five years, the French had seized U.S. ships at a much higher rate than the British. While the United States wanted both Britain and France to stop interfering with U.S. ships, why not declare war on France? Britain was the world's greatest naval power, and France was appreciably weaker. At least the U.S. Navy might have had a chance of defeating the French. While the British had impressed six to ten thousand U.S. sailors since the start of the Republic, that alone was probably not a justification for war. The vast majority of sailors who were impressed were actually British nationals.[2] Republican antipathy toward Britain and a hunger for Canadian territory probably had more to do with the decision to go to war than did the capture of U.S. ships.

The declaration of war on June 18, 1812, jeopardized American independence. No dispassionate observer could expect that the United States would defeat the British navy. The U.S. Navy consisted of just sixteen vessels, none as powerful as most of the British ships. The British had a thousand heavily armed vessels patrolling the world's oceans manned by tens of thousands of well-trained sailors. The U.S. Army had only 6,000 soldiers while the British had honed an army of 250,000. Yet President Madison, a man not known for passionate impulses, confidently predicted that the United States would vanquish Britain.[3] The declaration of war passed the House by a largely partisan vote of seventy-nine to forty-nine. Many Republican congressmen may have hoped that the Senate would reject the declaration of war and save the country from their own folly.[4] But the Senate approved the war by a vote of nineteen to thirteen with all the Federalists voting against.

British aggression toward American shipping gave the United States a convenient pretext for territorial expansion. Republicans dreamed of pushing Native American tribes farther west and annexing Canada (still a British colony at the time) in the north. The United States began the war with an ill-considered military assault on Canada. Republicans predicted that Canadians would refuse to defend British sovereignty and would welcome Americans as liberators.[5] Instead, the invasion of Canada showed how poorly prepared the Americans were to fight anyone. Americans suffered huge defeats at Detroit, Dearborn, and Mackinac that summer. In the spring of 1813, Americans won a single victory at York, then Canada's tiny capital with a population of only six hundred, including soldiers. Even there the Americans suffered disproportionate losses, including the death of their commanding general, the famed explorer Zebulon Pike. U.S. soldiers looted the Canadian treasury and burned York to the ground. The behavior of U.S. forces embarrassed the United States and enraged Canadians.

Along the western frontier, U.S. troops under the command of the future president William Henry Harrison struck brutally against the Creek tribe in Indiana. Despite their superior arms, the Americans suffered twice as many casualties as the more nimble Indians who were defending their homes and families.[6]

By 1813, the foolishness of the war was glaringly obvious. The British had crushed America's futile attempts to "liberate" Canada. American forces retreating across the border to Fort Niagara viciously burned the tiny village of Newark, leaving women and children homeless and barefoot in a snowstorm. In retaliation, the British sliced through upstate New York, took hundreds of prisoners, and burned Buffalo to the ground.[7] The states never appropriated sufficient funds to prosecute the war, and the U.S. economy withered under the Republicans' embargo against foreign trade. American military morale suffered while the British navy plied the U.S. coast like hungry sharks.

While the situation appeared dire for the United States, Marshall looked "with anxious solicitude—with mingled hope & fear to the great events which are taking place in the north of Germany." He thought that an end to the American war depended on the outcome of the Napoleonic Wars in Europe. If Britain defeated France, President Madison would seek to end the war quickly before Britain could focus its naval forces against the United States.[8] Marshall predicted that America's fate would turn on the battle between the Duke of Wellington and the Emperor Napoleon.[9] He did not know that the British had already crushed Napoleon at Leipzig and chased a panicked emperor back to Paris. The British would soon be free to turn their attention to the American "savages."[10]

While the war raged, Washington maintained a pretense of normality. The local newspapers carried little mention of the war. There were the usual advertisements for milliners and shoemakers, land offers, and rewards for runaway slaves. The upscale Washington Hotel opened across the street from the Executive Mansion, another sign of the capital's growth. Yet a sense of unease was growing between the lines. The *Daily National Intelligencer* warned the public, "The enemy now on the coast, and in our waters will and must get provisions, and perhaps attempt something more serious." The paper carried instructions for the national defense: Since the U.S. infantry was unable to respond rapidly to an invasion by the enemy, "[t]he individual defence consists in the knowledge of riding, and in the horse being well trained." A course for this purpose was offered for five dollars to teach "maneuvering and riding exercises, and the proper manner to train horses."[11] Congress had failed to provide soldiers, guns, or horses, so now the public was expected to defend itself.

What became known derogatively as Madison's War polarized the country. Southerners enthusiastically embraced the war to rid themselves of Indian tribes and bloody the British lion. Westerners lusted after more territory. But northerners overwhelmingly opposed Madison's War. New Englanders had no interest in annexing Canada or expanding west. First the embargo and now the war were strangling New England commerce. Yankees wanted normal relations with England and free trade for their merchants. In December 1814, representatives of the New England states gathered in Hartford, Connecticut, to discuss the possibility of secession. Madison was sufficiently alarmed to move federal troops to Albany to crush any insurrection. That proved unnecessary. Cooler heads prevailed; news of Napoleon's abdication convinced the flinty Yankees to postpone secession pending a peace settlement.[12] Madison's War dragged on pointlessly for nearly three years with British forces scoring the most victories. General Andrew Jackson's famous victory at the Battle of New Orleans came after a peace treaty had already been signed at Ghent in December 1814. Though British forces resented the generous terms offered to the Americans, Madison's War accomplished nothing.

IN APRIL 1812, just two months before Congress declared war, the *Emulous*, a U.S. merchant vessel owned in part by Joshua Delano, an American citizen, docked at Savannah, Georgia, where it loaded on board 550 tons of pine timber and other goods bound for Plymouth, England. Elijah Brown chartered the vessel as an agent for a group of merchants residing in London, including Elijah's brother, James, and a British firm, Christophe Ide, Brothers and Co. Before the vessel departed, federal agents enforcing the embargo against Britain stopped it. The master and Elijah Brown agreed to sail the ship to New Bedford, Massachusetts, where Delano resided. While the ship was docked in New Bedford, war was declared. After months of uncertainty, the timber was finally unloaded and stored in a nearby saltwater creek secured by booms and fastened by stakes driven into the briny mud. Not knowing how long the war would last, Delano persuaded Elijah Brown to sell the cargo. Brown sold the timber to his other brother, Armitz, who resided in Massachusetts.[13]

Brown apparently failed to pay Delano, and Delano informed the U.S. attorney in Boston of the sale. The U.S. attorney filed a libel on behalf of Delano, as the informant, against the timber as the property of an enemy alien. Armitz Brown argued that all three Brown brothers were U.S. citizens. The timber was lawfully acquired by his brother from a fellow citizen before the outbreak of war. The government had no right to confiscate it. Nonetheless, Justice Story, sitting as the circuit court judge, condemned the timber, and Armitz Brown appealed to the Supreme Court.[14]

Though the Browns were U.S. nationals, the original owners of the timber were British citizens. Brown's attorney argued that international law protected the property rights of enemy aliens.[15] Congress had not authorized the seizure of enemy alien property, and "no act or measure of the American government has ever indicated a disposition adverse to these humane and liberal provisions and usages of the common law and of the law of nations."[16]

The U.S. attorney general chose not to appear. Instead, he merely submitted Justice Story's circuit court opinion as the government's brief. In it, Story asserted the declaration of war implicitly gave the president the power to seize enemy alien property on U.S. soil.[17] Once Congress declared war, the only limitation on the president's power to wage war were "the rules of warfare established among civilized nations."[18]

Given Marshall's faith in a strong executive, he probably found Story's argument compelling, but he nevertheless held that the U.S. attorney had no authority to libel Brown's timber. Writing for the majority, Marshall analogized the seizure of enemy alien property to the confiscation of an enemy alien's private debt or credit. Marshall had defended Lord Fairfax's estate from being confiscated by Virginia. He was familiar with the practice of other countries with regard to confiscating enemy alien property, and the general practice of states was to respect private property. Marshall concluded "that war gives the right to confiscate, but does not itself confiscate the property of the enemy."[19] If Congress wanted to confiscate enemy property, it must say so explicitly.

Marshall reached this conclusion based on a novel theory of constitutional interpretation. Since the Constitution was framed at a time when respect for the rights of enemy aliens and their property was recognized "throughout the civilized world," courts should not construe the Constitution to permit a declaration of war to have an effect in the United States that it does not have in other countries.[20] Marshall applied the same principle he employed in *Charming Betsy*: Courts should interpret both the Constitution and acts of Congress consistent with the law of nations. So, for example, Marshall would presumably say that the Constitution does not permit the president to authorize acts prohibited by international law such as torture or war crimes.

It's noteworthy that Marshall wrote his opinion in *Brown v. United States* respecting the rights of British subjects as British forces were threatening Virginia. Marshall's magnanimous attitude reflected both his skepticism about Madison's War and his generous view of international law. Marshall firmly believed that if the United States acted with restraint, then it could expect other governments to act with restraint. Reciprocity was, after all, the code of genteel societies like nineteenth-century Virginia; Marshall expected no less from Europeans.[21]

THE SUPREME COURT'S TERM ended two weeks later, in mid-March 1814, and Marshall returned to the circuit court in Richmond for the spring while the war raged on. He always looked forward to his return home where he resumed the role of a private citizen. His casual dress and his informal manners made him approachable. One of his neighbors remarked that the judge "was regarded by old and young with affectionate reverence."[22] A delivery boy carrying a message to Marshall's house appeared to be unduly intimidated by Marshall's fame, and the chief justice made a point of setting the boy at ease by challenging him to a game of marbles.[23]

That summer, word reached Virginia that the Duke of Wellington's forces had defeated Napoleon. The emperor abdicated in April 1814 and was exiled to the island of Elba. As Britain focused its military superiority against the Americans, Marshall hoped that Madison would settle the war quickly, but Marshall would be disappointed.

In mid-August, British Major General Robert Ross arrived with a fleet of British warships and an army of battle-hardened soldiers in Chesapeake Bay. He landed at Benedict, Maryland, on the banks of the Patuxent River, where he met up with Rear Admiral George Cockburn. They marched five thousand sweaty troops toward the capital sixty miles away in a brutal blast of humidity and heat. Though Madison had been forewarned about a possible British invasion more than a month earlier, Secretary of War John Armstrong Jr. had dismissed the risk of an invasion. The secretary of war thought that the British would be more likely to attack the naval base at Annapolis. In fact, Armstrong detested Washington and wanted to move the nation's capital somewhere else, so perhaps he would not much mind if the British leveled the city. As a consequence, no forces guarded Chesapeake Bay, and the Department of War had no idea the British had landed until they approached the capital.[24]

Madison left Washington's defense to a puny force of five hundred soldiers under the command of a Baltimore attorney, William Winder, whose principal qualification was that he was the favorite nephew of the governor of Maryland. The British could not believe they met no resistance as they marched toward Washington. Scarcely six miles from the capital, General Winder engaged the British at Bladensburg, Maryland. The Americans were overwhelmed and quickly routed. Before dusk, two hundred British regulars led by Cockburn and Ross were spotted marching down Maryland Avenue toward the Capitol. The British seemed bewildered that the Americans had abandoned their capital. Nearly every government official had cut and run. One of the last to flee was Dolley Madison, who took the time to rescue some of her china and silver as well as Gilbert Stuart's famous painting of George Washington. At the corner of Second Street and Maryland Avenue, a single shot was fired from the home of Treasury Secretary Gallatin that killed General Ross's horse. The British responded by burning the house to the ground.[25]

The British wasted no time in avenging the burning of York. They set fire to the Capitol first. The blue-and-buff silk curtains in the Senate chamber burst into flames. The chamber burned so hot that the marble columns supporting the domed ceiling cracked and crumbled into ash. The invaders were especially careful to destroy the Supreme Court chamber below. They piled chairs and tables into the center of the courtroom and doused them with gunpowder.[26] Henry Adams wrote that the British "assumed that the American government stood beyond the pale of civilization; and in truth, a government which showed so little capacity to defend its capital, could hardly wonder at whatever treatment it received."[27]

British troops strolled down Pennsylvania Avenue astonished to find that even the President's House had been abandoned. Soldiers helped themselves to supper and wine at the president's table before looting and burning the mansion. The elaborate damask curtains, satin upholstery, and formal chairs that Dolley Madison had personally selected were incinerated, as were her clothing, jewelry, and wigs. None of the Madisons' personal items or artwork were spared. Only the mansion's thick exterior sandstone walls, now blackened by smoke, survived the fire.[28]

Next, soldiers burned the Treasury building while across town U.S. Commodore Thomas Tingey, commander of the federal naval yard, set fire to the navy's facilities before British troops could plunder their ships and supplies. In the suffocating August heat, the fires felt like blast furnaces. Eighteen British soldiers dropped dead from heat exhaustion. By nightfall, the sky glowed a demonic orange, and the inhabitants huddled in their homes, terrified and incensed that the government had left them defenseless.[29]

The following morning, the air tasted thick with smoke. The British rose early to their appointed task, systematically setting ablaze the War and State Departments and other government offices. Admiral Cockburn ordered his men to smash the presses of the *Daily National Intelligencer*, Washington's leading newspaper. Angry at the way he was portrayed by the national press, Cockburn instructed his men to be sure they destroyed all the Cs in the type sets "so that the rascals cannot any longer abuse my name."[30]

Then something remarkable happened: The sky abruptly darkened, and a torrent of rain fell. The winds picked up so powerfully that a British officer and his horse were blown to the ground. Small cannons were scattered like leaves. Lightning and thunder rolled ferociously, and the startled soldiers rushed to take cover as a freak tornado touched ground. In the harbor, two British ships broke free and were blown onto shore. Trees were uprooted, houses were thrown off their foundations, chimneys were toppled, roofs were torn away, furniture and featherbeds littered the deserted street.[31] The fires, collapsed buildings, wind, lightning, rain, and ensuing chaos looked apocalyptic. Admiral Cockburn shouted to a woman from a doorway, "God, Madam! Is this the kind of storm to which you are accustomed in this infernal country?" She boldly replied, "No, sir, this is a special interposition of Providence to drive our enemies from our city."[32] Indeed, it appeared as if the heavens had rendered judgment. Satisfied that they had done enough damage, General Ross gave orders to withdraw. The British marched south to rejoin their ships at Benedict while the rains extinguished the smoldering embers of the Capitol.[33]

At home in Richmond, Marshall read the first account of the British invasion and fire two days later in the local paper. It reported that "every public building in Washington is in a heap and the city and GeorgeTown in quiet possession of the British troops . . . You can scarcely conceive the distress, alarm and consternation that prevails in this place, women and children crying and screaming in every direction." Marshall's eyes widened in disbelief and horror at the humiliating spectacle. As Adams's secretary of state, he had personally supervised the completion of the President's House and the Capitol. Now all that work lay in ruins. The paper reported that across the Potomac in Alexandria, Virginians continued their quotidian lives with relative indifference. "You can have no idea of the apathy which prevailed there after the city was actually in the hands of the enemy . . . The young men generally were walking about the Taverns and streets smoking segars, and with great *sang froid* enquiring what the last express brought over." The British may have destroyed the federal capital, but the Commonwealth of Virginia still stood. The reporter despaired that "[i]f we depend on the Alexandrians, we shall soon 'repose in the arms of our legitimate sovereign.'"[34] Nearly twenty-five years after the Constitution's ratification, Virginians still did not consider themselves as Americans first. For Marshall, that may have been even more painful to confront than the destruction of the Capitol.

Though Marshall regarded Madison's War as a tragic mistake, he was by nature an optimist. He remained confident that the country would survive and move forward. After all, Marshall had experienced war before, and he had seen Richmond rise from the ashes after it was burned by the British during the Revolution. Marshall's life had been framed by three wars—the French and Indian War that left its imprint on the Virginia frontier, the Revolutionary War in which he had served, and the Quasi-War with France, which had shaped his public career. Once again the terrible experience of war left its mark, deepening Marshall's commitment to building a strong national government and fostering the civilizing influence of international law.

CHAPTER TWENTY-FIVE

FRIENDS AND ENEMIES

O nly days after the smoke cleared, members of Congress re-turned to Washington to survey the damage. Congress recon-vened on September 19, 1815, in a cramped room at the Patent Office, located inside Blodgett's Hotel on E Street Northwest. For the next six months, Congress debated whether to abandon the federal city perma-nently and return to Philadelphia. The motion in favor of moving north was narrowly defeated, and Congress agreed to borrow the money to re-build the Capitol, the President's House, and the other official buildings. In 1815, Congress moved to another, larger building northeast of the Capitol, on the site of the present-day Supreme Court building. That building, which became known as the Old Brick Capitol, housed Congress for another four years while the Capitol was rebuilt for the third time in twenty-five years.

Marshall returned to Washington in February, and it was a particularly painful experience for him. The Supreme Court chamber that the Court had occupied for only four years was decimated. Only its vaulted ceiling survived the fire. Once again, Congress made no provision for the Court, so the justices had to fend for themselves. Stelle's Hotel had survived, and the justices moved back into their old rooms.[1] They agreed to hold hearings in the home of the court clerk, Elias Caldwell. Caldwell owned a three-story Federal-style home on the corner of B Street and Pennsylvania Avenue Southeast, just opposite the Capitol, where the Library of Congress's John Adams Building now sits. Caldwell had fought the British at Bladensburg. When the battle was lost, Caldwell hurried to Washington on horseback to rescue the Supreme Court library before the British torched it. He frantically moved armfuls of law books as he dashed back and forth across the avenue to his home.[2]

The justices met in Caldwell's front parlor, crowded together in their black robes behind a long table. With the sound of Caldwell's eight small children shouting in the background, the lawyers sat on the parlor furniture waiting to argue. Spectators stood packed behind them in the parlor and spilled out into the hallway.[3]

The Court's February term was once again dominated by prize cases resulting from the war with Britain. Among these was the colorfully named *Thirty Hogsheads of Sugar v. Boyle.*[4] In July 1812, shortly after the United States had declared war, a British vessel en route to London was captured by a U.S. privateer and brought to Baltimore where it was libeled as enemy property. The cargo included thirty hogsheads (large casks) of sugar belonging to Adrian Bentzon, a Danish government official. The sugar had been grown on the Dane's plantation on the Danish island of Saint Croix (now part of the U.S. Virgin Islands). Denmark was a neutral country, and normally the property of a Danish national produced on a Danish island would be considered neutral and returned to the owner. However, British forces had captured the island shortly before the sugar was shipped, and British officers had ordered the sugar to be brought to London on a British vessel. The Maryland Circuit Court treated the cargo as enemy property, and the Danish owner appealed. The question for the Supreme Court was whether the sugar should be considered enemy property subject to capture because it was grown on soil claimed by Britain.

Bentzon was Danish by birth. He had purchased his plantation while the island was Danish territory before it was occupied by Britain. After the British seized the island, Bentzon returned to Denmark. He had never voluntarily submitted to British rule. Moreover, Britain's occupation of the island was only temporary, and it had since returned the island to Denmark. The equities seemed to favor Bentzon.

Writing for the Court in another unanimous decision, Chief Justice Marshall looked to customary international law. Where there was no governing treaty, he wrote, U.S. courts must consider "the decisions of the Courts of every country, so far as they are founded upon a law common to every country . . . not as authority, but with respect." Marshall insisted that U.S. courts should distill the customary international rule by looking at a range of countries.[5] Accordingly, Marshall found that the international customary rule was that the nationality of produce should be determined by the sovereign who possessed the soil regardless of the nationality of the individual owner of the land.[6] Regardless of the equities of the situation, the Dane was bound to share the same destiny as whatever sovereign claimed the island. When the island became British soil, its produce became British, and the sugar was rightfully condemned as enemy property.[7]

The significance of Marshall's decision in *Thirty Hogsheads* was his reliance on customary international law as part of our law. Marshall had forged a unanimous consensus in support of the principle that customary international law is a part of United States law, and this principle has since become a keystone of the American legal system.

A few days later, writing for a divided Court, Marshall issued another important opinion on the law of prizes that came to a different conclusion. On December 19, 1813, an American privateer, the *Governor Tompkins*, captured the *Nereide*, an armed British vessel sailing from Britain to Buenos Aires in a naval convoy. The *Nereide* was carrying cargo shipped by Manuel Pinto, a Spanish national born in Buenos Aires who now resided in London.[8] A New York district court condemned the vessel and cargo, and the circuit court upheld their decision. Pinto appealed, arguing that since he was the national of a neutral country, his cargo should not be subject to seizure under customary international law. The issue for the Supreme Court was whether cargo owned by the national of a neutral country transported on an armed British vessel should be treated as enemy property.

Again, Marshall began by looking to customary international law. He acknowledged that under customary international law the goods of a neutral found in an enemy vessel were not subject to capture.[9] Marshall opined that since it was not Pinto's decision to arm the British vessel or fire on the American privateer, this was not a basis for denying his property rights.[10]

However, the U.S. privateers argued that under Spanish law, U.S. property would be subject to condemnation in a comparable situation. Since Spain would not respect the rights of U.S. shippers, it seemed only fair that U.S. courts should treat the property of a Spanish national the same way. The principle of reciprocity—"An eye for an eye"—was as old as the Bible.

Marshall responded that deciding whether to retaliate against a foreign state's unjust treatment of U.S. citizens was a political judgment left to the president and Congress. It was not up to the courts to decide whether and how to retaliate. Until such time as Congress or the president chooses to retaliate, "the Court is bound by the law of nations which is part of the law of the land."[11] Therefore the Supreme Court decided to restore the goods to its Spanish owner.

Just as Marshall had denied the court's power to decide "political questions" in *Marbury*, and just as he found in *Schooner Peggy* and *Schooner Exchange* that it was up to the political branches to compensate owners for the illegal capture of a vessel, Marshall drew a bright line between foreign relations and questions of law. At the same time that the Court was deferring to the political branches, Marshall was also asserting the Supreme Court's authority to determine and apply international law.

Although *Nereide* and *Thirty Hogsheads of Sugar* came to opposite results—the former upheld the property rights of a neutral, while the latter denied them—these two decisions sent a clear signal that U.S. courts were bound by the law of nations. Though some Supreme Court justices have since argued that the opinions of foreign courts are not relevant in U.S. courts, Marshall believed that U.S. judges should look to foreign courts to determine customary international law.[12] Fifteen years earlier, as an American commissioner to France, Marshall had been asserting customary international law in defense of American commerce. Now he had established it as a foundational principle of U.S. law.

THOUGH THE SUPREME COURT'S two terms in winter and spring lasted only about eight weeks each, Marshall hated being away from his family and friends in Richmond. He enjoyed his colleagues on the Court, but he did not relish the accoutrements of public office. Dinners at the Executive Mansion, diplomatic receptions, parties with senators—these things did not matter to Marshall. "Since my being in this place I have been more in company than I wish & more than is consistent with the mass of business we have to go through," he complained to Polly. "I have been invited to dine with the President with our own secretaries & with the minister of France & tomorrow I dine with the British minister." It sounded glamorous, but "[i]n the midst of these gay circles my mind is carried to my own fire side & to my beloved wife. I conjecture where you are sitting & who is with you to cheer your solitary moments."[13] All Marshall really hoped for was some communication letting him know that she was fine as he constantly fretted over her deteriorating health.

By now, Marshall had achieved national celebrity, but he refused to take himself too seriously. Dressed in ill-fitting trousers and muddy boots, often without a coat or a hat, he never forgot where he came from. He brushed aside anyone who put him on a pedestal. When an attorney once praised the chief justice for reaching the "acme of judicial distinction," Marshall quickly dismissed the flattery. All that the "acme of judicial distinction" meant, Marshall replied, was "the ability to look a lawyer straight in the eyes for two hours and not hear a damned word he says."[14] For the same reason, Marshall avoided newspaper reporters and disdained any publicity: "I hope to God they will let me alone 'till I am dead."[15]

On Tuesday, March 4, 1817, Marshall swore in James Monroe as the newly elected president. No prior president had the good fortune to assume office at a time of both prosperity and peaceful relations with Britain and France. He was the fourth Virginian patrician to occupy the office, but unlike his close associates, Jefferson and Madison, he was more of a soldier and a politician than an intellectual. He had served with Marshall at Valley Forge and was wounded at the Battle of Trenton. Though he was intensely private and reserved, Monroe had no patience for ideas; he was all about politics.[16] It was Marshall's fourth inauguration, and this time he was genuinely pleased to administer the oath to one of his boyhood friends. Since their days together at Reverend Campbell's school in Washington parish, they had formed a bond that transcended political affiliations. Monroe may have grown into being Jefferson's lieutenant over the years, but Marshall continued to admire him despite their political differences. Though Monroe did not distinguish himself intellectually, no president since Washington was more respected by both voters and politicians for his integrity and good spirit. In fact, Monroe had won all but a single electoral vote in his contest against John Quincy Adams. Monroe's presidency ushered in the Era of Good Feelings, which brought a brief interlude in the squabbles between the Jeffersonians, who now had officially renamed their party as the Democratic-Republican Party, and the last die-hard Federalists.

Monroe's inauguration felt like a genuine celebration of the nation's resilience and unity following years of warfare and partisanship. The only sour note was the absence of the Speaker of the House, Henry Clay. Clay disdained the president-elect for choosing John Quincy Adams as secretary of state. Clay aspired to be president himself someday. Like so many before and since, he hoped that the position of secretary of state would be a stepping-stone to the presidency. Though Clay was one of the great states-men of his era, he could be petty and vindictive. President Monroe had planned the inauguration to be in the House chamber as was customary, but Speaker Clay denied the president-elect the use of *his* chamber. Clay claimed that he did not want the senators to add their plush upholstered chairs to the plain wooden chairs in the people's house.[17] Instead, the inauguration was held outside for the first time in front of the Old Brick Capitol.

Standing before an exuberant crowd of eight thousand in the brilliant sunshine of an unseasonably warm day, Marshall beamed as he adminis-tered the oath to his old school friend.[18] Winter was giving way to spring, and for the moment, it seemed that the whole country was suffused in the warm glow. Sitting in the front row were the other six members of the Su-preme Court. With Bushrod Washington being the only other Federalist remaining on the Court, Marshall had accepted without bitterness that he was among the last of a rapidly vanishing tribe. He began to wonder if the time was coming to step down.

AT SIXTY-ONE, MARSHALL looked far more robust and powerful than most men half his age. The gangly young man had filled out and matured into an august presence with snowy white hair and piercing dark eyes underneath a thatch of salt-and-pepper eyebrows. He'd retained both his sharp mind and his sense of humor. His stature had not robbed him of his humility, nor had age dimmed his sense of wonder. People of all social posi-tions and ages fascinated him. Visitors to Richmond marveled at the chief justice's accessibility.[19] One day in Richmond, while waiting for his carriage to be repaired, he struck up a conversation with the young son of his repair-man. Marshall learned that the boy, James Beale, had an interest in medi-cine. Marshall took the boy under his wing and eventually sponsored him to attend the Pennsylvania Medical School.[20] Dr. James Beale would later go on to become the president of the Medical Society of Virginia and a founding figure in the American Medical Association.[21] Marshall remained as engaged in the lives of his neighbors in Richmond as he was in parsing the details of the court cases he heard. When he was home, Marshall still played quoits regularly with the other members of the Barbecue Club. He never seemed more at ease than when he was gulping down mint juleps and trading stories over a roasted pig after a round pitching quoits in the hot sun.[22]

By contrast, Polly, at fifty, had aged poorly. She had shrunk into a skeletal, childlike figure. Time had magnified her neuroses and heightened her sensitivity to noise and light. Nighttime terrified her. Marshall had to reassure her that no one was hiding under her bed or in a cupboard. In addition to emotional stress, she suffered from severe anemia, chronic fatigue, and frequent fainting. Polly constantly complained of the cold. In the warm months when the humidity demanded that windows be left open, Polly was whisked away to the family's home at Oak Hill where she would not be disturbed by the clatter of carriages or the chatter of couples passing on the street below. Years of confinement to her room left her estranged from society. Polly's only pleasures were reading and the company of her husband. She rarely left the house unless accompanied by Marshall and then only to attend Sunday services at the Monumental Church a few blocks away. Though Marshall was a Unitarian and never joined a church, he happily escorted her for as long as she was able to go.[23]

For all of Polly's infirmities, Marshall remained devoted to her. Whenever he was away from Richmond, he worried about her, and he was always relieved to return to her side. He removed his shoes and padded around the house in slippers so that his footsteps would not aggravate Polly's nerves. In spring and summer he would read in the side yard under the dappled shade of a spreading elm. He would sit there for hours with a book propped on his crossed legs, glancing up to acknowledge a passing neighbor or sip a cool drink. He especially loved reading the novels of Jane Austen for her wry humor and vivid language.[24]

Marshall's devotion to Polly reflected his general regard for, and fascination with, women. Unlike most men of his time, he respected women as his equals and refused to tolerate improper language or humor referring to the feminine sex. Justice Story described Marshall's attitude as "romantic chivalry," but it was more than Marshall's placing women on a pedestal. Marshall believed "that national character as well as happiness depends more on the female part of society than is generally imagined."[25] Marshall remained an incurable flirt even into his sixties. He loved to flatter women and make them laugh. He even composed poetry to some of those he admired.

What should we conclude about his relationships with these women? One such poem was penned for Eliza Lambeth, an attractive young female singer. It read in part:

> Where learnt you the notes of that soul-melting measure?
> Sweet mimic, who taught you to carol that song?
> From Eliza 'twas caught, whom e'en birds hear with pleasure
> As brightly she trips the green meadow along.
> O breathe them again while with rapture I listen,
> Every beat of my heart is responsive to thee;
> And my eyes to behold thee with ecstasy glisten
> With the gray breast reclined on that high poplar tree.[26]

Marshall cryptically titled the poem "From the Chameleon to the Mocking Bird."

Why a chameleon? A chameleon is capable of disguising itself, of appearing to be something it is not. Is Marshall implying here that he was not always faithful to Polly? It would not be surprising if a man with his vitality and social opportunities felt tempted from time to time to stray from his long-suffering wife.

In March 1816, the Court heard the famous case of *Martin v. Hunter's Lessee.*[27] This was the latest and final incarnation of the case that Marshall had initiated a quarter of a century earlier on behalf of Lord Fairfax's estate. Fairfax's nephew and heir, Denny Martin, was suing to determine who had good title to the Virginia land once held by Fairfax. In 1796, Marshall had prepared to argue the issue before the Supreme Court, but fate intervened: The argument was postponed by the death of the opposing counsel, and soon after that, Marshall left for France. Now, two decades later, the case had finally returned to the Supreme Court. Since Marshall had purchased much of Martin's property, he was personally interested in the outcome, and for this reason, he recused himself from judging the case.

Of more than one thousand opinions issued by the Marshall Court, *Martin* is among the most significant, and yet it is one of the very few that Marshall did not write. While Justice Story signed the majority opinion, there is strong reason to suspect Marshall had a hand in drafting it. The language and arguments based on both constitutional law and the law of nations are written in Marshall's distinctive voice. Moreover, the underlying principles of the decision embody the core of Marshall's own beliefs about the nature of the Union and the role of treaties in domestic law. Marshall and Story had become such intimate associates that it was sometimes hard to know where one began and the other ended. Despite his republicanism and his Yankee detachment, Story gushed, "I am in love with [Marshall's] character, positively in love." Story loved Marshall's hearty laugh and admired "his good temper and unwearied patience" both on and off the bench.[28] Marshall's critics surely thought Story's decision bore Marshall's fingerprints, and even Justice Story later confessed that the chief justice "concurred in every word of it."[29]

This specific suit began twenty-five years earlier, in 1791, as an action brought by John Marshall on behalf of Denny Martin in a Virginia district court against David Hunter for trespass on the land Martin had inherited from his uncle. Virginia had expropriated this land during the Revolutionary War and sold it to Hunter in 1788. The case had come before Virginia's highest court, the Court of Appeals, which held that Martin did not have good title under the law of the commonwealth. The case was appealed to the Supreme Court in 1813. Story, writing for the majority, held that the Treaty of Paris ending the Revolutionary War had restored Martin's title. Relying on the supremacy clause in Article VI of the Constitution, Story found that since treaties were the "supreme law of the land," the treaty trumped even Virginia's prior statute. A writ was issued to the Virginia court to order Hunter's lessee off the property.

However, the Virginia court refused to comply. Virginia's Court of Appeals held that under the Constitution, the Supreme Court had no power to hear an appeal from a state's highest court.[30] In effect, the Virginia Court of Appeals asserted that the state and federal governments were sovereign equals and that each state's highest court was free to interpret the U.S. Constitution as it saw fit. A state court could, if it wished, nullify a federal law or, as in this case, a federal treaty.

Once again Martin petitioned the Supreme Court challenging the refusal of the Virginia Court of Appeals to give effect to the Supreme Court's order.[31] The petition framed two of the most fundamental questions in our constitutional system: Is the Supreme Court supreme over the state courts? And is federal law, including federal treaties, supreme over state law? If the Virginia Court of Appeals were correct, then the Constitution was merely a compact among sovereign states that the states were free to ignore, and the Supreme Court was not the final arbiter of its meaning. It would allow state courts to nullify federal law and make it impossible for any foreign government to rely on its treaties with the United States. These were the very issues that lay at the foundation of the Civil War forty-five years later.

There was also an intensely personal aspect to this case.[32] The Virginia Court of Appeals decision was authored by the court's president, Spencer

Roane. Roane and Marshall had a long history of professional and political conflict that dated back more than thirty years. Roane was the leader of Virginia's Republican Party, while Marshall was the leading Federalist. Roane was especially close to Jefferson and Madison. In fact, Roane would have been Jefferson's own candidate for chief justice of the United States if John Adams had not nominated Marshall. The bitter feud between Jefferson and Marshall continued between Roane and Marshall. Roane was well aware that Marshall was the real party in interest in Martin's suit, and he had no reason to accommodate Marshall. It would hardly be surprising if Roane had discussed his decision first with Jefferson, who no doubt would have encouraged him to confront Marshall.[33]

Marshall reciprocated Roane's disdain even though Marshall had the remarkable capacity to maintain friendships with people of all political affiliations. Throughout his career, he befriended his political and legal adversaries. He was even civil toward Jefferson. But the one man he could not suffer was Spencer Roane. And when Roane dared to suggest that the Supreme Court was not, in fact, supreme over the states, Marshall excoriated him publicly. Marshall wrote that the Supreme Court was not merely a "partial, local tribunal" like the Virginia Court of Appeals. It had been established by "the people of the United States" to decide "all national questions." Marshall continued that in every case before every other court in the nation, the Supreme Court's judgment "has been acquiesced in, and the jurisdiction of the court has been recognized." Quoting from Hamilton in *The Federalist,* Marshall concluded that Roane's decision in Martin's case was "the only example furnished by any court in the union of a sentiment favorable to that 'hydra in government,' from which, says the Federalist, 'nothing but contradiction and confusion can proceed.' "[34]

In perhaps his most important decision, Justice Story declared that "the constitution of the United States was ordained and established, not by the states in their sovereign capacities, but emphatically, as the preamble of the Constitution declares, by 'the people of the United States.'" In Story's view, the people had decided to limit the sovereign power of the states by the Constitution and make the states subordinate to federal laws and treaties.[35]

With a careful textual reading of the relevant portions of the Constitution, Story found that the state courts were required to submit to the Supreme Court's appellate jurisdiction.[36] Story pointed out that unless the Supreme Court had appellate jurisdiction over all the state courts, state judges might arrive at conflicting judgments about the meaning of constitutional provisions. In order to preserve a uniform interpretation of the Constitution and federal statutes and treaties, it was essential that the Supreme Court have appellate jurisdiction over the state courts.[37]

Story rejected the argument that the Supreme Court's appellate jurisdiction over state courts infringed on state sovereignty. He boldly insisted that the Constitution was intended to "restrain or annul the sovereignty of the states."[38] Story asserted that the individual will of each state was subordinate to the interest of the whole nation. "The security and happiness of the whole was the object, and to prevent dissension and collision, each surrendered those powers which might make them dangerous to each other."[39]

Today, *Martin* remains a cornerstone of the Union. Writing a century later, Supreme Court Justice Oliver Wendell Holmes wrote that "I do not think the United States would come to an end if we lost our power to declare an Act of Congress void. I do think the Union would be imperiled if we could not make that declaration as to the laws of the several States."[40]

Back in Virginia, no one doubted that Marshall had a hand in the Court's decision in *Martin*. It was followed by a line of decisions by the Marshall Court asserting the supremacy of federal law over the states. And it was the final act in Marshall's estrangement from his native Virginia.

CHAPTER TWENTY-SIX

THE SUPREME LAW

Alexander Hamilton persuaded Congress to approve the first Bank of the United States in 1791 as a temporary measure to refinance the country's Revolutionary War debt. Jefferson, Madison, and other Republicans opposed the creation of a national bank, which they argued exceeded the federal government's power. The charter of the first national bank lapsed in 1811, and Madison, who was then president, had no intention of renewing it. At that time there were some ninety state banks competing for business with the national bank. As a result of the national bank's demise, the number of state banks soared to 250. Each state bank printed its own bank notes, which had questionable value at any other bank. By 1814, the increase in the money supply created wild inflation and led to the collapse of the country's banking system, and even Jefferson, Madison, and Monroe shifted their views on the merits of a national bank. Pragmatism trumped ideology, as it eventually must.

In 1816, the Republican Congress agreed to charter the Second Bank of the United States to restore value to the money supply and refinance the national debt following the War of 1812.[1] The bank's initial capitalization

was thirty-five million dollars, which made it perhaps the largest corporation in the United States, if not the world. The bank could control the money
supply by issuing its own bank notes and trading in bank notes issued by
state banks. It also lent money to the federal government, the states, and
private borrowers. The federal government held 20 percent of the shares,
and private banks and investors, many of them British, held the majority of
the stock. When the bank opened its doors in 1817, it quickly prospered and
established branch offices in eighteen cities throughout the country.[2]

From the outset, state bankers and state officials viewed the bank with
suspicion. The bank's size and the wealth of its shareholders dominated the
market. The bank outcompeted state banks by offering loans at very favorable rates to land speculators with questionable credit. When commodity
prices slipped, the bank called in its loans to state banks and businesses.
Banks and businesses were unable to repay their loans. Depositors could
not be repaid. In the Panic of 1819, the economy plunged into the worst
depression since the Revolution. States blamed the national bank as the
source of misery. To make matters worse, the bank was not merely unsound; it was unsavory. Bank officers treated depositors' funds as their
own. The corruption was on an unprecedented scale.[3]

Republicans opposed to federal power, businesses and farmers facing insolvency, and state bankers pushed for state laws to exclude the national bank
from their states. The Maryland legislature imposed a stamp tax on bank
notes issued by the bank. The tax ranged from ten cents to twenty dollars
depending on the face value of the bank note. The manager of the Baltimore
branch of the national bank, James McCulloch, sought to challenge the state
statute. He refused to pay the tax, and an informer, John James, reported him
to Maryland officials for a reward of one hundred dollars. McCulloch was
convicted in Maryland state court of violating state law and appealed to the
Supreme Court.

Daniel Webster, one of the leading attorneys of the day, represented Mc-
Culloch along with Attorney General William Wirt and William Pinkney.

Luther Martin, Joseph Hopkinson, and Walter Jones defended Maryland's law. The Court set aside nine days to hear the historic argument.

After listening to William Pinkney's three-day summation of the bank's argument, Justice Story wrote that "never in my whole life, have I heard a greater speech."[4] The arguments raised fundamental questions about the relationship between the federal government and the states. If a federally chartered bank could be taxed by a state, what was the meaning of federal supremacy? But if the bank was immune from state taxes, what was the meaning of state sovereignty? These were not merely academic questions. For years Congress had bitterly debated various measures for improving the nation's infrastructure. Internal improvements, such as roads and canals, were vital to building a modern nationwide economy but were resisted by many Republicans, including Madison and Monroe, who believed that the Constitution limited the size of the federal government. If Congress could charter a national bank, then it had the authority to engage in other projects to stimulate commerce. And most important, if Congress could encroach on state sovereignty this way, southerners feared that Congress could also interfere with slavery.

On March 6, 1819, just three days after the closing arguments in *McCulloch v. Maryland*, Marshall delivered the Court's unanimous opinion, which was almost surely written before the arguments were heard. Borrowing liberally from Alexander Hamilton's memorandum to Washington that defended the constitutionality of the first United States Bank, Marshall addressed two broad issues: First, whether Congress had the power to charter a national bank, and second, whether a state had the power to tax it.[5]

Marshall held that even though the Constitution did not explicitly grant Congress the power to charter a national bank, reading the Constitution was not like reading a statute. Congress must be allowed to respond to circumstances and exigencies as they arose. The chief justice famously declared that "we must never forget it is a constitution we are expounding."[6] The Constitution gave Congress the power to make "all laws necessary and proper" to carry out any of its express powers.[7] Marshall interpreted this broadly: "Let the end be legitimate, let it be within the scope of the Constitution, and all means which are appropriate, which are plainly adapted to that end, which are not prohibited but consist with the letter and the spirit of the constitution, are constitutional." Since it would be "useful" and "convenient" to have a national bank in order for Congress to tax and spend and finance the army, therefore Congress had the power to charter a national bank.[8]

Maryland had argued that even assuming that Congress had the power to charter a bank, surely the state had the power to tax it as it would any other private entity. After all, the Constitution was nothing more than a compact among the states that ceded only limited power to the federal government while reserving the sovereign powers of each state. Maryland's case rested in part on the Kentucky and Virginia Resolutions, authored by Jefferson and Madison, which had asserted the states had the right to nullify federal laws.

Marshall responded that the Constitution was not made by the states; it was ratified by the people directly acting through the ratification conventions, and it expressed the popular will: "The government of the Union, then . . . is emphatically, and truly, a government of the people. In form and in substance it emanates from them."[9] Marshall was building on the controversial proposition first posited by Justice Story in the *Martin* opinion three years earlier that the Constitution was made not as a compact among the states but organically by the whole nation.

Marshall opined that when Congress chartered the Bank, its authority flowed from the popular will and was superior to the power of the states. Since the power to tax was equivalent to "the power to destroy," states could not assert tax authority over it. To allow Maryland to tax a federal agency would be tantamount to allowing Maryland to tax residents of other states who had no voice in the political process.[10] (Marshall had distorted the facts to make a point. Though the federal government owned a fifth of the bank's shares, the national bank was not a federal government entity. It was a privately owned profit-making enterprise, and a large portion of its share-holders were not even U.S. citizens.) Marshall once again introduced a new constitutional principle: that a government cannot impose burdens on people who are not represented. In a sense, he was echoing the cry of "no taxation without representation." But Marshall was taking that principle a step further by asserting that the Supreme Court could strike down laws whenever legislators act in a way that frustrates democratic accountability.[11] For example, Marshall was suggesting that if Congress were to pass a law that disenfranchised voters, it would impede democratic accountability, and the Supreme Court could strike it down under this principle.

McCulloch was probably the most controversial decision that Marshall ever wrote. Marshall left no doubt as to the supremacy of the federal government over the states. Only months after the decision was issued, the appellant, James McCulloch, and the president of the Baltimore branch, James Buchanan, were indicted for stealing $1.4 million, confirming in the public's mind that the bank was a corrupt institution.

McCulloch inflamed the South's worst fears that the federal government could end slavery. The proslavery Republican press repudiated Marshall's opinion in the most extreme language. One paper condemned it as a "deadly blow" to state sovereignty that threatened the "welfare of the union."[12] Republican leaders in Virginia, particularly Judge Spencer Roane, coordinated a campaign to discredit Marshall. Writing in the Richmond *Enquirer* under the pen name Hampden, Roane blasted the *McCulloch* decision as unconstitutional.[13]

McCulloch laid bare the debate over slavery and the question of whether slavery could be extended into the western territories. Jefferson accused the court of "constantly working underground to undermine the foundations of our confederated fabric."[14] Jefferson charged that the Federalists were dividing the states between free and slave in the name of "morality," but he bluntly asserted that "[m]oral the question certainly is not." In Jefferson's view, the whole debate over whether to extend slavery was not in the interests of the slaves themselves. After all, whether slaves moved west or not, they remained slaves. Incredibly, Jefferson argued that "by spreading [the slaves] over a larger surface, their happiness would be increased."[15] In fact, many Virginians feared the increasing number of African Americans and hoped to dilute the threat by pushing slavery farther west away from their commonwealth.[16]

"Our opinion in the bank case has roused the sleeping spirit of Virginia," Marshall confided to Justice Story. "It will I understand be attacked in the papers with some asperity; and as those who favor it never write for the publick it will remain undefended & of course be considered as *damnably heretical.*"[17] When Jefferson issued a public letter attacking the Court, Marshall wrote to Story that Jefferson "rather grieves than surprises me. It grieves me because his influence is still so great that many—very many will adopt his opinions however unsound they may be, & however contrary to their own reason." But Marshall saw through the retired president: "[H]e is among the most ambitious, & I suspect among the most unforgiving of men." Though he acquired power by "professions of democracy," Jefferson rejected any check on "the wild impulse of the moment" as a constraint on his power and looked "with ill will at an independent judiciary."[18]

The immediate consequence of the *McCulloch* decision was less clear. Marshall's holding was not readily enforceable, and some states, including Ohio and Georgia, ignored it. When the bank's branch office in Ohio refused to pay the taxes it owed the state, the Ohio state auditor, Ralph Osborn, forcibly stole one hundred thousand dollars from the bank's office for the Ohio treasury. When a federal court ordered Osborn to repay the funds, he refused, claiming that the Eleventh Amendment prohibited suits against state officials in a federal court. Speaking for a six-to-one majority, Chief Justice Marshall held in *Osborn v. Bank of the United States* that when a federal court issued an injunction to a state official, that official was not entitled to whatever sovereign immunity the state would otherwise be entitled to under the Eleventh Amendment.[19] The *Osborn* decision created another important precedent for holding state officials accountable for their official actions.

THE LONG-BREWING BATTLE over the supremacy of the Supreme Court and the Constitution reached its height the year following *McCulloch* in a criminal case concerning a Virginia law that prohibited the sale of out-of-state lottery tickets. In 1812, Congress had authorized the District of Columbia to establish a lottery to finance improvements in the capital city. The District established what it called the National Lottery with a grand prize worth $100,000. In 1820, Philip and Mendes Cohen were caught selling six tickets to the National Lottery out of their office at Maxwell's wharf in Norfolk, Virginia. The Cohens were convicted by a state court and appealed their conviction to the Supreme Court, arguing that the federal law trumped Virginia's ban on out-of-state lottery tickets.

The key question for the Supreme Court in *Cohens v. Virginia* was whether the Court could hear an appeal from a state court in a criminal case. Unlike the *Martin* case, which involved a suit between two private parties, this appeal was against the Commonwealth of Virginia. Virginia argued that the state courts were not subject to the Supreme Court's appellate review in a criminal lawsuit. Virginia rested its argument in part on the state's sovereignty and in part on the Eleventh Amendment, which barred federal courts from hearing suits against a state brought by citizens of another state.

On March 3, 1821, Marshall issued a unanimous opinion that asserted the Supreme Court's appellate jurisdiction over state courts in criminal cases. Marshall rejected the Eleventh Amendment argument that Virginia could not be sued in a federal court. In this case, Virginia had initiated the action by prosecuting the Cohen brothers. The Cohens had not brought suit, and therefore the Eleventh Amendment did not apply to an appeal to the federal courts.[20]

The bulk of Marshall's opinion reaffirmed the absolute supremacy of the federal Constitution over state law. "The constitution and laws of a State, so far as they are repugnant to the constitution and laws of the United States, are absolutely void."[21] This was strong language. Again, he echoed the argument in *Martin* and *McCulloch* that the Constitution was not a compact of the states. "The people made the constitution, and [only] the people can unmake it. It is the creature of their will, and lives only by their will." Marshall rejected the idea that states could nullify federal law. "[T]his supreme and irresistible power to make or to unmake, resides only in the whole body of the people, not in any subdivision of them."[22] Marshall reasoned that "[i]n war, we are one people. In making peace, we are one people. In all commercial regulations, we are one and the same people." The people chose to create one nation. To secure the advantages of the Union necessitated uniformity in interpreting the Constitution.[23]

Marshall's decision in *Cohens v. Virginia* bolstered the Supreme Court's holdings in *Martin* and *McCulloch* and ignited another firestorm of protest. Judge Roane, as the president of the Virginia Supreme Court, wrote more than a dozen articles excoriating the decision under the pen names Algernon Sidney and Hampden. Roane warned that if Marshall's opinion stood "the equilibrium established by the Constitution is destroyed, and the compact exists thereafter but in name." He accused the Supreme Court of succumbing to "that love of power, which all history informs us infects and corrupts all who possess it, and from which even the high and ermined judges, themselves, are not exempted." He joked that the only thing left for Marshall to claim was "divine right."[24] Roane attacked Marshall's holding as incompatible with the sovereignty of Virginia. "There is no tribunal before which the sovereign can be arraigned," he asserted. It is in the nature of sovereignty that a sovereign "is incapable of error." Marshall's judgment "must be refuted," or it "must ultimately prove fatal" to the sovereignty of the states.[25]

Marshall warned Story that a "deep design to convert our government into a meer [*sic*] league of States has taken strong hold of a powerful & violent party in Virginia. The attack upon the Judiciary is in fact an attack upon the union." And he had no doubt where the responsibility lay: "The whole attack, if not originating with Mr. Jefferson is obviously approved & guided by him."[26] Marshall did not see that the stridency of his opinion may have added fuel to the fire.

Marshall's opinions in *Martin, McCulloch,* and *Cohens* were seen by most southerners as a betrayal.[27] In their view, Marshall had chosen sides against his fellow southerners. Southern Republicans denounced this attack on states' rights. But what they meant by "states' rights" was not only some abstract principle of state sovereignty. In concrete terms, "states' rights" really meant slavery. Decades before the Civil War, the Supreme Court had become a focal point of the conflict on which the Union's survival depended.

CHAPTER TWENTY-SEVEN

THE PIRATE LOTTERY

Marshall dreaded his sojourns to Washington every February. The road from Richmond to Washington rambled obliquely through forested hills, and even a traveler familiar with the way could easily become lost. Since the roads were frequently flooded, they were often impassable. On a good day, a light coach could go as fast as two miles per hour. But Marshall usually plodded along on horseback, though at sixty-five, this was becoming increasingly uncomfortable for him. In June and the end of December, Marshall was also required to ride circuit in North Carolina, where travel was even more difficult. By the 1820s, Marshall's salary was five thousand dollars (about one hundred thousand dollars today). By comparison, an attorney in private practice could earn four times that amount without the inconvenience of riding circuit.[1] Lawmakers were unmoved by the apparent inequity. Then, as now, judges were expected to be both incorruptible and cheap.

The Supreme Court's docket was growing in the 1820s. The winter term ran about seven weeks, from late January or early February through mid-March. The justices packed in an average of three or four dozen decisions, hearing arguments from eleven in the morning until four in the afternoon without a break. Then they would walk back to their boardinghouse a few blocks away for supper and conferencing, which could last quite late.[2] Marshall did not look forward to the parties in the nation's capital, and he often avoided social engagements outside the close circle of the other justices.

Marshall wrote fewer of the court's opinions in the 1820s than he had in his first two decades on the court. The task of drafting opinions by hand became more onerous with age. He sometimes asked one of the other justices, particularly Justice Story, to draft the court's opinion, but the chief justice still played a role in crafting nearly every opinion.

Monroe's Era of Good Feelings did not last long. The question of slavery soon clouded over the warm sunshine of the Monroe administration. Though Marshall had seen the nation survive three wars in his lifetime, he worried now more than ever about the country's destiny. One is often disappointed when one's friends assume higher office, and Marshall could not help but doubt Monroe's leadership. Marshall thought that the country needed to spend more money to improve infrastructure; Monroe opposed such measures. And Monroe vacillated on the most critical issue of the day: whether to permit the spread of slavery into the new territories.[3]

Since Jefferson's acquisition of Louisiana, the states had divided over the question of whether the new territory would be slave or free. For the southern states, rejecting the growth of slavery was perceived as a threat to their economic viability and an indictment of their way of life. The issue came to a head with the debate over admitting Missouri as a state. Missourians petitioned Congress for the right to enter as a slave state. By 1819, there were eleven free states and eleven slave states. Admitting Missouri as slave or free would tip the balance in Congress. Southerners feared that if there were a majority of free states, Congress would legislate slavery out of existence. The North threatened the southern way of life. But the Northwest Ordinance signed by President Washington in 1789 had prohibited slavery anywhere in the Northwest Territory. The northern states feared that the balance of power in the Senate would tip in favor of the slave states if slavery were permitted to expand into the western territory.

While Congress bitterly debated the question of Missouri's admission, President Monroe remained silent, refusing to take a position on the most critical issue of his presidency. The president worried more about his own chances for reelection than the outcome of the debate.[4] It fell to House Speaker Henry Clay to craft a compromise: admit Missouri as a slave state and Maine as a free state and prohibit slavery in the future from other territories north of the parallel 36° 30'. The Missouri Compromise of 1820 saved the Union, at least for the time being.[5] But the debate had exposed the jagged fault line that cut through American politics. Writing from Monticello, Jefferson predicted that "this momentous question, like a fire bell in the night, awakened and filled me with terror. I considered it at once the knell of the Union. It is hushed indeed for the moment. But this is a reprieve only, not a final sentence."[6]

Slavery was the Constitution's original sin. The Framers had not merely tolerated slavery but had enshrined it in the Constitution. The original seven articles of the Constitution did not protect a citizen's right to speak, assemble, petition the government, vote, or worship; they did not assure that persons would be secure in their homes from unreasonable searches or seizures, prohibit cruel and unusual punishments, or guarantee a right to a jury trial or any other procedural right before the government could take away one's life, liberty, or property. The original Constitution did, however, preserve the right to buy, sell, and own slaves: The Constitution counted slaves as three-fifths of a person for purposes of apportioning representation in Congress. That dramatically increased the South's voting power in Congress at a time when roughly a third of all southerners were slaves.[7] The slave trade could not be regulated for twenty years—an immunity afforded to no other industry.[8] To safeguard slavery from excessive taxation, the state and federal governments were prohibited from imposing taxes on slaves or the products of slave labor.[9] This gave slaveholders a tax exemption that farmers and manufacturers in the free states did not enjoy. And unlike almost any other clause in the Constitution, these two provisions could not be amended.[10] To quiet the fears of a slave uprising, the federal government was obligated to protect the states against a slave revolt and was empowered to call up state militias to suppress uprisings.[11] The Constitution prohibited states from emancipating fugitive slaves and required states to return fugitives to their masters on demand.[12] The whole bicameral structure of Congress ensured that the sovereignty of the slave states would be protected from interference by free states.[13]

The slavery issue first arose before the federal courts in the context of the slave trade. Many southerners, including Jefferson, supported the ban on importing slaves. By 1807, there were about one million slaves in the United States, with all but around fifty thousand of them packed into the southern states.[14] This was more than enough to ensure an inexhaustible supply of slaves into the future. The roughly two million southern whites feared that the swelling population of slaves might overwhelm them.[15] Some slaveholders worried that the growing supply of slaves would lower the market value of their own slaves. Northern abolitionists and some anxious southerners forged an unlikely alliance against the slave trade.

In 1794, Congress prohibited U.S. citizens and residents from engaging in the slave trade, but the law did not apply to foreign nationals and foreign vessels.[16] In 1807, Congress went further and prohibited the import of all slaves to the United States effective January 1, 1808, the earliest date such a ban would be allowed under the Constitution. The president was authorized to send out naval vessels to seize any U.S. ships engaged in the slave trade even if they were outside U.S. territorial waters.[17] In 1819, Congress went one step further and authorized the president to seize any slave ship owned or commanded by U.S. citizens or residents even if it was flying a foreign flag in foreign waters. The 1819 act provided that any captured Africans on board should be freed and returned to Africa.

Despite these laws, unscrupulous American and foreign nationals entered the slave trade using vessels registered to Spain or Portugal, which had not yet banned the slave trade. These ships would cruise the southern coastline looking for an opportunity to land and quickly unload their precious cargo before the U.S. authorities seized their ships. They assumed that the law would punish only U.S. nationals and U.S. ships.

IN 1820, A SOUTH AMERICAN pirate ship, the *Colombia*, captured a U.S. slave ship with twenty-five slaves off the coast of Africa.[18] The *Colombia*, later known as the *Arraganta*, flew the flag of the Banda Oriental, a revolutionary independence movement centered in what is now Uruguay. In addition to the U.S. ship, the *Arraganta* seized several Portuguese slave ships, including the *Antelope,* and a Spanish slave vessel, capturing a total of around 280 Africans. The *Arraganta* and the *Antelope*, loaded with slaves, sailed back toward South America, but the *Arraganta* was wrecked off the northeast coast of Brazil. A number of crew members and about thirty Africans were lost at sea. The captain and some of the crew were seized for piracy by Portuguese ships. The remaining crew and their captives transferred to the *Antelope*, under the command of Captain John Smith, a U.S. citizen, and the *Antelope* proceeded toward Florida.

Captain Smith apparently intended to slip into a friendly port in Florida and sell his slaves there. Spain had recently agreed to cede Florida to the United States, but the treaty was not yet ratified, so for the time being Florida remained Spanish territory. As the *Antelope* hovered along the Florida coast, it was spotted by a U.S. revenue cutter, the *Dallas*. Captain John Jackson, the commander of the *Dallas,* suspected that the *Antelope* was either a pirate ship or a slave ship. After a brief chase, the *Dallas* captured the *Antelope* in Spanish waters. Jackson determined that the vessel was indeed a slave ship commanded by U.S. citizens in violation of U.S. law and brought the ship in for adjudication. The Africans were transported on the *Dallas* to the port of Savannah. As provided by the 1819 act, they were turned over to the federal marshal, who was responsible for their safekeeping while they awaited a judgment as to where they belonged.[19]

President Monroe, vacationing at his home in Albemarle, Virginia, faced the question of whether to return the slaves to Spain and Portugal or send them back to Africa. Initially, his instinct was to direct the district attorney to ask the district court to free the slaves as provided by the 1819 act. He was drafting an order to this effect when he received an unexpected visitor—the Portuguese ambassador, José Francisco Correia da Serra. Correia da Serra, a personal friend of Monroe's, insisted that the slaves be returned to the Portuguese government—a demand at odds with the Portuguese government's official position opposing the slave trade.[20] Monroe drew a line through his initial instructions to free the slaves and instead directed the U.S. attorney in Georgia to await instructions from Attorney General William Wirt.[21]

Monroe's decision would have raised eyebrows among the cabinet. At that time, the attorney general merely advised the president. The U.S. attorneys, who prosecuted cases, were independent from the attorney general. The president had every reason to expect that Wirt would side with the property rights of the slave traders. Wirt was a Maryland slave owner who had argued in favor of extending slavery to the Louisiana Purchase, and he believed that the federal government had no authority to curb the spread of slavery.[22] But the president's order to the U.S. attorney did not arrive on time. Without waiting for instructions from the president or the attorney general, the U.S. attorney for Georgia, Richard Wylly Habersham, decided to intervene on behalf of the Africans.

While the case proceeded, the U.S. marshal in Savannah kept the Africans locked up partly for their own protection from possible kidnappers and partly to prevent them from escaping. That summer Savannah was in the grip of a terrifying yellow fever epidemic. Georgia law prohibited ships from landing in Savannah during the summer months, when diseases spread like wildfire, but no one cared about exposing the Africans to yellow fever. Ten percent of the city's population died, including many of the Africans. By the fall, there were 212 Africans remaining.[23] Though the U.S. Navy paid for the cost of feeding the slaves, the thrifty mayor of Savannah insisted that the Africans should be put to work—for no wages. Fifty were ordered to work on the city's fortifications. Others were rented out to local residents. More than one hundred worked the steamy fields of the U.S. marshal's own plantation. All this was done under the authority of the federal court. President Monroe objected that the cost of feeding the Africans fell on the federal government, but he did not complain about the moral hypocrisy of the government exploiting the involuntary labor of persons that the U.S. government argued in court were free.[24]

The case reached U.S. District Judge William Davies in January 1821. Under the 1819 act, Captain Jackson would be entitled to receive a bounty of twenty-five dollars for each of the Africans he had freed. In addition to Captain Jackson, the Spanish and Portuguese vice-consuls and Captain John Smith filed claims for the ship and its cargo. Judge Davies held that even though the slave trade may be unjust and illegal under U.S. law, it was permissible under international law, and therefore the Africans should be returned as slaves to Spain and Portugal. The problem was that since no one knew for certain which Africans came from which ships, there was no way of knowing who belonged to which country. More than one hundred of the kidnapped Africans had either perished or escaped, so it was uncertain how many Africans were owed to Spain or Portugal. Under U.S. law, any Africans allocated to the United States would be freed. The court decided to allocate the Africans proportionately to Spain, Portugal, and the United States. The judge determined that 63 should be handed over to Spain, 142 to Portugal, and the remaining 7 to the United States. Captain Jackson received a quarter of the salvage value of the *Antelope* plus a bounty of $175 for the seven Africans freed to the United States. U.S. Attorney Habersham appealed to the circuit court—in defiance of the president's desire to end the litigation.[25]

Supreme Court Justice William Johnson heard the appeal as the circuit judge sitting in Milledgeville, then the booming capital of Georgia. Appointed by Jefferson when he was only thirty-three, Justice Johnson bore the smug assurance of his own intellectual superiority. John Quincy Adams described Justice Johnson as "restive, turbulent, hot-headed, flaringly independent."[26] Of all the men who served on the Marshall Court, Johnson was the least collegial.[27] He dissented more often than any other justice and always in harsh tones. His opinions did not fit into any coherent pattern but proceeded from some contrarian impulse.

The day the argument concluded, Johnson issued his opinion without a moment of deliberation. While he acknowledged that slavery was a "national evil," he rejected the argument that the slave trade was condemned by international law. "However revolting to humanity" this was, Johnson believed that slaves were no different from any other commercial cargo under the law of nations. Therefore a U.S. court could not enforce laws banning the slave trade against foreign slavers, and the slave traders were entitled to the return of their property. Johnson adjusted the number of Africans to be returned to Portugal and increased to sixteen the number of Africans to be freed to the United States.[28] Justice Johnson's opinion flew in the face of Congress's declaration that same year that the slave trade was "piracy" under international law punishable by death.[29]

Since the South American pirates had not kept records of which Africans had been captured from the American vessel, it was impossible to know which sixteen Africans should be freed. That alone might have given the court a reason to withhold its judgment, but Justice Johnson was not deterred by a lack of evidence: "[S]hall we refuse to act because we are not vested with the power of devination [sic]?" Johnson decided to organize a game of chance: The Africans could win their freedom by drawing lots. It would have been unthinkable that any jurist would hazard the freedom of a white man in a raffle, but Johnson had no such scruples when it came to Africans. "We can only do the best in our power, the lot must decide their fate, and the Almighty will direct the hand that acts in the selection."[30] The Almighty, however, was not paying attention.

Each African was assigned a number, and the numbers were copied on small slips of paper. The assembled Africans watched while the U.S. attorney's brother slowly drew sixteen slips from a box and called out their numbers. It is unknown whether the Africans really comprehended that their fate was being decided by lots, or whether they watched in anxious prayer. When all sixteen numbers were chosen, the rest were told they would be sold as chattel. In the guise of doing justice, the court dispensed freedom with a cruel capriciousness. The lives of 212 Africans were casually discarded as if they were losing lottery tickets.[31]

On Saturday, February 26, 1825, Attorney General William Wirt and Francis Scott Key appeared before the Supreme Court to argue the appeal on behalf of the Africans. Wirt's reputation as a brilliant litigator was undoubtedly due in part to his powerful appearance. He had a distinguished face with an intense glare and a strong jaw. His broad, noble forehead was crowned with a widow's peak and a dramatic swirl of long white curls. Key, who was a poet as well as an attorney, frequently argued before the Supreme Court. His flamboyant style of argument, not unlike the lyrics he wrote for "The Star-Spangled Banner," was full of fury and bombast. Both Key and Attorney General Wirt were slaveholders and appeared despite their outspoken support for slavery. Key, in particular, had prosecuted cases against abolitionists. Opposing them on behalf of the Spanish vice-consul were U.S. Senator John Macpherson Berrien of Georgia and Charles Jared Ingersoll. The Portuguese vice-consul was represented by Richard Henry Wilde. Wilde was a Georgia congressman and also a poet, who throughout four days of argument kept a curious silence.[32]

Key argued that since the slave trade was illegal in the United States, U.S. law must prevail in U.S. courts. The *Antelope* was a "piratical vessel." Though there was no treaty outlawing the slave trade, it violated natural law—a point that even the king of Spain had conceded.[33] The "time is at hand, if it has not already arrived," Key asserted, "when the slave trade is not only forbidden by the concurrent voice of most nations, but is denounced and punished as a crime of the deepest die." In fact, most European nations had at least condemned the slave trade.[34] Portugal and Spain had signed treaties with Britain in 1815 and 1816, respectively, promising to end the slave trade. And both had signed a declaration at the Congress of Vienna in 1815 condemning the slave trade as "repugnant to the principles of humanity and universal morality" and calling on all governments to abolish it.[35] Finally, Key pointed out that neither Spain nor Portugal had any proof of ownership beyond a lottery that would surely shock the conscience of any court.[36]

Counsel for Spain challenged the authority of the *Dallas* to seize a ship flying a foreign flag outside U.S. waters.[37] Berrien argued that the United States had no license to act as "censors of the morals of the world."[38] Moreover, the slave trade could not violate natural law. After all, it had been, until very recently, "universally tolerated and encouraged."[39] Berrien insisted that it would be hypocritical for the Supreme Court to condemn the slave trade while the Constitution safeguarded slavery at home.

Attorney General Wirt responded that Spain and Portugal had not met the burden of proving the Africans belonged to them. "Some of them are confessedly free . . . Which of them are slaves, it is impossible to determine by any rule of evidence known to our practice."[40] Wirt asserted that the Africans remained free both under the law of nature and the law of their own countries. "The mere possession of an African, claiming him as a slave by a Spanish ship, on the coast of Africa, would no more prove the African a slave, than the possession of a Spaniard, by an African ship on the coast of Spain, would prove the Spaniard a slave." And the persistence of slavery in the United States could not provide "any excuse or palliation; for perpetuating, and extending the guilt and misery of the slave trade."[41]

Just a week after administering the oath of office to President Monroe for his second term, Marshall delivered the Court's opinion. For Chief

Justice Marshall, *Antelope* must have been among the most emotionally wrenching decisions he faced on the Court. He had strong personal feelings on the subject. He was an outspoken opponent of the slave trade, a founding leader of the Society for the Colonization of Free People of Color, and the founder, president, and principal benefactor of the Virginia Society for Colonization until his death. He had defended slaves pro bono in Virginia, and as a member of the Virginia House, he had supported legislation to encourage the manumission of slaves.[42]

This was by no means the first time that Marshall had confronted racial injustice on the bench. Marshall once described to Justice Story a case he heard on the circuit involving a Virginia law that discriminated against free blacks. Marshall admitted that "I might have considered its constitutionality had I chosen to do so, but it was not absolutely necessary, &, as I am not fond of butting against a wall in sport, I escaped on the construction of the act."[43] Marshall preferred to deal with the issue of slavery and states' rights indirectly. As a circuit court judge, Marshall had decided a number of cases concerning the property rights and liabilities of slave owners and traders, but he had never been presented squarely with the question of whether the slave trade was consistent with the law of nations.[44] *Antelope* offered Marshall an opportunity to strike a blow against slave trading, but it would be difficult to reach that outcome. The Supreme Court now included Justices Smith Thompson, Joseph Story, Bushrod Washington, Gabriel Duvall, William Johnson, and Thomas Todd. Though Justices Duvall and Story had issued opinions critical of the slave trade, at least four of the justices were slaveholders.[45] All but Thompson and Story were southerners, and all but Washington and Marshall had been appointed by Republican presidents. Under the circumstances, it would be a challenge to cobble together a majority to reverse Justice Johnson's circuit court decision.

Marshall first considered the question of whether the slave trade violated international law. Marshall acknowledged that regardless of how much European states condemned the slave trade, "[t]he Christian and civilized nations of the world with whom we have most intercourse, have all been engaged in it." Only in the past couple of decades had the Europeans begun outlawing the trade, but still it persisted.[46] For example, even though Britain had outlawed the slave trade by statute, British courts were still divided on whether international law permitted the slave trade.[47] Though Marshall recognized that the slave trade violated natural law, he wrote that courts must distinguish morality from law.[48]

On behalf of the Africans, the U.S. attorney had argued that even if the slave trade was not illegal under international law, it was clearly outlawed by the United States, and a U.S. court should apply U.S. law. Marshall responded that since all sovereign nations are equal, "no one can rightfully impose a rule on another." Though the United States could outlaw slave trading by U.S. persons and on board U.S. ships, the Africans were enslaved on Portuguese and Spanish ships subject to the laws of those countries. "[T]his traffic remains lawful to those whose governments have not forbidden it."[49]

In fact, it was not clear what the law was in Spain and Portugal. Both governments had issued declarations against the slave trade, and both had signed treaties with Britain condemning it. But neither country had a statute clearly outlawing slave trade. Even assuming that Spain and Portugal intended to outlaw the slave trade, Marshall held that a U.S. court could not apply Spanish or Portuguese criminal laws prohibiting the slave trade. Though U.S. courts do apply foreign law in civil suits, such as contract or tort law, Marshall declared that "[t]he Courts of no country execute the penal laws of another."[50] This principle that U.S. courts will not enforce a foreign government's criminal law was another invention of Marshall's legal imagination that persists in our law today.

To resolve the sticky question as to which Africans belonged to Spain or Portugal, the Court decided that the claimants had the burden of proving who owed which slaves. The counsel for Portugal, Congressman Wilde, kept quiet. He had not presented an actual claim on behalf of Portugal but had confined himself to arguing that Portugal should not have to pay for the upkeep of the Africans while they were in federal custody. Marshall concluded that the "unaccountable absence, of any Portuguese claimant, furnishes irresistible testimony, that no such claimant exists, and that the real owner belongs to some other nation, and feels the necessity of concealment." The implication was clear that the real owner in interest was an unidentified American fearing prosecution. As it later turned out, the real claimant was hiding in plain view. Accordingly, the Court dismissed Portugal's claim.[51] Spain could show that its ship had originally carried ninety-three Africans, but since so many of the original captives had died or were lost, the court reduced the number of Africans that Spain was entitled to from the sixty-three awarded by the circuit court to thirty-nine.

The remaining 149 Africans were "freed," but they were not quite free. The president ordered them deported on a naval vessel to the newly created U.S. colony of Liberia. There they were placed under the close supervision of the euphemistically named United States Agency for Liberated Africans, which assigned them to housing units and jobs. The Africans had no choice but to comply.[52] After being kidnapped by slave traders, seized by pirates, rescued by the U.S. Navy, imprisoned by the federal authorities, enslaved by a U.S. marshal, and subjected to a dehumanizing lottery, they were finally "liberated" in a strange new country and indentured to work for the U.S. Agency— for the rest of their lives—as "free" men and women. Though they were compensated for their labor, they were only marginally freer than slaves.

While the "freed" Africans were forcibly deported, the thirty-nine consigned to Spain never left the United States. Another legal appeal was filed in the Supreme Court on their behalf, which extended their detention and delayed the final outcome until 1827, when the Supreme Court reaffirmed its prior decision. By then, it was clear that the Africans' real "owners" never stepped forward because they, too, were probably Americans who feared prosecution under U.S. law.[53] The Spanish vice-consul had simply acted as agent for the true owner. During seven years of litigation, the Spanish and Portuguese vice-consuls had accumulated legal fees and other costs associated with the Africans that exceeded the market value of the thirty-nine slaves. All this time, the fees were quietly paid by Congressman Wilde, the counsel to Portugal. Instead of repaying Wilde for his expenses, the Spanish and Portuguese vice-consuls agreed to transfer ownership of "their" Africans to Wilde.[54] The congressman later insisted that he had acted with "humane" motives: "My feelings toward those poor creatures induces me to wish them free. But if slavery is their destiny I desire to render it as endurable as slavery can be." Rather than sending them to Spain, Wilde sent them to Florida, which he called the "land of flowers," to work on his sugar plantation.[55] The ultimate beneficiary of the Court's decision was a U.S. congressman, who, contrary to the spirit if not the letter of U.S. law, profited from a depraved lottery and the piracy of a foreign slave ship.

PERSONALLY, MARSHALL VIEWED slavery and the slave trade as an abomination.[56] Marshall's decision in *Antelope* betrayed this conviction. Why did he step back from the opportunity to affirm an emerging principle of international law outlawing the slave trade? Marshall could surely see the arc of history bending in that direction.

Marshall's decision is especially difficult to explain in light of a decision by Justice Story on the Massachusetts circuit court just three years earlier. In a case arising out of the seizure of a French slave ship, the *Jeune Eugénie*, Story excoriated the slave trade and declared that it violated international law, which he affirmed rested on natural law and general principles of right and justice.[57] One must question why Marshall did not rely on Story's circuit opinion as precedent and hold that the slave trade was illegal.

One way to explain Marshall's opinion is that he believed obedience to the law trumped moral judgments.[58] According to this view, Marshall saw judges as neutral referees merely applying fixed legal rules. But that view does not square with his expansive interpretation of the Constitution. The man who wrote *Marbury* and *McCulloch* was not shy about inventing legal principles. Marshall understood that he was not just applying the law mechanically; he was also making law.

An alternative explanation might be that Marshall feared that a decision condemning the slave trade would threaten the Union.[59] But by 1825, it would hardly be controversial to assert that the slave trade violated international law. Congress had already outlawed the trade three times with broad support from southerners. And Marshall had not backed down in the past from issuing controversial opinions that threatened state sovereignty and slavery.

A third possibility is that Marshall rejected the view that natural law could bind sovereign states. The danger of imposing natural law on sovereign states is that it would give courts broad latitude to pluck legal principles from the air and interfere with the power of the political branches of government to manage foreign relations. By insisting that the United States could be bound only by its own consent to treaties or customary international law, Marshall once again reaffirmed the constitutional separation of powers. Yet this explanation is not entirely satisfactory either because in other contexts—his legal memoranda during the XYZ Affair and his later opinions on Indian sovereignty—Marshall references natural law as a source of international law. Moreover, the international legal authorities whom Marshall most frequently relied upon—Vattel, Grotius, Pufendorf, and Rutherford—accepted at least in part that natural law could be a foundation for international law.[60]

Perhaps Marshall was concerned not by the domestic impact of the court's decision but by its implications for foreign affairs. A decision that a U.S. cruiser could stop and search foreign vessels in peacetime would likely invite more naval conflicts with the European powers in the future. If the United States could assert its authority in international waters over foreign vessels, what would prevent France or Britain from doing the same against U.S. ships?

Whatever Marshall's reason for denying the Africans their freedom, he clearly felt conflicted. His opinion began with these words: "[T]his Court must not yield to feelings which might seduce it from the path of duty, and must obey the mandate of the law."[61] The contrast he drew between his feelings and his duty reveals something about Marshall's psychology. His early years were shaped by powerful male authority figures—his father, General Steuben, President Washington, and President Adams. Marshall had advanced professionally through his service to these authority figures. As the eldest in his large family, Marshall accepted responsibility at an early age to help to raise his siblings. His parents expected him to subordinate his own desires for the collective good of the family. Marshall distinguished himself as a young soldier for his self-discipline and willingness to endure hardship. As chief justice, Marshall often built consensus by compromising his own views. Throughout Marshall's career, duty demanded that he set aside his own emotions; service and conscience were antipodes. Personal values had to yield to higher authority. His instinct as a judge would be to choose the opposite of his own preference, to privilege rules over empathy.

Antelope revealed certain faults in Marshall's character: a readiness to submit to the authority of the law no matter how cruel or capricious it was and a failure of empathy for those seeking justice in his court. *Antelope* presented Marshall with the opportunity to strike a blow against the slave trade that might have sent ripples across the Atlantic. He failed this test. Though Marshall would not challenge slavery directly, he found another, indirect route—granting Congress authority to regulate the slave trade domestically. A steamboat provided the unlikely vehicle for Marshall's redemption.

CHAPTER TWENTY-EIGHT

THE GREAT
STEAMBOAT CASE

I n 1820, Chief Justice Marshall issued one of the most monumental decisions ever rendered on the scope of the federal government's powers and its relationship to the states. It was a decision that more than any other made it possible to forge a unified modern national economy out of the fragmented state governments that jealously feuded over resources and markets.

The Constitution granted Congress the "power to regulate commerce among the states," but what did that include? And what powers belonged exclusively to the states? The Constitution also eliminated trade barriers between states, yet state governments had issued monopolies to local businesses and jealously sought to protect local businesses from competition. A growing economy required a national infrastructure, and it was not clear whether the federal government had the power to create that infrastructure.

At the turn of the nineteenth century, the emergence of the steam engine held the promise of opening up the interior of the country and uniting the states in a genuine national market. James Rumsey and John Fitch had developed designs for a steamboat, which Fitch demonstrated to the amazement of the delegates to the Constitutional Convention in Philadelphia in 1787. Their demonstration helped to persuade the delegates of the value of granting the federal government the power to award patents. Despite their creativity, Fitch and Rumsey lacked the financial and political capital to create a successful business.[1]

In 1802, Robert Fulton, an ambitious engineer, and Robert Livingston, the former chancellor of New York State's highest court, formed a partnership to develop steamboats. Five years later, they were granted a U.S. patent—which most likely infringed on Fitch's design and may have been invalid. In 1808, Chancellor Livingston's political influence and wealth helped them to secure from the New York legislature a thirty-year monopoly to navigate steamboats in the waters of New York State that authorized them to seize any steamboats operated by an unlicensed party. The monopoly engendered resentment from the public, who were forced to pay higher transportation prices. Many people rightly viewed it as an example of influence peddling.[2] When some New Yorkers challenged the monopoly in court, the state's highest court ruled that until Congress enacted conflicting laws, the state had the sovereign authority to create monopolies for steamboats.[3]

At the same time that Fulton and Livingston were establishing their steamboat company, Aaron Ogden, a former New Jersey governor and U.S. senator, established a company of his own to run a ferry from New York City to Elizabethtown (now Elizabeth), New Jersey. Ogden was as combative as he was ambitious. Ogden lobbied New Jersey to pass a law that prohibited steamboats registered in New York from New Jersey waters. He used this to pressure Fulton to grant him a license to run his ferry in New York waters.[4]

Ogden then formed a partnership with Thomas Gibbons, a wealthy South Carolina lawyer. At first, Ogden and Gibbons were a great team, but Gibbons had a mean temper. After Ogden tried to interfere in a dispute between Gibbons and his daughter, Gibbons responded angrily. He challenged Ogden to a duel and even threatened him with a horsewhip.[5] The partnership collapsed. Gibbons sought revenge by establishing a new partnership with the young Cornelius Vanderbilt, the future titan of New York railroads and shipping, who captained Gibbons's ferry from Elizabethtown to New York. Gibbons received a license "to navigate the waters of any state by steamboat" from the federal government under the Federal Coasting Act of 1793. In 1820, Ogden won an injunction in a New York court to stop Gibbons from infringing on his exclusive license, and Gibbons appealed to the U.S. Supreme Court.[6] This battle set the stage for one of the most significant decisions of Marshall's era on the Court.

Though the controversy was popularly dubbed the Great Steamboat Case, much more was at stake. The real issue was how to define the powers of the states and the federal government. New York, Connecticut, and New Jersey had all asserted exclusive authority over their own waterways and prohibited steamships chartered by other states. The dispute threatened to spread and strangle navigation among the states at a time when Congress was again considering legislation to finance improvements to the nation's roads and canals. Both Presidents Madison and Monroe had vetoed such legislation on the grounds that in their view Congress had no power over internal improvements. Southern Republicans resisted any suggestion that the federal government could regulate commerce. If the national government could encroach on New York's waters in this way, what else might Congress do? Southerners worried that their "peculiar institution" might be vulnerable to federal regulations. Virginia Congressman John Randolph warned that if Congress had broad authority to regulate commerce "they may emancipate every slave in the United States."[7]

On Wednesday morning, February 4, 1824, the Supreme Court chamber was mobbed with attorneys, members of the press, and spectators who spilled out into the hallway. Massachusetts Senator Daniel Webster and Attorney General William Wirt represented Gibbons. Two former New York attorneys general—Thomas J. Oakley and the prominent lawyer Thomas

Addis Emmet—represented Ogden. A few minutes after eleven, Marshall dipped the nib of his pen, pulled up the sleeves of his robe, and nodded silently to Senator Webster to begin. Five days of brilliant and often fiery rhetoric followed.[8]

There were two basic questions before the Court: first, whether Congress had the power to regulate navigation, and if so, whether Congress had, in fact, displaced New York's authority over its own waterways. Webster argued that Congress's power to regulate commerce was comprehensive and exclusive. He asserted that the Constitution left no room for the states to grant any monopolies or restraints on trade. "The very object intended, more than any other, was to take away such power. If it had not so provided, the constitution would not have been worth accepting."[9] Webster pointed out that the states' powers to maintain roads and bridges, or impose quarantines, were merely "police powers" rather than the power to regulate commerce itself.[10] In enacting the 1793 act, Congress had granted to Gibbons a right to navigate the waters of any state, and under the Constitution, federal law must be supreme over conflicting state law.[11]

After Webster's powerful performance, the spectators wondered what Oakley could possibly argue in rebuttal, but Ogden's attorney did not seem rattled. He responded with the cool confidence of a master.[12] Rather than dispute the power of the federal government, Oakley asserted that nothing in the Constitution forbids states from exercising power over commerce.[13] The Constitution limited certain powers of states, such as the power to impose tariffs. Oakley suggested that this must mean that states retained concurrent authority to regulate other aspects of commerce.[14] All that New York State had done was to prohibit a steamboat from entering New York's waters. Oakley argued that restricting navigation was not the same thing as banning commerce. Nothing in the Constitution gave Congress an exclusive power to regulate navigation within the territory of the states.[15]

Wirt gave the final rebuttal to Ogden's lawyers. The Court stood at the threshold of a momentous decision whether to permit states to restrict the growth of the national market or whether to uphold the supremacy of federal law. Wirt warned that "if the spirit of hostility, which already exists in three of our States, is to catch by contagion, and spread among the rest . . . what are we to expect? Civil wars have often arisen from far inferior causes, and have desolated some of the fairest provinces of the earth." The attorney general solemnly concluded that "if you do not extirpate the seeds of anarchy which New-York has sown; you will have civil war."[16]

A few days after the argument, Marshall stumbled on the cellar door of his boardinghouse. He suffered bruises to his head and a dislocated shoulder that caused him enormous pain. Marshall was unable to deliver his opinion for three weeks while he recovered. On March 2, 1824, Marshall read the Court's unanimous decision with one arm in a sling. His voice was still weak, but his words struck a bold chord. He slowly read out his opinion—an opinion that would define the scope of federal power for centuries.

The chief justice began by rejecting a narrow reading of the Constitution's text. "It has been said, that these powers ought to be construed strictly. But why?" Nothing in the Constitution countenanced such a rule. "We do not, therefore, think ourselves justified in adopting it." Keeping faith with the Constitution required the Court to interpret it. The Court eschewed a "narrow construction, which would cripple the government, and render it unequal to the object for which it is declared to be instituted."[17] Marshall interpreted Article I of the Constitution granting Congress the "power to regulate commerce with foreign nations, and among the several States and with the Indian tribes." Ogden's counsel argued that commerce was limited to "traffic, to buying and selling, or the interchange of commodities." Ogden was ferrying people, not goods. Marshall affirmed that commerce is more than commodities; it is commercial "intercourse," which "[a]ll America understands . . . comprehends navigation."[18] In fact, this was far from clear. But Marshall insisted it would be "absurd, as well as useless," to grant Congress the power to regulate commerce and not include navigation.[19]

Did Congress's power to regulate navigation reach inside the territorial waters of a sovereign state? That depended on the meaning of commerce "among the several states." Here Marshall argued that "[a] thing which among others, is intermingled with them. Commerce among the States, cannot stop at the external boundary line of each state, but may be introduced into the interior."[20] This was another bold maneuver by Marshall, subordinating the territorial sovereignty of the states to the federal government's commerce powers. If Congress's regulatory powers stopped at the border of each state, the power to regulate commerce would be nugatory. "The deep streams which penetrate our country in every direction, pass through the interior of almost every State in the Union, and furnish the means of exercising this right. If Congress has the power to regulate it, that power must be exercised whenever the subject exists."[21] In other words, no territory was out of reach of the federal power.

What then is the power that Congress exercises? "This power, like all others vested in Congress, is complete in itself, may be exercised to its utmost extent, and acknowledges no limitations, other than are prescribed in the constitution."[22] The Constitution expressly prohibited certain acts like ex post facto laws (laws that punish people after the fact). But apart from these explicit limits, Congress's authority to regulate commerce was limited only by the political restraints exercised by the people on their elected representatives. Congress's power was plenary and as absolute as if it had been granted to a single government rather than a federal entity.[23] Marshall came close—but did not assert—that the federal power was exclusive and that states had no power to regulate commerce. Since Congress had exercised its authority by adopting the Federal Coasting Act under which Gibbons's steamboat was properly licensed, the New York law that prohibited Gibbons from the New York waters was invalid.

Marshall had been speaking for nearly an hour. He was exhausted, and the courtroom spectators leaned forward to hear his closing passage: "Powerful and ingenious minds, taking, as postulates, that the powers expressly granted to the government of the Union, are to be contracted by construction, into the narrowest possible compass, and that the original powers of the States are retained . . . may, by a course of well digested, but refined and metaphysical reasoning . . . explain away the constitution of our country, and leave it, a magnificent structure, indeed, to look at, but totally unfit for use."[24]

Justice Johnson wrote a concurring opinion that Marshall apparently participated in drafting.[25] It went even further than the Court's opinion and expressed what was almost certainly Marshall's own view of the federal government's power. Johnson traced the history leading up to the adoption of the Constitution and concluded, "The 'power to regulate commerce,' here meant to be granted, was that power to regulate commerce which previously existed in the States." The power to regulate commerce can only reside in one sovereign state, and therefore "the power must be exclusive . . . leaving nothing for the State to act upon."[26] This meant that if Congress repealed the Federal Coasting Act, New York still could not prohibit Gibbons from navigating New York's waters.[27] Once the states gave up their power to Congress, "[state] laws dropped lifeless from their statute books, for want of the sustaining power, that had been relinquished to Congress."[28] Though Marshall did not sign onto Johnson's concurrence, there's little doubt it expressed his own conviction that federal power was exclusive.

THE SUPREME COURT'S holding in the Great Steamboat Case was generally well received throughout the country. When the *United States*, a steamboat registered in Connecticut, arrived in New York Harbor a few days after the Court's decision, it was met by a huge cheering crowd. When two steamboats arrived at Augusta, Georgia, they were greeted by a band and rifles firing a salute.[29] The Supreme Court had liberated the steamboat industry from the constraints of monopoly. The *New-York Evening Post* called Marshall's opinion "one of the most able and solemn opinions that has ever been delivered by any Court . . . Many passages indicate a profoundness and a forecast, in relation to the destiny of our confederacy, peculiar to the great man who acted as the organ of our court."[30]

In its time, *Gibbons* was understood primarily as a blow against monopolies in favor of competition. Newspapers in the Northeast hailed Marshall's decision as increasing competition in their markets. A New Jersey newspaper proclaimed that "the waters are now free, and those who heretofore held with an iron gasp, and exercised with unfeeling perverseness, their precarious power will not perhaps lament, when it is too late, the rashness and severity which has involved them in embarrassment, if not ruin."[31]

More surprising, perhaps, was the response in the South. Newspapers in Kentucky, South Carolina, Virginia, and Georgia praised Marshall's decision for promoting transportation. One Missouri newspaper assured New Yorkers "that it is a decision approved of in their sister States."[32] Marshall's bold statement of federal power was overlooked perhaps because Marshall had not quite endorsed Johnson's arguments for an *exclusive* federal power. One of the few critical voices against Marshall's opinion was his own hometown newspaper. The *Richmond Enquirer* warned that Marshall's opinion threatened to "stretch the power of the Government by a most liberal construction" and warned that "the State Governments would moulder into ruins, upon which would rise up one powerful, gigantic and threatening edifice."[33]

By stripping away the monopoly that state legislatures had often corruptly granted to Fulton, the Supreme Court had opened up the country's interior and coastline and would hasten the creation of a national market. Farmers in the South would now be able to reach distant markets at a lower cost. Steamboat fares immediately fell throughout the country, and in New York alone, the number of steamboats serving the state rose from six to forty-three in the first year.[34]

Gibbons formed the foundation for the regulatory authority of the federal government. Virtually all the regulatory authority that the federal government exercises today—whether over the environment, occupational health and safety, banks, securities markets, labor, transportation, and even terrorism and crime—derives from Marshall's expansive reading of the commerce clause in *Gibbons*. Without Marshall's decision, a truly national economy would not have been possible. Instead, we would have had fifty competing state economies with different regulatory systems unable to harmonize their laws to promote the common good.

Just as the Supreme Court's opinions in *Marbury* and *Martin* ensured that there would be a uniform interpretation of the Constitution, Marshall's decisions in *McCulloch* that interpreted the necessary and proper clause broadly and in *Gibbons* that expanded the scope of Congress's power under the commerce clause ensured a uniform national system of regulation to facilitate economic growth.

CHAPTER TWENTY-NINE

PUBLIC AND PRIVATE

C orporations, both for-profit and nonprofit, were relatively scarce creatures in the eighteenth century. Until the dawn of the nineteenth century, most American corporations were municipal bodies created for a public purpose. Before the American Revolution, there were only seven private corporations in the entire country, and as late as 1790, there were only forty-two. After the Court's 1810 decision in *Fletcher v. Peck*, that number had grown to around three hundred.[1] Corporate charters were originally issued by royal decree either to enrich the king's favorites or advance the public interest. The development of a national economy required that investors have some assurance that their corporate entities would be secure from excessive state interference. At the same time, the demand for higher education required the creation of privately funded schools and colleges chartered by the states.

The Marshall Court played a critical role in defining the relationship between government and private market actors. In particular, the Marshall Court protected corporations from excessive regulation by the states, making possible the modern economy. The first important case the Supreme

Court faced on the rights of a corporation arose out of an obscure dispute concerning a small New England college.

In the 1760s, Reverend Eleazar Wheelock, a young Congregationalist pastor in Lebanon, Connecticut, sought to establish a college to teach Christianity to Indians. He raised funds from England and Scotland, and to assure his benefactors that their funds were spent properly, an English board of trustees was appointed under the direction of Lord Dartmouth, the secretary of state for the Colonies. An American board of trustees was also established to oversee the college's day-to-day operations. In 1769, the royal governor of New Hampshire, John Wentworth, invited Wheelock to move his college to New Hampshire, and he issued a royal charter to establish Dartmouth College "for civilizing and Christianizing children of pagans . . . and also of English youth and any others." The charter named a board of twelve trustees, including Reverend Wheelock, who was also named president. The trustees and Wheelock were empowered to appoint their successors "forever hereafter."[2]

Wheelock ruled the college like a benevolent despot, and the trustees never questioned him. Before he died in 1779, he named his twenty-five-year-old son, John, as president. John possessed his father's authoritarian tendency without his father's erudition or judgment. The result was unfortunate. He filled faculty positions with friends who were unqualified, the college's finances deteriorated, and his management style alienated the trustees. As the Second Great Awakening swept across New England in the first decade of the nineteenth century, Wheelock embraced the new Presbyterianism—to the chagrin of his old-line Congregationalist trustees. When the trustees named a professor of divinity over Wheelock's objections, Wheelock asked the New Hampshire legislature to remove Dartmouth's trustees. In retaliation, the board fired Wheelock in 1815 and appointed Reverend Francis Brown as Dartmouth's president.[3]

The following year, Republicans won a majority in the New Hampshire legislature. The Republican legislature viewed Dartmouth College with hostility. The college's royal charter and its self-perpetuating board were seen as a vestige of British aristocracy, and Congregationalism was practically synonymous with old-fashioned Federalism. Republicans believed that higher education should be open to all and opposed private colleges on principle. The Republican state legislature adopted a measure to give control over Dartmouth's board to the Republican governor and reconstituted the college as Dartmouth University. The college trustees opposed these changes to Dartmouth's royal charter. In 1817, the college treasurer, William Woodward, sided with the university, and the college trustees sued Woodward in the New Hampshire Superior Court for the college records and seal.

Daniel Webster, who happened to be a Dartmouth alumnus, represented the college trustees. Webster challenged the New Hampshire law under both the state and federal constitutions as well as general equitable principles. The New Hampshire court unanimously ruled that Dartmouth College was a public corporation chartered for a public purpose and that the legislature was free to reconstitute the board as it saw fit.

Webster appealed to the Supreme Court on the narrow question of whether the New Hampshire law violated the federal Constitution's Contract Clause. As the Court held in *Fletcher v. Peck*, the Contract Clause prohibits any state law "impairing the Obligation of Contracts."[4] Webster was arguing that a college's charter, or any corporation's charter, was a form of contract protected by the federal Constitution. This was a novel argument. By 1820, there were only thirty-five colleges or universities in the United States.[5] Colleges, like other corporations, were considered public entities chartered with a public mission.

The case reached the Supreme Court on March 10, 1818. The U.S. attorney general, William Wirt, and John Holmes appeared for the university. Webster addressed the Court in a fashionable blue coat with brass buttons, a white vest, a tie, and dark pants.[6] He began three days of argument with a four-hour oration. His argument rested on the Court's decision eight years earlier, in *Fletcher v. Peck*, that the state's grant was a contract and that the subsequent law impaired the contract in violation of the Constitution's Contract Clause. First, Webster argued that a charitable institution like a college was, in fact, a private corporation, not a public entity. If New Hampshire could take control of Dartmouth, then other private colleges were also at risk.

But if the college was not owned by private shareholders, who was really harmed by changes in the structure of the college? The original donors and incorporators were gone. The students were transitory. Webster insisted that academic freedom itself would be threatened. "No description of private property has been regarded as more sacred" than academic freedom, he declared. The faculty's rights must be protected by the Constitution, for academics are the estates and freeholds of "a most deserving class of men . . . who have consented to forego the advantages of professional and public employments, and to devote themselves to science and literature, and the instruction of youth in the quiet retreats of academic life." Webster admonished the court that it would be "indefensible" for the government to threaten a college's academic freedom.[7]

Then Webster moved to his principal argument that New Hampshire had violated the Contract Clause. He asserted that a grant of a corporate charter was as much a contract as the grant of land in *Fletcher*. The grant bound the state like a contract, and the benefactors contributed to the college with the expectation that the college would endure in perpetuity.[8] The college did not need a change in its structure. "That which it did need was the kindness, the patronage, the bounty of the legislature; not a mock elevation to the character of a university, without the solid benefit of a shilling's donation to sustain the character," Webster declared with his dark eyes flashing.[9] New Hampshire had clearly impaired the contract by reconstituting the board of trustees and changing the name and character of the college.

Webster concluded his argument with a stem-winding peroration that has seldom been equaled in the Supreme Court. He reminded the court what was at stake: "The case before the Court . . . affects not this college only, but every college, and all the literary institutions of the country . . . They have all a common principle of existence, the inviolability of their charters." Webster argued that if colleges lost their independence from state legislatures, benefactors would be less inclined to contribute and that scholars would be discouraged from devoting themselves to such institutions. "Colleges and halls will be deserted by all better spirits, and become a theater for the contention of politics. Party and faction will be cherished in the places consecrated to piety and learning."[10] Webster had reached an emotional crescendo. People in the courtroom had begun to weep.

Webster turned to face the chief justice: "Sir, you may destroy this little institution; it is weak, it is in your hands! . . . But, if you do so, you must carry through your work! You must extinguish, one after another, all those greater lights of science which, for more than a century, have thrown their radiance over our land!" The chief justice, who rarely showed any emotion, struggled to hold back tears as Webster concluded: "It is, sir, as I have said, a small college. And *yet there are those who love it.*"[11]

The Court was divided, and Marshall announced the next day that the Court would reconsider the case the following year. Webster believed that Justices Marshall and Washington would support the college trustees while Justices Todd and Duvall were opposed. He thought that Justice Story might be undecided.[12] While the justices mulled over their decision, Harvard appointed Story to its board of overseers, and both Harvard and Princeton awarded doctors of law degrees to Justices Johnson and Livingston. Whether or not these events had any effect on the justices' ruling, Republicans later accused the Court of improper influence.[13]

The case was scheduled for rehearing on February 2, 1819. The Court met for the first time in its new courtroom, the fifth since Marshall had joined the Court. It was located underneath the north wing of the Capitol in an obscure corner of the basement at the end of a long hallway. The chamber was a cramped, oddly shaped triangular room with three windows and a profusion of arches supporting the ceiling. On one wall was a marble bas-relief of Fame gesturing at the Constitution and Justice balancing a scale. The justices sat on a long bench on a raised platform.[14] Webster was prepared to resume the argument but no doubt wondered what more he could possibly add after his heroic performance the previous winter. William Pinkney, who represented New Hampshire, had not yet arrived when to Webster's astonishment—and relief—Marshall pulled a stack of pages from the sleeve of his black cloak and began reading the Court's majority opinion.[15] Justices Washington and Story wrote concurring opinions in which Livingston also concurred. Justice Todd had missed the entire term due to "indisposition," and Justice Duvall dissented without writing an opinion.

First, Marshall described the history of Dartmouth College. The fact that it was chartered for the purpose of propagating Christianity among the Indians did not transform Dartmouth into a public entity. "A corporation is an artificial being, invisible, intangible, and existing only in contemplation of law." As such, corporations possess only the characteristics conferred by their charter. "But nothing confers on a private corporation the status of being a public entity. It does not have any political power, or a political character . . . It is no more a State instrument, than a natural person exercising the same powers would be."[16]

Was the 1769 charter a contract with the trustees that bound the state not to interfere? Marshall found that it was a contract that the donors had relied on when making contributions to the college.[17] Marshall conceded that the rights of a corporation were "not particularly in the view of the Framers of the constitution" when they drafted the clause prohibiting states from impairing contracts. But the Framers' intentions were not necessarily controlling where the Constitution's words appear to govern.[18] Marshall left no doubt that private corporations were protected by the Constitution. And to the New Hampshire attorneys' argument that there was no way to remove incompetent or malevolent trustees, Marshall responded that the mere chance that the college could be badly governed did not justify violating the Contract Clause.[19]

Marshall then addressed the question of whether the contract had been impaired by New Hampshire's legislation. The New Hampshire legislature had tried to impose the "will of the State" over "the will of the donors, in every essential operation of the college." Therefore the state's law violated the Constitution's protection for contracts. For the first time, the Supreme Court had declared a state law unconstitutional.

The public response to the Court's holding was surprisingly muted after such a long public battle. One Vermont newspaper hailed the Court's decision as promising to prevent "much evil" in the future.[20] Of course, many New England Republicans criticized the decision, echoing the complaints of southern Republicans that Marshall had changed the "original compact between the general and state governments" by infringing on the state's sovereignty. One New Hampshire newspaper charged that the Supreme Court's decision was "not the only 'novel principle' that has been advanced" by the Marshall Court and warned that the Court's decision would lead to "wide destruction."[21] New Hampshire Republicans threatened to put Dartmouth College out of business by imposing heavy taxes. But the nation's colleges and other charitable institutions breathed a sigh of relief. The trustees resumed control of Dartmouth College, and Dartmouth University was disbanded.[22]

The *Dartmouth College* opinion created the underpinnings for modern corporate law. Marshall shattered the lingering concept that corporations were merely instruments of the state intended to serve a public mission. Marshall's opinion recognized that corporate charters were contracts protected by the Constitution and that corporations were private persons with many of the same powers as natural persons. So a corporation like Dartmouth could have an interest in property that was protected by the Constitution.

As a consequence of *Dartmouth College*, corporations began to proliferate throughout the nineteenth century, and dozens more religiously affiliated private colleges sprung up throughout New England. Over the next four decades following the *Dartmouth College* decision, the number of U.S. for-profit corporations surged from three hundred to more than twenty thousand with a total authorized capital of six to seven billion dollars.[23]

A FEW WEEKS LATER, the Marshall Court issued another significant decision expanding the Constitution's protection for property and contract rights. Republicans had long voiced concerns that it would be difficult to defend republican values in a country with a growing class of workers without property. Madison worried that demagogues would appeal to the working poor by promising to take from the rich. The Republican solution was to appropriate more land for settlers by pushing Indians farther west if necessary. Nevertheless, the disparity of wealth was becoming more apparent by the 1820s. Rhode Island, New York, Pennsylvania, and Connecticut had adopted laws to help debtors by allowing them to declare bankruptcy or insolvency.[24] The question arose whether such laws impaired the contract rights of creditors.

In March 1811, Josiah Sturges lent Richard Crowninshield $1,543.74 (about $27,000 today) to be paid the following August. Crowninshield was the dissolute son of George Crowninshield Jr., a wealthy and powerful Massachusetts merchant. He was living in New York City at the time, and he had squandered his fortune and flirted with debtors' prison. In April, the New York legislature passed a bill for the relief of insolvent debtors, and shortly thereafter, Crowninshield declared bankruptcy and was relieved from his debt to Sturges. Then he returned to his family in Massachusetts and began a profitable textile company. Crowninshield's success attracted the attention of his former creditor. Sturges sued Crowninshield on the promissory notes in the federal circuit court in Massachusetts. Sturges challenged the New York law as unconstitutional on two grounds: First, he claimed that the Constitution gave Congress an exclusive right to adopt a nationwide bankruptcy law and that the states had no such power. Second, he argued that the state law impaired his contract with Crowninshield in violation of the Contract Clause.[25]

The circuit court included Justice Story, who had represented the Crown-inshield family and who owed much of his success to their support.[26] But despite his personal loyalty to the Crowninshields, Story had pushed for Congress to adopt a national bankruptcy code. He thought that the Consti-tution precluded states from legislating on bankruptcy. Story believed that laws regulating commerce should be made uniform throughout the nation by Congress.[27] The other judge on the circuit court was District Judge John Davis. In order to ensure that the case would eventually be settled by the Supreme Court, Story and Davis agreed to issue conflicting opinions so the Supreme Court would have no choice but to accept the case.[28]

Sturges v. Crowninshield was a more complex case involving contract or property rights than the Marshall Court had previously considered. In *Fletcher* and *Dartmouth College,* the Marshall Court had defended the rights of property holders, but bankruptcy cases were not so simple. Both creditors and debtors possessed property interests, and the issue for a court was how to allocate the property that remained.[29]

Marshall personally disfavored laws for the relief of debtors, and he thought that such laws had contributed to the failure of the Articles of Con-federation.[30] Initially, the other Supreme Court justices were divided on whether to uphold the New York bankruptcy law. Justices Story, Washing-ton, and possibly Todd questioned the validity of any state bankruptcy law. Justices Johnson, Livingston, and Duvall thought that the states should be free to pass bankruptcy laws concurrent with the federal power.[31] Never-theless, just days after the oral argument ended, Marshall cobbled together a unanimous opinion that papered over their differences.

Marshall wrote that Article I of the Constitution gave the authority to

Congress to establish "uniform laws on the subject of bankruptcies throughout the United States" but that Congress had not yet adopted a bankruptcy code. In the absence of any congressional action, could the states adopt their own bankruptcy statutes? The Constitution expressly prohibited states from doing certain things, such as making treaties with foreign powers, but it did not mention bankruptcy laws. From this, Marshall inferred that "the mere grant of a power to Congress, did not imply a prohibition on the States to exercise the same power."[32] If and when Congress eventually adopted a bankruptcy code, it would extinguish any conflicting state insolvency laws.[33]

Then Marshall turned to the question of whether the New York law impaired the obligation of contracts. The New York bankruptcy law discharged any debts whether contracted before or after the enactment of the state law. Marshall considered the circumstances in which the Framers drafted the Contract Clause. In response to "the general distress" that followed the American Revolution, states had adopted laws that harmed the rights of creditors. "These were the peculiar evils of the day. So much mischief was done . . . that general distrust prevailed, and all confidence between man and man was destroyed." To restore confidence and prevent a recurrence of these dangers, the Framers prohibited state laws impairing the obligation of contracts.[34] Because the New York law operated retroactively to discharge debts that existed prior to the statute, the Court unanimously agreed it was invalid.

Nevertheless, Marshall noted that since the Contract Clause applied only against state laws, Congress could pass bankruptcy laws that provided debtors with relief retroactively. This was a compromise that Marshall had struck between those justices opposed to any state bankruptcy law and those who would permit at least some state bankruptcy laws. The question as to whether state bankruptcy laws could apply prospectively to debts contracted after the state law took effect was not decided by the Court until eight years later, in *Ogden v. Saunders*.[35]

By 1827, Congress still had not enacted a comprehensive federal bankruptcy law that might have superseded state laws. John Saunders, a citizen of Kentucky, sought to enforce a debt owed by George Ogden, a New York citizen. Ogden filed for bankruptcy under the New York statute that was adopted prior to his contract with Saunders.[36] President John Quincy Adams had just appointed Robert Trimble, a moderate Republican from Kentucky, to fill the vacancy left by the death of Justice Todd, another Kentucky Republican. Justices Trimble, Washington, Johnson, and Thompson agreed that the New York law applied, and Ogden was discharged from paying his debt. Unlike the issue in *Sturges*, the debt in this case was incurred after the New York law was adopted.

For the first and only time in his thirty-four years on the Court, Chief Justice Marshall found himself dissenting in a constitutional case. He was joined by Justices Story and Duvall. Marshall wrote a long and strident dissent. The chief justice argued that a state law could never alter an existing or future contract, that the right to contract existed in a state of nature, and that the Contract Clause safeguarded the rights of private parties against the heavy hand of the state.[37]

The outcome in *Ogden* demonstrated that the chief justice no longer exercised the same influence over the Court. His ideas about the sanctity of private property and contract were now being challenged. Nevertheless, Marshall had already shaped the contour of American capitalism. In less than two decades, the Marshall Court had liberated the market from the constraints of monopolies and the heavy hand of state regulation. It had guaranteed the sanctity of contracts and private property rights. And it had empowered Congress to adopt national regulations that would harmonize state laws. In so doing, the Marshall Court helped create the conditions for free enterprise to flourish in the nineteenth century.

CHAPTER THIRTY

RIGHT REMAINS
WITH THE STRONGEST

In 1828, Marshall, now seventy-two, spent at least a month every summer at Oak Hill. He built a home there for his son Thomas on the land that his father had left him. There, between the rolling blue shadows of the Cobbler Mountains and the muddy green water of Goose Creek, the chief justice looked forward to retiring with his wife. "A person as old as I am feels that his home is his place of most comfort, and his old wife the companion in the world in whose society he is most happy," he wrote to Polly.[1] Headaches, fatigue, and anxiety still racked her frail body, but in the honeyed stillness of the valley, Polly could sit outside undisturbed by city noises.

In August, Marshall received word that his colleague Justice Robert Trimble, twenty years his junior, had died of malarial fever.[2] Trimble had served only two years on the Court. Marshall was especially fond of Justice Trimble who, like Justice Story, was a moderate Republican and a proponent of a strong federal government. The unexpected death of his "friend and brother" gave Marshall reason to reflect on his own mortality.[3] Marshall could look back on his long record of public service and wonder what would endure. By the late 1820s, Marshall could feel confident that the country would remain independent from Britain and France. America was still weak relative to the European powers, but her immense size and her distance from Europe assured that the country would remain free to prosper or fail on its own.

Over time, Marshall's thoughts on the Revolution had matured. For him, it was not a war against Britain or a tyrannical monarch. Marshall judged that Jefferson's Declaration of Independence had stretched the truth: "The long list of tyrannical acts which is found [there]" was "judiciously inserted as tending to produce unanimity," but it was not the true story. "[T]he time is arrived when the truth may be declared," he wrote to Congressman Edward Everett of Massachusetts. "The war was a war of principle, against a system hostile to political liberty, from which oppression was to be dreaded, not against actual oppression."[4] The real revolutionary document was the Constitution, not Jefferson's Declaration. The Constitution was a fence against the kind of corruption that the British Parliament had succumbed to. The Constitution transformed the parochial interests of competing states into one nation. It safeguarded the rights of individuals and property from the tyranny of the majority, and it established a judicial system that would become the envy of the world.

But Marshall fretted over the future of the Constitution and the Supreme Court. Marshall had welcomed the elections of Monroe and John Quincy Adams after the acrimonious years of Jefferson and Madison, but the country's mood had quickly soured during both presidencies. The Supreme Court had defended property rights and upheld the power of Congress to create a national economy, but neither Monroe nor Adams had made much progress knitting the country's farms and cities together. Meanwhile, the country was increasingly divided on the toxic question of slavery in the Louisiana Purchase. Marshall was especially concerned by the approaching election of 1828. Three decades in Washington had taught

Marshall that men with the character of Washington and the genius of Hamilton were a rare breed.

Marshall worried that Andrew Jackson's presidential campaign roused an insidious spirit in the American people. Ever since Jackson's loss to John Quincy Adams in 1824, his Democratic supporters had engaged in a perpetual campaign of accusation against the president and his heir apparent, Henry Clay, the secretary of state. The masses were "animated with the most hostile feelings towards each other," Marshall wrote. This new phenomenon was a permanent campaign that polarized the country by region. Marshall thought that it "threatens the most serious danger to the public happiness. The passions of men are enflamed to so fearful an extent, large masses are so embittered against each other, that I dread the consequences." He feared that the Constitution would not survive a Jackson victory.[5] Marshall even speculated that it might be better to let the Senate choose the president in the future.[6] His one consolation was that "I shall not live to witness and bewail the consequences of those furious passions which seem to belong to man."[7]

As chief justice, Marshall felt that he should refrain from voting for president or endorsing any candidate. But now a Baltimore newspaper quoted him saying that he would probably vote in the upcoming election "from the strong sense I felt of the injustice of the charge of corruption [by Jackson and his supporters] against the President and Secretary of State."[8] It was a serious faux pas, and he knew it. It was considered that Supreme Court justices ought never to comment on presidential candidates. Secretary Clay thanked Marshall for his public support and expressed his regret that it "will subject you to a part of that abuse which is so indiscriminately applied to all and to every thing standing in the way of the elevation of a certain individual."[9] Marshall's fears were soon realized when Jackson was swept into office on a populist landslide.

Marshall returned to Washington in February 1829 anticipating the arrival of the man who threatened to overturn the federal government and bend the Supreme Court to his will. Marshall worried that even if Jackson was inclined to be more conciliatory, "he is brought in by a hungry and vindictive party" that is less responsible and that will make demands on the new chief executive. Though he wished success to every new administration, he "perceive[d] much more to fear than to hope for the future."[10]

Despite the usual buzz of social events, the city held its breath in anticipation of Jackson's arrival. The weather cast a funereal light over the city, which seemed appropriate given that the president-elect's wife, Rachel, had suddenly died of a heart attack at their home in Tennessee less than two months earlier. Marshall, too, was in mourning as Marshall's son Thomas had lost his wife and his infant son in childbirth a few weeks earlier. Marshall could not help imagining the loss of his own wife. "A man who at [Jackson's] age loses a good wife loses a friend whose place cannot be supplied," he wrote to Polly.[11]

Marshall was increasingly aware of his wife's mortality. That winter Polly's condition continued to deteriorate. "Your general health is so delicate, your spirits so liable to depression that I cannot controul my uneasiness," he wrote to her.[12] He followed that with a love poem that concluded:

> Now age with hoary frost congeals
> Gay fancy's flowing stream,
> And the unwelcome truth reveals
> That life is but a dream;
> Yet still with homage true I bow
> At Woman's sacred shrine
> And if she will a wish avow
> That wish must still be mine.[13]

For the eighth time in thirty-two years, Chief Justice Marshall administered the oath of office to the president. Both candidates had emerged from the campaign soiled. The Jacksonians had accused President Adams of corruption, and Adams's campaign responded by accusing Jackson and his wife of bigamy and adultery. Still smarting from the attacks, Jackson refused to pay the customary visit to President Adams, and Adams, in turn, boycotted the inauguration. Fifteen thousand people—the largest crowd ever to gather in the capital city—flocked to the inauguration on the steps of the Capitol. After weeks of cutting cold, the day was unusually mild. When Jackson was done speaking, the crowd followed him to the Executive Mansion and overran the reception, leaving the furnishings in ruins. The president had to be hustled back to his boardinghouse to avoid being crushed by the adoring masses. Marshall avoided the raucous celebrations. He had no desire to celebrate Jackson's election.[14]

Only two days later, President Jackson nominated Postmaster General John McLean for the seat vacated by the death of Justice Trimble. McLean was originally appointed postmaster by President Monroe and reappointed by President John Quincy Adams. Though McLean was a Whig, like his rival Henry Clay, he had endorsed Jackson for president. As postmaster, McLean stood in the way of Jackson's appointing more postmasters as patronage for his supporters. Jackson decided to move McLean out of the way by placing him on the Court where presumably he would be less trouble. Jackson also hoped that he would prevent McLean from challenging him in the next presidential election.[15] Marshall had favored John Crittenden, the former senator from Kentucky, who had been nominated for Justice Trimble's seat by President Adams. The Senate, however, decided to defer voting on the nomination until Jackson assumed office. Marshall greeted McLean's nomination with relief.[16] McLean was a pragmatic centrist who years later would be one of only two justices to dissent against the Supreme Court's decision in *Dred Scott* to uphold slavery. (McLean later sought the Republican nomination for president, but he lost to Abraham Lincoln.) Marshall soon found that McLean had a fiercely independent mind.

President Jackson won office as an authentic populist with his rough manners and fiery rhetoric. He was seen as the "champion of the common man." Jackson opposed big government, corporations, and financial interests. He favored laissez-faire economic policies, cutting federal spending, and political reform to extend the suffrage to nearly all white men. Jackson was also fiercely racist, anticlerical, and nationalistic. He defended slavery and wanted to extend it into the Louisiana Purchase. He opposed abolitionists and other faith-based movements. And he ruthlessly pursued land occupied by Spain and the tribal nations. It was inevitable that Marshall's Court would have to face the consequences of Jackson's political program.

THE FERTILE PROVINCE of West Florida stretched below the thirty-first parallel like a narrow belt fronting the Gulf of Mexico from the Perdido River across what is today southern Georgia, the Florida Panhandle, and parts of Alabama, Mississippi, and Louisiana as far as the eastern bank of the Mississippi River. It included two valuable ports, Mobile and Pensacola, and was only sparsely settled with a sprinkling of pirates, fugitive slaves, Indians, revolutionaries, and outlaws. Spain held a tenuous grasp on both East Florida and West Florida, and Americans hungered after both Floridas as if they were ripened fruit ready to drop off the branch.[17]

In 1800, Napoleon Bonaparte "persuaded" Spain that it was in her own best interest to cede Spain's territory west of the Mississippi to France as a buffer against the Americans, who lusted after Mexican gold. The deal was sealed secretly that year in the Treaty of San Ildefonso. Nothing in the treaty referred to the Floridas, which were east of the Mississippi. Three years later France sold Spain's territory to the United States as the Louisiana Purchase. Remarkably, the agreement never spelled out the precise boundaries of the Louisiana Territory, but at the time Spain still claimed both Floridas, and France and the United States acknowledged that.[18] President Jefferson, who had hoped to purchase both Floridas from Spain, confidently predicted that the Floridas "cannot fail to fall into our hands."[19]

In 1804, Congress adopted the Mobile Act, which asserted U.S. jurisdiction over West Florida and authorized President Jefferson to impose taxes there. For the next six years, fighting erupted periodically along the Florida border until a band of wayward Americans proclaimed a short-lived Republic of West Florida. President Madison, who certainly knew better, now claimed that the Louisiana Purchase had included West Florida. Using the rebellion as a pretext, Madison issued a declaration annexing the territory in 1813.

Two years before this declaration of annexation, two Americans, James Foster and Pleasants Elam, purchased from a subject of Spain two thousand acres of land in West Florida in the Feliciana District just thirty miles east of the Mississippi River. Foster and Elam, both U.S. citizens, were speculators, and for a long time, they did nothing to improve the property while Spain continued to occupy the Floridas.

While border skirmishes continued, slaves fleeing from South Carolina, Georgia, and Alabama found sanctuary in the Florida swamps among the Seminole tribe. When white settlers intruded on Seminole lands in pursuit of slaves or gold, the Indians fought back with attacks on white settlements. In 1818, President Madison ordered then Major General Andrew Jackson to clear the Seminoles out of the territory along Florida's northern border.[20] Jackson exceeded his orders. In addition to suppressing the Seminoles, he drove out the Spanish forces and captured both Floridas. In 1819, Secretary of State John Quincy Adams and Spanish Ambassador Luis de Onís signed the Transcontinental Treaty, by which Spain ceded West and East Florida to the United States for five million dollars and an empty promise that the United States would renounce any future claims to Spanish territory from the Mississippi to the Pacific.[21] That promise was soon forgotten.

In 1826, seven years after the Transcontinental Treaty was signed, Foster and Elam discovered David Neilson squatting on their land. They went to court in Louisiana to seek an order to remove him for trespass.[22] Neilson had no legal claim to the land, but that did not prevent him from alleging that neither Foster nor Elam had good title to the property either. Neilson constructed a fanciful argument that before Spain had sold the land to Foster and Elam it had secretly transferred West Florida to France in the Treaty of San Ildefonso and that France had resold West Florida to the United States as part of the Louisiana Purchase.[23] In sum, Neilson's argument was that Spain had sold land that Spain no longer owned to Foster and Elam.

Despite overwhelming evidence that Spain had never transferred the territory to France, the district court in Louisiana agreed with Neilson that Foster and Elam had purchased the land after Spain had ceded West Florida to France and after it had been acquired by the United States. Foster and Elam appealed to the U.S. Supreme Court, which heard the case in February 1829.

As counsel for Foster and Elam, Daniel Webster pointed out that neither the Treaty of San Ildefonso nor the Louisiana Purchase ever mentioned the Floridas.[24] Moreover, the 1819 Transcontinental Treaty with Spain explicitly provided that all land grants made by Spain before January 24, 1818, "shall be ratified and confirmed to the person in possession of the lands, to the same extent that the same grants would be valid if the territories had remained under the dominion of his catholic majesty."[25] Here was irrefutable proof that the United States had promised to respect private property in the Floridas held under Spanish law before 1818. Since the Constitution provided that all treaties are the "supreme law of the land," Foster and Elam's title must be upheld.[26]

This case pitted the property rights of two U.S. citizens who had paid good money against a squatter with no title from anyone. Time and again Marshall had acted to protect private property rights. The claim arose out of the actions of a foreign government, and Marshall had previously held that U.S. courts should defer to foreign law in foreign territory. Marshall's legal career defending the rights of British creditors and landholders under the Treaty of Paris was premised on the idea that treaties trumped the narrow prejudices of domestic courts. And the Marshall Court had reaffirmed the supremacy of treaties in the *Martin* case thirteen years earlier. For all these reasons, Webster anticipated that the Court would hold in favor of his clients.

On March 9, 1829, Chief Justice Marshall issued the court's unanimous opinion in *Foster & Elam v. Neilson*. Despite the fact that both France and Spain agreed that the Floridas were not included in the Louisiana Purchase, Marshall found that a U.S. court should not be swayed by the intentions of foreign parties in a dispute over an international boundary: "In questions of this character, political considerations have too much influence over the conduct of nations, to permit their declarations to decide the course of an independent government in a matter vitally interesting to itself."[27] Instead, he averred that "[i]n a controversy between two nations concerning the national boundary, it is scarcely possible that the courts of either should refuse to abide by the measures adopted by its own government."[28]

Marshall was not entirely convinced by the U.S. government's position, but in the absence of any international tribunal to decide the boundaries of the territory, "the right remains with the strongest." He felt that courts were not competent to judge this question and should defer to Congress.[29]

This was a classic illustration of how Marshall viewed international law through the lens of the U.S. Constitution. The court faced a dilemma— whether to defer to the consistent position of a foreign sovereign or whether to side with the somewhat less persuasive claims of the U.S. government. Rather than base his opinion on the facts before him, he deferred to Congress, because courts should not interfere with foreign relations. Congress had enacted a series of measures, including the Mobile Act of 1804, and the Court was not free to adopt an opposing view.[30]

But in the eighth article of the Transcontinental Treaty, the United States had agreed that Spanish land grants in the Floridas shall be "ratified and confirmed to the persons in possession of the lands, to the same extent that the same grants would be valid" under Spanish law. Did the 1819 treaty trump the earlier Mobile Act of 1804?[31] The Constitution provided that treaties, like federal statutes, were the law of the land.[32] Nevertheless,

Marshall asserted that *some* treaties were *not* intended to have an effect on domestic law until Congress passed implementing legislation.[33] Marshall drew a distinction between treaties that had an immediate effect on domestic law and treaties that required subsequent legislation. There was no such distinction in contemporary international law; Marshall invented it. The question then became whether the 1819 treaty was "self-executing" or whether it required implementing legislation.

Marshall interpreted the eighth article of the Transcontinental Treaty to mean that the parties anticipated there would be some additional action by Congress before the land grants would take effect domestically. Since Congress had not acted to ratify and confirm the land grants, Foster and Elam's title should not be recognized in a court.[34]

No court in the United States had ever held that a treaty had no effect on domestic law. Marshall had invented a new distinction between what has become known as "self-executing" and "non-self-executing" treaties. While maintaining the appearance of deferring to Congress, Marshall left it up to the courts to decide whether to give treaties effect in domestic law. Once again Marshall had expanded the Court's power while appearing to defer to Congress. *Foster & Elam* was a breathtaking example of Marshall's capacity for invention.

Why did Marshall create a doctrine that would undermine the supremacy of at least some treaties? Marshall did not have to reach the question whether the Transcontinental Treaty was self-executing. He could have decided either that Spain had ceded the territory to France before the purchase of the property, or he could have held that Congress had superseded the treaty with subsequent legislation barring such land claims. Instead, Marshall now raised a fundamental question about the supremacy of treaties under U.S. law.

Marshall later acknowledged that he had misread the treaty. Just three years after deciding *Foster & Elam,* he reversed his own interpretation of the eighth article of the 1819 treaty and held that the provision was, in fact, self-executing in a case brought by Juan Percheman to enforce his title to property granted by Spain.[35] In *U.S. v. Percheman*, Marshall held that international law requires that once territory is transferred to a new sovereign, private rights are preserved. The law of nations "would be violated; that sense of justice and of right which is acknowledged and felt by the whole civilized world would be outraged if private property should be generally confiscated and private rights annulled." After a change in sovereignty, people's "relation to their ancient sovereign is dissolved; but their relations to each other and their rights of property, remain undisturbed."[36]

Marshall could not reconcile the holding in *Foster & Elam* with the *Percheman* decision. Instead, he blamed the inconsistency on the fact that in *Foster & Elam*, the court relied on a mistranslation of the eighth article of the Transcontinental Treaty. Now the court possessed an official translation of the eighth article, which provided that land grants "shall *remain ratified* and confirmed to the person in possession of them" rather than "shall *be ratified* and confirmed." Marshall thought that the new translation sounded less like the parties intended for Congress to adopt implementing legislation. Thus Marshall concluded that the eighth article was, in fact, self-executing and no further congressional action was needed.[37]

Foster & Elam is too important to dismiss as simply a case of mistaken translation. It remains a foundational case for the proposition that not all treaties have a direct effect on domestic U.S. law. *Foster & Elam* was probably not a mistake at all. Marshall knew exactly what he was doing. He was trying to avoid another collision with the strident Jacksonians not only on the sensitive question of whether the United States had purchased Florida from France—or seized Florida from Spain.

Marshall was anxiously looking over the darkening horizon at another approaching storm that threatened the judiciary and the Union: the cataclysmic confrontation over the sovereignty of the Indian tribes and the enforcement of Indian treaties. President Jackson and his party were challenging the legitimacy of the various treaties with the Indian nations.

Marshall imagined that by drawing a distinction between self-executing and non-self-executing treaties, he created the possibility for compromise: Leave it to the courts to prune back treaty commitments that might otherwise impede westward movement.

But as events later proved, the Jacksonians had no patience for compromise. They would not allow the Supreme Court to block their path. They were determined to seize the moment and, with it, the continent.

CHAPTER THIRTY-ONE

AN EXTRAVAGANT PRETENSE

G eneral Andrew Jackson forged his celebrity as an Indian fighter even before the Battle of New Orleans solidified his reputation as the unbreakable Old Hickory. Jackson welcomed the War of 1812 as an opportunity to expel the Indians from the frontier and open up the West.[1] He regarded Indian treaties as "an absurdity."[2] In his inaugural address, he pledged "to observe toward the Indian tribes within our limits a just and liberal policy, and to give that humane and considerate attention to their right and their wants."[3] But Jackson had no intention of honoring such commitments.

Jacksonian Democrats, especially in the South and the West, believed it was their destiny to expand "freedom" westward. They saw no contradiction between their imperial ambition to conquer the territory of others and the country's commitment to human liberty. The presence of Indians along the frontier was an obstacle to progress. Alabama, Georgia, and Mississippi passed laws to abrogate the independence of the tribal nations. They offered the Indians a stark choice—submit to state authority or move. Jacksonians argued that "uncivilized" tribes would be safer far removed from white settlers.[4]

As often happens when a nationalist leader is elected to office by vilifying other ethnic groups, a wave of racism swept across the country. Racial animosity turns especially ugly when there are economic interests at stake, and that is what happened in 1828 when gold was discovered on Indian land in Georgia. Jackson asked Congress to designate a territory west of the Mississippi for the Indians to occupy and appropriate funds for Indian removal. President Jackson offered the Cherokee and their Creek cousins a "choice": move farther west voluntarily or the federal government would move them.[5] The aptly named Senator Hugh White of Tennessee proposed the Indian Removal Act to force the Indians to move west. However, northeastern liberals were generally sympathetic to the tribal nations.

The leading opponent of the Removal Act, New Jersey Senator Theodore Frelinghuysen, argued that the United States must abide by its treaties. "Do the obligations of justice change with the color of the skin?" he bluntly asked.[6]

Georgia Senator John Forsyth responded that Indians were a "race not admitted to be equal . . . treated somewhat like human beings, but not admitted to be freemen." Forsyth accused northern liberals of trying to arrest the "progress" of southern states by protecting Indians.[7]

After months of bitter arguments in both chambers, Congress adopted the Indian Removal Act in May 1830. Ethnic cleansing was now the law of the land.

SEVEN YEARS EARLIER, the Marshall Court had considered the Indians' right to possess their land in *Johnson v. M'Intosh*. That case arose out of a dispute over title to western land. In 1763, King George III issued a proclamation reserving all the territory west of the Allegheny Mountains for the native peoples. The British were motivated more by a desire to keep the peace with the Indians than by genuine altruism. The prohibition on settlers acquiring land from the tribal nations became a source of friction between Britain and her American subjects. Virginians were especially opposed to the king's proclamation, which became a primary reason that Virginians supported independence.

In 1773, William Murray purchased two vast tracts from the Illinois Indians for twenty-four thousand dollars on behalf of the Illinois Company, a land syndicate. Together these two tracts covered roughly twenty-three thousand square miles lying east of the Mississippi, northwest of the Ohio, and west of the Great Miami rivers in present-day Illinois. Two years later, Murray paid the Piankashaw tribe about thirty-one thousand dollars for another pair of tracts covering parts of present-day Indiana and Illinois on behalf of a related land syndicate, the Wabash Company. One of these purchases straddled the Wabash River while the other ran from the Ohio River to the White River. The shareholders in the Illinois and the Wabash companies, which later merged, included many well-connected financiers and political figures such as Lord Dunmore, the royal governor of Virginia. After independence, Virginia claimed all the western land at issue and invalidated any title to the property acquired from Indian tribes. Virginia reserved a portion of this territory as a bounty for the militiamen who served in the Revolutionary War, and the chief justice's father was appointed to oversee the veterans' land claims. He surveyed the territory and drew up plans to disburse two hundred acres to each enlisted man and more to officers.[8]

The other states envied Virginia's western empire. They demanded that Virginia cede the territory to the Continental Congress to help finance the war debt. Maryland even refused to sign the Articles of Confederation until Virginia relinquished its western land claim. In 1781, Virginia begrudgingly agreed to surrender its claim to Congress on condition that a portion of the land would be set aside to compensate Virginia's veterans. Congress eventually designated that portion of the territory as Kentucky, and Kentucky agreed to reserve land for the Virginia militiamen.

In 1803 and 1805, the federal government purchased the land previously sold to the Wabash and Illinois companies by the Illinois and the Piankashaw tribes. (This did not include the Kentucky territory.) Congress planned to resell the property to finance the national debt. Meanwhile, the shareholders in the Wabash Company repeatedly petitioned Congress to recognize their title to the property. The investors offered to sell their property to the federal government, but Congress refused to recognize their title to the property.[9]

The following year, one of the original investors in the merged Illinois-Wabash Company, Thomas Johnson, died. Johnson had served as a delegate to the Continental Congress, the governor of Maryland, and briefly as an associate justice of the U.S. Supreme Court. The executor of his estate was Robert Goodloe Harper, a former congressman and Supreme Court advocate who had defended Justice Chase from impeachment. And Harper had also invested in the Wabash Company.[10] By now, the Wabash investors felt they had no recourse but to file a lawsuit to assert their property rights. Harper thought that Johnson's estate would make an especially appealing plaintiff in federal court. Johnson, like Marshall, had been a prominent Federalist and a close associate of both Marshall's father and George Washington. Harper could reasonably expect to find a sympathetic audience in Marshall's court.

Harper's biggest procedural hurdle in clearing Johnson's title would be proving the Illinois and Wabash companies had purchased good title to their land. There was little documentation and no eyewitnesses to the transaction with the Piankashaw and Illinois tribes. To sidestep this problem, Harper needed to find a cooperative defendant who would stipulate to the fact that the investors had paid for good title. Harper found his man in William M'Intosh.

M'Intosh was a Scottish speculator who resided in Vincennes, Indiana, then the capital of the Indiana Territory. In 1818, M'Intosh had purchased about twelve thousand acres of Illinois land from the federal government. M'Intosh waged an ongoing battle against both his neighbors and the local authorities, who regarded him as a disagreeable and shady character. A federal judge once described M'Intosh as "an arrant knave, a profligate villain, a dastardly cheat, a perfidious rascal, an impertinent puppy, an absolute liar and a mean cowardly person."[11] William Henry Harrison, the territorial governor and future president, clashed repeatedly with M'Intosh and won a slander suit against him. When M'Intosh took a former slave as his common-law wife, the "good people" of Vincennes had had enough. They drove him out of town, and M'Intosh settled in a remote part of the territory seething with resentment.[12]

M'Intosh agreed to cooperate with Harper as a way to get even with his enemies. Harper would sue to eject M'Intosh from the property owned by the Wabash Company. Although M'Intosh was one of the largest landowners in the region, he had little to lose from the litigation. In reality, his property did not overlap with any of the property claimed by the Wabash Company.[13] It appears that Harper promised M'Intosh shares in the Wabash Company as compensation. The lawsuit gave M'Intosh a chance to challenge the property rights of his former neighbors and embarrass Harrison, who had purchased millions of acres of Indian lands on behalf of the federal government.[14]

Johnson's estate sued for an order to eject M'Intosh from his land, and in 1823, the case reached the Supreme Court. The issue was whether Johnson or M'Intosh had good title to the property. Harper hired Daniel Webster as his co-counsel. M'Intosh was represented by two less experienced advocates, Henry Murray and William Winder, the brigadier general whose disastrous defeat at the Battle of Bladensburg led to the burning of Washington. Both men were apparently hired by Harper.[15] Since M'Intosh was colluding with Johnson's attorneys, it hardly mattered who represented him.

On behalf of M'Intosh, Murray and Winder argued that Indians could not convey good title to the property: If the tribes had ever been a sovereign people, they had long ceased to be so. They were "an inferior race of people, without the privileges of citizens." The tribes were nomadic. They merely occupied the land without owning any of it. They "never had any idea of individual property in lands."[16] In reality, these assertions grossly misrepresented the tribal nations. Not all tribes were nomadic. And the Indian nations had varied complex concepts of property rights that included both collective and personal rights.[17]

The attorneys for M'Intosh insisted that the source of all property rights was the "discovery" of the continent, and these rights were originally vested in the British Crown and passed through Virginia to the federal government. The defendant was asking the Supreme Court, in effect, to expropriate the entire continent from the Indians in a single blow.

From an equitable perspective, it should have been an easy win for Johnson and the Wabash investors: The Indians had occupied the continent since time immemorial, and the treaties between tribes and Europeans implicitly acknowledged the right of the Indians to possess the land. There were many instances of Americans, including George Washington and Benjamin Franklin, joining land syndicates to buy property from Indian tribes. Johnson purchased the land from the Piankashaw more than four decades before M'Intosh bought it from the federal government. Once the land was sold to Johnson, it could not be sold a second time, and the federal government could not deny the preexisting private property rights of a U.S. citizen. The Fifth Amendment to the Constitution expressly provided that the government could take private property only for public use and only if it paid fair compensation to the owner. Marshall was personally sympathetic to the Indians, and of course, he was himself a land speculator. For all these reasons, one might expect that the court would hold in favor of the estate of their former colleague, Justice Johnson.

That worried political leaders in Virginia and Georgia. Both states had tribal nations scattered across substantial portions of their frontiers. Georgia wanted to seize the land occupied by the Creek and Cherokee tribes along its western frontier, which held the prospect of large gold deposits. Virginia wanted to expel any doubt that it had good title to the land that Kentucky set aside for Virginia's veterans. A holding in favor of Johnson would negate the promise made to Virginia's veterans. It would leave the gold beyond the grasp of Georgia's legislature. And it would deny the claims of all states to the tribal lands within their borders.

Before the case was even argued, Marshall drafted an opinion brimming with historical—though not necessarily accurate—details of the original settlement of the country. Marshall cribbed this history from his first volume of his *The Life of George Washington*.[18] Marshall's opinion traced a somewhat mythologized history of discovery, conquest, and colonialism in North America. Marshall acknowledged that the Europeans had claimed land based on the principle of "discovery." But the Europeans were unable to conquer the tribal nations, and discovery did not displace the Indians from the land they inhabited. Indians remained "the rightful occupants of the soil, with a legal as well as just claim to retain possession of it."[19]

The principle of discovery meant that each European power was bound to recognize the claim of any other European country that first "discovered" a territory. Practically speaking, discovery meant that the Indians could not sell a freehold interest in land to other Europeans. The European sovereign had an exclusive right to purchase title from the tribes and sell a freehold stake in the property.[20] But unless the European sovereign acquired title from the tribe—which usually involved paying for it—the Indians were free to occupy and use the land and sell the same rights to other private purchasers to occupy and use the land.

Marshall admitted that the principle of discovery was a fiction. The Europeans did not "discover" a continent that was already inhabited and cultivated by millions of indigenous people. Nor was discovery the same as conquest. The Europeans may have stuck a flag in the ground, but they had neither the will nor the capacity to subdue the tribal nations. The Indians were "as brave and as high spirited as they were fierce, and were ready to repel by arms every attempt on their independence."[21] Marshall mocked the European powers: "The potentates of the old world found no difficulty in convincing themselves that they made ample compensation to the inhabitants of the new, by bestowing on them civilization and Christianity, in exchange for unlimited independence."[22] He described the Europeans' "pompous claims" to the country and the "frequent and bloody wars," in which Europeans were usually the aggressors pushing the Indians deeper and deeper into the forests and denying the Indians those fundamental rights that humanity and the law of nations required.[23]

It is curious that Marshall relied on the doctrine of discovery.[24] Marshall knew that Europeans had abandoned the doctrine of discovery centuries earlier.[25] In Marshall's well-worn copy of *The Law of Nations,* Emer de Vattel rejected the doctrine of discovery, and he expressly denied that Europeans had a right to claim more territory than they could actually cultivate.[26] Nevertheless, Marshall wrote that discovery was a convenient fiction that U.S. courts had to accept: "However extravagant the pretension of converting discovery of an inhabited country into conquest may appear, if the principle has been converted in the first instance, and afterwards sustained; if a country has been acquired and held under it; if the property of the great mass of the community originates in it, it becomes the law of the land, and cannot be questioned."[27]

Why did Marshall reinvent the discredited doctrine of discovery? He could have rested his decision entirely on the king's proclamation of 1763 that prohibited the original acquisition of land by the Illinois-Wabash Company. That would have settled the narrow question as to whether M'Intosh had good title. But Marshall wanted to clarify the relationship between the states, the federal government, and Indian tribes. Marshall saw this as an opportunity to affirm the supremacy of federal sovereignty over both the states and the tribes while also protecting the right of Indians to use and occupy their land without interference by the states. At the same time, Marshall wanted to reaffirm the property rights of all those who purchased land from the federal government.

Marshall had one other relevant purpose in defining the relationship between the states and the federal government. Marshall wanted to ensure that the land reserved for Virginia's militiamen remained protected. The chief justice, like many Virginians of the Revolutionary generation, was committed to honoring the promise made more than forty years earlier to the veterans who fought the Revolutionary War. By relying on the doctrine of discovery, Marshall confirmed that Virginia had the original right to the property and could therefore transfer title to Congress conditioned on the rights of the militiamen.[28]

Marshall was sympathetic to the tribal nations. As a young legislator in the Virginia House of Delegates, Marshall fought alongside Madison for legislation to punish whites who committed crimes against Indians. He also supported a bill authored by Patrick Henry to provide subsidies to whites who married Indians.[29] Though this may have been motivated in part by a paternalistic desire to "civilize" the indigenous tribes, it was a repudiation of the notion that the Indians were racially inferior. (It took another 180 years before the Supreme Court reached the same conclusion about interracial marriage.)

But Marshall once again set aside his own moral sentiments just as he had in *Antelope*. He wrote, "We will not enter into the controversy, whether agriculturists, merchants and manufacturers, have a right, on abstract principles, to expel hunters from the territory they possess, or to contract their limits."[30] Marshall was not disparaging the natural rights of native Americans; he was asserting that federal law trumped natural rights.[31] Marshall believed that natural rights existed only in a state of nature. Once a person entered into civil society, he exchanged his natural rights for whatever rights the state afforded him.[32] That was a surprisingly modern idea of law that anticipated the rise of legal positivism at the end of the nineteenth century.

Johnson v. M'Intosh is another example of how Marshall guarded the boundaries between the branches of the federal government. Marshall declared that "[c]onquest gives a title that the courts of the Conqueror cannot deny, whatever the private and speculative opinions of individuals may be, respecting the original justice of the claim which has been successfully asserted." He chose his words carefully. The decision rested on the doctrine of discovery, but Marshall spoke of "conquest." Conquest referred to military power, which belonged exclusively to Congress and the president.[33] In other words, "[i]t is not for the Courts of this country to question the validity of this title, or to sustain one which is incompatible with it."[34] Once again Marshall based his decision on the idea that certain policy questions lie beyond the domain of judges. Property rights as well as sovereignty derived from an "extravagant pretense," but courts could not contest these matters without calling into question their own legitimacy: "Conquest gives a title that the courts of the Conqueror cannot deny."

Marshall wove his opinion in *Johnson v. M'Intosh* as if it were fine damask. On one side *Johnson* appeared to deny the property rights of Indian tribes. But turned over, it revealed the opposite pattern: Marshall actually preserved the right of Indians to occupy and use their land without interference from the state or federal governments, and the right to sell their land either to the federal government or a private purchaser. A person who acquired title from the Indians had the same right to occupy, but they did not possess a freehold.[35] Investors such as the Illinois and Wabash companies could occupy the land until such time as the Indians sold it to the United States.[36] If the federal government wanted to acquire the land, it was expected to pay for it. Since private land speculators could not acquire a freehold interest in the property from the Indian tribes, the tribes would be denied the fair market value of their land. In other words, the federal government could purchase Indian land at a price below what the private market might be willing to pay. Marshall's decision cleared the way for the federal government to develop the West.[37]

A few years later, Justice Story sent the chief justice a copy of a speech he delivered on Indian rights: "What can be more melancholy than their history? By a law of nature, they seem destined to a slow, but sure extinction. Everywhere, at the approach of the white man, they fade away. We hear the rustling of their footsteps, like that of the withered leaves of autumn, and they are gone forever."[38] Marshall replied that the time had "unquestionably arrived" when the United States should "give full indulgence to those principles of humanity and justice which ought always to govern our conduct towards the aborigines when this course can be pursued without exposing ourselves to the most afflicting calamities." He regretted that "every oppression now exercised on a helpless people . . . impresses a deep stain on the American character." And he expressed his "indignation" with the treatment of Indians in Georgia.[39]

He would soon have an opportunity to set the matter straight.

CHAPTER THIRTY-TWO

IN THE
CONQUEROR'S COURT

S tanding before the chief justice of the United States was an extraordinary figure of such singularity that Marshall stumbled for the
right words. Barbara O'Sullivan Addicks appeared at Marshall's door-
step in Richmond dressed in a well-tailored man's suit and trousers. She was
selling subscriptions for a French grammar text she wrote for children. In
Boston such a character would perhaps raise eyebrows; in Richmond she
might incite a riot.

Regaining his composure, Marshall politely invited her into his sitting
room. Recently widowed, Mrs. Addicks shared Marshall's love of French
culture. Her nonconformity and her cosmopolitan affect surely reminded
him of the buoyant Madame de Villette, whom he had not seen in more
than thirty years. She was fascinating.

It was not by accident that Mrs. Addicks had knocked at Marshall's
door. She wanted his legal advice. Over refreshments, she explained her
remarkable story. Her father had been a British military officer in the
Revolutionary War, and her first husband was a wealthy Philadelphia

merchant. She was still married to him when she began a torrid affair with a German businessman that resulted in an ugly divorce and a quick second marriage. Her second husband had recently died. She had six children with her two husbands. Her first husband was waging an ugly custody battle for the return of his offspring, which she was contesting. She had one further legal problem: She had married her second husband unaware that under Pennsylvania law an adulterous woman was not permitted to marry her paramour during the lifetime of her prior spouse. In other words, her second marriage was invalid, and her children from that marriage may not have been legitimate. After her second husband died, she was left with his considerable debts. Around this time, weighted under the twin burdens of debt and litigation, she began dressing as a man. She hoped by so doing that she would command the attention of men.[1]

Mrs. Addicks certainly had everyone's attention—even the president's. She was not the kind of woman who was easily turned away, and she did not hesitate to drop in on President John Quincy Adams at least twice at the Executive Mansion. The president later snarled, "Mrs. O'Sullivan came again with her tale of misery and distress, her children, her man's attire, and her book, for which she is soliciting subscriptions." Adams quipped: "It is a difficult thing to persevere in kindness with a half-insane man—with a half-insane woman, impossible."[2]

In spite of her audacity and her odd costume, she endeared herself to the chief justice, who reassured her in a paternal way that "the ties between parent and child are too strong to be absolutely severed." She was so moved by his generous reception—something she clearly had not experienced elsewhere—that she dedicated her next book to him—a dubious honor that he might have preferred to decline.[3] Marshall touched many lives this way. Perhaps it was a reaction to Polly's isolation that made Marshall even more open to people from all walks of life.

THINGS WERE MUCH HARDER for Marshall at home. By this time, Polly felt too weak to leave the house even to attend church. Instead, the chief justice would read to her on Sundays in his soft voice from the *Book of Common Prayer*. Polly forbade anyone in the household to work on the Lord's Day; even the slaves and the horses were commanded to sit idle. Only the steady beat of the French Empire clock punctuated the hush that suffused the house. The stillness was occasionally broken by visits from one of their twenty-six grandchildren, but mostly the chief justice and his wife sat quietly reading.[4]

Throughout their married life, Marshall had spared no effort to shelter Polly's emotional frailty. At times, this required extraordinary measures of subterfuge to conceal uncomfortable truths. In 1792, they had lost their three-year-old daughter, Mary Anne. That same month their four-month-old son, John James, fell ill with fever. At one point he stopped breathing, and Polly became hysterical with grief. Marshall tore her from the bedside and carried her out of the infant's room. He returned expecting to find the infant dead, but his son had miraculously resumed breathing. Since Marshall assumed that his son's death was inevitable, he thought it would be harder for Polly if he raised her hopes only to lose the child a second time, so he sent his grieving wife across the square to her mother's house while he tended his dying son. He never admitted that he had hid from her the fact that their son survived for several more agonizing days. Such were the lengths that Marshall went to insulate Polly from harsh realities.[5]

Marshall's constant anxiety over Polly's frailty, depression, and migraines was aggravated by his sons' continuing financial difficulties. Marshall complained to James that "I am surprised as well as grieved at the magnitude of your debts." John, too, squandered his money on his own amusement rather than taking responsibility for his debts.[6] Ultimately,

Marshall felt compelled to pay off his sons' debts. For a man who was entirely self-made, he could only be disappointed in them.

AFTER JEFFERSON'S PASSING IN 1826, Marshall was recognized as one of the three elder statesmen of Virginia along with Presidents Monroe and Madison. They were the last giants from Virginia's Revolutionary generation who dominated national politics. Though Marshall was often the scourge of the Jeffersonians and Jacksonians, his historical status was now undeniable.

In 1829, he was invited to be a delegate to the Virginia Constitutional Convention to draft a new state constitution. Though he initially declined the invitation, he eventually yielded after repeated efforts to draft him. He wrote to Story that he had no interest in another public position, but after he relented, he confessed, "I have acted like a girl addressed by a gentleman she does not positively dislike, but is unwilling to marry. She is sure to yield to the advice and persuasion of her friends."[7]

IN JANUARY 1831, Marshall resumed his duties at the Supreme Court. "Every thing goes on as usual," he wrote to his wife. "I take my walk in the morning, work hard all day, eat a hearty dinner, sleep sound at night and sometimes comb my head before I go to bed. While this operation is performing I always think with tenderness of my sweet barber in Richmond. It is the most delightful sentiment I have."[8]

But despite his cheery letters home, the Court's close fraternity had disintegrated. Justice Bushrod Washington, Marshall's dear friend, trusted colleague, and publishing partner, passed away in November 1829. That was an especially difficult loss for the chief justice. They had worked together like brothers for more than thirty years, ever since President Washington had corralled them to run for Congress.

President Jackson nominated Pennsylvania Congressman Henry Baldwin to replace Justice Washington, and he was confirmed by the Senate. Baldwin, who came from an upper-crust Connecticut family, was nonetheless a strident supporter of the president's and a passionate defender of states' rights. Baldwin opposed the expansion of the Supreme Court's power and believed in a literal reading of the Constitution that put him at odds with his colleagues, especially Marshall and Story. Baldwin soon grew frustrated by his inability to influence the other justices, and he was increasingly belligerent, shattering the collegiality that had long characterized the Court. After only a few months on the bench, he first threatened to resign and then took an extended leave of absence. He returned to the Court, and over time, it emerged that Baldwin was mentally unstable. Despite frequent bouts of emotional illness and long unexplained absences, he clung tenaciously to his black robes for fourteen stormy years.

With the passing of Bushrod Washington, the chief justice was the only one of the original members of the Marshall Court to survive. Despite his longevity, his influence over his younger colleagues was slipping away. There were more frequent dissents and more heated disagreements. Since life in the capital city had become somewhat more civilized, Justices Johnson and McLean had brought their wives to Washington. The two couples chose to live apart from the other bachelor justices, who still shared a rooming house with the chief justice.[9] Each year it was becoming more difficult to find suitable housing for the justices. As the city's population grew, rooms became scarce, and rents soared.

The Supreme Court began to reflect the polarization of the nation's politics as the Jacksonian age dawned. Justice Story remained Marshall's one constant friend. Story once observed of Marshall: "I love his laugh, it is too hearty for an intriguer, and his good temper and unwearied patience are equally agreeable on the bench and in the study."[10] As Marshall aged, he increasingly depended on Story. The chief justice had a portrait of himself sent to Story as a token of his affection. Marshall thought more often of retiring to Oak Hill, but he also felt more keenly than ever that the Union was at a critical juncture, and he was needed on the Court.

The South had begun talking openly of secession. The latest secession crisis was precipitated by the fight over tariffs. Tariffs protected northern manufacturers, but they disadvantaged the southern states that depended on selling cotton and tobacco abroad. They also raised the price that southerners had to pay for imports and manufactured goods from New England. Marshall warned Story: "The crisis of our constitution is now upon us. A strong disposition to prostrate the judiciary has shown itself and has succeeded to a considerable extent. I know not what is in reserve."[11]

THE CREEK AND THE CHEROKEE once occupied a large arc along Georgia's western frontier. As white settlers moved farther west in search of larger tracts, the proud tribes defended their ancestral homeland. Georgia forced the Creek to move west, but it could not persuade the Cherokee to leave their homes. After the discovery of gold on Cherokee land in 1828, Georgia enacted a series of laws aimed at pushing the Cherokee off their land. Georgia pushed through legislation that voided Indian law and asserted jurisdiction over the tribal members and their land effective June 1, 1830. Indians would be denied the most basic civil rights. They could not appear in court against a white man. The state seized control over the gold mines and forbade Indians to work there. The state militia was posted to protect mining operations from the native inhabitants.[12]

But the Cherokee were not without allies. Incensed by Georgia's treatment of the Indians, New England Congregationalists protested, raised money, and sent missionaries to help the Cherokee. National Republicans, such as Webster and Clay, also aligned with the Cherokee in opposition to the Jacksonian Democrats. At Webster's recommendation, the Cherokee Nation hired former Attorney General William Wirt, who in 1831 sought an injunction in the U.S. Supreme Court to prevent Georgia from exercising jurisdiction over the Indians in violation of federal law. He was assisted by his co-counsel, John Sergeant, another prominent Supreme Court advocate. The Supreme Court usually hears only appeals from lower courts, but it can conduct trials where a case is brought by a foreign government against a U.S. state. Wirt asserted that since the Cherokee Nation was a foreign sovereign, it had the right to sue the state before the U.S. Supreme Court without first suing in the state courts.

Webster and Wirt had another reason for filing this case in the Supreme Court. They hoped that a Court decision would become an issue in the 1832 presidential election. Both Webster and Wirt had ambitions of running against Jackson, and they hoped that a decision in favor of the Indians would embarrass Jackson.[13]

The stakes in *Cherokee Nation v. Georgia* could not have been higher. While secessionist talk hung in the air, Georgia framed the issue as one of states' rights: States should be free to control their Indians just as they controlled their slaves. Georgia Senator John Forsyth argued on the Senate floor that the State of Georgia controlled both Indian territory and its inhabitants. The rights of Indians could be disposed of either by "trifling presents" and "poisonous potations" or by "the sword," Forsyth asserted.[14]

While the case was pending before the Supreme Court, President Jackson, already committed to the forced removal of the Indians, warned the Indians that his plan to remove them was more "liberal" and humane than the alternative—extermination: "Humanity has often wept over the fate of the aborigines of this country," Jackson acknowledged, "but its progress has never for a moment been arrested, and one by one have many powerful tribes disappeared from the earth." The president continued that this was just an unfortunate but unavoidable fact of nature like "the extinction of one generation to make room for another." After all, "[w]hat good man would prefer a country covered with forests and ranged by a few thousand savages to our extensive Republic, studded with cities, towns, and prosperous farms, embellished with all the improvements which art can devise or industry execute, occupied by more than 12,000,000 happy people, and filled with all the blessings of liberty, civilization, and religion?"[15]

Georgia chose not to appear before the Supreme Court. The governor cavalierly insisted that since the Court had no jurisdiction there was no reason for the state to defend against the meritless claims of "savages." Wirt and Sergeant presented their argument on behalf of the Cherokee Nation over two days. There were members of the Cherokee tribe present in the public section of the crowded courtroom. Some wept openly as Wirt described how the state had set out to crush a once proud and independent nation. The chief justice listened intently while shifting uncomfortably in his chair and grimacing. It was not the argument that troubled him; Marshall was beginning to experience acute abdominal pain that was later diagnosed as bladder stones.[16] The *Daily National Intelligencer* later lauded Wirt's argument as "one of the most splendid discourses ever pronounced in that court, and as powerful in argument as it was beautiful in diction." The *New York Journal of Commerce* called it "sublime."[17]

On March 18, 1831, four days after the argument concluded, Marshall read his opinion from the bench. As in prior cases involving slaves and Indians, Marshall began by acknowledging the need to divorce moral imperatives from legal requirements: "If courts were permitted to indulge their sympathies, a case better calculated to excite them can scarcely be imagined. A people once numerous, powerful, and truly independent, found by our ancestors in the quiet and uncontrolled possession of an ample domain, gradually sinking beneath our superior policy, our arts and our arms, have yielded their lands by successive treaties."[18]

The real issue in the case was whether the Cherokee had the same right as a foreign government would have to file a case in the U.S. Supreme Court, or were the Cherokee forced to seek a remedy in the unsympathetic courts of Georgia. Marshall acknowledged that the Cherokee had some of the characteristics of a sovereign state, but they were not, strictly speaking, a "foreign nation" like any other. Their land formed part of the United

States, and the relations between the federal government and the tribes were "marked by peculiar and cardinal distinctions which exist no where else."[19] Accordingly, the Court denied the request for an injunction against Georgia.[20] That appeared to leave the state free to impose its will on the Cherokee and left the Indians with no legal remedy in a federal court.

But what then were the Indian nations if they were not "foreign sovereigns"? Indians were not considered U.S. citizens, so Marshall invented a new legal status to describe the indigenous tribes: "domestic dependent nations." In essence, this meant that the tribes were "wards" of the federal government in a perpetual "state of pupilage." In words dripping with paternalism, Marshall explained that the tribes "look to our government for protection; rely upon its kindness and its power; appeal to it for relief to their wants; and address the president as their great father." He pointed out that foreign governments regarded the Indians as "completely under the sovereignty and dominion of the United States" and that any attempt by a foreign state to form a relationship with a tribe would be "an invasion of our territory, and an act of hostility."[21]

Just as he had done in *Marbury*, Marshall ducked a direct confrontation with the president by denying the Court's jurisdiction. There was reason to doubt that the opinion represented Marshall's genuine beliefs. The Court was divided in this case, with only two justices, Thompson and Story, voting in favor of the Cherokee. If Marshall had joined them, they would still be the minority. From a pragmatic perspective, if Marshall had not voted with the majority, the majority's decision would have been written by Justice Johnson because of his seniority. As it was, Johnson wrote a racially inflammatory concurrence that dismissed the idea that any "people so low in the grade of organized society" could ever be thought of as a "state."[22] Johnson asserted that under the law of nations, Indian tribes were "nothing more than wandering hordes, held together only by ties of blood and habit, and having neither laws or government, beyond what is required in a savage state."[23]

By voting with the majority, Marshall blocked Johnson from writing the Court's opinion. Marshall could be criticized for being unprincipled, but here he was choosing what he saw as the lesser evil. Since Marshall did not usually circulate his draft opinions to the other justices, he did not have to take into consideration Johnson's views. And he was able to craft an opinion that left the door open to challenge Georgia's treatment of the Indians in a future case. Marshall hinted that the "mere question of right might perhaps be decided by this court in a proper case with proper parties."[24] He was signaling a willingness to try again to forge a court majority in support of Indian sovereignty.

Privately, Marshall asked Justices Thompson and Story to respond to Justice Johnson's racist concurrence by issuing a strong dissent.[25] Justice Thompson's dissent demonstrated that the federal government had consistently accorded to tribal nations the same dignity it accorded independent foreign sovereigns and that the tribes were "not within the jurisdiction nor under the government of the states within which they were located." Therefore the Indians should be entitled to remain on their territory unimpeded by the states.[26] If there was any doubt that Thompson's views more closely reflected Marshall's, the chief justice secretly arranged with the Supreme Court's reporter to republish Thompson's dissent in a special volume to educate the public about the rights of the tribal nations.

After the Court's decision, Marshall claimed that he "had not time to consider the case in its various bearings," and that if he had thought about it longer he would have been more explicit that states have no authority over tribal nations.[27] Marshall would soon have one last opportunity to right this historical wrong.

MARSHALL'S ABDOMINAL PAIN worsened over the next several months. Marshall decided it was time to draft a last will and testament. To his beloved Polly and each of his sons, he left the property they were then residing on. Then he added an unconventional provision: "I have for some time thought that the provision intended by a parent for a daughter ought in common prudence to be secured to herself and children so as to protect her under any casualties which may happen, from distress." Rather than leaving property to his son-in-law as was customary, Marshall provided that his son-in-law would hold the property in trust for his daughter and her children: "The property thus given in trust for my daughter and her family is for her and their separate use, not to be subject to the control of her husband or for his debts."[28] As in so many other ways, Marshall's view of women was ahead of his time.

In September 1831, at age seventy-six, Marshall left Richmond by steamboat down the James River for Philadelphia, where he hoped that the famous American surgeon Dr. Philip Syng Physick could relieve the agonizing pain from his bladder stones. The operation was painful and risky, especially given Marshall's age, but the chief justice preferred death to this torturous suffering.[29] Given his infirmity and the bad weather, he had hoped to slip quietly into Philadelphia, but news of his arrival preceded him, and his appearance was greeted by a public spectacle. Marshall was paraded through a series of events in his honor—a reception by the bar association, an address to the Young Men of Philadelphia, an appearance at Masonic Hall, and a speech to the Free Trade Convention. A portrait of him was commissioned, and he had to sit for hours in exquisite pain while the artist, Henry Inman, applied paint to canvas. He had aged greatly in the past few years. His strong jaw and chin were surrounded by puffy pink skin, and his pain was visible in his tight, crooked mouth. His dark eyes were buried behind thick lines and protruding bags, but his hypnotic stare retained its intensity.[30]

The following day, Dr. Physick, sixty-three and also in failing health, performed a lithotomy on the chief justice. Without the benefit of anesthesia, Marshall was tied to a table and pinned down by assistants as the elderly doctor slowly and skillfully removed thousands of tiny stones. The operation was a complete success, and after nearly a month spent recovering in the doctor's care, Marshall sailed back to Richmond at the end of November for the beginning of the circuit court's new term.[31]

Marshall was still weak when he reached home in early December. During the two months he was away, Polly had taken a turn for the worse. She lay "dangerously ill" and confined to her bedroom with an unspecified illness. Though Polly had been ill for most of their married life, this was different. Marshall's "fears were stronger than [his] hopes." For weeks he sat by her bedside stroking her tiny hand and laying a cool wrist on her fevered brow. There seemed little left of her. As he had so often in the past, he read books to her as she faded in and out of consciousness. There was nothing that could be done for her except pray.

On Christmas Eve, Polly sat up and with trembling hands removed the gold locket she had worn around her neck since their engagement. It contained the lock of hair she had given to Marshall as a sign of her devotion, entwined with a lock of his own hair. She asked him now to wear the locket for safekeeping. The following day, Polly's long suffering finally ended. She was sixty-four, and it was just nine days shy of their forty-ninth wedding anniversary. Marshall buried "Dearest Polly" nearby at Shockoe Hill Cemetery.[32]

The cheery light of Christmas was now overshadowed with grief. "Never can I cease to feel the loss and to deplore it," he wrote. He had relied on her counsel for five decades, and he had never "regretted the adoption of her opinion." To others, she appeared frail and dour, but in private Polly "possessed a good deal of chaste delicate and playful wit." She was a talented mime, a good storyteller, and a sophisticated reader. "I have lost the solace of my life!" Marshall exclaimed. He was inconsolable.[33]

Marshall had been looking forward to retirement for a long time, imagining quiet days with Polly on the porch of their house in Oak Hill gazing out over his grassy pastures. He had already outlived most of his contemporaries and five of his children. He felt that he should retire before age dulled his judgment. He was too proud to allow himself to "hazard the disgrace of continuing in office, a meer [sic] inefficient pageant." If he stepped down now, he could take pride in all that the Court had accomplished. And yet he hesitated to quit. Marshall feared that their progress in securing the judiciary's independence and galvanizing the Union could be undone: "I cannot be insensible to the gloom which lours [sic] over us," he confided to Story, and he worried that he would be "abandoning" his colleague at a critical moment. Since his surgery, he was feeling more vigorous. Perhaps he would postpone a decision to retire at least for a little while longer.[34] After Polly's death, the emerald dream of retirement no longer beckoned.

IN MARCH 1831, a group of white missionaries living in Cherokee territory was arrested in Georgia. An 1830 Georgia statute prohibited any white person from residing on Indian land unless they held a state license and swore an oath of allegiance to Georgia. Georgia's legislature had no patience for northern troublemakers stirring up the passions of "savages." One of the missionaries arrested was the redoubtable Samuel Worcester, a Congregationalist minister sent from Vermont to preach the Gospel. Worcester persuaded the others to file a petition in a state court challenging their arrest as an unconstitutional intrusion in Indian territory. After the *Cherokee Nation* opinion, Worcester hoped to use their arrest as a way of dragging Georgia into court.[35]

Worcester's case was filed with the State Superior Court of Gwinnett County where Judge Augustin Clayton upheld the Georgia law but released Worcester and the others on a technicality. Clayton held that since Worcester served as postmaster for New Echota, the Cherokee capital, he and his fellow ministers were federal agents immune from state prosecution. Worcester returned to minister to the Cherokee.[36] That might have ended the matter, except that Georgia Governor George Gilmer wanted to punish these "insolent" northerners. Gilmer asked the president to remove Worcester as local postmaster, and Jackson obliged. In July, the Georgia Guard rearrested Worcester and nine others. A jury took only fifteen minutes to convict all ten missionaries, and Judge Clayton imposed the maximum penalty of four years hard labor for the crime of spreading the word of God.[37]

At this point Governor Gilmer offered pardons to all the missionaries if they agreed not to return to the Cherokee territory without a license as required by law. Only Worcester and one other missionary, Elizur Butler, refused pardons and were sent to prison. The ubiquitous William Wirt offered to represent them pro bono and appealed their convictions to the Supreme Court. The Georgia legislature responded by authorizing newly elected Governor Wilson Lumpkin to "resist and repel" any order from the Supreme Court.[38]

Meanwhile, Wirt was nominated as the presidential candidate of the Anti-Masonic Party. He would challenge President Jackson and the National Republican candidate, Henry Clay, in the 1832 election. Georgia's persecution of the Cherokee emerged as a central issue in the campaign. Northern newspapers featured stories portraying the missionaries as Christian martyrs; southern Democratic papers urged Jackson to oppose any Supreme Court order that infringed on Georgia's sovereignty.[39]

The Court heard the case on February 20, 1832. The courtroom was packed with members of Congress, reporters, members of the public, and Cherokees. The latter were easily identified by their skin caps and leather breeches as they sat scattered among ladies in silk dresses and feathered hats and men in well-tailored broadcloth suits.[40] Still recovering from his surgery four months earlier, Marshall's voice was so thin that he was barely audible. It was fortunate that Justice Johnson, who authored the biting concurrence in *Cherokee Nation*, was absent, so Marshall would have a chance to forge a consensus.[41]

Wirt and his co-counsel, Thomas Sergeant, constructed their argument based upon Marshall's prior decisions in *Johnson* and *Cherokee Nation*. Both cases had acknowledged that the federal government had authority over the tribal nations. Wirt and Sergeant argued that Congress's authority meant that Georgia had no jurisdiction over the Cherokee territory, that the Georgia act of 1830 was invalid, and that the missionaries must be freed.[42] Justice Story did not even wait for Wirt to sit down. He interrupted counsel to express his admiration for Wirt's "uncommonly eloquent" argument. Story later remarked, "I blush for my country, when I perceive that such legislation, destructive of all faith and honor towards the Indians is suffered to pass with the silent approbation of the present Government of the United States."[43]

Under the luminous glare of public scrutiny, the chief justice waited a few days longer than he had in the *Cherokee Nation* case before issuing his opinion. A decision upholding Worcester's conviction would shut the federal courts forever to the tribes and lead inexorably to the forcible removal of the Indians. But a decision overturning Worcester's conviction meant denying Georgia's sovereignty and risking secession. Moreover, it would be difficult if not impossible to compel Georgia to comply with an order to release the missionaries and abandon its claim to the Indian lands.

On March 3, Marshall read the Court's decision in a strained voice barely above a whisper. He was still weak from his operation and grief-stricken from the loss of his wife. Members of the bar and the press crowded around the bench and leaned forward, straining to catch his words.[44] Justices Story, Duvall, and Thompson joined Marshall's opinion, while Justice Baldwin dissented on technical grounds. Once again Marshall began with the history of discovery, but the tone in his writing had shifted: "It is difficult to comprehend the proposition that the inhabitants of either quarter of the globe could have rightful original claims of dominion over the inhabitants of the other, or over the lands they occupied."[45] Discovery did not give the Europeans the right to dispossess the Indians, Marshall insisted; discovery merely gave them the right to purchase whatever land the tribes were willing to sell and no more. "The extravagant and absurd idea, that the feeble settlements made on the sea coast" somehow gave whites a legitimate right to "occupy the lands from sea to sea, did not enter the mind of any man," he wrote.[46]

Marshall focused his analysis not on the Constitution but on the development of international law. Never had the British Crown asserted the right to control the internal affairs of the tribal nations.[47] And from the first treaty made with the Delaware in 1778, Congress had consistently treated the Indians as sovereign nations.[48] The Cherokee had made peace with the United States in the Treaty of Hopewell in 1785, accepting the protection of the federal government and affirming that Congress alone had the power to manage Indian affairs.[49] But at the same time, the treaty expressly recognized "the national character of the Cherokees, and their right of self government."[50] While *Cherokee Nation* emphasized that Indian land formed part of the territory of the United States, Marshall now found that "[t]he treaties and laws of the United States contemplate the Indian territory as completely separated from that of the states."[51] The Indians "had always been considered distinct, independent political communities, retaining their natural rights, as the undisputed possessors of the soil, from time immemorial," subject only to the exclusive right of the United States government to purchase good title to their property.[52]

Marshall continued that Cherokee dependence on the federal government for protection in no way diminished their territorial sovereignty: "A weak state, in order to provide for its safety, may place itself under the protection of one more powerful, without stripping itself of the right of government, and ceasing to be a state," he asserted, citing de Vattel for authority.[53] Just as he had looked to customary international law to shed light on the Constitution's meaning in *Brown*, here Marshall found that the law of nations implied a limit on the states' power over tribal land. For these reasons, Georgia's legislation was "repugnant to the constitution, laws, and treaties of the United States."[54] And so Marshall held that

Worcester's conviction was unlawful and that the Superior Court of Gwinnett County should release him.

The chief justice left no room for doubt or evasion. He held nothing back as if he intended this to be a sort of valedictory. Though his weak delivery was hard to hear, the old chief justice had at last found his voice. Marshall had survived for so long by the art of compromise, forging a pragmatic path between competing ideologies and often sacrificing his own preferences in the interest of consensus. Now he could no longer mask his reaction to the sheer injustice of driving an ancient people from their ancestral lands. Perhaps it was the loss of his beloved wife or the reality of his own mortality that had liberated him at long last to express his genuine moral outrage.

One newspaper noted that the original manuscript in Marshall's trembling hand "should be preserved; and the friends of the Union and of the Constitution will look upon it with veneration, when its author shall be removed from amongst us."[55] Justice Story privately exulted: "Thanks be to God the Court can wash their hands clean of the iniquity of oppressing the Indians." Marshall had redressed his own opinion in *Cherokee Nation* and redeemed the Supreme Court.[56]

But the question remained whether Georgia would submit willingly or whether President Jackson would compel Georgia to comply. Georgia's governor stubbornly refused to comply with the Court's decision and release the missionaries. Horace Greeley, the Whig editor of the *New-York Tribune*, reported that Jackson had responded to the decision by saying, "John Marshall has made his decision; now let him enforce it."[57] Though Greeley invented that quote, Jackson made it clear that he would do nothing to force Georgia to comply. Jackson remarked, "The decision of the supreme court has fell still born, and they find they cannot coerce Georgia to yield to its mandate."[58] For the first time in American history, a president refused to enforce a decision of the Supreme Court.

In Jackson's next annual message to Congress, the president cheerfully reported that "the wise and humane policy of transferring from the eastern to the western side of the Mississippi the remnants of our aboriginal tribes, with their own consent and upon just terms, has been steadily pursued, and is approaching, I trust, its consummation."[59] The Cherokee rejected the government's offer to relocate them, but Jackson left no doubt that he would compel them to succumb.

Justice McLean, apparently on his own initiative, met privately with the Cherokee in Washington and advised them that the Court's decision would have no practical effect in preventing their removal. McLean, who had concurred with the Court's decision, told the Indians to accept the "liberal" terms Jackson offered to them to abandon their ancestral homeland.[60] The Cherokee must have found the white man's justice strange indeed: What justice was there when the loser stole victory from the hands of the victor?

After President Jackson was reelected in 1832, the Union faced two existential threats: Georgia refused to comply with the Supreme Court's order to free the missionaries, and South Carolina refused to enforce a new federal tariff enacted by Congress to protect the North's industries from import competition. Both states invoked Jefferson's "doctrine of nullification," the pernicious theory that states had a right to void federal laws and federal court judgments. In November 1832, South Carolina issued its Nullification Ordinance, asserting its power to void any federal law or Supreme Court opinion. President Jackson replied in kind with a Nullification Proclamation that threatened to use military force against any state that refused to comply with federal law. Jackson had no desire to interfere on behalf of the Cherokee, but the president would not tolerate nullification, and he was determined to enforce the tariff over South Carolina's objections. Jackson was afraid that if the missionaries sought an order from the Supreme Court that was specifically addressed to the president to enforce the Court's order, it would aggravate the nullification crisis. To avoid that risk, Jackson sent his lieutenants to persuade Georgia Governor Lumpkin to pardon the missionaries. After many months of hard labor in the blazing heat, the missionaries reluctantly accepted pardons, and the Nullification Crisis was averted.[61]

Georgia, President Jackson, and the Supreme Court were off the hook. With the missionaries out of prison, no one would have standing to challenge the state's continuing plan to remove the Indians. Marshall breathed easier knowing he would not have to face another legal action on behalf of the Cherokee against either Georgia or the president. The Republic was spared, but not so the Cherokee. Feeling the weight of his mortality, Marshall must have wondered how many more constitutional crises the country could survive before the centrifugal forces of regionalism would tear the political center apart.

CHAPTER THIRTY-THREE

A UNION PROLONGED
BY MIRACLES

By the summer of 1832, as the federal government proved unable or unwilling to compel either South Carolina or Georgia to comply with federal law, the Union seemed to be dissolving. Marshall worried that "[t]hings to the south wear a very serious aspect." From Richmond, he reported to Story that the governors of South Carolina and Georgia were "determined to risk all the consequences of dismemberment." Even though Marshall thought Virginia "was always insane enough to be opposed to the bank of The United States," he doubted Virginia would "embrace this mad and wicked measure." On the other hand, he feared the talk of secession in New England as well. "New Hampshire and Maine seem to belong to the tropics."[1] Though Story heard these secessionist rumblings up in Boston, he could not imagine how more depressing it was for a native Virginian committed to the Union. "The union has been prolonged thus far by miracles," Marshall concluded. And he added, "I [fear] they cannot continue."[2]

By autumn, many southerners spoke openly about forming a "southern confederacy." Marshall thought that "[t]he people are not at present ripe for it. But their political prejudices are so skillfully cultivated as to inspire serious fears that the bitter fruit may soon be gathered." Marshall prayed that South Carolina was not "so absolutely mad as to have made her declaration of war against The United States" without the support of Virginia. "In the mean time our people will be inextricably entangled in the labyrinth of their state right theories, and the feeble attachment they still retain for the union will be daily weakened. 'We have fallen on evil times.'"[3]

As a cholera epidemic swept through the Eastern Seaboard in August and September, Marshall took refuge at the home of his son James at Leeds, Virginia. On August 31, while Marshall was relaxing in the house, a burst of lightning struck the house, knocking his sons James and Edward and three grandchildren unconscious before his eyes. Incredibly, the seventy-six-year-old chief justice was untouched, although he was unnerved by seeing his children and grandchildren violently thrown to the floor. They lay there unconscious for twenty terrifying minutes while Marshall frantically doused them with ice water.[4] This incident was a terrifying portent of what would follow.

THE CHIEF JUSTICE returned to Washington for the Supreme Court term in January 1833 and boarded with Justice Story at the home of the Ringgold family at F and Eighteenth Streets. By now, Marshall's judicial fraternity had dissolved, and the justices had scattered to different boardinghouses. After a summer marked by the threat of secession, cholera, and a lightning strike, he was glad to see his friend Story. President Jackson had struck a conciliatory tone in his annual message to Congress by combining a stern warning against nullification with a generous offer to reduce the tariffs that South Carolina protested. To Marshall's amusement, Jackson's Democrats now denounced their party's leader as a closet Federalist. Marshall mused, "To have said he was ready to break down and trample on every other department of the government would not have injured him but to say he was a Federalist—a convert to the opinions of Washington was a mortal blow under which he is yet staggering." The deep partisanship that now divided the nation also fractured the Democratic Party. Marshall laid the blame on his own state: These were the "bitter fruits of the tree . . . planted by Mr. Jefferson, and so industriously and perseveringly cultivated by Virginia."[5]

To cheer themselves up, Marshall and Story went to see a play performed by Fanny Kemble, a well-known English actress touring America. When they entered their box at the theater, the audience rose to acknowledge the chief justice and applauded wildly. Marshall's spirits lifted. A few days later, President Jackson invited all the justices to dinner. Jackson warmly received the chief justice and jokingly called Justice Story "the most dangerous man in America." It would have been unthinkable a year earlier, but in the present political crisis, Marshall and Story found themselves in an awkward alliance with the president to save the Union. "Who would have dreamed of such an occurrence?" Story wondered.[6]

In November 1833, yet another tragedy darkened Marshall's family. The chief justice's son John Marshall Jr. died from alcoholism. The shock left Marshall depressed and anxious for his son's family.[7] Ever since his expulsion from Harvard, John Jr.—Marshall called him his "culpable son"—had been a bitter disappointment. He was a drunk and a spendthrift who left behind a wife and three children with a mountain of debt, which his grieving father assumed along with financially supporting his son's family.[8] Of Marshall's ten children, only five—Thomas, Jaquelin, Mary, James Keith, and Edward—still survived.

The following year, Justice Johnson was too ill to attend the Supreme Court's term. He died later that summer. Johnson's contributions to the Court were not always appreciated by his brethren, and his death created a new vacancy on the court, with all the attendant anxieties about the person President Jackson might appoint. Jackson nominated James Wayne, a

Democratic congressman from Georgia, who presumably might assuage some of the South's secessionist sentiments.

Soon after that, in 1835, Justice Duvall retired. Jackson nominated Roger Taney from Maryland. Taney had served as Jackson's acting secretary of the treasury and his former attorney general. However, Taney was a highly controversial choice. The Senate had refused to confirm him as treasury secretary after he removed federal government deposits from the Second Bank of the United States and placed them in state banks that Jackson favored instead. The president was censured by Congress for this action, and Taney was attacked for his "servility" to Jackson.[9] The Whigs strongly opposed Taney's nomination, and after a bitter public battle that dragged on for months, the Senate rejected him.

In his place, Jackson nominated Philip Barbour, a Virginia congressman and wealthy slaveholder whose most notable achievement was his fierce defense of slavery and states' rights. He was staunchly opposed to Marshall's broad interpretation of the Constitution and the expansion of the judiciary's powers. His appointment spelled trouble for Marshall's legacy on the Court. By now, Jackson had appointed four of the seven justices. Marshall and Story were outnumbered by Democratic appointees.

FOR THREE DECADES, Marshall had regretted the time spent away from Richmond and Polly. Now, returning to Richmond and an empty house, he missed Story's companionship in Washington. Story attributed their extraordinary friendship to Marshall's virtuous character, "where there is nothing to regret, and nothing to conceal; no friendships broken; no confidence betrayed; no timid surrenders to popular clamour; no eager reaches for popular favour."[10] Marshall often turned to Story for support as he fretted over the growing polarization between the North and South. "[T]he present is gloomy enough," he lamented in a letter to Story, and "the future presents no cheering prospect." Even southerners who supported the president personally opposed the national government. And those who opposed the president were even more extreme in their support for nullification and secession. Marshall could see no way out of this political crisis.[11]

The long months on his own at the Richmond house felt dark and empty. His household now consisted of Robin Spurlock and four other slaves. They were more than he needed, but he could not bring himself to either emancipate or sell them. When a visitor asked him if he was feeling melancholy since Polly's passing, Marshall's eyes filled with tears: "I do indeed feel the absence of a companion, so kind and good, and with whom I had lived with so much harmony, love, and happiness, for more than forty years." And he would "submit with meekness and humility to the just will of Him, at whose appointed time we must all depart."[12] According to one account, Marshall at seventy-nine was still "tall, majestic, bright-eyed . . . old by chronology, by the lines on his composed face, and by his services to the republic; but so dignified, so fresh, so present to the time."[13]

Marshall decided that the Richmond house was too much for him to manage now and that he preferred to live closer to his son James at Oak Hill. Marshall designed a modest addition to the house he had given James—a small sitting room and a bedchamber for himself and a cellar for his slaves.[14] He began the tedious process of packing up and moving a lifetime of books, papers, and furniture to Fauquier County. The most vexing detail was arranging to move his vast collection of Madeira. The wine would have to be transferred from the bottles into large wooden casks and freighted by boat. Though he worried that much of his precious wine might be spilled or spoiled, this was the best option he could come up with.[15]

As he neared the end of his life, the chief justice felt freer to dispense wisdom on a wide range of subjects—American history, French politics, the Russian invasion of Turkey, the resettlement of former slaves in Liberia, the construction of a monument in Washington for its eponymous hero. Marshall took a special interest in counseling his grandchildren on their education. Marshall thought that a classical education in Greek and Latin was essential even though he had little formal education himself. He promised his grandson that if he kept up his Latin, "[y]ou will not be reduced to the mortification of saying '*fugit interea, fugit irreparabile tempus.*'" (It flies, irretrievable time flies.) Instead, he told his grandson, "You may rejoice . . . that in youth you have observed the valuable injunction '*Carpe horam,*' [seize the hour] and turned every hour to the best account."[16] On the moral education of children, Marshall remarked in his typically self-effacing manner, "I have been croaking on about this subject when I could get anybody to listen to me these thirty years, but have made no other progress than to get myself placed among those old men who are always extolling the times that are past at the expense of the present."[17]

MARSHALL WAS NOT LOOKING FORWARD to the journey home at the end of the Court's 1835 term. He would miss Story's camaraderie, and he knew that there would not be many more opportunities for them to sit together on the bench. "We have an immensely severe winter," he wrote his grandson from the capital. "I have fears that I shall not have a very comfortable journey to Richmond. But patience is sorrows best salve."[18]

Marshall's foreboding proved true. The winter of 1834–1835 held on tenaciously. Marshall headed back home on the spring equinox, but the roads were still thick with ice. On the way to Richmond, his carriage skidded and rolled over. Marshall's spine was seriously damaged, but he survived and returned to Richmond to recuperate. He was in severe pain and confined to his room, unable to sit up or write for several weeks.[19] From his sick bed, he struggled to supervise the shipping of furniture and books from Richmond to Oak Hill. He anxiously looked forward to joining his son James and his newest grandson, Thomas, there, but his recovery was slow.[20] Marshall's pain increased. He could not eat. His energy flagged, and he lost weight. He struggled to resume his morning walks, now reduced to half a mile—just enough to visit Polly's gravesite a few blocks away. He tried to cheer up when guests came, and assured his colleagues by post that he would return to the Court in January.[21] He considered whether he should return to Philadelphia for back surgery, but he feared that "my old worn out frame cannot . . . be repaired." Marshall mused that if he could "find the mill which would grind old men, and restore youth, I might indulge the hope of recovering my former vigor and taste for the enjoyments of life. But that is impossible."[22]

It was not simply the agonizing pain or the loss of Polly that had lessened his taste for life. Marshall saw with cold clarity that he had become irrelevant in the age of Jackson. His time had passed. He was still admired—the way one might admire a fine old house, well-built but no longer in fashion. Marshall's reasoned voice could no longer be heard above the din that threatened to shatter the Union.

By late May, he sat with the circuit court in Richmond although he was still in terrible discomfort. His son Edward persuaded him in June to seek medical help, and so Marshall and Edward boarded a steamboat to Philadelphia via Baltimore and lodged at the home of a Mrs. Crim on Walnut Street. Two prominent Philadelphia doctors, Nathaniel Chapman and Jacob Randolph, examined Marshall and determined that his back pain was the least of his problems: Marshall had an enlarged liver with several large abscesses and the pressure on his stomach prevented him from absorbing nutrients.[23]

After several weeks, Marshall was too weak to eat. A month passed as he lay in bed drifting along the shore between life and death. By late June, it appeared he would not make it. Marshall's son Thomas raced to Philadelphia to see his father one last time, stopping in Baltimore en route, where he was caught in a sudden windstorm and took cover in a courthouse. A strong gust toppled the courthouse chimney, raining stones through the roof. A brick struck Thomas in the head, shattering his skull. Thomas died two days later, on June 29.[24] It was an inauspicious sign of the times to come: An ill wind brought the collapse of a courthouse and cost America's greatest jurist his favorite son. Now only four of his ten children remained. But Marshall's infirmity spared him from learning of this one last family tragedy.

On July 4, the same day that John Adams and Thomas Jefferson had died nine years earlier, John Marshall rallied. He sat up for the first time in weeks. He was completely lucid and felt well enough to compose an epitaph for his gravestone. Two days later, on July 6, 1835, Marshall's breathing stopped at six in the evening. The chief justice slipped away peacefully.

The Supreme Court had lost its lion. The Union had lost its compass.

THE NATION MOURNED the loss of the chief justice with the kind of somber ceremony and affection that it had mourned Washington. Marshall was the last giant of the Revolutionary generation to pass into history. In Philadelphia there was a mass funeral procession from Marshall's lodgings to the boat that would carry his body home to be laid to rest next to Polly's in Shockoe Hill Cemetery. Throughout the nation, flags flew at half-mast for an extended period. The citizens of Philadelphia met to approve a resolution that "the nation suffers a peculiar and irreparable loss . . . Seldom has an individual died more universally or more justly admired, esteemed, cherished, or deplored."[25]

Newspapers overflowed with eulogies. The *Daily National Intelligencer* wrote that Marshall "has now descended to the tomb crowned with a larger share of public esteem and public regret, than any citizen since the departure of Washington."[26] The *National Gazette* declared that a "nearly unanimous chorus of fervent eulogy and heartfelt regret is resounding on every side . . . All this speaks well for the country. It shows that however pernicious may have been the operation of faction . . . it has not yet destroyed the knowledge of what is right in the land."[27] Even the *Richmond Enquirer,* which often criticized Richmond's most famous citizen, wrote that Marshall was "as much loved as he was respected. There was about him so little of the 'insolence of office,' and so much of the benignity of the man, that his presence always produced the most delightful impressions. There was something irresistibly winning about him."[28]

Justice Story observed that after Alexander Hamilton John Marshall was "the greatest and wisest man of this country." Story suggested his epitaph should read "Here lies the expounder of the Constitution."[29]

President Jackson conceded that he often disagreed with Marshall's reading of the Constitution, but "in the revolutionary struggles for our National independence, and . . . in the subsequent discussions which established the forms and settled the practice of our system of Government, the opinions of John Marshall . . . gave him a rank amongst the greatest men of his age."[30]

Former Senator Jeremiah Mason of New Hampshire wrote that if "John Marshall had not been Chief Justice of the United States, the Union would have fallen to pieces before the General Government had got well under way . . . John Marshall has saved the Union, if it is saved."[31]

But the country was not universal in its praise for Marshall's service. The editor of the New-York Evening Post, William Leggett, acknowledged that Marshall was "a good and exemplary man" who loved his country, but Leggett expressed his "satisfaction" that Marshall was removed from his station. He accused Marshall of being hyperpartisan, "ultra federal or aristocratic," and for distrusting "the virtue and intelligence of the people."[32] Leggett's editorial triggered a ferocious response from other newspapers that called the Post "fiends . . . hyenas . . . vampyres . . . monsters" and attacked Leggett as a "rabid Jacobin . . . miserable maniack . . . savage . . . unfortunate malignant . . . crazy."[33] Partisanship did not pause for Marshall's passing.

To fill the chief justice's seat, President Jackson once more nominated his friend and ally Roger Taney. Despite the fact that Taney had been rejected twice by the Senate as a nominee for the Treasury and for the Supreme Court, Jackson now had the votes to confirm Taney as the fifth chief justice. Taney's unfortunate tenure on the Court was overshadowed by his ill-fated decision in *Dred Scott v. Sandford* to deny citizenship to any person descended from slaves and guarantee the right to own slaves beyond the slave states.[34] Taney's misguided effort to resolve the slavery question in *Dred Scott* was precisely the kind of overreaching that Marshall had wisely avoided. Taney not only damaged the Court's legitimacy for a generation, his decision in *Dred Scott* tore apart the Union that Marshall had fought to preserve.

Marshall's judicial legacy was now threatened not only by Taney's appointment but also by President Jackson's ruthless persecution of the Indians. Just months before Marshall's death, President Jackson wrote a threatening letter to the Cherokee again, demanding their removal from their traditional lands. In defiance of the Supreme Court's decision in *Worcester*, Jackson warned that "as certain as the sun shines to guide you in your path, so certain is it that you cannot drive back the laws of Georgia from among you. Every year will increase your difficulties." Resistance by the Indians was futile. "This cannot be allowed. Punishment will follow, and all who are engaged in these offences must suffer."[35]

In 1835, Jackson pressured one Cherokee leader, Major Ridge, to sign the Treaty of New Echota that surrendered all the Cherokee lands in exchange for federal land promised out west. Ridge represented only a tiny fraction of the Cherokee, and other tribal leaders rejected the treaty. The Senate barely ratified the treaty by a single vote.

What followed three years later was the catastrophic forced removal of some fifteen thousand Cherokee by U.S. troops under the command of General Winfield Scott. Federal troops brutally marched Indians hundreds of miles. The army failed to provide proper food, water, shelter, or clothing for these civilians. As a result, about four thousand Cherokee men, women, and children died on the Trail of Tears.[36] No other president has acted so overtly in contempt of a Supreme Court decision. And few other presidents have acted so inhumanely. The Trail of Tears was surely one of the ugliest episodes in American history, and it was a complete repudiation of the Marshall Court by the nation's highest law enforcer.

IT IS TEMPTING to contrast Marshall's life and legacy with Jefferson's. Until Jefferson's passing, they lived as mirror opposites for half a century in almost every way. No Marshall biography can avoid taking sides in their conflicted relationship. That is not to say that Marshall was always right or that Jefferson was always wrong. Both were exceptional and entirely human. They were flawed, and sometimes they erred. Yet both Marshall and Jefferson were indispensable to the founding of the Republic.

Jefferson was an eloquent writer who more than any other Founder gave voice to the philosophy behind American democracy. Jefferson drafted the Declaration of Independence; established and led the Republican Party; served as Virginia's first governor, minister to France, secretary of state, vice president, and president; acquired the Louisiana Purchase; and built the University of Virginia. Any one of these accomplishments would have been praiseworthy and deserves historical recognition.

Jefferson lived a life of privilege and never had to work to support himself. He depended on an army of plantation slaves, and his extravagant lifestyle ultimately depleted his estate. His cousin Marshall was born in a log cabin on the frontier, the eldest of fifteen children. He grew up poor and without Jefferson's education or advantages. As an adult, Marshall prospered both as an attorney and a landholder, and left behind a significant estate. Unlike Jefferson, who was groomed for leadership as a member of the elite, Marshall had to invent himself, and the experience of self-invention gave him the confidence and imagination to reinvent the law.

While Marshall suffered the winter at Valley Forge as a rifleman in the Virginia regiment, Jefferson, as governor, was preoccupied with the design of his new state capital. And when the British invaded Richmond and Charlottesville, Jefferson ran away. Captain Marshall and his men fought the invaders. And while both served in the state's government, Jefferson was disgraced by his failure to properly prepare the state's defenses and never sought state office again.

As the American minister, Jefferson was a popular figure in France. Perhaps imprudently, he became entangled with the French revolutionaries. His correspondence from Paris misrepresented the violence and the terror of the French Revolution, and even after he returned to the States, he continued to romanticize it. Marshall's tenure in Paris was less successful than Jefferson's, and though he initially sympathized with the French Revolution, his time there taught him not to trust the French government.

While Jefferson was in Paris, he did not support the adoption of the federal Constitution. Marshall helped Madison lead the fight for the Constitution's ratification at the critical Virginia Ratifying Convention. Without Marshall's successful lobbying, the Constitution might never have been ratified by the nation's largest and most important state. When Jefferson returned from Paris, he fought for a more limited federal government and supported states' rights and nullification while Marshall championed federal power and opposed states' rights.

Both Jefferson and Marshall, like so many of their contemporaries, were slaveholders, and neither freed their own slaves during their lifetimes. But Marshall seemed to have a more generous and humane relationship with his slaves, perhaps, in part, because he was not a plantation owner with a large number of slaves working the fields under an overseer. As an attorney, Marshall defended slaves pro bono against their masters. As a member of the Virginia General Assembly, Marshall opposed slavery and the slave trade, and as chief justice, he ultimately upheld the rights of Indian tribes to their own land.

As secretary of state, Jefferson often had a stormy relationship with Washington's cabinet. He sided with the French against the British during the French Revolutionary Wars, and he secretly conspired with the French ambassador, Citizen Genet, in ways that undermined Washington's neutrality policy. Privately, Jefferson criticized Washington. Later, as Adams's vice president, Jefferson commissioned slanderous publications against President Adams. By contrast, Marshall defended the neutrality policy, criticized Genet, and lauded Washington and Adams.

Jefferson and Marshall had a fundamentally different relationship to authority figures. Jefferson was often skeptical and even disloyal, especially toward Washington and Adams; Marshall's whole career was defined by his loyalty to Washington, General Steuben, and Adams. Jefferson was as fiercely loyal to his ideology as Marshall was to his leaders. Marshall would compromise his own opinions before he would compromise his associates. On a personal level, Marshall was warmer and more gregarious; Jefferson preferred the world of books and ideas.

Marshall and Jefferson fought on opposing sides of every major political issue. Washington persuaded Marshall to run for Congress to oppose the growing influence of Jefferson's political party. Marshall supported President Adams's decision to extradite Jonathan Robbins to face trial in Britain for mutiny; Jefferson used that political issue against Adams. Though Marshall did not publicly oppose the Alien and Sedition Acts at the time they were first proposed, Jefferson did. And while Marshall defended Jay's Treaty, Jefferson and his partisans attacked it. As secretary of state, Marshall maintained neutrality but privately favored Britain over France while Jefferson boasted that he looked forward to having dinner with a victorious Napoleon in London. As chief justice, Marshall defended the judiciary's independence from Jefferson and the Republican Party. Jefferson's disregard for judicial independence was demonstrated by his support for the repeal of the circuit courts, the impeachment of Justice Chase, and his involvement in Burr's treason trial. Time and again, Jefferson and his lieutenants criticized Marshall's decisions and sought to undermine his authority on the Court.

Jefferson, as the heir to wealth and privilege, romanticized the common man; Marshall, as the common man, defended the rights of landholders and creditors. Jefferson may have posed as the revolutionary, but his republican ideology was more about preserving the agrarian past, the plantation system, slavery, and states' rights than the country's future. Jefferson was suspicious of cities, finance, and manufacturing. He did not foresee the creation of a truly national market. Marshall's defense of property rights may have appeared conservative, but his expansive reading of the Constitution made possible the creation of the modern federal government and the modern national economy. Marshall's Constitution was truly revolutionary. In the final analysis, Jefferson's localized vision of a republic of yeoman farmers proved anachronistic, while Marshall's robust federalism triumphed.

MARSHALL WAS NO PURER than his contemporaries. He was at best naïve when he dealt with Talleyrand. As chief justice, his motives were sometimes too overtly partisan. He did not always recuse himself from cases in which he had a clear interest, most notably *Marbury v. Madison.* In *Marbury,* he most likely solicited a perjured affidavit from his own brother in order to prove the existence of a commission. Even in *Martin v. Hunter's Lessee,* Marshall allegedly helped draft the majority's opinion even though the case concerned Fairfax's property, which he had a personal investment in. When he was faced with real moral dilemmas, he abandoned his own moral principles and applied legal rules without regard for their human consequences. His opinions in *Antelope* and *Cherokee Nation v. Georgia,* for example, caused untold misery for African captives and Indians, respectively. Jefferson accused Marshall of "twistification" in the Burr trial, and it is true that Marshall often reached decisions in ways that were inconsistent.

But Marshall's inconsistency and his failure to follow his own moral instincts were not symptoms of intellectual dishonesty. Time and again

Marshall acted to forge consensus on the Court and avert constitutional crises. Marshall tried to persuade his brethren to his point of view when he could, and when he could not, he sought common ground. Marshall did not see compromise or pragmatism as a moral failing. Nor should we. Compromise and pragmatism made possible the Union.

Chief Justice Marshall lived in a revolutionary age in which the country was deeply polarized by competing ideologies. The politics of his day were every bit as negative and ruthless as the politics of our own time. Though he did not have the benefit of precedent, Marshall creatively navigated his way through a thicket of domestic and international controversies, choosing his battles prudently and forging consensus where none seemed possible. Though the Revolutionary generation was governed by certain rules of civility—rules that have since been forgotten—men were no less mean-spirited, petty, jealous, avaricious, or corruptible than in our own time.

Democracy requires practical jurists and statesmen who prefer compromise to chaos and who understand that the single-minded pursuit of one's own ideology at the expense of all else is the path to civil war.

More than any other American, John Marshall set the foundations of the Republic that have guided the nation for more than two centuries. He had the courage of his imagination, the wisdom to find common ground, and the grace to hold together a fragile union. With his passing, who would save the Union now?

ACKNOWLEDGMENTS

I am grateful for the research support I received from the University of California Hastings College of the Law, especially from my librarian, Vince Moyer, and his colleagues who worked tirelessly over seven years gathering materials for this book. I was fortunate to have the assistance of student researchers, including George Croton, Noah Glazier, Greg Greenberg, Ken Laslavic, Scott Malzahn, Robert Moutrie, and Nick Smith. Special thanks go to Michelle Hernandez, Serena Salem, Drew Stark, Daniel Wilson, and Jakob Zollmann, who helped with translating, gathering materials at the Bibliothèque Nationale de France and the Archives Nationales, and reading hundreds of documents and newspaper accounts.

I am also grateful for the assistance of Catherine Dean and Jennifer Hurst on the staff of Preservation Virginia at the John Marshall House in Richmond; Thomas Lester at the Massachusetts Historical Society; Jennifer Harbster at the Library of Congress; James Cronan at the British National Archives; Phyllis Scott at the Fauquier County Records Office; and the staffs of the British Library, the British National Archives, the Doe Memorial Library at the University of California at Berkeley, the Harvard Law School and Widener Libraries, the Library of Congress, the New York Public Library, the San Francisco Public Library, the South Caroliniana Library at the University of South Carolina, and the Virginia State Library.

I also appreciate the contributions of my friends and colleagues who read drafts, filled gaps in my knowledge, and supported my work, in particular Paul Aron, Lucinda Eubanks, Chimène Keitner, Elise Kroeber, Nell Jessup Newton, Zach Price, Margaret Russell, Reuel Schiller, and Joan Williams.

I am especially indebted to my friend and teacher Professor Robert A. Gross for his generous feedback on an earlier draft. He has inspired me throughout my career.

Of course, this book would not be possible without the help of my literary agent, Roger Williams, and my editor and friend, Jake Morrissey, and his colleagues at Riverhead Books.

Finally, my special thanks for the encouragement of my friends and family, in particular Jane Shulman, Rick Steele, and Charles Uerhke. I am blessed having each of you in my life.

NOTES

CHAPTER 1. THE FRONTIER SOLDIER

1 Thomas Fleming, *Washington's Secret War: The Hidden History of Valley Forge* (New York: Harper-Collins, 2005), 180.

2 Paul Lockhart, *The Drillmaster of Valley Forge: The Baron de Steuben and the Making of the American Army* (New York: HarperCollins, 2008), 73–74.

3 Charles H. Lesser, *The Sinews of Independence* (Chicago: University of Chicago Press, 1976), 59; Fleming, *Secret War*, 15, 30, 214, 263.

4 James R. Gaines, *For Liberty and Glory: Washington, Lafayette, and Their Revolutions* (New York: W. W. Norton, 2007), 104.

5 Louis Clinton Hatch, *The Administration of the American Revolutionary Army* (New York: Longmans, Green, and Co., 1904), 93.

6 Ron Chernow, *Washington: A Life* (New York: The Penguin Press, 2010), 325.

7 Hatch, *Administration*, 92.

8 E. Wayne Carp, *To Starve the Army at Pleasure: Continental Army Administration and American Political Culture, 1775–1783* (Chapel Hill: University of North Carolina Press, 1984), 179.

9 Fleming, *Secret War*, 134.

10 Chernow, *Washington*, 326.

11 John R. Alden, *A History of the American Revolution* (New York: Da Capo Press, 1969), 300.

12 Fleming, *Secret War*, 186, as quoted in Chernow, *Washington*, 329.

13 There is some disagreement about Azor's breed, which some sources refer to as an Italian greyhound. However, that seems unlikely since Azor was described as much larger than an Italian greyhound would ordinarily have been. Lockhart, *Drillmaster*, 49.

14 Joseph H. Jones, ed., *The Life of Ashbel Green, V.D.M.*, as quoted in Benson Bobrick, *Angel in the Whirlwind* (New York: Penguin Books, 1997), 333.

15 James Thomas Flexner, *George Washington in the American Revolution (1775–1783)* (Boston: Little, Brown, 1968), 261; Fleming, *Secret War*, 214.

16 Flexner, *Washington in the American Revolution*, 262.

17 Fleming, *Secret War*, 14.

18 Fleming, *Secret War*, 22–24, 160; Chernow, *Washington*, 325.

19 Fleming, *Secret War*, 137.

20 Fleming, *Secret War*, 131–133; Alden, *American Revolution*, 446.

21 Fleming, *Secret War*, 33.

22 Flexner, *Washington in the American Revolution*, 260; Gaines, *For Liberty*, 96.

23 Fleming, *Secret War*, 163, 263.

24 Flexner, *Washington in the American Revolution*, 282.

25 Albert J. Beveridge, *The Life of John Marshall* (Boston: Houghton Mifflin, 1916), 1:118–119; Joseph J. Ellis, *His Excellency: George Washington* (New York, Alfred A. Knopf, 2004), 112–118; Jane Carson, *Colonial Virginians at Play* (Williamsburg: University Press of Virginia, 1965), 180–182; Jean Edward Smith, *John Marshall: Definer of a Nation* (New York: Henry Holt, 1996), 64.

26 Gaines, *For Liberty*, 104; Beveridge, *Marshall*, 1:119–120.

27 Alden,*American Revolution*, 390;Fleming, *Secret War*, 217–222, 229; Lockhart, *Drillmaster*, 108–113.

28 Fleming, *Secret War*, 230, 263–277.

29 Fleming, *Secret War*, 222, 233.

30 John Marshall, *The Life of George Washington* (New York: Walton Book Company, 1930) 1:268–269; Smith, *Marshall*, 65–66, 82–85; Gaines, *For Liberty*, 105.

31 Beveridge, *Marshall*, 1: 119–120; Lockhart, *Drillmaster*, 21; Marshall, *Life of George Washington*, 1:254.

32 Marshall to James Monroe, Jan. 3, 1784, in Charles F. Hobson, Herbert A. Johnson, Charles T. Cullen, and Nancy G. Harris, eds., *The Papers of John Marshall* (Chapel Hill: University of North Carolina Press, 1974–2006) 1:113 (hereafter cited as MP).

33 Marshall, *Life of George Washington*, 1:408–419, 2:66–67.

34 Lockhart, *Drillmaster*, 42–43; William E. Benemann, *Male-Male Intimacy in Early America: Beyond Romantic Friendship* (New York: Routledge, 2012), 102–106. Steuben, who never married or expressed an interest in women, lavished his attention on younger men. At Valley Forge he formed a particularly close bond with his aide, Captain Benjamin Walker, whom he called his "angel."

35 Lockhart, *Drillmaster*, 44–49.

36 Lockhart, *Drillmaster*, 53, 65–66.

37 Smith, *Marshall*, 29.

38 Beveridge, *Marshall*, 1:33–56.

39 Smith, *Marshall*, 24–25.

40 Beveridge, *Marshall*, 1:12–18; Smith, *Marshall*, 29–30; Dumas Malone, *Jefferson the Virginian* (Charlottesville: University of Virginia Press, 1948), 10–20.

41 John Marshall, *An Autobiographical Sketch*, ed. John Stokes Adams (Ann Arbor: University of Michigan Press, 1991), xx, 4; Beveridge, *Marshall*, 1:18, 53–57.

42 Marshall, *Autobiographical Sketch*, 4.

43 Smith, *Marshall*, 35.

44 Marshall, *Autobiographical Sketch*, xix.

45 Michael A. McDonnell, *The Politics of War: Race, Class, and Conflict in Revolutionary Virginia* (Chapel Hill: University of North Carolina Press, 2007), 24–29.

46 Beveridge, *Marshall*, 1:60–61.

47 Jack P. Greene, *Political Life in Eighteenth-Century Virginia* (Williamsburg, VA: Colonial Williamsburg Foundation, 1986), 10, 45–46; John Selby, *The Revolution in Virginia, 1775–1783* (Williamsburg, VA: Colonial Williamsburg Foundation, 1988), 30, 33, 39.

48 Edwin S. Gaustad, *Revival, Revolution, and Religion in Early Virginia* (Williamsburg, VA: Colonial Williamsburg Foundation, 1994), 16–19, 23–27; Selby, *Revolution in Virginia*, 33–35, 154–157.

49 Selby, *Revolution in Virginia*, 15–16, 21–22; Greene, *Political Life*, 29–31.

50 Rhys Isaac, *The Transformation of Virginia: 1740-1790* (Chapel Hill: University of North Carolina Press, 1982), 137.

51 McDonnell, *Politics of War*, 47–49.

52 Selby, *Revolution in Virginia*, 1–5.

53 Selby, *Revolution in Virginia*, 7–8, 41–43, 66–67.

54 Beveridge, *Marshall*, 1:67–68; R. Kent Newmyer, *John Marshall and the Heroic Age of the Supreme Court* (Baton Rouge: Louisiana State University Press, 2001), 2–3; Smith, *Marshall*, 44.

55 Isaac, *Transformation*, 256–258; Smith, *Marshall*, 45–46.

56 Smith, *Marshall*, 47–51.

57 Marshall, *Life of George Washington*, 1:82.

CHAPTER 2. A REVOLUTIONARY CAPITAL

1 Marianne Buroff Sheldon, "Black-White Relations in Richmond, Virginia: 1782–1820," *The Journal of Southern History* 45, no. 1 (February 1979): 27–29.

2 Harry M. Ward and Harold E. Greer Jr., *Richmond During the Revolution: 1775–1783* (Charlottesville: University Press of Virginia, 1977), 8–10, 16; Beveridge, *Marshall*, 1:171; Frances Norton Mason, *My Dearest Polly: Letters of Chief Justice Marshal to His Wife, with Their Background, Political and Domestic, 1779–1831* (Richmond, VA: Garrett & Massie, 1961), 13; Smith, *Marshall*, 88.

3 Alf J. Mapp, Jr., *Thomas Jefferson: A Strange Case of Mistaken Identity* (New York: Madison Books, 1987), 133, 140; R. B. Bernstein, *Thomas Jefferson* (New York: Oxford University Press, 2003), 45; Selby, *Revolution in Virginia*, 236, citing Julian Boyd, Charles Cullen, John Catanzariti, and Barbara Oberg,eds., *The Papers of Thomas Jefferson* (Princeton, NJ: Princeton University Press, 1950), 1:602–603.

4 Selby, *Revolution in Virginia*, 236; Mapp, *Jefferson*, 133, 140; Bernstein, *Jefferson*, 45.

5 Mapp, *Jefferson*, 140; Selby, *Revolution in Virginia*, 235–236, 246; Ward and Greer, *Richmond During the Revolution*, 38.

6 Marshall, *Autobiographical Sketch*, 5–6; Beveridge, *Marshall*, 1:151–153.

7 Law notes, MP, 1:37–41; Smith, *Marshall*, 17–18.

8 Beveridge, *Marshall*, 1:41, 154; Law notes, MP, 1:39.

9 Smith, *Marshall*, 82.

10 Jon Meacham, *Thomas Jefferson: The Art of Power* (New York Random House Trade Paperbacks, 2013), 133–136; Ward and Greer, *Richmond During the Revolution*, 80–81; Smith, *Marshall*, 83.

11 Meacham, *Jefferson*, 137–138; Mapp, *Jefferson*, 141–156; Ward and Greer, *Richmond During the Revolution*, 82.

12 Beveridge, *Marshall*, 1:153, 165; Mason, *My Dearest Polly*, 19; Smith, *Marshall*, 85.

13 Beveridge, *Marshall*, 1:166–167, 171.

14 Harry Ammon, *James Monroe: The Quest for National Identity* (Charlottesville: University of Virginia Press, 1990), 37–38, 45.

15 Randolph to James Madison, Nov. 29, 1782, in Smith, *Marshall*, 92.

16 Pendleton to James Madison, Nov. 25, 1782, in David John Mays, ed., *The Letters and Papers of Edmund Pendleton, 1734–1803* (Charlottesville: University Press of Virginia, 1967), 1:429.

17 Beveridge, *Marshall*, 1:203–209.

18 Harry M. Ward, *Public Executions in Richmond, Virginia: 1782–1907* (Jefferson, NC: McFarland & Co., 2012), 17–19.

19 Smith, *Marshall*, 95–96.

20 Ward and Greer, *Richmond During the Revolution*, 108.

21 Joseph Jones to James Monroe, April 15, 1785, in Daniel Preston and Marlena C. DeLong, eds., *The Papers of James Monroe: Selected Correspondence and Papers, 1776–1794* (Westport, CT: Greenwood Press, 2006), 2:207.

22 Charles F. Hobson, "The Recovery of British Debts in the Federal Circuit Courts of Virginia, 1790 to 1797," *Virginia Magazine of History and Biography* 92, no. 2 (April 1984): 183–185; Newmyer, *Marshall*, 96; Smith, *Marshall*, 155.

23 Newmyer, *Marshall*, 96–97.

24 Beveridge, *Marshall*, 1:183; Smith, *Marshall*, 104; Jean Edward Smith, "Marshall Misconstrued: Activist? Partisan? Reactionary?" *John Marshall Law Review* 33, no. 4 (2000): 1122; Newmyer, *Marshall*, 34–35.

25 Beveridge, *Marshall*, 1:198; Mason, *My Dearest Polly*, 41–43, 57–61; Smith, *Marshall*, 107.

26 Margaret Good Myers, *A Financial History of the United States* (New York: Columbia University Press, 1970), 40; E. James Ferguson, *The Power of the Purse: A History of American Public Finance, 1776–1790* (Chapel Hill: University of North Carolina Press), 242–243.

27 Ferguson, *Power of the Purse*, 238–244, citing *Worcester Magazine* (July 1787), 3.

28 Patrick T. Conley, "Rhode Island: Laboratory for the Lively Experiment," in Patrick T. Conley and John P. Kaminksi, eds., *The Bill of Rights and the States: The Colonial and Revolutionary Origins of American Liberties* (Madison, WI: Madison House Publishers, 1992), 124–160.

29 Marshall, *Life of George Washington*, 2:137.

30 David P. Szatmary, *Shays' Rebellion: The Making of an Agrarian Insurrection* (Amherst: University of Massachusetts Press, 1980), 19–20, 66; Robert A. Gross, ed., *In Debt to Shays: The Bicentennial of an Agrarian Rebellion* (Charlottesville: University Press of Virginia, 1993), 7–8.

31 Leonard L. Richards, *Shays's Rebellion: The American Revolution's Final Battle* (Philadelphia: University of Pennsylvania Press, 2002), 7–61; Gross, *In Debt to Shays*, 3.

32 Richards, *Shays's Rebellion*, 116–117.

33 Samuel E. Morison and Henry S. Commager, *The Growth of the American Republic* (New York: Oxford University Press, 1962), 1:272–276.

34 Marshall to James Wilkinson, Jan. 5, 1787, in MP, 1:200–201.

CHAPTER 3. DEBATING THE CONSTITUTION

1 Account book, MP, 1:409; Smith, *Marshall*, 122–124.

2 Newmyer, *Marshall*, 50–51.

3 John P. Kaminski, Gaspare J. Saladino, et al., eds, *The Documentary History of the Ratification of the Constitution by the States: Virginia* (Madison: Wisconsin Historical Society Press, 1990), 9:897.

4 Smith, *Marshall*, 122–123; Hugh Blair Grigsby, *The History of the Virginia Federal Convention of 1788* (New York: Da Capo Press, 1969), 1:25–26; Mason, *My Dearest Polly*, 51; Newmyer, *Marshall*, 54.

5 Ralph Ketcham, *James Madison: A Biography* (Charlottesville: University Press of Virginia, 1990), 51–52, 89; Richard Brookhiser, *James Madison* (New York: Basic Books, 2011), 4.

6 *Baron v. Baltimore*, 32 U.S. 243, 250 (1833).

7 Washington to Lafayette, April 1, 1788, in Kaminski et al., eds., *Documentary History*, 9:768.

8 Ellis, *His Excellency*, 180–183; Chernow, *Washington*, 543–547.

9 Dumas Malone, *Jefferson and the Rights of Man* (Boston: Little, Brown and Co., 1951), 164–169.

10 Jefferson to John Adams, Nov. 13, 1787, in Boyd, ed., *Papers of Jefferson*, 12:349.

11 Jefferson to W. S. Smith, Nov. 13, 1787, in Paul Leicester Ford, ed., *The Writings of Thomas Jefferson* (New York: G. P. Putnam's Sons, 1909), 4:466–467.

12 Malone, *Jefferson and the Rights of Man*, 171–178.

13 Jeff Broadwater, *James Madison: A Son of Virginia and a Founder of the Nation* (Chapel Hill: University of North Carolina Press, 2012), 70.

14 Ketcham, *Madison*, 254; Grigsby, *Virginia Federal Convention*, 1:67–68.

15 Newmyer, *Marshall*, 52, citing Henry, June 5, 1788, in Kaminski et al., eds., *Documentary History* 9:962.

16 Jack N. Rakove, *James Madison and the Creation of the American Republic* (New York: Longman, 2002), 88–89.

17 Rakove, *Madison*, 88–89; Broadwater, *Madison*, 70; Ketcham, *Madison*, 258–259.

18 Bernard Bailyn, ed., *The Debate on the Constitution: Federalist and Antifederalist Speeches, Articles, and Letters During the Struggle over Ratification* (New York: Library of America, 1993), 2:596.

19 Grigsby, *Virginia Federal Convention*, 1:157; Newmyer, *Marshall*, 53.

20 Grigsby, *Virginia Federal Convention*, 1:176, 181–183.

21 Monroe to Thomas Jefferson, July 12, 1788, as quoted in Pauline Maier, *Ratification: The People Debate the Constitution, 1787–1788* (New York: Simon & Schuster Paperbacks, 2010), 310.

22 Speech, June 10, 1788, MP, 1:260–262.

23 Speech, June 20, 1788, MP, 1:276–277; *Marbury v. Madison*, 5 U.S. 137 (1803).

24 Smith, *Marshall*, 133–134; Ward and Greer, *Richmond During the Revolution*, 51.

25 Ketcham, *Madison*, 263.

26 Speech by Patrick Henry, June 24, 1788, Virginia Ratifying Convention, http://www.constitution .org/rc/rat_va_20.htm. accessed June 30, 2012.

27 Monroe to Thomas Jefferson, July 12, 1788, in Boyd, ed., *Papers of Thomas Jefferson*, 13:351–354.

28 Grigsby, *Virginia Federal Convention*, 1:319–320, n241.

29 Kaminski et al., eds., *Documentary History*, 9:951.

CHAPTER 4. SLAVES AND HYPOCRITES

1 Smith, *Marshall*, 145.

2 Jefferson to James Madison, June 29, 1792, in Ford, ed., *Writings of Thomas Jefferson*, 7:129–130.

3 Newmyer, *Marshall*, 35.

4 Frances Howell Rudko, "Pause at the Rubicon, John Marshall and Emancipation: Reparations in the Early Period?" *John Marshall Law Review* 35, no. 1 (2002): 79. The average household in 1784 had five slaves according to census figures. James Sidbury, *Ploughshares into Swords: Race, Rebellion, and Identity in Gabriel's Virginia, 1730–1810* (New York: Cambridge University Press, 1997), 164.

5 Sidbury, *Ploughshares into Swords*, 161.

6 Edmund S. Morgan, *American Slavery, American Freedom: The Ordeal of Colonial Virginia* (New York: W. W. Norton, 1975), 376–387.

7 Edmund S. Morgan, *Virginians at Home: Family Life in the Eighteenth Century* (Williamsburg, VA: Colonial Williamsburg Foundation, 1952), 68–70; Sidbury, *Ploughshares into Swords*, 185–187; Marie Tyler-McGraw and Gregg D. Kimball, *In Bondage and Freedom Antebellum Black Life in Richmond* (Chapel Hill: Valentine Museum and University of North Carolina Press, 1998), 14, 24–27, 35–39, 49–50, 63–64; Ward and Greer, *Richmond During the Revolution*, 121–122.

8 Marshall to Timothy Pickering, March 20, 1826, in MP, 10:277.

9 James H. Broussard, *The Southern Federalists, 1800–1816* (Baton Rouge: Louisiana State University Press, 1976), 313–319.

10 *The Antelope*, 23 U.S. 66, 124 (1825).

11 Jefferson sold or transferred by gift 161 slaves between 1784 and 1794, separating parents and children. Joseph J. Ellis, *American Sphinx: The Character of Thomas Jefferson* (New York: Vintage Books, 1996), 144–145. When slaves misbehaved, Jefferson ordered his overseers to flog or sell them. Ibid., 149. See also Fawn M. Brodie, *Thomas Jefferson: An Intimate History* (New York: Bantam Books, 2011), 377–378. Twenty-three of Jefferson's slaves ran away. Alan Taylor, *The Internal Enemy: Slavery and War in Virginia, 1772–1832* (New York: W. W. Norton, 2013), 28. Jefferson justified slavery based on his belief that blacks were inherently inferior to whites. Bernstein, *Jefferson*, 61–62; Mapp, *Jefferson*, 167–173.

12 Newmyer, *Marshall*, 414–418; Ellis, *American Sphinx*, 149; Mapp, *Jefferson*, 170–171.

13 Sidbury, *Ploughshares into Swords*, 68–69, 95–99, 118–121.

14 Broussard, *Southern Federalists*, 319.

15 Rudko, "Pause at the Rubicon," 84–88; Smith, *Marshall*, 489–490.

16 Ward and Greer, *Richmond During the Revolution*, 124–125.

17 Rudko, "Pause at the Rubicon," 80–81.

18 Mason, *My Dearest Polly*, 139, 235.

19 Smith, *Marshall*, 162.

20 Smith, *Marshall*, 163.

21 Smith, *Marshall*, 162.

22 *Pleasants v. Pleasants*, MP, 5:541–549.

23 Newmyer, *Marshall*, 91–92.

24 Newmyer, *Marshall*, 92; Founders Online, "Editorial Note: The Debt to Farell & Jones and the Slave Ship *The Prince of Wales*," found at http://founders.archives.gov/documents/Jefferson/0-15-02-0620-0001, accessed on Nov. 25, 2015.

25 Argument in the Court of Appeals, MP, 5:148–158.

26 *Wayles's Executors v. Randolph et al.* (1795–1799), MP, 5:117–120, 159–160; Newmyer, *Marshall*, 91.

27 Jefferson to Jean Nicolas Démeunier, Jan. 24, 1786, in Additional Questions and Answers in Ford, ed., *Writings of Jefferson*, 5:12.

28 Meacham, *Jefferson*, 23–25.

29 Bernstein, *Jefferson*, 110.

CHAPTER 5. INNOCENCE LOST

1 Marshall, *Autobiographical Sketch*, 13.

2 Gordon S. Wood, *Empire of Liberty: A History of the Early Republic, 1789–1815* (New York: Oxford University Press, 2009), 175; Jay Winik, *The Great Upheaval: America and the Birth of the Modern World, 1788–1800* (New York: Harper, 2007), 448.

3 Jefferson to Abigail Adams, August 9, 1786, in Boyd, ed., *Papers of Jefferson*, 10:203.

4 Jefferson to George Washington, Dec. 4, 1788, in Boyd, ed., *Papers of Jefferson*, 14:330.

5 Christopher Hibbert, *The French Revolution* (London: Penguin Books, 1982), 82.

6 Jefferson to John Jay, July 19, 1789, in John Gabriel Hunt, ed., *The Essential Thomas Jefferson* (Avenel, NJ: Portland House, 1994), 119.

7 Wood, *Empire*, 179–180; Harlow Giles Unger, *Lafayette* (New York: John Wiley & Sons, 2002), 226–227; Malone, *Jefferson and the Rights of Man*, 216–225, 229–233; Conor Cruise O'Brien, *The Long Affair: Thomas Jefferson and the French Revolution, 1785–1800* (Chicago: University of Chicago Press, 1996), 52–63.

8 Jefferson to Thomas Paine, Sep. 13, 1789, in Boyd, ed., *Papers of Jefferson*, 15:424.

9 Hibbert, *French Revolution*, 96; George Rudé, *The French Revolution: Its Causes, Its History, and Its Legacy After 200 Years* (New York: Grove Press, 1988), 30.

10 As quoted in Hibbert, *French Revolution*, 93.

11 Simon Schama, *Citizens: A Chronicle of the French Revolution* (New York: Alfred A. Knopf, 1989), 501–509.

12 As quoted in Hibbert, *French Revolution*, 116.

13 Hibbert, *French Revolution*, 145–176.

14 Winik, *Great Upheaval*, 134.

15 Chernow, *Washington*, 658–659.

16 Dumas Malone, *Jefferson and the Ordeal of Liberty* (Boston: Little, Brown, 1962), 56–57.

17 Winik, *Great Upheaval*, 459.

18 Joel Richard Paul, *Unlikely Allies: How a Merchant, a Playwright, and a Spy Saved the American Revolution* (New York: Riverhead Books, 2009), 218–220, 333–334.

19 Samuel Flagg Bemis, *Jay's Treaty: A Study in Commerce and Diplomacy* (New Haven, CT: Yale University Press, 1962), 261.

20 Winik, *Great Upheaval*, 460–461.

21 Wood, *Empire*, 182; Stanley Elkins and Eric McKitrick, *The Age of Federalism: The Early American Republic, 1788–1800* (New York: Oxford University Press, 1995), 337–341; Chernow, *Washington*, 690–691; Malone, *Ordeal of Liberty*, 69–70.

22 Washington to Thomas Jefferson, April 12, 1793, in John H. Rhodehamel, ed., *George Washington: Writings* (New York: Library of America, 1997), 837, as quoted in Chernow, *Washington*, 690.

23 Though political factions associated with federalists and anti-federalists emerged during the debates to ratify the Constitution, there were no formalized political parties. In the first two congressional elections, candidates did not run for office on party tickets. Organized political parties did not emerge until sometime around 1794. This author capitalizes references to the Republican and Federalist parties from that date.

24 As quoted in Wood, *Empire*, 177, citing letter from Hamilton, May 8, 1793, in Harold C. Syrett, ed., *The Papers of Alexander Hamilton* (New York: Columbia University Press, 1972), 16:475–476.

25 Wood, *Empire*, 177–178.

26 As quoted in Winik, *Great Upheaval*, 463.

27 O'Brien, *Long Affair*, 136.

28 Jefferson to William Short, Jan. 3, 1793, in Boyd, ed., *Papers of Jefferson*, 25:14.

29 Jefferson to Lafayette, April 2, 1790, in Boyd, ed., *Papers of Jefferson*, 16:293.

30 Jefferson to John Adams, Sep. 4, 1823, in Merrill D. Peterson, ed., *Jefferson: Writings* (New York: Library of America, 1984), 1478.

31 Wood, *Empire*, 181.

32 As quoted in Winik, *Great Upheaval*, 463.

33 Malone, *Ordeal of Liberty*, 62.

34 As quoted in Wood, *Empire*, 181, citing Jefferson to William Carmichael, Dec. 15, 1787, in Boyd, ed., *Papers of Jefferson*, 12:424.

35 Jefferson to James Madison, Aug. 28, 1789, in Boyd, ed., *Papers of Jefferson*, 15:364; Malone, *Ordeal of Liberty*, 62–66.

36 Jefferson to William Branch Giles, April 27, 1795, in Boyd, ed., *Papers of Jefferson*, 28:337.

37 Wood, *Empire*, 183; Winik, *Great Upheaval*, 470.

38 As quoted in Malone, *Ordeal of Liberty*, 61, citing *National Gazette*, April 20, 1793.

39 Smith, *Marshall*, 153.

40 Hobson, "Recovery of British Debts," 185; Newmyer, *Marshall*, 96–97.

41 *Jones v. Walker*, Federal Circuit Court, Charlottesville, Virginia (1791).

42 *Jones v. Walker*, MP, 5:264–268.

43 Replications and demurrer, from *Jones v. Walker*, July 26, 1791, MP, 5:276–278.

44 Amended pleas, Nov. 23, 1791, MP, 5:280–287; Rejoinder, Nov. 23, 1791, MP, 5:289–291; Smith, *Marshall*, 155.

45 Newmyer, *Marshall*, 98–100.

46 Maeva Marcus, ed., *The Documentary History of the Supreme Court of the United States, 1789–1800* (New York: Columbia University Press, 1989), 2:209–212.

47 Marcus, ed., *Documentary History of the Supreme Court*, 6:210–215, 261–311; Julius Goebel, Jr., *History of the Supreme Court of the United States: Antecedents and Beginnings to 1801* (New York: Macmillan, 1971), 750.

48 Smith, *Marshall*, 164–165.

49 Editorial note, MP, 2:145–146.

50 To Mary Marshall, Feb. 3, 1796, MP, 3:3–4.

51 John Adams to Abigail Adams, Feb. 8, 1796, in Charles Francis Adams, ed., *Letters of John Adams to His Wife*, (Boston: Charles C. Little and James Brown, 1841), 2:195.

52 Marcus, ed., *Documentary History of the Supreme Court*, 7:203.

53 Marcus, ed., *Documentary History of the Supreme Court*, 6:2.

54 Argument, *Ware v. Hylton*, Feb. 9, 1796, MP, 3:7–11; Philip B. Kurland and Gerhard Casper, eds., *Landmark Briefs and Arguments of the Supreme Court of the United States* (Bethesda, MD: University Publications of America, 1975), 1:209–220.

55 Argument, Feb. 9, 1796, MP, 3:11–14.

56 Argument, Feb. 9, 1796, MP, 3:9.

57 *Ware v. Hylton*, 3 Dallas 281.

58 *Ware v. Hylton*, 3 Dallas 242–243.

59 *Ware v. Hylton*, 3 Dallas 199.

CHAPTER 6. CITIZEN GENET

1 Meade Minnigerode, *Jefferson, Friend of France, 1793: The Career of Edmond Charles Genet* (New York: G. P. Putnam's Sons, 1928), 34; Elkins and McKitrick, *Age of Federalism*, 330.

2 Minnigerode, *Friend of France*, 128–129.

3 As quoted in Harry Ammon, *The Genet Mission* (New York: W. W. Norton, 1973), 26–27.

4 George C. Herring, *From Colony to Superpower: U.S. Foreign Relations Since 1776* (New York: Oxford University Press, 2008), 70; Ammon, *Genet Mission*, 27–29.

5 Wood, *Empire*, 103.

6 As quoted in Elkins and McKitrick, *Age of Federalism*, 332.

7 Ammon, *Genet Mission*, 11–13, 23.

8 Wood, *Empire*, 185.

9 Alden, *American Revolution*, 412–416.

10 Ammon, *Genet Mission*, 30; Elkins and McKitrick, *Age of Federalism*, 334–335.

11 Wood, *Empire*, 185–186; Elkins and McKitrick, *Age of Federalism*, 335; Ammon, *Genet Mission*, 44–45.

12 Elkins and McKitrick, *Age of Federalism*, 335–336; Ammon, *Genet Mission*, 46–47.

13 *Commonwealth v. Randolph*, MP, 2:161–162.

14 *Commonwealth v. Randolph*, MP, 2:163–167; Smith, *Marshall*, 150–151.

15 Malone, *Ordeal of Liberty*, 69–71; Chernow, *Washington*, 690–691.

16 Ammon, *Genet Mission*, 47–49; Herring, *From Colony to Superpower*, 69–70; Elkins and McKitrick, *Age of Federalism*, 337–340; Malone, *Ordeal of Liberty*, 74–79.

17 Elkins and McKitrick, *Age of Federalism*, 337–341; Malone, *Ordeal of Liberty*, 70–71.

18 James F. Simon, *What Kind of Nation: Thomas Jefferson, John Marshall and the Epic Struggle to Create a United States* (New York: Simon & Schuster Paperbacks, 2002), 33, citing Hamilton to Carrington, in Syrett, ed., *Papers of Hamilton*, 11:439.

19 Malone, *Ordeal of Liberty*, 70, citing Jefferson to Monroe, May 5, 1793, in Ford, ed., *Writings of Jefferson*, 6:238–239.

20 Malone, *Ordeal of Liberty*, 88, citing Jefferson to Madison, Jun. 9, 1793, in Ford, ed., *Writings of Jefferson*, 6:290–292.

21 Neutrality Proclamation, Apr. 22, 1793, in W. W. Abbot, Dorothy Twohig, Philander D. Chase, et al., eds., *The Papers of George Washington*. The Presidential Series. (Charlottesville: University of Virginia Press, 1987–), 12:472.

22 Militia Duty, MP, 2:181–182.

23 Chernow, *Washington*, 691–692.

24 Ron Chernow, *Alexander Hamilton* (New York: The Penguin Press, 2004), 438–439; Winik, *Great Upheaval*, 468; Malone, *Ordeal of Liberty*, 92–93.

25 As quoted in Chernow, *Hamilton*, 439.

26 Ketcham, *James Madison*, 342–343; Ammon, *Genet Mission*, 55–57.

27 John Ferling, *John Adams: A Life* (New York: Henry Holt, 1992), 337.

28 As quoted in Chernow, *Hamilton*, 439.

29 From Morris, Jan. 6, 1793, in Abbot et al., eds., *The Papers of George Washington*, 11:593.

30 Jefferson to Madison, May 19, 1793, in Boyd, ed., *Papers of Jefferson*, 26:62.

31 Ammon, *Citizen Genet*, 59; Chernow, *Washington*, 693.

32 Chernow, *Hamilton*, 438; Ammon, *Genet Mission*, 51–52.

33 Ammon, *Genet Mission*, 60.

34 Malone, *Ordeal of Liberty*, 58–59.

35 Ammon, *Genet Mission*, 63–65.

36 Jefferson to James Madison, May 19, 1793, in Boyd, ed., *Papers of Jefferson*, 26:62.

37 Ammon, *Genet Mission*, 63.

38 Malone, *Ordeal of Liberty*, 96.

39 Elkins and McKitrick, *Age of Federalism*, 342; Malone, *Ordeal of Liberty*, 99.

40 Malone, *Ordeal of Liberty*, 63.

41 Elkins and McKitrick, 349–350; Malone, *Ordeal of Libertyl*, 106–108; Ammon, *Genet Mission*, 82–84.

42 Jefferson to Monroe, Jun. 4, 1793, in Boyd, ed., *Papers of Jefferson*, 26:190.

43 Ammon, *Genet Mission*, 66–68; Malone, *Ordeal of Liberty*, 100.

44 Jefferson to James Monroe, Jun. 28, 1973, in Boyd, ed., *Papers of Jefferson*, 26:593.

45 Elkins and McKitrick, *Age of Federalism*, 350; Malone, *Ordeal of Liberty*, 100–101.

46 From Genet, July 9, 1793, in Boyd, ed., *Papers of Jefferson*, 26:456–459; Ammon, *Genet Mission*, 86–87.

47 Jefferson to James Madison, Jul. 7, 1793, in Boyd, ed., *Papers of Jefferson*, 26:444.

48 Jefferson to James Madison, Aug. 3, 1793, in Boyd, ed., *Papers of Jefferson*, 26:606.

49 Marshall to Augustine Davis, Sep. 11, 1793, MP, 2:202–206.

50 From George Washington, Jul. 22, 1793, in Boyd, ed., *Papers of Jefferson*, 26:550; Notes of Cabinet Meeting on Genet, Jul. 23, 1793, in Boyd, ed., *Papers of Jefferson*, 26:553–555.

51 Notes on Cabinet Meeting, Aug. 2, 1793, in Boyd, ed., *Papers of Jefferson*, 26:601–602.

52 Notes on Cabinet Meeting, Aug. 2, 1793, in Boyd, ed., *Papers of Jefferson*, 26:601–604.

53 Jefferson to George Washington, Jul. 31, 1793, in Boyd, ed., *Papers of Jefferson*, 26:593.

54 Flexner, *Washington*, 293–294.

55 Elkins and McKitrick, *Age of Federalism*, 285.

56 Chernow, *Washington*, 693.

57 Pacificus No. 1, Jun. 29, 1793, in Morton Frisch, ed., *The Pacificus-Helvidius Debates of 1793–1794* (Indianapolis, IN: Liberty Fund, 2007), 9. In eighteenth-century America, pseudonyms like "Pacificus" or "Publius" were commonly used as a way that writers could remain anonymous. It was not just a matter of personal modesty. It also allowed prominent figures like Hamilton and Madison to use stronger language contesting their opponents' arguments and character without fear of having to fight a lawsuit or a duel. In fact, the elite knew or suspected who was writing what, but by using a pseudonym no one had to acknowledge attribution. Roman names were typically used to suggest a link to classical thought.

58 Pacificus No. 1, Jun. 29, 1793, in Frisch, ed., *Pacificus-Helvidius Debates*, 13.

59 Jefferson to James Madison, Jul. 7, 1793, in Boyd, ed., *Papers of Jefferson*, 25:444.

60 Helvidius I, Aug. 24, 1793, in Frisch, ed., *Pacificus-Helvidius Debates*, 59–62.

61 Americanus II, Feb. 7, 1794, in Frisch, ed., *Pacificus-Helvidius Debates*, 115.

62 Chernow, *Hamilton*, 505–506.

CHAPTER 7. ENTANGLING ALLIANCES

1 John K. Alexander, "The Philadelphia Numbers Game: An Analysis of Philadelphia's Eighteenth-Century Population." *Pennsylvania Magazine of History and Biography* 98, no. 3 (July 1974): 314, 324.

2 Chernow, *Hamilton*, 448–449.

3 Harry Ammon, "The Genet Mission and the Development of American Political Parties." *The Journal of American History* 52, no. 4 (March 1966): 728–730; Harry Ammon, "Agricola Versus Aristides: James Monroe, John Marshall, and the Genet Affair in Virginia." *Virginia Magazine of History and Biography* 74, no. 3 (July 1966): 314; Ammon, *Genet Mission*, 114–115, 132–133.

4 Walter Stahr, *John Jay: Founding Father* (New York: Hambledon and London, 2005), 306–307.

5 From Monroe, Sep. 3, 1793, in Boyd, ed., *Papers of Jefferson*, 27:26–27.

6 Ammon, *Genet Mission*, 135–140; Smith, *Marshall*, 173; Newmyer, *Marshall*, 107.

7 Resolutions, Aug. 17, 1793, MP, 2:196–197.

8 Address, reprinted from *Virginia Gazette*, Sep. 11, 1793, MP, 2:198–199.

9 From James Madison, Sep. 2, 1793, in Boyd, ed., *Papers of Jefferson*, 27:15-16.

10 Beveridge, *Marshall*, 98–99, 102–103; Marshall to Archibald Stuart, Mar. 27, 1794, MP, 2:261–262.

11 Philip Marsh, "James Monroe as 'Agricola' in the Genet Controversy, 1793" *Virginia Magazine of History and Biography* 62, no. 4 (October 1954): 472–476.

12 Ammon, "Agricola Versus Aristides,", 316.

13 Marshall, *Autobiographical Sketch*, 14.

14 Ammon, *James Monroe*, 106.

15 Marshall to Augustine Davis, Sep. 8, 1793, MP, 2:202–206.

16 Ammon, "Agricola Versus Aristides," 317.

17 Ammon, "Agricola Versus Aristides," 318.

18 Marshall to Augustine Davis, Nov. 20, 1793, MP, 2:238–247.

CHAPTER 8. JAY'S TREATY

1 Marshall to Archibald Stuart, Mar. 27, 1794, MP, 2:262.

2 Marshall to Henry Lee, Jul. 28, 1794, MP, 2:276–278; Smith, *Marshall*, 176–177.

3 Acting Attorney General, MP, 2:290.

4 Deed, Feb. 1, 1794, MP, 2:254–257.

5 Fairfax Lands, MP, 2:140–149.

6 Marshall to Archibald Stuart, Jan. 22, 1794, MP, 2:253.

7 From George Washington, Aug. 26, 1795, MP, 2:319–320.

8 Marshall to George Washington, Aug. 31, 1795, MP, 2:320.

9 From Thomas Marshall, Nov. 6, 1795, MP, 2:324.

10 Smith, *Marshall*, 178.

11 Marshall, *Autobiographical Sketch*, 14–16.

12 Jefferson to James Madison, Nov. 26, 1795, in Boyd, ed., *Papers of Jefferson*, 28: 539; Smith, *Marshall*, 177–178.

13 Bemis, *Jay's Treaty*, 210–216.

14 Bemis, *Jay's Treaty*, 238–240.

15 Stahr, *John Jay*, 313–316.

16 Bemis, *Jay's Treaty*, 318–325.

17 Stahr, *John Jay*, 324–330.

18 Stahr, *John Jay*, 331–332.

19 Bemis, *Jay's Treaty*, 355–359; Henry Adams, *The Life of Albert Gallatin* (Philadelphia: J. B. Lippincott & Co., 1879), 158.

20 As quoted in Donald L. Stewart, *The Opposition Press of Federalist Period* (Albany NY: SUNY Press, 1969), 218, from the Charleston *South–Carolina State-Gazette*.

21 Stahr, *John Jay*, 337.

22 Bemis, *Jay's Treaty*, 261, 371–373; Thomas L. Hungerford, *CRS Report on U.S. Federal Government Revenue: 1790 to Present* (Washington, D.C.: Library of Congress, 2006.) 3–4.

23 Newmyer, *Marshall*, 109.

24 Newmyer, *Marshall*, 110.

25 Indeed, the Constitutional Convention hammered out the treaty clause as a carefully drawn compromise that ensured that all states, regardless of population, would have an equal voice in the Senate in adopting a treaty. Joel Richard Paul, "The Geopolitical Constitution," *California Law Review* 86, no. 4 (1998): 730–737.

26 Article 9, Treaty of Amity, Commerce and Navigation between His Brittanick Majesty and the United States, U.S. Treaty Series, 1794.

27 Harlow Giles Unger, *John Marshall: The Chief Justice Who Saved the Nation* (Boston: Da Capo Press, 2014), 111.

28 Marshall, *Autobiographical Sketch*, 18–19.

29 Marshall to Hamilton, Apr. 25, 1796, MP, 3:24.

30 Marshall to Hamilton, Apr. 25, 1796, MP, 3:23.

31 Marshall, *Autobiographical Sketch*, 19–20.

32 Marshall to George Washington, Jul. 11, 1796, MP, 3:32.

33 See, generally, Paul, *Unlikely Allies*.

34 From Chevallié, Oct 5, 1792, MP, 2:126, *n*6.

35 As quoted in Joseph J. Ellis, *Founding Brothers* (New York: Vintage Books, 2000), 224–225.

36 Winik, *Great Upheaval*, 516.

37 Malone, *Ordeal of Liberty*, 316.

38 Beveridge, *Marshall*, 2: 211.

39 Marshall, *Autobiographical Sketch*, 21–22.

40 Smith, *Marshall*, 185–186; Mason, *My Dearest Polly*, 86.

41 Mason, *My Dearest Polly*, 89–90.

42 To Mary Marshall, Jun. 24, 1797, MP, 3:92.

43 To Mary Marshall, Jul. 5, 1797, MP, 3:95.

44 To Mary Marshall, Jul. 10, 1797, MP, 3:97.

45 To Mary Marshall, Jul. 3, 1797, MP, 3:94 and notes.

46 To Mary Marshall, Jul. 3, 1797, MP, 3:94 and notes.

47 To Mary Marshall, Jul. 11, 1797, MP, 3:99.

48 To Mary Marshall, Jul. 14, 1797, MP, 3:102.

49 To Mary Marshall, Jul. 11, 1797, MP, 3:99–100.

50 To Mary Marshall, Jul. 12, 1797, MP, 3:100.

51 From Pickering, Jul. 15, 1797, MP, 3:102–119.

52 To Mary Marshall, Jul. 20, 1797, MP, 3:120–121.

CHAPTER 9. TALLEYRAND

1 To Mary Marshall, Aug. 3, 1797, MP, 3:122; To Mary Marshall, Jul. 20, 1797, MP, 3:121–122.

2 Beveridge, *Marshall*, 3:229.

3 Rudé, *French Revolution*, 150–151; Jan-Pieter Smits, Edwin Horlings, and Jan Luiten van Zanden, *Dutch GNP and Its Components, 1800–1913* (Groningen, The Netherlands: N. W. Posthumus Institute, 2000), 100.

4 Marshall to George Washington, Sep. 15, 1797, MP, 3:139–141.

5 Marvin R. Zahniser, *Charles Cotesworth Pinckney: Founding Father* (Chapel Hill: University of North Carolina Press, 1967), 30–35.

6 James Madison, *Notes of Debates in the Federal Convention of 1787* (New York: W. W. Norton, 1987), 281, 505–507.

7 Frances Leigh Williams, *A Founding Family: The Pinckneys of South Carolina* (New York: Harcourt Brace Jovanovich, 1978), 291, 295.

8 To Mary Marshall, Sep. 9, 1797, MP, 3:130.

9 From Vans Murray, Sep. 2, 1797, MP, 3:128.

10 Marshall to George Washington, Sep. 15, 1797, MP, 3:146.

11 Marshall to Pickering, Sep. 9, 1797, MP, 3:134–135.

12 Marshall to Charles Lee, Sep. 22, 1797, MP, 3:148.

13 Marshall to George Washington, Oct. 24, 1797, MP, 3:268–269.

14 MP, 3:147, *n*6.

15 Zahniser, *Pinckney*, 165.

16 To Mrs. Gerry, Nov. 25, 1797, in Russell W. Knight, ed., *Elbridge Gerry's Letterbook: Paris 1797–1798* (Salem, MA: The Essex Institute, 1966), 22; Harold Cecil Vaughan, *The XYZ Affair 1797–1798: The Diplomacy of the Adams Administration and an Undeclared War with France* (New York: Franklin Watts, 1972), 48; *Paris Journal*, MP, 3:158; Smith, *John Marshall*, 200.

17 Clinton Rossiter, *1787: The Grand Convention* (New York: W. W. Norton, 1966), 85–85; Max Farrand, ed., *The Records of the Federal Convention, of 1787* (New Haven, CT: Yale University Press, 1966) 3:329; Walter Isaacson, *Benjamin Franklin* (New York: Simon & Schuster, 2003), 456; Farrand, *Records of the Federal Convention*, 3:88; From Vans Murray, Sep. 24, 1797, MP, 3:150.

18 *Paris Journal*, MP, 3:242–243.

19 *Paris Journal*, MP, 3:159.

20 Duff Cooper, *Talleyrand* (New York: Grove Press, 1997), 34–43.

21 David Lawday, *Napoleon's Master: A Life of Prince Talleyrand* (New York: Thomas Dunne Books, 2007), 56–57.

22 Lawday, *Napoleon's Master*, 65.

23 Cooper, *Talleyrand*, 56–61; Lawday, *Napoleon's Master*, 72.

24 Lawday, *Napoleon's Master*, 45–46, 76–77.

25 Lawday, *Napoleon's Master*, 77.

26 Cooper, *Talleyrand*, 73–79; Lawday, *Napoleon's Master*, 86.

27 Jean Orieux, *Talleyrand: The Art of Survival*. Translated by Patricia Wolf (New York: Alfred A. Knopf, 1974), 163–168.

28 Cooper, *Talleyrand*, 84– 85.

29 Rosalynd Pflaum, *Talleyrand and His World* (Afton, MN: Afton Press, 2010), 171.

30 *Paris Journal*, MP, 3:159–160; Marshall to Charles Lee, Oct. 12, 1797, MP, 3:246–248.

31 From Paine, Oct. 11, 1797, MP, 3:243–245.

32 *Paris Journal*, MP, 3:160–161; Paul, *Unlikely Allies*, 299; Marshall to Charles Lee, Oct. 12, 1797, MP, 3:248.

33 William Stinchcombe, "Talleyrand and the American Negotiations of 1797–1798," *Journal of American History* 62, no. 3 (December 1975): 577, 584.

34 William Stinchcombe, "The Diplomacy of the WXYZ Affair." *William and Mary Quarterly* 34, no. 4 (October 1977): 596; Stinchcombe, "Talleyrand and the American Negotiations," 582.

35 Talleyrand, "Memoirs on relations between France and the United States," in Stinchcombe, "A Neglected Memoir by Talleyrand on French-American Relations." *Proceedings of the American Philosophical Society* 121, no. 3 (1977): 204–207.

36 Talleyrand, "Memoirs on Relations between France and the United States,"in William Stinchcombe, "A Neglected Memoir by Talleyrand on French-American Relations," *Proceedings of American Philosophical Society*, 121, no. 3 (June 1977): 207.

37 Speech of the President to Congress, May 16, 1797, Philadelphia.

38 Talleyrand, "Memoirs on Relations between France and the United States," in Stinchcombe, "Neglected Memoir," *Proceedings of American Philosophical Society*, 206.

39 *Paris Journal*, MP, 3:161–162; Marshall to Pickering, Oct. 22, 1797, MP, 3:256–257.

CHAPTER 10. NOT A SIXPENCE

1 To Mary Marshall, Nov. 27, 1797, MP, 3:299.

2 *Paris Journal*, MP, 3:162–163.

3 Marshall to Pickering, Oct. 22, 1797, MP, 256–257; Stinchcombe, "WXYZ Affair," 597–598.

4 *Paris Journal*, MP, 3:163.

5 *Paris Journal*, MP, 3:164–165; Stinchcombe, "WXYZ Affair," 598.

6 *Paris Journal*, MP, 3:165–166.

7 Marshall to George Washington, Oct. 24, 1797, MP, 3:268–270.

8 *Paris Journal*, MP 3:166–167; Marshall to Pickering, Oct. 22, 1797, MP, 3:260–265.

9 *Paris Journal*, MP, 3:167; Marshall to Pickering, Oct. 22, 1797, MP, 3:261–262.

10 *Paris Journal*, MP, 3:167–168.

11 *Paris Journal*, MP, 3:167–168.

12 *Paris Journal*, MP, 3:168–169.

13 *Paris Journal*, MP, 3:168–169; Stinchcombe, "WXYZ Affair," 599.

14 *Paris Journal*, MP, 3:169–170.
15 *Paris Journal*, MP, 3:169–171.
16 *Paris Journal*, MP, 3:171.
17 *Paris Journal*, MP, 3:171.
18 *Paris Journal*, MP, 3:171–174.
19 *Paris Journal*, MP, 3:174.
20 *Paris Journal*, MP, 3:174–176; Stinchcombe, "WXYZ Affair," 600.
21 *Paris Journal*, MP, 3:176.
22 *Paris Journal*, MP, 3:177–178; Cooper, *Talleyrand*, 104–118.
23 *Paris Journal*, MP, 3:179–183.
24 Stinchcombe, "Talleyrand and the American Negotiations," 585–586.
25 Lawday, *Napoleon's Master*, 98–100; Pflaum, *Talleyrand*, 171.
26 As quoted in Smith, *Marshall*, 194–195.

CHAPTER 11. LOVE AND WAR

1 Delamétherie, *Journal de Physique, de Chimie, d'Histoire Naturelle et des Arts*, Dugour, (1798), 3:135–141.
2 *Paris Journal*, MP, 3:185; Marshall to Charles Lee, Nov. 3, 1797, MP, 273–274.
3 *Paris Journal*, MP, 3:185, 188.
4 Marshall to Talleyrand, Nov. 11, 1797, MP, 3:293–294.
5 *Paris Journal*, MP, 3:185–186.
6 From Beaumarchais, Nov. 7, 1797, MP, 3:275–276; Stinchcombe, "WXYZ Affair," 601–602.
7 *Paris Journal*, MP, 3:188–189.
8 To Mary Marshall, Nov. 27, 1797, MP, 3:299.
9 To Mrs. Gerry, Nov. 25, 1797, in Knight, ed., *Gerry's Letterbook*, 22.
10 To Mary Marshall, Nov. 27, 1797, MP, 3:300–301.
11 Monique Ferrero, *Voltaire la nommait Belle et Bonne: La marquise de Villette, un coeur dans la tourmente*. (Bourg-en-Bresse, France: M & G Editions, 2007), 12–15.
12 Jean Stern, *Belle et Bonne: Une Fervente Amie de Voltaire (1757–1822)* (Paris: Librairie Hachette, 1938), 15.
13 Ian Davidson, *Voltaire: A Life* (New York: Pegasus Books, 2010), 447; Ferrero, *Voltair la nommait*, 15–17; Stern, *Belle et Bonne,* 13–15.
14 Stern, *Belle et Bonne*, 30; Ferrero, *Voltaire la nommait*, 20.
15 William Stinchcombe, *The XYZ Affair* (Westport, CT: Greenwood Press, 1980), 67; Ferrero, *Voltaire la nommait*, 22; Stern, *Belle et Bonne*, 42; Louis Crompton, *Homosexuality and Civilization* (Cambridge, MA: The Belknap Press, 2003*)*, 514, 518, 525–526.
16 Stern, *Belle et Bonne*, 28; Jeffrey Merrick and Bryant T. Ragan Jr., eds., *Homosexuality in Modern France* (New York: Oxford University Press, 1996), 31–32; Roger Pearson, *Voltaire Almighty: A Life in Pursuit of Freedom* (New York: Bloomsbury, 2005), 369; Michael Sibalis, "Villette, Marquis," in Robert Aldrich and Garry Wotherspoon, eds., *Who's Who in Gay and Lesbian History: From Antiqurty to World War II* (New York: Routledge, 2001) 1:464.
17 Merrick and Ragan, *Homosexuality in Modern France*, 32, 36–40; Davidson, *Voltaire*, 447; Pearson, *Voltaire Almighty*, 370; Ferrero, *Voltaire la nommait*, 18, 26; Stern, *Belle et Bonne*, 28.
18 Stern, *Belle et Bonne*, 95.
19 To Mrs. Gerry, Nov. 25, 1797, in Knight, ed., *Gerry's Letterbook*, 25, *n* 3; Stern, *Belle et Bonne*, 168–171; Stinchcombe, *XYZ*, 67–68.
20 To Mrs. Gerry, Nov. 25, 1797, in Knight, ed., *Gerry's Letterbook*, 22–23.
21 MP 3:300, *n*7.
22 Mary Pinkney to Margaret Manigault, Mar. 9, 1798, *Manigault Family Papers*, South Caroliniana Library, University of South Carolina.
23 Michel Poniatowski, *Talleyrand et Le Directoire, 1796–1800* (Paris: Librairie Académique Perrin, 1982), 563.
24 Marshall to Pickering, Dec. 24, 1797, Exhibit C, MP, 3:322.
25 *Paris Journal*, MP, 3:190–191.
26 *Paris Journal*, MP, 3:191.

27 *Paris Journal*, MP, 3:192–193.
28 To Pinckney, Dec. 17, 1797, MP, 3:311–312.
29 Marshall to King, MP, 3:315–316.
30 Mary Pinckney to Margaret Manigault, Jan. 23, 1798, *Manigault Family Papers*, South Caroliniana Library, University of South Carolina.
31 Mary Pinckney to Margaret Manigault, Mar. 9–12, 1798, *Manigault Family Papers*, South Caroliniana Library, University of South Carolina.
32 Beveridge, *Marshall*, 2:297.
33 Marshall to Talleyrand, Jan. 17, 1798, MP, 3:332.
34 Marshall to Talleyrand, Jan. 17, 1798, MP, 3:333.
35 Marshall to Talleyrand, Jan. 17, 1798, MP, 3:333–334.
36 Marshall to Talleyrand, Jan. 17, 1798, MP, 3:334.
37 Marshall to Talleyrand, Jan. 17, 1798, MP, 3:334.
38 Marshall to Talleyrand, Jan. 17, 1798, MP, 3:334–335.
39 Marshall to Talleyrand, Jan. 17, 1798, MP, 3:338.
40 Marshall to Talleyrand, Jan. 17, 1798, MP, 3:352–355.
41 Marshall to Talleyrand, Jan. 17, 1798, MP, 3:339–342. Marshall cited Emer de Vattel in support of this argument. Marshall had studied Vattel, and he carried an English translation of Vattel's principal work, *The Law of Nations*, with him to Paris. Vattel wrote that belligerents had the right to search neutral ships and seize ordinary non–military goods owned by belligerents, and he rejected a right of armed neutrality. Vattel, *The Law of Nations*, eds., Béla Kapossy and Richard Whitmore, 3:114. Vattel's rule favored major naval powers, like Britain, at the expense of weaker naval powers, like France and the United States, that did not have the capacity to stop and search hundreds of merchant vessels crossing the ocean.
42 The U.S. position on armed neutrality was consistent since its founding and indeed was included in the Plan of 1776, the country's model treaty for commercial relations. Eric A. Belgrad, "John Marshall's Contributions to American Neutrality Doctrines," *William & Mary Law Review* 9 (1967–1968): 430, 434.
43 Carl J. Kulsrud, "Armed Neutralities to 1780," *American Journal of International Law* 29, no. 3 (July 1935): 423. In 1780, for example, the Empress of Russia, Catherine II, formed a League of Armed Neutrality that endorsed the principle that "free ships make free goods," and that contraband should be narrowly defined to include only munitions of war and not supplies that could be used for non-military purposes. The League included Spain, France, Denmark, Sweden, Prussia, Austria, Portugal, the Kingdom of the Two Sicilies, as well as the United States. After the outbreak of the French Revolutionary Wars, the League became an anachronism since virtually all of continental Europe was pulled into the war as belligerent parties. The United States was the only neutral party remaining in the League. Philip C. Jessup, *American Neutrality and International Police* (World Peace Foundation Pamphlet Series 1, 1928), 374.
44 Marshall to Talleyrand, Jan. 17, 1798, MP, 3:350–355.
45 *Journal de Physique*, 135–139.
46 *Paris Journal*, MP, 3:195.
47 *Paris Journal*, MP, 3:198–199.
48 *Paris Journal*, MP, 3:199.
49 *Paris Journal*, MP, 3:199.
50 *Paris Journal*, MP, 3:195–197.
51 C. C. Pinckney to Thomas Pinckney, Feb. 22, 1798, *Pickering Papers*, Massachusetts Historical Society, as quoted in *Paris Journal*, MP, 3:197.
52 *Paris Journal*, MP, 3:196–197.

CHAPTER 12. TOSSED INTO THE SEINE

1 Mary Pinckney to Margaret Manigault, Mar. 9, 1798, 12–14, *Manigault Family Papers*, South Caroliniana Library, University of South Carolina.
2 Mary Pinckney to Margaret Manigault, Mar. 9, 1798, 3–4, *Manigault Family Papers*, South Caroliniana Library, University of South Carolina.

3 Mary Pinckney to Margaret Manigault, Mar. 9, 1798, 4, *Manigault Family Papers*, South Caroliniana Library, University of South Carolina.
4 Stinchcombe, *XYZ*, 78, 82–83, 94–97.
5 From Nathaniel Cutting, Feb. 17, 1789, MP, 3:383–386.
6 Stinchcombe, *XYZ*, 109, citing Cutting to James Monroe, Feb. 22, 1798, *Cutting Papers*, Massachusetts Historical Society.
7 Stinchcombe, *XYZ*, 109, citing Skipwith to Thomas Jefferson, Mar. 17, 1789, *Wolcott Papers*, 12,
   Connecticut Historical Society.
8 Stinchcombe, *XYZ*, 110, citing Skipwith to Thomas Jefferson, Mar. 17, 1798, *Wolcott Papers*, 12,
   Connecticut Historical Society.
9 Zahniser, *Pinckney*, 176; Alexander DeConde, *The Quasi-War: The Politics and Diplomacy of the
   Undeclared War with France 1797–1801* (New York: Charles Scribner's Sons, 1966), 51–52. But see
   Smith, *Marshall*, 218; Stinchcombe, *XYZ*, 68.
10 Orieux, *Voltaire*, 37–38.
11 Note, MP, 3:155.
12 Stinchcombe, *XYZ*, 52.
13 Stinchcombe, *XYZ*, 55, 67, 96, 108; Smith, *Marshall*, 215, 592.
14 Stinchcombe, *XYZ*, 59, 68; Smith, *Marshall*, 215.
15 The British had budgeted close to one million pounds in an unprecedented spying operation directed by William Wickham that deployed agents of various nationalities. The British hoped to
   undermine France's efforts to organize a massive invasion of Britain, and they hoped to foment an
   insurrection against the Directory. See generally, Liam Sumption, "Confidential Gentlemen on
   Confidential Service," unpublished manuscript, British Library YA.1997.b.2793.
16 Stern, *Belle et Bonne*, 171–172.
17 Smith, *Marshall*, 218.
18 Paul, *Unlikely Allies*, 169–170, 178–182, 254–256.
19 Though there is no evidence that the "lady" referred to was Madame de Villette, Marshall's biographer Beveridge concluded that it was de Villette, and there is no evidence to the contrary. Smith
   has suggested that the woman in question could be Madame de la Forest, but there is no evidence
   to support that. Smith, *Marshall*, 593.
20 Pinckney Memorandum, Dec. 21, 1797, MP, 2:318–319.
21 The editors of Marshall's Papers concluded that there was no indication he suspected de Villette
   was working for Talleyrand. Note, MP, 3:155.
22 *Paris Journal*, MP, 3:200–201.
23 Paul, *Unlikely Allies*, 149–151.
24 *Paris Journal*, MP, 3:201.
25 *Paris Journal*, MP, 3:201–202.
26 Marshall to Talleyrand, Feb. 26, 1798, MP, 3:388–394.
27 Gerry to President Adams, Jul 5, 1799, in Knight, ed., *Gerry's Letterbook*, 54.
28 Mary Pinckney to Margaret Manigault, Mar. 9, 1789, 13–15, *Manigault Family Papers*, South Caroliniana Library, University of South Carolina.
29 *Paris Journal*, MP, 3:202.
30 *Paris Journal*, MP, 3:202–203.
31 *Paris Journal*, MP, 3:219.
32 *Paris Journal*, MP, 3:203.
33 *Paris Journal*, MP, 3:204.
34 *Paris Journal*, MP, 3:205–206.
35 Stinchcombe, "Talleyrand and the American Negotiations," 584–585.
36 *Paris Journal*, MP, 3:207.
37 Stinchcombe, "WXYZ Affair," 601, confirming that Beaumarchais reported to Talleyrand.
38 *Paris Journal*, MP, 3:208–209.
39 *Paris Journal*, MP, 3:211.
40 *Paris Journal*, MP, 3:211–215.
41 *Paris Journal*, MP, 3:213–214.
42 *Paris Journal*, MP, 3:214.

43 Mary Pinckney to Margaret Manigault, Mar. 9, 1798, 2, *Manigault Family Papers*, South Caroliniana Library, University of South Carolina.
44 *Paris Journal*, MP, 3:215.
45 *Paris Journal*, MP, 3:215.
46 *Paris Journal*, MP, 3:216–217.
47 *Paris Journal*, MP, 3:217.
48 *Paris Journal*, MP, 3:217–218.
49 *Paris Journal*, MP, 3:218–219.
50 Marshall to Charles Lee, Mar. 4, 1798, MP, 3:395–397.
51 *Paris Journal*, MP, 3:220–221.
52 *Paris Journal*, MP, 3:223.
53 *Paris Journal*, MP, 3:224.
54 *Paris Journal*, MP, 3:225.
55 *Paris Journal*, MP, 3:225–226.
56 *Paris Journal*, MP, 3:228.
57 *Paris Journal*, MP, 3:229–230.
58 *Paris Journal*, MP, 3:230–231.
59 Marshall to George Washington, Mar. 8 1798, MP, 3:399–402.
60 *Paris Journal*, MP, 3:399, n5.
61 *Paris Journal*, MP, 3:231–232.
62 Ville de Paris Annuaire de L'Observatoire Municipal de Montsouris, 80, 108; Mary Pinckney to Margaret Manigault, Mar. 12, 1798, 5, *Manigault Family Papers*, South Caroliniana Library, University of South Carolina.
63 *Paris Journal*, MP, 3:233.
64 *Paris Journal*, MP, 3:234.
65 *Paris Journal*, MP, 3:234–235.
66 To Mrs. Gerry, Mar. 26, 1798, in Knight, ed., *Gerry's Letterbook*, 33–34.
67 Marshall to Talleyrand, Apr. 3, 1798, MP, 3:431–432, 439.
68 Marshall to Talleyrand, Apr. 3, 1798, MP, 3:447–448.
69 *Paris Journal*, MP, 3:236.
70 *Paris Journal*, MP, 3:237.
71 *Paris Journal*, MP, 3:237–238.
72 *Paris Journal*, MP, 3:238.
73 *Paris Journal*, MP, 3:238–241.
74 Marshall to Beaumarchais, Apr. 15, 1798, MP, 3:462–463.
75 Marshall to Skipwith, Apr. 21, 1798, MP, 3:464.
76 Marshall to Pinckney, Apr. 21, 1798, MP, 3:463.
77 Marshall to George Washington, Sep. 15, 1797, MP, 3:141.
78 Marshall to George Washington, Sep. 15, 1797, MP, 3:145–146.

CHAPTER 13. THE XYZ PAPERS

1 MP, 3:255.
2 Note 7, MP, 3:132.
3 Marshall to Pickering, Jan. 8, 1789, MP, 3:325–326.
4 David McCullough, *John Adams* (New York: Simon & Schuster, 2001) 495–496; John Ferling, *Adams v. Jefferson: The Tumultuous Election of 1800* (New York: Oxford University Press, 2004), 352–353.
5 Ferling, *Adams*, 353.
6 Jefferson to James Madison, Mar. 21, 1798, in Boyd, ed., *Papers of Jefferson* 30:189–190.
7 As quoted in Adams, *Life of Albert Gallatin*, 200.
8 Adams, *Life of Albert Gallatin*, 200–201.
9 Vaughan, *XYZ Affair*, 64.
10 Adams, *Life of Albert Gallatin*, 54.
11 DeConde, *Quasi-War*, 66–73; Smith, *Marshall*, 226.
12 Jefferson to James Madison, Apr. 6, 1798, in Boyd, ed., *Jefferson Papers* 30:250–251.

13 Madison to Thomas Jefferson, Apr. 15, 1798, Hunt, *Writings of Madison*, 6:315, as quoted in Smith, *Marshall*, 226.
14 Adams, *Life of Albert Gallatin*, 200–201.
15 Gallatin to wife, Mar. 6, 1789, as quoted in Adams, *Life of Albert Gallatin*, 195.
16 DeConde, *Quasi-War*, 74.
17 DeConde, *Quasi-War*, 72–73.
18 From Washington, Dec. 4, 1787, MP, 3:307–308.
19 Boyd, ed., *Jefferson Papers*, 30:525 notes.
20 DeConde, *Quasi-War*, 74–82.
21 Smith, *Marshall*, 234–235.
22 DeConde, *Quasi-War*, 93.
23 Beveridge, *Marshall*, 2:347.
24 Note, MP, 3:156.
25 Jefferson to Elbridge Gerry, Jan. 26, 1799, in Boyd, ed., *Jefferson Papers*, 30:648–649.
26 Malone, *Ordeal of Liberty*, 382.
27 Beveridge, *Marshall*, 2:346, 348–349, 358; From Jefferson, Jun. 23, 1798, MP, 3:471; MP, 3:468, *n*3.
28 Smith, *Marshall*, 237.
29 As quoted in Malone, *Ordeal of Liberty*, 386–387; DeConde, *Quasi-War*, 100–101; Ferling, *Adams*, 365.
30 As quoted in Geoffrey R. Stone, *Perilous Times: Free Speech in Wartime* (New York: W. W. Norton, 2004), 20.
31 Meacham, *Jefferson*, 315.
32 Smith, *Marshall*, 239; McCullough, *Adams*, 506–507.
33 Marshall to a Freeholder, Oct. 2, 1798, MP, 3:505.
34 Gerry to Thomas Jefferson, Jan. 15, 1801, in Knight, ed., *Gerry's Letterbook*, 78.

CHAPTER 14. THE JONATHAN ROBBINS AFFAIR

1 Mason, *My Dearest Polly*, 122–123.
2 Marshall, *Autobiographical Sketch*, 25–26; Smith, *Marshall*, 240–241.
3 Smith, *Marshall*, 242–244.
4 Smith, *Marshall*, 245–248; Beveridge, *Marshall*, 2:396–397.
5 Henry to Archibald Blair, Jan. 8, 1799, in William Wirt Henry, ed., *Patrick Henry: Life, Correspondence, and Speeches* (New York: Charles Scribner and Sons, 1891), 1:592–593.
6 Smith, *Marshall*, 245.
7 Malone, *Ordeal of Liberty*, 399–408; Meacham, *Thomas Jefferson*, 318–319; Beveridge, *Marshall*, 2:397–400.
8 Jefferson to John Taylor, Jun. 4, 1798, in Boyd, ed., *Jefferson Papers*, 30:388–389.
9 To James Marshall, Apr. 3, 1799, MP, 4:10.
10 Smith, *Marshall*, 248–249.
11 Greene, *Political Life in Eighteenth-Century Virginia*, 22–25; Beveridge, *Marshall* 2:415.
12 Smith, *Marshall*, 250; Newmyer, *Marshall*, 124.
13 From Thomas Marshall, Sep. 9, 1796, MP, 3:45.
14 Mason, *My Dearest Polly*, 131.
15 Beveridge, *Marshall* 2:434–438, 445–456; Smith, *Marshall*, 254.
16 Mason, *My Dearest Polly*, 135–136; as quoted in Smith, *Marshall*, 255.
17 Speech, Dec. 19, 1799, MP, 4:46–47.
18 Editorial note, MP, 4:33.
19 Beveridge, *Marshall* 2:440–444.
20 See generally, Ruth Wedgwood, "The Revolutionary Martyrdom of Jonathan Robbins," *Yale Law Journal* 100 (1990–1991).
21 Jefferson to Pinckney, Oct. 29, 1799, in Ford, ed., *Writings of Thomas Jefferson*, 9:87.
22 Beveridge, *Marshall*, 2:459–460.
23 Wedgwood, "Revolutionary Martyrdom," 329–333.
24 Speech, Mar. 7, 1800, MP, 4:108, referring to Livingston's speech.

25 Editorial note, MP, 4:35.
26 Mason, *My Dearest Polly*, 138.
27 Speech, Mar. 7, 1800, MP, 4:84–85, 93–94.
28 MP, 4:104.
29 Mason, *My Dearest Polly*, 139.
30 Ida Brudnick, "Salaries of Members of Congress," Sep. 17, 2015, 12, Table I, Congressional Research Service Report.
31 Chernow, *Alexander Hamilton*, 613.
32 Marshall, *Autobiographical Sketch*, 27–28.
33 Chernow, *Alexander Hamilton*, 614–615.
34 DeConde, *Quasi-War*, 222.
35 Beveridge, *Marshall*, 2:539, n1.
36 Marshall, *Autobiographical Sketch*, 28.
37 Marshall, *Autobiographical Sketch*, 29.

CHAPTER 15. PRIVATEERS AND PIRATES

1 Editorial note, MP, 4:158.
2 Editorial note, MP, 4:158; McCullough, *Adams*, 541–542; Winik, *Great Upheaval*, 578–579; Elkins and McKitrick, *Age of Federalism*, 172–181.
3 Editorial note, MP, 4:158.
4 DeConde, *Quasi-War*, 178–183.
5 Editorial note, MP, 4:158.
6 Editorial note, MP, 4:158.
7 Smith, *Marshall*, 269.
8 Editorial note, MP, 4:159–160.
9 Editorial note, MP, 4:158–160; From *Commissioners of the District of Colombia*, Jul. 3, 1800, MP, 4:175; Smith, *Marshall*, 270–271.
10 Department of State Office of the Historian, Buildings of the Department of State, https://history .state.gov/departmenthistory/buildings/section21, accessed on August 10, 2014.
11 Marshall to King, Aug. 23, 1800, MP, 4:237.
12 Marshall to Adams, Jun. 24, 1800, MP, 4:169.
13 Marshall to King, Aug. 23, 1800, MP, 4:237.
14 From King, Jun. 6, 1800, MP, 4:161.
15 Editorial note, MP, 4:158–159; To Adams, July 21, 1800, MP, 4:184.
16 From Adams, Aug. 1, 1800, MP, 4:198.
17 Marshall to Adams, Aug. 12, 1800, MP, 4:214–215.
18 From Adams, Aug. 22, 1800, MP, 4:229.
19 Marshall to King, Aug. 23, 1800, MP, 4:237.
20 Marshall to King, Aug. 23, 1800, MP, 4:238.
21 Smith, *Marshall*, 272–273.
22 Denver Brunsman, *The Evil Necessity: British Naval Impressment in the Eighteenth-Century Atlantic World* (Charlottesville: University of Virginia Press, 2013), 304. This includes the years from 1793–1802, which is the most reliable reference available.
23 Marshall to Adams, Jun 24, 1800, MP, 4:169.
24 Marshall to King, Sep. 20, 1800, MP, 4:283–285.
25 Marshall to King, Sep. 20, 1800, MP, 4:286.
26 Marshall to King, Sep. 20, 1800, MP, 4:286–287.
27 Marshall to King, Sep. 20, 1800, MP, 4:288–291.
28 Marshall to Talleyrand, Jan. 17, 1798, MP, 3:352–355.
29 Marshall to King, Sep. 20, 1800, MP, 4:292.
30 Marshall to King, Sep 20, 1800, MP, 4:293–294.
31 Marshall to King, Sep. 20, 1800, MP, 3:294.
32 Marshall to King, Sep. 20, 1800, MP, 3:294–295.
33 Marshall to Benjamin Lincoln, Oct. 30, 1800, MP, 3:335.

34 Brunsman, *The Evil Necessity,* 177.
35 Marshall to King, Sep. 20, 1800, MP, 4:295–296.
36 Walter R. Borneman, *1812: The War That Forged a Nation* (New York: HarperCollins, 2004), 20.
37 DeConde, *Quasi-War,* 224–225, 232.
38 DeConde, *Quasi-War,* 226–227.
39 DeConde, *Quasi-War,* 231–232, 235–237.
40 DeConde, *Quasi-War,* 240–241.
41 Rudé, *French Revolution,* 130–131.
42 Marshall to Adams, Aug. 25, 1800, MP, 3:240.
43 From American Envoys, Aug. 15, 1800, MP, 3:220.
44 Smith, *Adams,* 1039; McCullough, *Adams,* 545; DeConde, *Quasi-War,* 280–282; Wood, *Empire,* 272–274.
45 Marshall to Adams, Sep. 17, 1800, MP, 4:279.
46 From American envoys, Oct. 4, 1800, MP, 4:315–319.
47 DeConde, *Quasi-War,* 254–255.
48 From de Yruzo, Jul. 7, 1800, MP, 4:178–180.
49 Marshall to Adams, Jul. 26, 1800, MP, 4:190–191.
50 Marshall to Adams, Sep.6, 1800, MP, 4:260–261.
51 *Pinckney Treaty of Friendship, Limits and Navigation between Spain and the United States,* 1795, Art. 5; From de Yrujo, Jul. 8, 1800, MP, 4:180–181.
52 Marshall to Adams, Aug. 12, 1800, MP, 4:213–214; Marshall to de Yrujo, Aug. 15, 1800, MP, 4:222.
53 Marshall to David Humphreys, Sep. 23, 1800, MP, 4:301.
54 *Pinckney Treaty of Friendship, Limits and Navigation between Spain and the United States,* 1795, Art. 6.
55 Marshall to David Humphreys, Sep. 8, 1800, MP, 4:266–267.
56 Marshall to David Humphreys, Sep. 8, 1800, 266–269.
57 Marshall to David Humphreys, Sep. 8, 1800, MP, 4:270–271.
58 Marshall to David Humphreys, Sep. 8, 1800, MP, 4:272.
59 John H. Pryor, *Geography, Technology, and War* (New York: Press Syndicate of the University of Cambridge, 1988), 192.
60 Herring, *From Colony to Superpower,* 98.
61 *Treaty of Peace and Friendship of 1796 Between the United States and the Bey of Tripoli,* Art. 11.
62 Marshall to J. Q. Adams, Jul. 24, 1800, MP, 4:189.
63 Marshall to Richard O'Brien, Jul. 29, 1800, MP, 4:193.
64 Frances Howell Rudko, *John Marshall and International Law: Statesman and Chief Justice* (Westport, CT: Greenwood Press, 1991), 105; Marshall to Adams, Jul. 24, 1800, MP 4:187; Marshall to King, Aug, 16, 1800, MP, 4:225.
65 Herring, *From Colony to Superpower,* 99–101; Dumas Malone, *Jefferson the President: First Term,* 1801–1805 (Boston: Little Brown, (1970), 98.

CHAPTER 16. THE NEW ORDER OF THINGS

 1 As quoted in Smith, *Adams,* 1037.
 2 As quoted in Smith, *Adams,* 1034–1035.
 3 As quoted in Chernow, *Hamilton,* 613.
 4 Malone, *Ordeal of Liberty,* 488; Chernow, *Hamilton,* 619–624.
 5 As quoted in Chernow, *Hamilton,* 617.
 6 McCullough, *Adams,* 548–551.
 7 McCullough, *Adams,* 551–552.
 8 As quoted in McCullough, *Adams,* 553.
 9 Marshall to Pinckney, Nov. 20, 1800, MP, 6:16–17.
10 Malone, *Ordeal of Liberty,* 489–493.
11 McCullough, *Adams,* 539. 556, 558; Chernow, *Hamilton,* 612–618.
12 As quoted, McCullough, *Adams,* 556.
13 From Jefferson, Dec. 28, 1800, MP 6:45–46.
14 Jefferson to Madison, Dec. 26, 1800, in Boyd, ed., *Jefferson Papers* 32:358.

15 Malone, *Ordeal of Victory*, 495–496.
16 Marshall to Pinckney, Dec. 18, 1800, MP, 6:41.
17 Marshall to Polly, Aug. 8, 1800, MP, 4:210.
18 Hamilton to Sedgwick, May 4, 1800, in Syrett, ed., *Papers of Alexander Hamilton*, 10:371.
19 To Hamilton, Jan. 1, 1801, MP, 6:46–47.
20 Jefferson to Tench Coxe, Dec. 31, 1800, in Boyd, ed., *Jefferson Papers*, 31:375.
21 From Monroe, Jan. 6, 1801, in Boyd, ed., *Jefferson Papers*, 31:403–404.
22 Marshall to John Jay, Dec. 22, 1800, MP, 6:42.
23 As quoted in Stahr, *John Jay*, 363–364.
24 Marshall, *Autobiographical Sketch*, 30.
25 Beveridge, *Marshall*, 539, n1.
26 Beveridge, *Marshall*, 557.
27 Judiciary Act of Feb. 13, 1801, ch. 4, 2 Stat. 89.
28 Organic Act of Feb. 27, 1801, ch. 15, 2 Stat. 103.
29 From Monroe, Jan. 18, 1801, in Boyd, ed., *Jefferson Papers*, 31:481.
30 From Gerry, Jan. 15, 1801, in Boyd, ed., *Jefferson Papers*, 31:466.
31 Jefferson to Burr, Feb. 1, 1801, in Boyd, ed., *Jefferson Papers*, 32:528.
32 Jefferson to Martha Jefferson Randolph, Feb. 5, 1801, in Boyd, ed., *Jefferson Papers*, 32:556–557.
33 Malone, *Ordeal of Liberty*, 502–505.
34 Jefferson to Pinckney, Mar. 4, 1801, in Boyd, ed., *Jefferson Papers*, 32:89.
35 First Inaugural Address, in Boyd, ed., *Jefferson Papers*, 33.
36 First Inaugural Address, in Boyd, ed., *Jefferson Papers*, 33.
37 Jefferson to Pinckney, Mar. 4, 1801, MP, 6:89–90.

CHAPTER 17. SHOWDOWN

1 Beveridge, *Marshall*, 3:4; George Haskins and Herbert A. Johnson, *History of the Supreme Court of the United States: Foundations of Power: John Marshall, 1801–1815*, Vol. 2. (New York: Macmillan, 1981), vol 2: 75–77.
2 White House Historical Association. "History of the White House Fence, found" at https://www .whitehousehistory.org/press-room-old/history-of-the-white-house-fence, accessed on June 19, 2017.
3 Haskins and Johnson, *History*, 2:82.
4 Haskins and Johnson, *History*, 2:86.
5 Beveridge, *Marshall*, 3:7; Simon, *What Kind of Nation*, 152.
6 As quoted in Beveridge, *Marshall*, 4:88.
7 Beveridge, *Marshall*, 4:87.
8 Adams, *Life of Albert Gallatin*, 272–273.
9 As quoted in Beveridge, *Marshall*, 3:11.
10 As quoted in Beveridge, *Marshall*, 3:13.
11 As quoted in Charles F. Hobson, *The Great Chief Justice: John Marshall and the Rule of Law* (Lawrence: University Press of Kansas, 1996), 17.
12 *Talbot v. Seeman*, 5 U.S. 1, 5, (1 Cranch 1) (1801).
13 "Ballads of Rhode Island," 1782, quoted in Louis Arthur Norton, *Captains Contentious: The Dysfunctional Sons of the Brine* (Columbia: University of South Carolina Press, 2009), 63.
14 Smith, *Marshall*, 291.
15 *Talbot v. Seeman*, 5 U.S. 1, 6, 15.
16 *Talbot v. Seeman*, 5 U.S. 1, 27–42.
17 *Talbot v. Seeman*, 5 U.S. 1, 43.
18 *Talbot v. Seeman*, 5 U.S. 1, 44–45.
19 Jefferson to Dickinson, Dec. 19, 1801, in Boyd, ed., *Jefferson Papers*, 36:165–166.
20 As quoted in Beveridge, *Marshall*, 3:22.
21 Marshall to James Madison, Nov. 29, 1790, MP, 2:66.
22 As quoted in Haskins and Johnson, *History*, 2:211.

CHAPTER 18. A STRATEGIC RETREAT

1 Malone, *Jefferson the President: First Term*, 144–145.

2 David F. Forte, "Marbury's Travail: Federalist Politics and William Marbury's Appointment as Justice of the Peace," *Catholic University Law Review* 45, no. 2 (Winter 1996): 349.

3 Peter Charles Hoffer, *Law and People in Colonial America* (Baltimore: The Johns Hopkins Press, 1998), 7–8, 96; Forte, "Marbury's Travail," 354.

4 D.C. Organic Act of Feb. 27, 1801, ch. 52, 2 Stat. 103, 107 (1801).

5 As quoted in Charles Warren, *The Supreme Court in United States History* (Boston: Little, Brown, 1926), 1:204.

6 Simon, *What Kind of Nation*, 176.

7 11 Annals of Congress 38 (1801), as quoted in James M. O'Fallon, "*Marbury*," *Stanford Law Review* 44, no. 2 (1991–1992) 219, 224–225.

8 Marshall to Patterson, Apr. 6, 1802, MP, 6:105–106; Marshall to Cushing, Apr. 19, 1802, MP, 6:108; From Chase, Apr. 24, 1802, MP 6:109–116.

9 Marshall to Patterson, May 3, 1802, MP, 6:117; From Patterson, Jun. 11, 1802, MP, 6:120.

10 Marshall to Patterson, Apr. 19, 1802, MP, 6:109.

11 From *Judge Bassett's Protest*, reprinted in Bruce Ackerman, *The Failure of the Founding Fathers: Jefferson, Marshall, and the Rise of Presidential Democracy* (Cambridge, MA: The Belknap Press, 2005), 283–284, 289.

12 Smith, *Marshall*, 328.

13 Beveridge, *Marshall*, 3:223–224.

14 Marshall, *Life of George Washington*, 1:218.

15 Marshall, *Life of George Washington*, 2:530.

16 Beveridge, *Marshall*, 3:235–240.

17 Beveridge, *Marshall*, 3:229–230.

18 Beveridge, *Marshall*, 3:227–228; Smith, *Marshall*, 330–331.

19 As quoted in Beveridge, *Marshall*, 3:268.

20 *Stuart v. Laird*, 5 U.S. 299, 302 (1803).

21 Haskins and Johnson, *Foundations of Power*, 2:211–215.

22 As quoted in Haskins and Johnson, *Foundations of Power*, 2:205.

23 Jefferson, *Weather Observations*, Massachusetts Historical Society.

24 *Marbury v. Madison*, 5 U.S. 137, 142–145; William Michael Treanor, "The Story of *Marbury v. Madison*: Judicial Authority and Political Struggle" in Vicki C. Jackson and Judith Resnik, eds., *Federal Courts Stories* (New York: Foundation Press, 2010), 47–48.

25 *Marbury v. Madison*, 5 U.S. 137, 146 (1803).

26 Newmyer, *Marshall*, 159–160; Smith, *Marshall*, 319.

27 To James Marshall, Mar. 18, 1801, MP, 6:90.

28 Jefferson, *Weather Observations*, Massachusetts Historical Society.

29 *Marbury v. Madison*, 5 U.S. 137, 154–162.

30 *Marbury v. Madison*, 5 U.S. 137, 163–168.

31 *Marbury v. Madison*, 5 U.S. 137, 169–170.

32 *Marbury v. Madison*, 5 U.S. 137, 173–174.

33 *Marbury v. Madison*, 5 U.S. 137, 176.

34 *Marbury v. Madison*, 5 U.S. 137, 177.

35 *Dred Scott v. Sandford*, 60 U.S. 393 (1857).

36 See, e.g., *Trevett v. Weeden* (Rhode Island, 1786).

37 Marshall, Jun. 20, 1788, in Kaminski et al., eds., *Documentary History*, 10:1431.

38 *Martin v. Hunter's Lessee*, 14 U.S. 304 (1816).

39 Section 13 of the Judiciary Act of 1789, 1 Stat. 73.

40 Bloch, "The Marbury Mystery," 18 Const. Comment, 607, 612 (2001).

41 Beveridge, *Marshall*, 3:153.

42 Warren, *Supreme Court*, 1:248–254.

43 Warren, *Supreme Court*, 1:257–261; e.g., Jefferson to Archibald Rowan, Sep. 26, 1798, in Boyd, ed., *Jefferson Papers*, 30:528.

44 Smith, *Marshall*, 324–325.
45 *Stuart v. Laird*, 5 U.S. 299, 309 (1803).

CHAPTER 19. PRIZES OF WAR

1 Benjamin Munn Ziegler, *The International Law of John Marshall: A Study in First Principles* (Chapel Hill: University of North Carolina Press, 1939), 12.
2 Joel Richard Paul, "The Cost of Free Trade," *The Brown Journal of World Affairs*, 22, no. 1 (Fall/Winter 2015) 194.
3 *U.S. v. Schooner Peggy*, 1 Cranch 103, 109–110 (1801).
4 Malone, *Jefferson the President: First Term*, 4:194–199.
5 Marshall to C. C. Pinckney, Nov. 21, 1802, MP, 6:124–126.
6 Frederick C. Leiner, "The Charming Betsy and the Marshall Court," *American Journal of Legal History* 45, no. 1 (2001): 3–4.
7 *Murray v. Schooner Charming Betsy*, 6 U.S. 64, 65–67. (1804).
8 Leiner, "Charming Betsy," 10.
9 James H. Kettner, *The Development of American Citizenship, 1608–1870* (Chapel Hill: University of North Carolina Press, 1978), 269–277; Smith, *Marshall*, 339.
10 Justice Story, for example, thought that expatriation required legislative permission and could not be done without a good-faith change of residence. Kettner, *American Citizenship*, 276.
11 Wood, *Empire*, 247–250.
12 Ziegler, *International Law of John Marshall*, 93–99; Smith, *Marshall*, 339.
13 *Murray v Schooner Charming Betsy*, 6 U.S. 64, 120 (1804).
14 Kettner, *American Citizenship*, 277–278.
15 *Murray v Schooner Charming Betsy*, 6 U.S. 64,113 (1804).
16 In a subsequent case, Marshall reaffirmed that unless Congress expressly stated that it intended to violate international law, "the Court is bound by the law of nations which is part of the law of the land." The Nereide, 9 Cranch 388, 422 (1815).
17 *Murray v Schooner Charming Betsy*, 6 U.S. 64, 120 (1804).
18 *Murray v Schooner Charming Betsy*, 6 U.S. 64, 121 (1804).
19 Leiner, "Charming Betsy," 14.
20 Joel Richard Paul, "Comity in International Law," *Harvard International Law Journal* 32, no. 1 (1991): 19–24. Though the term "comity" was only introduced into U.S. law later by Justice Joseph Story, the sense of mutual respect and reciprocity informed Marshall's views of the law.
21 *Respublica v. De Longchamps*, 1 Dallas (Pa.) 111, 116 (1784).
22 Federal Constitution, Art. I (8)(10).
23 See, e.g., "The *Charming Betsy* Canon, Separation of Powers and Customary International Law," *Harvard Law Review* 121, no. 4 (February 2008): 1215.
24 Ziegler, *International Law of John Marshall*, 5–6.
25 Leiner, "Charming Betsy," 18.
26 Non-Intercourse Act, ch. 2, section 1, 3 Stat. 613 (1799).
27 *Little v. Barreme*, 6 U.S. (2 Cranch) 170, 171 (1804).
28 *Little v. Barreme*, 6 U.S. 170–173 (1804).
29 *Little v. Barreme*, 6 U.S. 170, 174–175 (1804).
30 *Little v. Barreme*, 6 U.S. 170, 176–177 (1804).
31 Act of Sep. 29, 1789, ch. 25, section 3, 1 Stat. 95 (1789).
32 *Little v. Barreme*, 6 U.S. 170, 177 (1804).
33 *Little v. Barreme*, 6 U.S. 170, 179 (1804).
34 *Little v. Barreme*, 6 U.S. 170, 179 (1804).

CHAPTER 20. HIGH CRIMES

1 To Mary Marshall, Jan. 2, 1803, MP, 6:145–146.
2 Mason, *My Dearest Polly*, 153–155.
3 Richard E. Ellis, *The Jeffersonian Crisis: Courts and Politics in the Young Republic* (New York: Oxford University Press, 1971), 77–80.

4 Newmyer, *Marshall*, 178–179; Peter Charles Hoffer and N. E. H. Hull, *Impeachment in America, 1635-1805* (New Haven, CT: Yale University Press, 1984), 181–190.
5 Jefferson to Nicholson, May 13, 1803, in Boyd, ed., *Jefferson Papers*, 40:371–372.
6 Adams, *History*, 1:403.
7 Haskins and Johnson, *Foundations of Power*, 2:224.
8 Haskins and Johnson, *Foundations of Power*, 2:242–243.
9 To James Marshall, Apr. 1, 1804, MP, 6:278.
10 Samuel H. Smith and Thomas Lloyd, eds., *Trial of Samuel Chase* (Washington, D.C.: Samuel Smith, 1805 [reprinted San Bernadino, CA: BiblioLife, 201]), 1:22–23.
11 Haskins and Johnson, *Foundations of Power*, 2:243.
12 Adams, *History*, 1:419.
13 Adams, *History*, 1:450–451; Nancy Isenberg, *Fallen Founder: The Life of Aaron Burr* (New York: Penguin Books, 2007), 272–273; Ellis, *Jeffersonian Crisis*, 92.
14 Isenberg, *Fallen Founder*, 274–278.
15 Notes of Major William Pierce (Maryland), Federal Convention of 1787, found at http://avalon.law .yale.edu/18th_century/pierce.asp, accessed on March. 28, 2016.
16 As quoted in C. Peter Magrath, *Yazoo: Law and Politics in the New Republic* (Providence, RI: Brown University Press, 1966), 65.
17 Magrath, *Yazoo*, 41.
18 Smith and Lloyd, eds., *Trial of Samuel Chase*, 1:255.
19 Smith and Lloyd, eds., *Trial of Samuel Chase*, 1:256.
20 Smith and Lloyd, eds., *Trial of Samuel Chase*, 1:33–34.
21 Smith and Lloyd, eds., *Trial of Samuel Chase*, 1:259.
22 Smith and Lloyd, eds., *Trial of Samuel Chase*, 1:260.
23 Adams, *History*, 1:452–463; Ellis, *Jeffersonian Crisis*, 104–105.
24 Adams, *History*, 1:463.
25 Marshall to Spencer Roane, Sep. 6, 1819, as quoted, Newmyer, *Marshall*, 179; Jefferson to William Branch Giles, Apr. 20, 1807, in Ford, ed., *Writings of Jefferson*, 10:384.
26 Adams, *History*, 1:465.

CHAPTER 21. TREASON

1 Aurora, Mar. 8, 1805, in MP, 6:379.
2 Isenberg, *Fallen Founder*, 252–255.
3 Andro Linklater, *An Artist in Treason: The Extraordinary Double Life of General James Wilkinson* (New York: Walker Publishing Co., 2009), 215.
4 Isenberg, *Fallen Founder*, 282–283.
5 Linklater, *An Artist in Treason*, 221.
6 R. Kent Newmyer, *The Treason Trial of Aaron Burr: Law, Politics, and the Character Wars of the New Nation* (New York: Cambridge University Press, 2012), 25–28.
7 Newmyer, *Treason*, 25, referencing articles in the Kentucky's *Western World*, summer 1806.
8 Newmyer, *Treason*, 31–33.
9 Newmyer, *Treason*, 30, citing Mary-Jo Kline and Joanne Wood, eds., *Political Correspondence and Public Papers of Aaron Burr* (Princeton, NJ: Princeton University Press, 1983): 2:973–986.
10 Newmyer, *Treason*, 38.
11 Linklater, *An Artist in Treason*, 6.
12 Linklater, *An Artist in Treason*, 218–219, 237–239.
13 Newmyer, *Treason*, 28–29, 33–35.
14 Linklater, *An Artist in Treason*, 204–206, 219.
15 Linklater, *An Artist in Treason*, 210.
16 Dumas Malone, *Jefferson the President: Second Term* (Boston: Little, Brown, 1974), 275–279.
17 Newmyer, *Treason*, 34.
18 Newmyer, *Treason*, 36–38.
19 As quoted in Malone, *Jefferson the President: Second Term*, 277.
20 Isenberg, *Fallen Founder*, 315.
21 Linklater, *An Artist in Treason*, 244.

22 Letter to Giles, Apr. 20, 1807, in Ford, ed., *Writings of Jefferson*, 10:387.

23 Newmyer, *Treason*, 54.

24 Note that the D.C. Circuit Court, unlike the other federal circuit courts, was established by the D.C. Organic Act of 1801. Thus, when the Congress abolished all the circuit courts created by the 1801 Judiciary Act, they left the D.C. Circuit Court in place.

25 One treason case was appealed to the Supreme Court on a procedural motion, but the Court did not reach the substance of the case. *U.S. v. Hamilton*, 3 U.S. 17 (1795). The issue there was whether the defendant could be released on bail.

26 Punishment of Crimes Act of 1790, ch. 9, 1 stat 112.

27 Newmyer, *Treason*, 56–57.

28 Ex Parte Bollman and Ex Parte Swartwout, 8 U.S. 75, 126–127, 131, 135 (1807).

29 *The Enquirer* (Richmond), Apr. 3, 1807, p. 2.

30 Isenberg, *Fallen Founder*, 330; Newmyer, *Treason*, 70.

31 Aaron Burr, *The Examination of Col. Aaron Burr upon the Charges of a High Misdemeanor and of Treason* (Richmond, VA.: S. Grantland, 1807), 34.

32 Burr, *The Examination of Col. Aaron Burr*, 35.

33 *Virginia Argus* (Richmond), Apr. 17, 1807, p. 3.

34 *Richmond Enquirer*, Apr. 10, 1807, p. 3.

35 *Impartial Observer* (Richmond), May 9, 1807, p. 1; Newmyer, *Treason*, 146.

36 E.g., *Impartial Observer* (Richmond), May 27 1807, p. 1–5.

37 Newmyer, *Treason*, 80

38 Newmyer, *Treason*, 41; Letter to Giles, Apr. 20, 1807, in Ford, ed., *Writings of Jefferson*, 10:383–388.

39 Isenberg, *Fallen Founder*, 347–348.

40 Newmyer, *Treason*, 120–121.

41 Federal Judicial Center, Charles F. Hobson, "Aaron Burr Treason Trial," found at https://www.fjc .gov/history/famous-federal-trials/u.s.-v.-aaron-burr-treason-trial accessed on June 22, 2017.

42 Newmyer, *Treason*, 112–114.

43 Cite to Marshall's opinion in *U.S. v. Burr.*

44 Newmyer, *Treason*, 162–165.

45 *Richmond Enquirer*, "Portrait of the Chief Justice," Nov. 6, 1807, p. 3.

46 *Virginia Argus* (Richmond), Dec. 4, 1807, p. 3.

47 Beveridge, *Marshall*, 3:535; Newmyer, *Treason*, 166.

48 *Virginia Argus* (Richmond), Dec. 4, 1807, p. 2.

49 As quoted in Newmyer, *Treason*, 157.

50 Jefferson to James Madison, May 25, 1810, in Ford, ed., *Writings of Thomas Jefferson*, 11:139.

51 Letter to Giles, Apr. 20, 1807, in Ford, ed., *Writings of Thomas Jefferson*, 10:386–387.

52 Newmyer, *Treason*, 177.

CHAPTER 22. ESTRANGEMENT

1 Architect of the Capitol, "Old Senate Chamber," found at https://www.aoc.gov/capitol-buildings /old-senate-chamber, accessed on June 22, 2017.

2 Architect of the Capitol, "Old Senate Chamber," found at https://www.aoc.gov/capitol-buildings /old-senate-chamber, accessed on June 22, 2017.

3 Smith, *Marshall*, 350.

4 Smith, *Marshall*, 351.

5 To Louis Marshall, Dec. 23, 1816. MP, 8:146.

6 To Louis Marshall, Dec. 7, 1817, MP, 8:160.

7 To Mary Marshall, Feb. 16, 1818, MP, 8:179.

8 Smith, *Marshall*, 395–396.

9 Smith, *Marshall*, 371.

10 Marshall to Willing & Francis, May 2, 1815, MP, 8:89–90.

11 Magrath, *Yazoo*, 2–4.

12 Magrath, *Yazoo*, 6–7.

13 Magrath, *Yazoo*, 14–15.

14 Magreth, *Yazoo*, 21–22.

15 Magreth, *Yazoo*, 48.
16 Magreth, *Yazoo*, 69.
17 *Fletcher v. Peck*, 10 U.S. 87, 128 (1810).
18 *Fletcher v. Peck*, 10 U.S. 87, 130–131 (1810).
19 *Fletcher v. Peck*, 10 U.S. 87, 132–133 (1810).
20 *Fletcher v. Peck*, 10 U.S. 87, 135–137 (1810).
21 *Fletcher v. Peck*, 10 U.S. 87, 138–139 (1810).

CHAPTER 23. THE MEANING OF SOVEREIGNTY

1 Ketcham, *Madison*, 107–108.
2 Marshall to Pinckney, Oct. 19, 1808, MP, 7:184.
3 *Daily National Intelligencer*, Feb. 12, 1813, p. 1.
4 Ketcham, *Madison*, 478; Wood, *Empire*, 663.
5 Marshall to James Madison, Oct. 15, 1810, in Ford, ed., *Writings of Jefferson*, 111:152–153.
6 To James Marshall, Nov. 21, 1808, MP, 7:186.
7 Marshall to Pinckney, Oct. 19, 1808, MP, 7:185.
8 Wood, *Empire*, 623.
9 Wood, *Empire*, 646; Bradford Perkins, *Prologue to War: England and the United States, 1805–1812* (Berkeley: University of California Press, 1961), 74.
10 Wood, *Empire*, 625.
11 Jerry L. Mashaw, *Creating the Administrative Constitution: The Lost One Hundred Years of American Administrative Law*. The Yale Law Library Series in Legal History and Reference (New Haven, CT: Yale University Press, 2012), 103.
12 Mashaw, *Creating the Administrative Constitution*, 96.
13 Joel Richard Paul, "The Myth of Economic Interdependence," *Waseda Proceedings of Comparative Law* 11, no. 3 (Spring 2009): 293, 301.
14 Marshall to Harry Heth, Mar. 2, 1812, MP, 7:306.
15 *The Schooner Exchange v. McFaddon*, 7 Cranch 116, 123–126.
16 *The Schooner Exchange v. McFaddon*, 7 Cranch 116, 126–129 (1812).
17 *The Schooner Exchange v. McFaddon*, 7 Cranch 116, 129–130; e.g., Thomas Rutherford, *Institutes of Natural Law* (Clark, NJ: Lawbook Exchange, 2004), 2:489–490.
18 *The Schooner Exchange v. McFaddon*, 7 Cranch 116, 126–130 (1812).
19 *The Schooner Exchange v. McFaddon*, 7 Cranch 116, 133.
20 *The Schooner Exchange v. McFaddon*, 7 Cranch 116, 135–136.
21 *The Schooner Exchange v. McFaddon*, 7 Cranch 116, 136.
22 Ziegler, *International Law of John Marshall*, 65.
23 *The Schooner Exchange v. McFaddon*, 7 Cranch 116, 137.
24 *The Schooner Exchange v. McFaddon*, 7 Cranch 116, 141.
25 Ziegler, *International Law of Marshall*, 83.
26 *U.S. v. Richard Peters*, 3 Dallas 121 (1795).
27 For example, Rutherford had written that "every state has authority to determine, by positive laws, upon what occasions, for what purposes, and in what numbers, foreigners shall be allowed to come within the territories . . ." Rutherford, *Institutes*, 2:488. Rutherford treated diplomatic immunity as the only exception to the broad rule that "Every nation has a right to judge for itself, how far its intercourse, either of the commercial or of the friendly sort, is likely to be detrimental to itself," including the power to exclude foreign persons or property. Rutherford, *Institutes*, 2:489.
28 Emer de Vattel, *The Law of Nations*. Béla Kapossy and Richard Whatmore, eds. Indianapolis, IN: Liberty Fund, 2008): 4:706. Marshall tried to extend this principle of diplomatic immunity by analogy: "Equally impossible is it to conceive, whatever may be the construction as to private ships, that a prince who stipulates a passage for his troops, or an asylum for his ships of war in distress, should mean to subject his army or his navy to the jurisdiction of a foreign sovereign." *The Schooner Exchange v. McFaddon*, 7 Cranch 116, 143.
29 *The Schooner Exchange v. McFaddon*, 7 Cranch 116, 145–146.
30 *The Schooner Exchange v. McFaddon*, 7 Cranch 116, 146–147.

31 Nearly twenty years later the U.S. government did, in fact, conclude an agreement with France to pay the heirs of McFaddon and Greetham a total of $109,133.62, including interest. "A Note on Exchange versus M'Faddon," *American Journal of International Law* 18, no. 2 (April 1924): 320.

32 Marshall to Robert Smith, Jul. 27, 1812, MP, 7:338.

33 Marshall to John Randolph, Jun. 18, 1812, MP, 7:332.

34 Marshall to Robert Smith, Jul. 27, 1812, MP, 7:338.

CHAPTER 24. WASHINGTON BURNING

1 Wood, *Empire*, 659.

2 Brunsman, *The Evil Necessity*, 248, 304. In fact, about one-third of all sailors on U.S. ships were British citizens. Wood, *Empire*, 642, 646; Borneman, *1812*, 48. Impressment had been a standard form of military conscription since at least the reign of Elizabeth I.

3 Wood, *Empire*, 659.

4 Borneman, *1812*, 51.

5 Borneman, *1812*, 57.

6 Wood, *Empire*, 675, 685.

7 Borneman, *1812*, 170–171.

8 Borneman, *1812*, 178.

9 Marshall to Pickering, Dec. 11, 1813, MP, 7:417.

10 Borneman, *1812*, 177–179.

11 *Daily National Intelligencer*, Jun. 7, 1813, vol. I, No. 135, p. 1.

12 Wood, *Empire*, 693.

13 *Brown v. U.S.*, 12 U.S. 110, 110–111 (1814).

14 *Brown v. U.S.*, 12 U.S. 110, 111–112.

15 *Brown v. U.S.*, 12 U.S. 110, 112.

16 *Brown v. U.S.*, 12 U.S. 110, 114.

17 *Brown v. U.S.*, 12 U.S. 110, 134–135, 151.

18 *Brown v. U.S.*, 12 U.S. 110, 153–154.

19 *Brown v. U.S.*, 12 U.S. 110, 125.

20 *Brown v. U.S.*, 12 U.S. 110, 125.

21 Marshall's decision in *Brown* limited the power of the commander in chief. During the Cold War, Story's dissenting view that the president possesses broad plenary authority to act as commander in chief without congressional authorization eclipsed Marshall's more limited view of executive power. More than a quarter of a century after the collapse of the Soviet Union, perhaps it is time to return to Marshall's formulation of a president subject to the will of Congress. See, generally, Paul, "The Geopolitical Constitution," 671.

22 C.M.S., "Home Life of Chief Justice Marshall," *William & Mary Quarterly* 12, no. 1 (Jan. 1932), 68.

23 Beveridge, *Marshall*, 4:80–81.

24 Borneman, *1812*, 222–223.

25 Borneman, *1812*, 223–229.

26 Anthony S. Pitch, *The Burning of Washington: The British Invasion of 1814* (Annapolis, MD: Naval Institute Press, 1998), 110.

27 Adams, *History*, 1013–1014.

28 Pitch, *Burning Washington*, 120–121.

29 Pitch, *Burning Washington*, 81.

30 Adams, *History*, 1015.

31 Pitch, *Burning Washington*, 139–140.

32 Kevin Ambrose, Dan Henry, and Andy Weiss, *Washington Weather: The Weather Sourcebook for the D.C. Area* (Washington, D.C.: Historical Enterprises, 2002), 31–32.

33 Adams, *History*, 1015.

34 "Latest from Camp," *Richmond Enquirer*, Aug. 31, 1814, p. 3.

CHAPTER 25. FRIENDS AND ENEMIES

1 Smith, *Marshall*, 420–421.

2 Robert Pohl, "Lost Capitol Hill: The Caldwell House," *The Hill*, November 15, 2010. Found at www .thehillishome/2010/h/lost-capitol-hill-the-caldwell-house.

3 Beveridge, *Marshall*, 4:130–131.

4 *Thirty Hogsheads of Sugar v. Boyle*, 13 U.S. 191 (1815).

5 *Thirty Hogsheads of Sugar v. Boyle*, 13 U.S. 191, 198 (1815).

6 The "Phoenix," 5 C. Rob. 21 (1803); The "Vrow Anna Catharina," 5 C. Rob. 167 (1783).

7 *Thirty Hogsheads of Sugar v. Boyle*, 13 U.S. 191, 199.

8 *The Nereide*, 13 U.S. 388 (1815). This was one of the rare occasions in which both Justices Johnson and Story dissented.

9 *The Nereide*, 13 U.S. 388, 418.

10 *The Nereide*, 13 U.S. 388, 423–429.

11 *The Nereide*, 13 U.S. 388, 422–423.

12 E.g., Norman Dorsen, "The Relevance of Foreign Legal Materials in U.S. Constitutional Cases: A Conversation Between Justice Antonin Scalia and Justice Stephen Breyer," *International Journal of Constitutional Law* 3, no. 4 (October 2005): 519–541.

13 To Mary Marshall, Feb. 14, 1817, MP, 8:149.

14 As quoted, Beveridge, *Marshall*, 4:82–83.

15 As quoted, Beveridge, *Marshall*, 4:89.

16 Ammon, *James Monroe*, xvi–xix, 12–13.

17 Merrill D. Peterson, *The Great Triumvirate: Webster, Clay, and Calhoun* (New York: Oxford University Press, 1987), 50.

18 Ammon, *James Monroe*, 367–368.

19 Smith, *Marshall*, 493–494.

20 Mason, *My Dearest Polly*, 286.

21 N. S. Davis, *History of the American Medical Association* (Philadelphia: Lippincott, Grambo & Co., 1855), 101.

22 Beveridge, *Marshall*, 4:76–78.

23 Mason, *My Dearest Polly*, 233–234, 273; Beveridge, *Marshall*, 4:69.

24 Marshall to Story, Nov. 26, 1826, MP, 10:315.

25 Citing North American Review, xx:444–445, Beveridge, *Marshall*, 4:72.

26 Mason, *My Dearest Polly*, 276–277.

27 *Martin v. Hunter's Lessee*, 14 U.S. 304 (1816).

28 As quoted in Beveridge, *Marshall* 4:81.

29 As quoted in Beveridge, *Marshall*, 4:145.

30 *Martin v. Hunter's Lessee*, 14 U.S. 304, 312–313.

31 Editorial note, MP, 8:117–118.

32 Newmyer, *Marshall*, 360–362.

33 Beveridge, *Marshall*, 4:145–146.

34 *Federalist Papers Number 80*, as quoted in Newmyer, *Marshall*, 360.

35 *Martin v. Hunter's Lessee*, 14 U.S. 304, 325.

36 *Martin v. Hunter's Lessee*, 14 U.S. 304, 326–337.

37 *Martin v. Hunter's Lessee*, 14 U.S. 304, 340–341.

38 *Martin v. Hunter's Lessee*, 14 U.S. 304, 343.

39 *Martin v. Hunter's Lessee*, 14 U.S. 304, 373–374.

40 Oliver Wendell Holmes, *Collected Legal Papers* (New York: Harcourt, Brace & Co., 1921), 295–296.

CHAPTER 26. THE SUPREME LAW

1 Myers, *Financial History*, 80–82.

2 Myers, *Financial History*, 83.

3 Warren, *Supreme Court*, 1:504–506.

4 Story to Stephen White, Mar. 13, 1819, *Life and Letters of Story*, 1:325, as cited in Smith, *Marshall*, 442.

5 *Opinion on Constitutionality of Bank*, Feb. 23, 1791, in Syett, ed., *Papers of Alexander Hamilton*, 8:113.

6 *McCulloch v. Maryland*, 17 U.S. 316, 407.

7 U.S. Constitution, Art. I(8)(18).

8 *McCulloch v. Maryland*, 17 U.S. 316, 421.

9 *McCulloch v. Maryland*, 17 U.S. 316, 405.

10 *McCulloch v. Maryland*, 17 U.S. 316, 435–436.
11 This theory of democratic-representation reinforcement is developed by John Hart Ely, *Democracy and Distrust* (Cambridge, MA: Harvard University Press, 1980).
12 *Weekly Register*, as quoted in Beveridge, *Marshall*, 4:310.
13 Beveridge, *Marshall*, 4:309.
14 Jefferson to Ritchie, Dec. 25, 1820, in Ford, ed., *Writings of Thomas Jefferson*, 12:177.
15 Jefferson to Albert Gallatin, Dec. 26, 1820, in Ford, ed., *Writings of Thomas Jefferson*, 12:186–187.
16 Taylor, *Internal Enemy*, 405.
17 Marshall to Joseph Story, Mar. 24, 1819, MP, 8:280.
18 Marshall to Joseph Story, Jul. 13, 1821, MP, 9:179.
19 *Osborn v. Bank of the United States*, 22 U.S. 738 (1824). The Eleventh Amendment provided that a state cannot be sued in a federal court by a citizen of another state or a foreign state.
20 *Cohens v. Virginia*, 19 U.S. 264, 407–412.
21 *Cohens v. Virginia*, 19 U.S. 264, 414.
22 *Cohens v. Virginia*, 19 U.S. 264, 389.
23 *Cohens v. Virginia*, 19 U.S. 264, 416.
24 As quoted in White, *Marshall Court*, 521; Algernon Sidney, "On the Lottery Decision," *The Enquirer (Richmond)*, May 25, 1821, p. 80, as cited in Margaret E. Horsnell, *Spencer Roane: Judicial Advocate of Jeffersonian Principles* (New York: Garland Publishing, Inc., 1986), 158; Hampden, "Cohens v. Virginia," *Washington Gazette*, Jul. 25, 1821, p. 2.
25 Hampden, "*Cohens v. Virginia*," *Washington Gazette*, Jun. 21, 1821, p. 2.
26 Marshall to Joseph Story, Sep. 18, 1821, MP, 9:184.
27 Susan Dunn, *Dominion of Memories: Jefferson, Madison, and the Decline of Virginia* (New York: Basic Books, 2007), 145–148.

CHAPTER 27. THE PIRATE LOTTERY

1 Haskins and Johnson, *History*, 2:163.
2 Haskins and Johnson, *History*, 2:160–161.
3 Warren, *Supreme Court*, 1:595–596.
4 Ammon, *James Monroe*, 450–451.
5 Peterson, *The Great Triumvirate*, 59–62.
6 Jefferson to John Holmes, Apr. 22, 1820, in Ford, ed., *Writings of Jefferson*, 17:158.
7 U.S. Constitution, Art. I(2).
8 U.S. Constitution, Art. I(9).
9 U.S. Constitution, Art. I(2),(9), and (10).
10 U.S. Constitution, Art. V.
11 U.S. Constitution, Art. I(8) and Art. IV(4).
12 U.S. Constitution, Art. IV(2).
13 William Wiecek, *The Sources of Antislavery Constitutionalism in America 1760–1848* (1977), 62–63.
14 U.S. Census, 1810; Economic History Association, www.http://eh.net/encyclopedia/slavery-in-the-united-states/.
15 Taylor, *Internal Enemy*, 20.
16 An Act to Prohibit the Slave Trade of 1794, 1 U.S. Statutes at Large 348.
17 Act to Prohibit Importation of Slaves of 1807, 2 Stat. 426 (1807).
18 *The Antelope*, 23 U.S. (10 Wheat.) 66 (1824).
19 *The Antelope*, 23 U.S. (10 Wheat.) 66, 67–68 (1824); The Act in Addition to the Acts Prohibiting the Slave Trade, March 2, 1819, Statutes at Large III, 532.
20 *The Antelope*, 23 U.S. (10 Wheat.) 66, 76. Portugal had signed a treaty with Britain in 1815 promising to end the slave trade. And at the Congress of Vienna in 1815 Portugal had signed a declaration with the other European powers condemning the slave trade as "repugnant to the principles of humanity and universal morality" and calling on all states to abolish it. David King, *Vienna 1814: How the Conquerors of Napoleon Made Love, War, and Peace at the Congress of Vienna* (New York: Three Rivers Press, 2008), 217.
21 John T. Noonan Jr., *The Antelope: The Ordeal of the Recaptured Africans in the Administrations of James Monroe and John Quincy Adams* (Berkeley: University of California Press, 1990), 39.
22 Noonan, *The Antelope*, 6.

23 Noonan, *The Antelope*, 31–32, 46–47.

24 Noonan, *The Antelope*, 46–49.

25 Noonan, *The Antelope*, 57–61.

26 J. Q. Adams, diary, Mar. 27, 1820, in Charles Francis Adams, *Memoir of John Quincy Adams: Comprising Portions of His Diary from 1795 to 1898*. (Philadelphia: J. B. Lippincott & Co., 1875), 3:43.

27 G. Edward White, *History of the Supreme Court of the United States: The Marshall Court and Cultural Change, 1815–1835* (New York: Macmillan, 1988), 333–336.

28 Noonan, *The Antelope*, 62–64. Johnson's circuit court opinion is reproduced in Carol Necole Brown, "Casting Lots: The Illusion of Justice and Accountability in Property Allocation," *Buffalo Law Review 53*, no. 65, (Winter 2005):130–140.

29 Act to Protect the Commerce of the United States and Punish the Crime of Piracy, May 15, 1820, 3 Statutes 600 (1820).

30 *Case of the Antelope*, Vol. 103, Minute Book 1816–1823, pp. 192–198, Div. Savannah, Georgia, Circuit Courts, Records Group 21, U.S. District Court, National Archives—Southeast Region (Atlanta) as reprinted in, Brown, "Casting Lots," 143.

31 *The Case of the Antelope*, Circuit Court of Georgia, May 11, 1821. discussed in Noonan, *The Antelope*, 64–66.

32 *The Antelope*, 23 U.S. 66 (1825).

33 *The Antelope*, 23 U.S. 66, 74–75 (1825).

34 *The Antelope*, 23 U.S. 66, 76 (1825).

35 King, *Vienna 1814*, 217.

36 *The Antelope*, 23 U.S. 66, 80–81 (1825).

37 *The Antelope*, 23 U.S. 66, 82–83 (1825).

38 *The Antelope*, 23 U.S. 66, 86 (1825).

39 *The Antelope*, 23 U.S. 66, 90–91 (1825).

40 *The Antelope*, 23 U.S. 66, 107–108 (1825).

41 *The Antelope*, 23 U.S. 66, 111 (1825).

42 Rudko, "Pause at the Rubicon," 80–88; Smith, *Marshall*, 489–490; Ward and Greer, *Richmond During the Revolution*, 124–125.

43 Marshall to Joseph Story, Sep. 26, 1823, MP, 9:338.

44 E.g., *The Brig Caroline*, 1 Brockenbrough 384 (Virginia Circuit Court, 1819).

45 See, e.g., *Mima Queen v. Hepburn*, 7 Cranch 290, 298–299 (1813), J. Duvall dissenting; *U.S. v. The La Jeune Eugenie*, 2 Mason 409, (Mass. Cir. Ct. 1822), 26 Fed. Cas. 832, 847.

46 *The Antelope*, 23 U.S. 66, 114–116 (1825).

47 Marshall was particularly persuaded by a decision by Sir William Scott, the leading British authority on admiralty law, holding that the slave trade was permitted by international law. *The Antelope*, 23 U.S. 66, 118–119, citing *The Louis*, 2 Dodson's Rep. 210, 238 (1817). Cf., *The Amedie*, 1 Acton's Rep. 240 (1810), holding that the American claimant had no rights "upon principles of universal law, to claim restitution in a prize Court of human beings carried as his slaves."

48 *The Antelope*, 23 U.S. 66, 120–121 (1825).

49 *The Antelope*, 23 U.S. 66, 122 (1825).

50 *The Antelope*, 23 U.S. 66, 123 (1825).

51 *The Antelope*, 23 U.S. 66, 130 (1825).

52 Noonan, *The Antelope*, 135–136.

53 Editorial Note, MP, 10:158.

54 Noonan, *The Antelope*, 142–143.

55 Wilde to Berrien, May 22, 1827, University of North Carolina MS (Berrien Collection), as quoted in Noonan, *The Antelope*, 145.

56 Marshall to Pickering, Mar. 20, 1826. MP, 10:277.

57 *U.S. v. La Jeune Eugenie*, 2 Mason 409, 26 F. Cas. 832 (1822).

58 E.g., Newmyer, *Marshall*, 433–434; Ziegler, *International Law of Marshall*, 307–310.

59 Newmyer, *Marshall*, 434; Smith, *Marshall*, 488.

60 For example, Rutherford recognized that the law of nature was distinguishable from the law of nations, which he said was based on the positive consent of states. However, he asserted that "all nations . . . are obliged to follow the same law of nature." And he concluded that, "there is no law of

nations which is wholly positive." Rutherford, *Institutes of Natural Law*, Book II, C.IX: I and IV, pp. 483, 485.
61 *The Antelope*, 23 U.S. 66, 114 (1825).

CHAPTER 28. THE GREAT STEAMBOAT CASE

1 Herbert A. Johnson, *Gibbons v. Ogden: John Marshall, Steamboats, and the Commerce Clause* (Lawrence: University Press of Kansas, 2010), 26–28.
2 Johnson, *Gibbons v. Ogden*, 26–30; Stites, "A More Perfect Union: The Steamboat Case," in John W. Johnson, ed., *Historic U.S. Court Cases: An Encyclopedia* (New York: Routledge, 2001), 357–358.
3 *Livingston v. Van Ingen*, 9 Johns. 507 (1811).
4 Thomas H. Cox, *Gibbons v. Ogden: Law and Society in the Early Republic* (Athens: Ohio University Press, 2009), 70–73.
5 Michael Birkner, *Samuel L. Southard: Jeffersonian Whig* (Madison, NJ: Fairleigh Dickinson University Press, 1984), 36–37.
6 Cox, *Gibbons v. Ogden*, 70–74, 93–100.
7 As quoted in Henry Adams, *John Randolph* (Boston: Houghton, Mifflin & Co., 1882), 276.
8 Cox, *Gibbons v. Ogden*, 143.
9 *Gibbons v. Ogden*, 22 U.S. 1 (1824), 13.
10 *Gibbons v. Ogden*, 22 U.S. 1 (1824), 18–20.
11 *Gibbons v. Ogden*, 22 U.S. 1 (1824), 27–29.
12 "Steam Boat Cause," *Middlesex* (Connecticut) *Gazette*, Feb. 11, 1824, p. 3.
13 *Gibbons v. Ogden*, 22 U.S. 1 (1824), 37–41, 45.
14 *Gibbons v. Ogden*, 22 U.S. 1 (1824), 60.
15 *Gibbons v. Ogden*, 22 U.S. 1 (1824), 71–74.
16 *Gibbons v. Ogden*, 22 U.S. 1 (1824), 184–185; "Steam Boat Case," *Hartford Advertiser*, Feb. 17, 1824, p. 3.
17 *Gibbons v. Ogden*, 22 U.S. 1 (1824), 187–188.
18 *Gibbons v. Ogden*, 22 U.S. 1 (1824), 189–190.
19 *Gibbons v. Ogden*, 22 U.S. 1 (1824), 191.
20 *Gibbons v. Ogden*, 22 U.S. 1 (1824), 194.
21 *Gibbons v. Ogden*, 22 U.S. 1 (1824), 195.
22 *Gibbons v. Ogden*, 22 U.S. 1 (1824), 196.
23 *Gibbons v. Ogden*, 22 U.S. 1 (1824), 197.
24 *Gibbons v. Ogden*, 22 U.S. 1 (1824), 222.
25 Beveridge, *Marshall*, 3:443. Beveridge concluded that Marshall used Justice Johnson, as a Republican from South Carolina, to express Marshall's true opinion that the federal power was exclusive.
26 *Gibbons v. Ogden*, 22 U.S. 1 (1824), 227.
27 *Gibbons v. Ogden*, 22 U.S. 1 (1824), 231.
28 *Gibbons v. Ogden*, 22 U.S. 1 (1824), 226.
29 Warren, *Supreme Court*, 615.
30 *New-York Evening Post*, Mar. 5, 1824, p. 2, cols. 2–3, as cited in Warren, *Supreme Court*, 613.
31 As quoted in Warren, *Supreme Court*, 614.
32 Warren, *Supreme Court*, 613–615.
33 *Richmond Enquirer*, Mar. 16, 1824, as cited in Warren, *Supreme Court*, 618.
34 Warren, *Supreme Court*, 615.

CHAPTER 29. PUBLIC AND PRIVATE

1 Morton J. Horwitz, *The Transformation of American Law, 1780–1860* (New York: Oxford University Press, 1992), 112.
2 *Trustees of Dartmouth College v. Woodward*, 17 U.S. (1819), 518, 524–525.
3 Francis N. Stites, *Private Interest & Public Gain: The Dartmouth College Case, 1819* (Amherst: University of Massachusetts Press, 1972), 7–11.
4 Federal Constitution, Art. I (10)(1).
5 1820 Federal Census, Occupation and Economic Data, https://www.archives.gov/research/census/ 1790.

6 Robert V. Remini, *Daniel Webster: The Man and His Time* (New York: W. W. Norton, 1997), 154.
7 *Trustees of Dartmouth College v. Woodward*, 17 U.S. 518, 583–584.
8 *Trustees of Dartmouth College v. Woodward*, 17 U.S. 518, 592.
9 *Trustees of Dartmouth College v. Woodward*, 17 U.S. 518, 597.
10 *Trustees of Dartmouth College v. Woodward*, 17 U.S. 518, 598–599.
11 As quoted in Remini, *Daniel Webster*, 156. This quotation does not appear in the official court report but was reconstructed based on eyewitness accounts. The reaction in the courtroom was later reported by Justice Story. White, *Marshall Court*, 615–617; Stites, *Private Interest & Public Gain*, 64.
12 Stites, *Private Interest & Public Gain*, 69.
13 Stites, *Private Interest & Public Gain*, 87.
14 Warren, *The Supreme Court*, 1:460–461.
15 Remini, *Daniel Webster*, 117, 161; White, *The Marshall Court*, 3:178.
16 *Trustees of Dartmouth College v. Woodward*, 17 U.S. 518, 634–636.
17 *Trustees of Dartmouth College v. Woodward*, 17 U.S. 518, 644.
18 *Trustees of Dartmouth College v. Woodward*, 17 U.S. 518, 645.
19 *Trustees of Dartmouth College v. Woodward*, 17 U.S. 518, 650.
20 "From the Palladium: The Dartmouth College Case," *Vermont Intelligencer*, May 10, 1819, p. 2.
21 "Our Country," (republished from *New-Hampshire Patriot*), *Vermont Republican & American Yeoman*, Apr. 5, 1819, p. 2.
22 Ironically, the university president, William Allen, became president of Bowdoin College, where he later invoked the precedent of the *Dartmouth College* case to defend Bowdoin from similar interference by the State of Maine. Stites, *Private Interest & Public Gain*, 101–103.
23 Robert E. Wright, "Rise of the Corporate Nation," in Douglas A. Irwin & Richard Sylla, eds., *Founding Choices: American Economic Policy in the 1790s* (Chicago: University of Chicago Press, 2011), 218–220.
24 White, *Marshall Court*, 629–630.
25 *Sturges v. Crowninshield*, 17 U.S. 122 (1819), 122–128, 131–132; Gerald T. Dunne, *Justice Joseph Story and the Rise of the Supreme Court* (New York: Simon & Schuster, 1970), 18, 158.
26 R. Kent Newmyer, *Supreme Court Justice Joseph Story: Statesman of the Old Republic* (Chapel Hill: University of North Carolina Press, 1985), 48–51.
27 Newmyer, *Story*, 210–211; White, *Marshall Court*, 2:634.
28 White, *Marshall Court*, 633–634.
29 White, *Marshall Court*, 632.
30 Marshall, *Life of George Washington*, 2:120–121.
31 White, *History of the Supreme Court*, 2:633–636.
32 *Sturges v. Crowninshield*, 17 U.S. 122 (1819), 193.
33 *Sturges v. Crowninshield*, 17 U.S. 122 (1819), 195–196.
34 *Sturges v. Crowninshield*, 17 U.S. 122 (1819), 204.
35 *Ogden v. Saunders*, 25 U.S. 213 (1827).
36 The case was first argued in 1824, but the Court was split, and Justice Todd missed the entire session. The case was held over for reconsideration when Todd returned, but he never did.
37 *Ogden v. Saunders*, 25 U.S. 213, 332, 346.

CHAPTER 30. RIGHT REMAINS WITH THE STRONGEST

1 To Mary Marshall, Mar. 12, 1826, MP, 10:276.
2 Smith, *Marshall*, 492.
3 Marshall to Joseph Story, Oct. 29, 1828, MP, 11:179.
4 Marshall to Edward Everett, Aug. 2, 1826, MP, 10:299.
5 Marshall to Joseph Story, May 1, 1828, MP, 11:94.
6 Marshall to James Hillhouse, May 26, 1830, MP, 11:377.
7 Marshall to Joseph Story, Dec. 30, 1827, MP, 11:65.
8 Marshall to John H. Pleasants, Mar. 29, 1828, MP, 11:92. Though it may seem remarkable that Marshall did not vote in presidential elections, in fact, only about one-quarter of eligible white males voted in presidential elections. Michael F. Holt, *The Rise and Fall of the American Whig Party: Jacksonian Politics and the Onset of the Civil War* (New York: Oxford University Press, 1999), 8.

9 From Clay, Apr. 8, 1828, MP, 11:92.
10 Marshall to Joseph Hopkinson, Mar. 18, 1829, MP, 11:225.
11 To Mary Marshall, Feb. 1, 1829, MP, 11:199.
12 To Mary Marshall, Feb. 28, 1829, MP, 11:205.
13 Poem, Feb. 1829, MP, 11:206.
14 To Mary Marshall, Feb. 19, 1829, MP, 11:203–204; To Mary Marshall, Mar. 5, 1829, MP, 11:207; Jon Meacham, *American Lion: Andrew Jackson in the White House* (New York: Random House, 2008), 57–62.
15 Newmyer, *Marshall*, 406.
16 Smith, *Marshall*, 503.
17 Wood, *Empire*, 366.
18 *Foster & Elam v. Neilson*, 27 U.S. 253, 305 (1829). After the transaction was concluded, the wily Talleyrand advised the Americans with a sly wink that while he could not sell them West Florida, "you have made a noble bargain for yourselves and I suppose you will make the most of it." Livingston to James Madison, May 20, 1803, Papers of Madison: 5:19, as quoted in Wood, *Empire*, 374.
19 Jon Kukla, *A Wilderness So Immense: The Louisiana Purchase and the Destiny of America* (New York: Alfred A. Knopf, 2003), 289.
20 Meacham, *American Lion*, 35–36.
21 Herring, *From Colony to Superpower*, 109–111.
22 *Foster & Elam v. Neilson*, 27 U.S. 253, 255.
23 *Foster & Elam v. Neilson*, 27 U.S. 253, 256.
24 *Foster & Elam v. Neilson*, 27 U.S. 253, 293–299.
25 *Foster & Elam v. Neilson*, 27 U.S. 253, 274.
26 *Foster & Elam v. Neilson*, 27 U.S. 253, 274–277.
27 *Foster & Elam v. Neilson*, 27 U.S. 253, 306.
28 *Foster & Elam v. Neilson*, 27 U.S. 253, 307.
29 *Foster & Elam v. Neilson*, 27 U.S. 253, 307.
30 *Foster & Elam v. Neilson*, 27 U.S. 253, 309.
31 *Foster & Elam v. Neilson*, 27 U.S. 253, 313.
32 *Foster & Elam v. Neilson*, 27 U.S. 253, 314.
33 *Foster & Elam v. Neilson*, 27 U.S. 253, 314–315.
34 *Foster & Elam v. Neilson*, 27 U.S. 253, 314–315.
35 Spain granted Percheman two thousand acres of land on the banks of the St. Johns River in Ocklawaha, East Florida. After Spain ceded Florida to the United States, the East Florida commission appointed to register land titles rejected Percheman's title to the property. Percheman sued under an 1830 federal statute adopted to provide for the settlement of Florida land claims.
36 *U.S. v. Percheman*, 32 US 51, 86–87 (1832).
37 *U.S. v. Percheman*, 32 US 51, 88–89 (1832).

CHAPTER 31. AN EXTRAVAGANT PRETENSE

1 H. W. Brands, *Andrew Jackson: His Life and Times* (New York: Doubleday, 2005), 175.
2 Ronald N. Satz, *American Indian Policy in the Jacksonian Era* (Lincoln: University of Nebraska Press, 1975), 10.
3 Jackson Inaugural, Mar., 1829, as quoted in Satz, *American Indian Policy*, 12.
4 Satz, *American Indian Policy*, 10–11, 19.
5 Jackson, State of the Union, Dec. 8, 1829; Satz, *American Indian Policy*, 12–13, 18–21.
6 Debates in Congress, 1st Cong., 1st sess., 309–312, as quoted in Satz, *American Indian Policy*, 22.
7 Debates in Congress, 1st Cong., 1st sess., 326–328, as quoted in Satz, *American Indian Policy*, 24.
8 Lindsay G. Robertson, *Conquest by Law: How the Discovery of America Dispossessed Indigenous Peoples of Their Lands* (New York: Oxford University Press, 2005), 87.
9 *Johnson v. McIntosh*, Note, MP 9:280–281.
10 Eric Kades, "History and Interpretation of the Great Case of *Johnson v. M'Intosh*." *Law and History Review* 19, no. 1 (Spring 2001): 92.
11 *From Indiana Gazette*, Aug. 27, 1804, as quoted in Robertson, *Conquest*, 52.
12 Robertson, *Conquest*, 51–53.

13 Eric Kades, "The Dark Side of Efficiency: *Johnson v. M'Intosh* and the Expropriation of American Indian Lands," *University of Pennsylvania Law Review* 148 (April 2000): 1091–1093.

14 Kades, "History and Interpretation of the Great Case," 94–95; Robertson, *Conquest*, 53–56.

15 Smith and Lloyd, *Trial of Samuel Chase*, 1:293–295. Harper had also called Winder as a witness in his defense of Justice Chase.

16 *Johnson v. M'Intosh*, 21 U.S. 543, 568–570 (1823).

17 Kenneth H. Bobroff, "Retelling Allotment: Indian Property Rights and the Myth of Common Ownership," *Vanderbilt Law Review* 54 (2001): 1559, 1571–1592.

18 The new edition was republished in 1824 and retitled as *A History of the Colonies Planted by the English on the Continent of North America*. (Philadelphia: Abraham Small, 1824).

19 *Johnson v. M'Intosh*, 21 U.S. 543, 574 (1823).

20 Nell Jessup Newton, "Federal Power over Indians: Its Sources, Scope, and Limitations," *University of Pennsylvania Law Review* 132 (January 1984): 207–208; David E. Wilkins, *American Indian Sovereignty and the U.S. Supreme Court: The Masking of Justice* (Austin: University of Texas Press, 1997), 31–34.

21 *Johnson v. M'Intosh*, 21 U.S. 543, 590.

22 *Johnson v. M'Intosh*, 21 U.S. 543, 573 (1823).

23 *Johnson v. M'Intosh*, 21 U.S. 543, 590–591.

24 Francesco de Vitoria, Hugo Grotius, Samuel von Pufendorf, Samuel Wharton, and Emerich de Vattel all rejected the principle of discovery as the basis for European colonization of the Americas. Vattel conceded that if discovery were followed by genuine occupation of the land, it could serve a basis for ownership. However, Vattel cautioned that a sovereign could not claim more land by discovery than it could reasonably cultivate. Andrew Fitzmaurice, "Discovery, Conquest, and Occupation of Territory," in Bardo Fassbender and Anne Peters, *Oxford Handbook of the History of International Law* (Oxford, UK: Oxford University Press, 2012), 842–844.

25 Gregory Ablavsky, "Beyond the Indian Commerce Clause," *Yale Law Journal* 124 (2015): 1012, 1071; Sarah H. Cleveland, "Powers Inherent in Sovereignty: Indians, Aliens, Territories, and the Nineteenth Century Origin of Plenary Power over Foreign Affairs," *Texas Law Review* 81, no. 1 (November 2002): 33. Marshall was well aware that for three centuries the leading international legal scholars had rejected the idea that mere discovery alone vested title in a European sovereign.

26 Vattel, *The Law of Nations*, 1:208–209, 215–217.

27 *Johnson v. M'Intosh*, 21 U.S. 543, 591. The term "extravagant pretense" was a familiar idiom in nineteenth-century America. The Archbishop of Canterbury Thomas Cranmer, one of the leaders of the English Reformation in the sixteenth century, disparaged the doctrines of the Roman Catholic Church as an "extravagant pretense." By the eighteenth century, the term was in common usage in America and Britain to describe any false idea worthy of debunking.

28 Robertson, *Conquest*, 76–80,

29 Beveridge, *Marshall*, 1:237–241.

30 *Johnson v. M'Intosh*, 21 U.S. 543, 588.

31 White, *Marshall Court*, 710–711.

32 White, *Marshall Court*, 703–710.

33 Stuart Banner, *How the Indians Lost Their Land: Law and Power on the Frontier* (Cambridge, MA: The Belknap Press, 2005), 186.

34 *Johnson v. M'Intosh*, 21 U.S. 543, 588–589.

35 Cohen, Original Indian Title, 32 Minn. L. Rev. 28, 48–50 (1947); Newton, "Federal Power over Indians," 132 U. PA. L. Rev. 195, 207–211.

36 Note, MP, 9:282–283.

37 Kades, "History and Interpretation of the Great Case," 113–114.

38 Story, ed., *The Miscellaneous Writings of Joseph Story*, 408–474, as quoted in MP, 11:179.

39 Marshall to Joseph Story, Oct. 29, 1828, MP, 11:178.

CHAPTER 32. IN THE CONQUEROR'S COURT

1 Note 1, MP, 11:227.

2 Note 1, MP, 11:227.

3 Marshall to Barbara O'Sullivan, Mar. 18, 1829, MP, 1:226–228.

4 Mason, *My Dearest Polly*, 322.
5 Marshall to Joseph Story, Jun. 26, 1831, MP, 12:94.
6 To James Marshall, Dec. 21, 1828, MP, 11:185.
7 Marshall to Joseph Story, Jun. 11, 1829, MP, 11:260.
8 To Mary Marshall, Jan. 31, 1830, MP, 11:343.
9 To Mary Marshall, Jan. 31, 1830, MP, 11:343.
10 Joseph to Samuel Fay, Feb. 25, 1808, as quoted in William W. Story, ed., *The Life and Letters of Joseph Story* (London: John Chapman, 1851), 1:167.
11 Marshall to Joseph Story, Jan. 8, 1830, MP, 11:332.
12 Editorial note, MP, 12:42.
13 Newmyer, *Marshall*, 447.
14 Register of Debates, VI, 333–334, Apr. 15, 1830, as quoted in Editorial Note, MP, 12:49.
15 Jackson annual message, Dec. 6, 1830, Compilation of Messages and Papers, 3:1082–1086, as quoted in Brands, *Andrew Jackson*, 491–492.
16 Marshall in Philadelphia, Sep. 28, 1831, editorial note, MP, 12:105.
17 As quoted in *Niles Register*, Mar. 26, 1831, 67–68.
18 *Cherokee Nation v. Georgia*, 30 U.S. 1, 15.
19 *Cherokee Nation v. Georgia*, 30 U.S. 1, 16.
20 *Cherokee Nation v. Georgia*, 30 U.S. 1, 19 (1831).
21 *Cherokee Nation v. Georgia*, 30 U.S. 1, 17–18.
22 *Cherokee Nation v. Georgia*, 30 U.S. 1, 21.
23 *Cherokee Nation v. Georgia*, 30 U.S. 1, 27.
24 *Cherokee Nation v. Georgia*, 30 U.S. 1, 20.
25 White, *Marshall Court*, 730.
26 *Cherokee Nation v. Georgia*, 30 U.S. 1, 50–60.
27 Marshall to Richard Peters, May 19, 1831, MP, 12:66–67.
28 Revoked Will and Codicils, Sep. 24, 1831, MP, 12:102.
29 Marshall in Philadelphia, Sep. 28, 1831, MP, 12:105.
30 Andrew Oliver, *The Portraits of John Marshall* (Charlottesville: University Press of Virginia, 1977), 135.
31 Marshall in Philadelphia, Sep. 28, 1831, MP, 12:105–109; To Mary Marshall, Nov. 8, 1831, MP, 12:121.
32 Smith, *Marshall*, 514; Mason, *My Dearest Polly*, 343.
33 Eulogy for Mary W. Marshall, Dec. 25, 1832, MP, 12:251–252.
34 Marshall to Joseph Story, Oct. 12, 1831, MP, 12:119–120.
35 *Worcester v. Georgia*, editorial note, Mar. 3, 1832, MP, 12:150–151.
36 *Worcester v. Georgia*, editorial note, Mar. 3, 1832, MP, 12:151.
37 *Worcester v. Georgia*, editorial note, Mar. 3, 1832, MP, 12:151.
38 *Worcester v. Georgia*, editorial note, Mar. 3, 1832, MP, 12:152.
39 *Worcester v. Georgia*, editorial note, Mar. 3, 1832, MP, 12:153.
40 Mason, *My Dearest Polly*, 330.
41 Marshall to Henry Clay and Philemon Thomas, Feb. 10, 1832, MP, 12:146; To Edward C. Marshall, Feb. 15, 1832, MP, 12:147.
42 *Worcester v. Georgia*, 31 U.S. 515, 535 (1831).
43 Story to Mrs. Story, Feb. 26, 1832, Story, *Life and Letters*, 2:84–85, as quoted in *Worcester v. Georgia*, editorial note, Mar. 3, 1832, MP, 12:153.
44 *Worcester v. Georgia*, editorial note, Mar. 3, 1832, MP, 12:153.
45 *Worcester v. Georgia*, 31 U.S. 515, 543.
46 *Worcester v. Georgia*, 31 U.S. 515, 544–545.
47 *Worcester v. Georgia*, 31 U.S. 515, 547.
48 *Worcester v. Georgia*, 31 U.S. 515, 549.
49 *Worcester v. Georgia*, 31 U.S. 515, 552.
50 *Worcester v. Georgia*, 31 U.S. 515, 556. Similarly, the Treaty of Holston in 1791 recognized the "national character of the Cherokees, and their right of self government; thus guarantying their lands; assuming the duty of protection, and of course pledging the faith of the United States for that protection."

51 *Worcester v. Georgia*, 31 U.S. 515, 557.
52 *Worcester v. Georgia*, 31 U.S. 515, 559.
53 *Worcester v. Georgia*, 31 U.S. 515, 561.
54 *Worcester v. Georgia*, 31 U.S. 515, 561.
55 *Worcester v. Georgia*, editorial note, Mar. 3, 1832, MP, 12:153.
56 White, *Marshall Court*, 736.
57 Meacham, *American Lion*, 204.
58 Satz, *American Indian Policy*, 49.
59 Andrew Jackson, Annual Message to Congress, Dec. 4, 1832.
60 *Worcester v. Georgia*, editorial note, Mar. 3, 1832, MP, 12:156.
61 White, *Marshall Court*, 737–738; Joseph C. Burke, "The Cherokee Cases: A Study in Law, Politics, and Morality," *Stanford Law Review* 21 (February 1969): 530.

CHAPTER 33. A UNION PROLONGED BY MIRACLES

 1 Marshall to Joseph Story, Aug. 2, 1832, MP, 12:226–227.
 2 Marshall to Joseph Story, Sep. 22, 1832, MP, 12:238.
 3 Marshall to William Gaston, Dec. 20, 1832, MP, 12:246.
 4 To James Marshall, Sep. 15, 1832, MP, 12:236, n2.
 5 Marshall to Joseph Story, Dec. 25, 1832, MP, 12:248–249.
 6 Marshall to S. W. Story, Jan. 20, 1833, as quoted in White, *Marshall Court*, 739.
 7 To Jaquelin Marshall, Feb. 13, 1834, MP, 12:349.
 8 Smith, *Marshall*, 424–425.
 9 Warren, *Supreme Court*, 798–800.
10 From Story, Jan. 1833, MP, 12:257.
11 Marshall to Joseph Story, Oct. 6, 1834, MP, 12:421–422.
12 Interview with John Frazee, May 22, 1834, MP, 12:413.
13 Meeting with Harriet Martineau, Feb. 1, 1835, MP, 12:453.
14 To James Marshall, Oct. 14, 1833, MP, 12:304.
15 To James Marshall, Apr. 13, 1835, MP, 12:483; To James Marshall, May 22, 1835, MP, 12:487–488.
16 To John Marshall Jr., Mar. 11, 1835, MP, 12:474. The quote is from *Virgil*.
17 See e.g., Marshall to James Garnett, Dec. 17, 1833, MP, 12:313.
18 To John Marshall Jr., Mar. 11, 1835, MP, 12:474.
19 Marshall to J. Y. Campbell, Apr. 4, 1835, MP, 12:480.
20 To James Marshall, Apr. 13, 1835, MP, 12:483.
21 Interview with James Kent, May 16, 1835, MP, 12:486.
22 Marshall to Richard Peters, Apr. 30, 1835, MP, 12:485–486.
23 Nathaniel Chapman to John Brockenbrough, Jul. 6, 1835, MP, 12:492, n1.
24 Marshall's Final Illness, Jun. 11, 1835, MP, 12:489–490.
25 "Funeral Honors to the Late Chief Justice Marshall," *Paul Pry* (Washington, D.C.), Jul. 18, 1835, vol. 4, no. 32, p. 4.
26 *National Intelligencer*, July 9, 1835, as quoted in White, *Marshall Court*, 775.
27 *National Gazette*, Jul. 25, 1835, as quoted in Warren, *Supreme Court*, 1:806.
28 *Richmond Enquirer*, Jul. 10, 1835, as quoted in Smith, *Marshall*, 524.
29 As quoted in Warren, *Supreme Court*, 1:796, 813.
30 Jackson to Horace Binney, Sep 18, 1835, Jackson papers, Library of Congress, as quoted in Smith, *Marshall*, 524.
31 Jeremiah Mason to Joseph Story, Feb. 16, 1828, as quoted in Warren, *Supreme Court*, 1:807.
32 *New-York Evening Post*, July 8, 1835, as quoted in White, *Marshall Court*, 774–775.
33 *New-York Evening Post*, July 29, 1835, as quoted in White, *Marshall Court*, 776.
34 *Dred Scott v. Sandford*, 60 U.S. 393 (1857).
35 Jackson to the Cherokee Tribe, Mar. 16, 1835, as quoted in John Ehle, *Trail of Tears: The Rise and Fall of the Cherokee Nation* (New York: Anchor Books, 1989), 278.
36 Ehle, *Trail of Tears*, 390–391.

SELECTED BIBLIOGRAPHY

PRIMARY SOURCES

Abbot, W. W., Dorothy Twohig, Philander D. Chase, et al., eds. *The Papers of George Washington: Presidential Series*. 19 vols. Charlottesville: University of Virginia Press, 1987–.

Adams, Charles Francis, ed. *Letters of John Adams to His Wife*. Boston: Charles C. Little and James Brown, 1841.

Bailyn, Bernard, ed. *The Debate on the Constitution: Federalist and Antifederalist Speeches, Articles, and Letters During the Struggle over Ratification*. 2 vols. New York: Library of America, 1993.

Boyd, Julian, Charles Cullen, et al., eds. *The Papers of Thomas Jefferson*, 42 vols. Princeton, NJ: Princeton University Press, 1950–.

Brockenbrough, John W., ed. *Reports of Cases Decided by the Honourable John Marshall in the Circuit Court of the United States*. 2 vols. Philadelphia: James Kay & Brother, 1837.

Bryson, William Hamilton. *Census of Law Books in Colonial Virginia*. Charlottesville: University of Virginia Press, 1978.

Burr, Aaron. *The Examination of Col. Aaron Burr upon the Charges of a High Misdemeanor and of Treason*. Richmond, VA: S. Grantland, 1807.

Carnegie Endowment for International Peace. *Official Documents Bearing on the Armed Neutrality of 1780 and 1800*. Pamphlet No. 27. Buffalo, NY: William Hein & Co., 2000.

———. *Documents Relating to the Controversy over Neutral Rights Between the United States and France, 1797–1800*, Pamphlet No. 24. Washington, D.C.: 1917.

Farrand, Max, ed. *The Framing of the Constitution of the United States*. New Haven, CT: Yale University Press, 1913.

Ford, Paul Leicester, ed. *The Writings of Thomas Jefferson*. 10 vols. New York: G. P. Putnam's Sons, 1909.

Frisch, Morton, ed. *The Pacificus-Helvidius Debates of 1793–1794*. Indianapolis, IN: Liberty Fund, 2007.

Henry, William Wirt, ed. *Patrick Henry: Life, Correspondence, and Speeches*. 3 vols. New York: Charles Scribner and Sons, 1891.

Hickey, Donald R., ed. *The War of 1812: Writings from America's Second War of Independence*. New York: Library of America, 2013.

Hobson, Charles F., Herbert A. Johnson, Charles T. Cullen, and Nancy G. Harris, eds. *The Papers of John Marshall*. 12 vols. Chapel Hill: University of North Carolina Press, 1974–2006.

Hunt, Gaillard, ed. *The Writings of James Madison.* 9 vols. New York: Knickerbocker Press, 1900–1910.

Hunt, John Gabriel, ed. *The Essential Thomas Jefferson.* Avenel, NJ: Portland House, 1994.

Kaminski, John P., Gaspare J. Saladino, et al., eds. *The Documentary History of the Ratification of the Constitution by the States: Virginia.* Vols. 8–10. Madison: Wisconsin Historical Society Press, 1990.

Knight, Russell W., ed. *Elbridge Gerry's Letterbook: Paris, 1797–1798.* Salem, MA: The Essex Institute, 1966.

Madison, James. *Notes of Debates in the Federal Convention of 1787.* New York: W. W. Norton, 1987.

Marcus, Maeva, ed. *The Documentary History of the Supreme Court of the United States, 1789–1800.* 8 vols. New York: Columbia University Press, 1986–2007.

Mays, David John, ed. *The Letters and Papers of Edmund Pendleton, 1734–1803.* 2 vols. Charlottesville: University Press of Virginia, 1967.

Preston, Daniel, and Marlena C. DeLong, eds. *The Papers of James Monroe.* 6 vols. Westport, CT: Greenwood Press, 2003.

Rutland, Robert A., Robert J. Brugger, Charles F. Hobson, John C. A. Stagg, Jeanne Kerr Cross, and Susan Holbrook Perdue, eds. *The Papers of James Madison: Presidential Series.* 9 vols. Charlottesville: University of Virginia Press, 1984–.

Servies, James A., ed. *A Bibliography of John Marshall.* U.S. Commission for the Celebration of the Two Hundredth Anniversary of the Birth of John Marshall, 1956.

Smith, Samuel H., and Thomas Lloyd, eds. *Trial of Samuel Chase.* 2 vols. Washington, D.C.: Samuel Smith, 1805 (reprinted San Bernardino, CA: BiblioLife, 2014).

Syrett, Harold C., ed. *The Papers of Alexander Hamilton.* 27 vols. New York: Columbia University Press, 1961–1987.

NEWSPAPERS

Albany Gazette
Albany Register
Alexandria Daily Advertiser
American Mercury (Hartford)
Aurora (Philadelphia)
Carolina Gazette (Charleston)
City of Washington Gazette
Courier of New Hampshire (Concord)
Daily National Intelligencer (Washington, D.C.)
Daily National Journal (Washington, D.C.)
Federal Gazette and Philadelphia Daily Advertiser
Gazette of the United States (Philadelphia)
Georgia Gazette (Savannah)
Impartial Observer (Richmond)
Independent Gazetteer (Worcester)
Newburyport Herald and Country Gazette
New-London Gazette
New York Commercial Advertiser
New-York Evening Post
New-York Spectator
Paul Pry (Washington, D.C.)
Philadelphia Gazette
Philadelphia Inquirer
Providence Journal, and Town and Country Advertiser
Providence Patriot
Recorder (Richmond)
Richmond Enquirer
Southern Patriot (Charleston)
Staunton Eagle
Vermont Republican and American Yeoman (Windsor, VT)
Virginia Argus (Richmond)

Virginia Chronicle and Norfolk & Portsmouth General Advertiser
Virginia Gazette, and General Advertiser (Richmond)
Washington Federalist
Washington Gazette

SECONDARY SOURCES

Ablavsky, Gregory. "Beyond the Indian Commerce Clause." Yale Law Journal 124 (2015): 1012–1090.
Ackerman, Bruce. The Failure of the Founding Fathers: Jefferson, Marshall, and the Rise of Presidential Democracy. Cambridge, MA: The Belknap Press, 2005.
Adams, Charles Francis. Memoir of John Quincy Adams: Comprising Portions of His Diary from 1795 to 1898. 7 vols. Philadelphia: J. B. Lippincott & Co., 1875.
Adams, Henry. The Life of Albert Gallatin. Philadelphia: J. B. Lippincott & Co., 1879.
——. John Randolph. Boston: Houghton, Miflin & Co., 1882.
——. History of the United States of America During the Administrations of James Madison, 1809–1817. New York: Library of America, 1986.
——. History of the United States of America During the Administrations of Thomas Jefferson, 1801–1809. New York: Library of America, 1986.
Alden, John R. A History of the American Revolution. New York: Da Capo Press, 1969.
Aldrich, Robert, and Garry Wotherspoon, eds. Who's Who in Gay and Lesbian History. 2 vols. New York: Routledge, 2001.
Alexander, John K. "The Philadelphia Numbers Game: An Analysis of Philadelphia's Eighteenth-Century Population." Pennsylvania Magazine of History and Biography 98, no. 3 (July 1974): 314–24.
Ambrose, Kevin, Dan Henry, and Andy Weiss. Washington Weather: The Weather Sourcebook for the D.C. Area. Washington, D.C.: Historical Enterprises, 2002.
Ammon, Harry. James Monroe: The Quest for National Identity. Charlottesville: University of Virginia Press, 1990.
——. "Agricola Versus Aristides: James Monroe, John Marshall, and the Genet Affair in Virginia." The Virginia Magazine of History and Biography 74, no. 3 (July 1966): 312–20.
——. "The Genet Mission and the Development of American Political Parties." The Journal of American History 52, no. 4 (March 1966): 725–41.
——. The Genet Mission. New York: W. W. Norton, 1973.
Aron, Paul. Founding Feuds: The Rivalries, Clashes, and Conflicts That Forged a Nation. Williamsburg: Colonial Williamsburg Foundation, 2016.
Bailey, Thomas A. A Diplomatic History of the American People. New York: Meredith Corporation, 1969.
Bailyn, Bernard. The Ideological Origins of the American Revolution. Cambridge, MA: The Belknap Press, 1976.
Baker, Leonard. John Marshall: A Life in the Law. New York: Macmillan, 1974.
Ball, Milner S. "John Marshall and Indian Nations in the Beginning and Now." John Marshall Law Review 33, no. 4 (Summer 2000): 1183–1195.
Banner, Stuart. How the Indians Lost Their Land: Law and Power on the Frontier. Cambridge, MA: The Belknap Press, 2005.
Belgrad, Eric A. "John Marshall's Contributions to American Neutrality Doctrines." William & Mary Law Review 9 (1967–1968): 430–451.
Bemis, Samuel Flagg. The Diplomacy of the American Revolution. Bloomington: Indiana University Press, 1967.
——. Jay's Treaty: A Study in Commerce and Diplomacy. New Haven, CT: Yale University Press, 1962.
Benemann, William. Male-Male Intimacy in Early America: Beyond Romantic Friendship. New York: Routledge, 2012.
Bernstein, R. B. Thomas Jefferson. New York: Oxford University Press, 2003.
Beveridge, Albert J. The Life of John Marshall. 4 vols. Boston: Houghton Mifflin, 1916.
Birkner, Michael. Samuel L. Southard: Jeffersonian Whig. Madison, NJ: Fairleigh Dickinson University Press, 1984.

Black, Jeremy. *British Foreign Policy in an Age of Revolutions, 1783-1793*. Cambridge, UK: Cambridge University Press, 1994.

Blackstone, William. *Commentaries on the Laws of England*. Thomas M. Cooley, ed. 4 vols. Chicago: Callaghan and Co., 1899.

Blanning, T. C. W. *The French Revolutionary Wars 1787-1802*. New York: Arnold, 1996.

Bobroff, Kenneth H. "Retelling Allotment: Indian Property Rights and the Myth of Common Ownership," *Vanderbilt Law Review* 54 (2001): 1559-1597.

Bobrick, Benson. *Angel in the Whirlwind*. New York: Penguin Books, 1997.

Borneman, Walter R. *1812: The War That Forged a Nation*. New York: HarperCollins, 2004.

Brands, H. W. *The Heartbreak of Aaron Burr*. New York: Anchor Books, 2012.

———. *Andrew Jackson: His Life and Times*. New York: Doubleday, 2005.

Broadwater, Jeff. *James Madison: A Son of Virginia and a Founder of the Nation*. Chapel Hill: University of North Carolina Press, 2012.

Brodie, Fawn M. *Thomas Jefferson: An Intimate History*. New York: Bantam Books, 1974.

Brookhiser, Richard. *James Madison*. New York: Basic Books, 2011.

———. *Alexander Hamilton*. New York: The Free Press, 1999.

———. *Founding Father: Rediscovering George Washington*. New York: The Free Press, 1996.

Broussard, James H. *The Southern Federalists, 1800-1816*. Baton Rouge: Louisiana State University Press, 1976.

Brown, Glenn. *History of the United States Capitol*. 2 vols. Washington, D.C.: Government Printing Office, 1903.

Brunsman, Denver. *The Evil Necessity: British Naval Impressment in the Eighteenth-Century Atlantic World*. Charlottesville: University of Virginia Press, 2013.

Burke, Edmund. *Reflections on the Revolution in France*. New York: Viking Penguin, 1968.

Burke, Joseph C. "The Cherokee Cases: A Study in Law, Politics, and Morality." *Stanford Law Review* 21 (February 1969): 500-531.

Campbell, Bruce Arthur. *Law and Experience in the Early Republic: The Evolution of the Dartmouth College Doctrine, 1780-1819*. Michigan State University (Ph.D. thesis), 1973.

Carlyle, Thomas. *The French Revolution: A History*. New York: Modern Library, 2002.

Carp, E. Wayne. *To Starve the Army at Pleasure: Continental Army Administration and American Political Culture, 1775-1783*. Chapel Hill: University of North Carolina Press, 1984.

Carpenter, William W. "The United States and the League of Neutrals of 1780." *American Journal of International Law* 15 (1921): 511-522.

Carrington, Elizabeth Ambler. "An Old Virginia Correspondence." *Atlantic Monthly* 84 (1899): 535-547.

Carson, Jane. *Colonial Virginians at Play*. Williamsburg, VA: Colonial Williamsburg Foundation, 1965.

Chernow, Ron. *Alexander Hamilton*. New York: The Penguin Press, 2004.

———. *Washington: A Life*. New York: The Penguin Press, 2010.

Cleveland, Sarah H. "Powers Inherent in Sovereignty: Indians, Aliens, Territories, and the Nineteenth Century Origin of Plenary Power over Foreign Affairs." *Texas Law Review* 81, no. 1 (November 2002): 1-284.

Clinton, Robert Lowry. "Classical Legal Naturalism and the Politics of John Marshall's Constitutional Jurisprudence." *John Marshall Law Review* 33, no. 875 (Summer 2000): 935-971.

Cohen, Felix S. "Original Indian Title." *Minnesota Law Review* 32 (1947-1948): 28-59.

Combs, Jerald A. *The Jay Treaty: Political Background of the Founding Fathers*. Berkeley: University of California Press, 1970.

Cometti, Elizabeth. *Social Life in Virginia During the War for Independence*. Williamsburg: Virginia Independence Bicentennial Commission, 1978.

Conley, Patrick T., and John P. Kaminski, eds. *The Bill of Rights and the States: The Colonial and Revolutionary Origins of American Liberties*. Madison, WI: Madison House Publishers, 1992.

Cooper, Duff. *Talleyrand*. New York: Grove Press, 1997.

Cornell, Saul. *The Other Founders: Anti-Federalism and the Dissenting Tradition in America, 1788-1828*. Chapel Hill: University of North Carolina Press, 1999.

Corwin, Edward S. *John Marshall and the Constitution*. New Haven, CT: Yale University Press, 1919.

Cox, Thomas H. *Gibbons v. Ogden: Law, and Society in the Early Republic*. Athens: Ohio University Press, 2009.

Craigmyle, Thomas Shaw. *John Marshall in Diplomacy and in Law*. New York: Charles Scribner's Sons, 1933.

Crompton, Louis. *Homosexuality and Civilization*. Cambridge, MA: The Belknap Press, 2003.

Cronin, Vincent. *Louis & Antoinette*. New York: William Morrow & Co., 1975.

Crowe, Justin. *Building the Judiciary: Law, Courts, and the Politics of Institutional Development*. Princeton, NJ: Princeton University Press, 2012.

Dark, Sidney. *Twelve Bad Men*. London: Hodder and Stoughton, 1928.

Davidson, Ian. *Voltaire: A Life*. New York: Pegasus Books, 2010.

Davis, David Brion. *Slavery in the Colonial Chesapeake*. Williamsburg, VA: Colonial Williamsburg Foundation, 1986.

DeConde, Alexander. *The Quasi-War: The Politics and Diplomacy of the Undeclared War with France 1797–1801*. New York: Charles Scribner's Sons, 1966.

Dewey, Donald O. *Marshall Versus Jefferson: The Political Background of Marbury v. Madison*. New York: Alfred A. Knopf, 1970.

Dickinson, H. T., ed. *Britain and the French Revolution, 1789–1815*. New York: St. Martin's Press, 1989.

Draper, Theodore. *A Struggle for Power: The American Revolution*. New York: Times Books, 1996.

Dunn, Susan. *Dominion of Memories: Jefferson, Madison, and the Decline of Virginia*. New York: Basic Books, 2007.

———. *Jefferson's Second Revolution: The Election Crisis of 1800 and the Triumph of Republicanism*. Boston: Houghton Mifflin, 2004.

———. *Sister Revolutions: French Lightning, American Light*. New York: Faber and Faber, 1999.

Dunne, Gerald T. *Justice Joseph Story and the Rise of the Supreme Court*. New York: Simon & Schuster, 1970.

Durey, Michael. *William Wickham, Master Spy: The Secret War Against the French Revolution*. London: Pickering & Chatto, 2009.

———. "William Wickham, the Christ Church Connection and the Rise and Fall of the Security Service in Britain, 1793–1801." *English Historical Review* 71, no. 492 (2006): 714–745.

Earl, John L. III. "Talleyrand in Philadelphia, 1794–1796." *The Pennsylvania Magazine of History and Biography* 91, no. 3 (July 1967): 282–298.

Ehle, John. *Trail of Tears: The Rise and Fall of the Cherokee Nation*. New York: Anchor Books, 1989.

Elkins, Stanley, and Eric McKitrick. *The Age of Federalism: The Early American Republic, 1788–1800*. New York: Oxford University Press, 1995.

Ellis, Joseph J. *His Excellency: George Washington*. New York: Alfred A. Knopf, 2004.

———. *Founding Brothers: The Revolutionary Generation*. New York: Vintage Books, 2000.

———. *American Sphinx: The Character of Thomas Jefferson*. New York: Vintage Books, 1996.

Ellis, Richard E. *The Jeffersonian Crisis: Courts and Politics in the Young Republic*. New York: Oxford, University Press, 1971.

Farrand, Max, ed. *The Records of the Federal Convention of 1787*. 3 vols. New Haven, CT: Yale University Press, 1966.

Fassbender, Bardo, and Anne Peters. *Oxford Handbook of the History of International Law*. Oxford, UK: Oxford University Press, 2012.

Ferguson, E. James. *The Power of the Purse: A History of American Public Finance, 1776–1790*. Chapel Hill: University of North Carolina Press, 1961.

Ferling, John. *Adams v. Jefferson: The Tumultuous Election of 1800*. New York: Oxford University Press, 2004.

———. *John Adams: A Life*. New York: Henry Holt, 1992.

Ferrero, Monique. *Voltaire la nommait Belle et Bonne: La marquise de Villette, un coeur dans la tourmente*. Bourg-en-Bresse, France: M & G Éditions, 2007.

Fleming, Thomas. *Duel: Alexander Hamilton, Aaron Burr and the Future of America*. New York: Basic Books, 1999.

———. *Washington's Secret War: The Hidden History of Valley Forge*. New York: HarperCollins, 2005.

Flexner, James Thomas. *Washington: The Indispensable Man*. Boston: Little, Brown, 1974.

———. *George Washington in the American Revolution (1775–1783)*. Boston: Little, Brown, 1968.

——. *George Washington*. 4 vols. Boston: Little, Brown, 1965–1972.

Forte, David F. "Marbury's Travail: Federalist Politics and William Marbury's Appointment as Justice of the Peace." *Catholic University Law Review* 45, no. 2 (Winter 1996): 349–402.

Frankfurter, Felix, and James M. Landis. *The Business of the Supreme Court: A Study in the Federal Judicial System*. New York: Macmillan, 1928.

Gaines, James R. *For Liberty and Glory: Washington, Lafayette, and Their Revolutions*. New York: W. W. Norton, 2007.

Gaustad, Edwin S. *Revival, Revolution, and Religion in Early Virginia*. Williamsburg, VA: Colonial Williamsburg Foundation, 1994.

Gelbach, Clyde Christian. "*Spencer Roane of Virginia, 1762–1822: A Judicial Advocate of State Rights*." PhD diss., University of Pittsburgh, 1955.

Glickstein, Jed. "After Midnight: The Circuit Judges and the Repeal of the Judiciary Act of 1801." *Yale Journal of Law and Humanities* 24, no. 2 (2012): 543–578.

Goebel, Julius, Jr. *History of the Supreme Court of the United States. Vol 1: Antecedents and Beginnings to 1801*. Oliver Wendell Holmes Devise History of the Supreme Court of the United States. New York: Macmillan, 1971.

Goldstone, Lawrence. *The Activist: John Marshall, Marbury v. Madison, and the Myth of Judicial Review*. New York: Walker & Co., 2008.

Graber, Mark A., and Michael Perhac, eds. *Marbury Versus Madison: Documents and Commentary*. Washington, D.C.: CQ Press, 2002.

Greene, Jack P. *Political Life in Eighteenth-Century Virginia*. Williamsburg, VA: Colonial Williamsburg Foundation, 1986.

Grigsby, Hugh Blair. *The History of the Virginia Federal Convention of 1788*. 2 vols. Richmond: Virginia Historical Society, 1890. Reprint, New York: Da Capo Press, 1969.

Gross, Robert A., ed. *In Debt to Shays: The Bicentennial of an Agrarian Rebellion*. Charlottesville: University Press of Virginia, 1993.

Grotius, Hugo. *The Rights of War and Peace*. Edited by Richard Tuck. 3 vols. Indianapolis: Liberty Fund, 2005.

Gunther, Gerald. "Unearthing John Marshall's Major Out-of-Court Constitutional Commentary." *Stanford Law Review* 21, no. 3 (February 1969): 449–547.

Gutzman, Kevin R. C. *James Madison and the Making of America*. New York: St. Martin's Press, 2012.

Hamilton, Alexander, John Jay, and James Madison. *The Federalist*. New York: Willey Book Co., 1901.

Haskins, George Lee, and Herbert A. Johnson. *History of the Supreme Court of the United States. Vol 2: Foundations of Power: John Marshall, 1801–1815*. New York: Macmillan, 1981.

Hatch, Louis Clinton. *The Administration of the American Revolutionary Army*. New York: Longmans, Green, and Co., 1904.

Hendrickson, Robert A. *The Rise and Fall of Alexander Hamilton*. New York: Van Nostrand Reinhold, 1981.

Herring, George C. *From Colony to Superpower: U.S. Foreign Relations Since 1776*. New York: Oxford University Press, 2008.

Hibbert, Christopher. *The French Revolution*. London: Penguin Books, 1982.

Hill, Peter P. *Napoleon's Troublesome Americans: Franco-American Relations, 1804–1815*. Washington, D.C.: Potomac Books, 2005.

——. *French Perceptions of the Early American Republic, 1783–1793*. Philadelphia: American Philosophical Society, 1988.

Hobson, Charles F. *The Great Chief Justice: John Marshall and the Rule of Law*. Lawrence: University Press of Kansas, 1996.

——. "The Recovery of British Debts in the Federal Circuit Courts of Virginia, 1790 to 1797." *Virginia Magazine of History and Biography* 92, no. 2 (April 1984): 176–200.

Hoffer, Peter Charles. *Law and People in Colonial America*, Baltimore: The Johns Hopkins Press, 1998.

——. and N. E. H. Hull. *Impeachment in America, 1635–1805*. New Haven, CT: Yale University Press, 1984.

Holmes, Oliver Wendell. *Collected Legal Papers*. New York: Harcourt, Brace & Co., 1921.

Holt, Michael F. *The Rise and Fall of the American Whig Party: Jacksonian Politics and the Onset of the Civil War*. New York: Oxford University Press, 1999.

Holton, Woody. *Unruly Americans and the Origins of the Constitution*. New York: Hill and Wang, 2007.
——. *Forced Founders: Indians, Debtors, Slaves & the Making of the American Revolution in Virginia*. Chapel Hill: University of North Carolina Press, 1999.
Horsnell, Margaret E. *Spencer Roane: Judicial Advocate of Jeffersonian Principles*. New York: Garland Publishing, Inc., 1986.
Horwitz, Morton J. *The Transformation of American Law, 1780–1860*. New York: Oxford University Press, 1992.
Huebner, Timothy S. "Lawyer, Litigant, Leader: John Marshall and His Papers." *American Journal of Legal History* 48 (July 2006): 314–326.
——. *The Southern Judicial Tradition: State Judges and Sectional Distinctiveness, 1790–1890*. Athens: University of Georgia Press, 1999.
——. "The Consolidation of State Judicial Power: Spencer Roane, Virginia Legal Culture, and the Southern Judicial Tradition." *Virginia Magazine of History and Biography* 102, no. 1 (January 1994): 47–72.
Hungerford, Thomas L. *CRS Report on U.S. Federal Government Revenue: 1790 to Present*. Washington, D.C.: Library of Congress, 2006.
Irons, Peter. *A People's History of the Supreme Court*. New York: Penguin Books, 1999.
Irwin, Douglas A., and Richard Sylla, eds. *Founding Choices: American Economic Policy in the 1790s*. Chicago: University of Chicago Press, 2011.
Isaac, Rhys. *The Transformation of Virginia: 1740–1790*. Chapel Hill: University of North Carolina Press, 1982.
——. *Worlds of Experience: Communities in Colonia Virginia*. Williamsburg, VA: Colonial Williamsburg Foundation, 1999.
Isaacson, Walter. *Benjamin Franklin: An American Life*. New York: Simon & Schuster, 2003.
Isenberg, Nancy. *Fallen Founder: The Life of Aaron Burr*. New York: Penguin Books, 2007.
Jessup, Philip C. *American Neutrality and International Police*. World Peace Foundation Pamphlet Series 1, 1928.
Johnson, Herbert A. *Gibbons v. Ogden: John Marshall, Steamboats, and the Commerce Clause*. Lawrence: University Press of Kansas, 2010.
——. *The Chief Justiceship of John Marshall, 1801–1835*. Columbia: University of South Carolina Press, 1997.
Johnson, John W., ed., *Historic U.S. Court Cases: An Encyclopedia*. New York: Routledge, 2001.
Kades, Eric. "History and Interpretation of the Great Case of *Johnson v. M'Intosh*." *Law and History Review* 19, no. 1 (Spring 2001): 67–116.
——. "The Dark Side of Efficiency: *Johnson v. M'Intosh* and the Expropriation of American Indian Lands." *University of Pennsylvania Law Review* 148 (April 2000): 1065–1190.
Keitner, Chimène. "The Forgotten History of Foreign Official Immunity," *New York University Law Review* 87, no. 3 (June 2012): 704–761.
Kerber, Linda K. *Federalists in Dissent: Imagery and Ideology in Jeffersonian America*. Ithaca, NY: Cornell University Press, 1980.
Ketcham, Ralph. *James Madison*. Charlottesville: University Press of Virginia, 1990.
Kettner, James H. *The Development of American Citizenship, 1608–1870*. Chapel Hill: University of North Carolina Press, 1978.
Kierner, Cynthia A. *Scandal at Bizarre: Rumor and Reputation in Jefferson's America*. New York: Palgrave Macmillan, 2004.
King, David. *Vienna 1814: How the Conquerors of Napoleon Made Love, War, and Peace at the Congress of Vienna*. New York: Three Rivers Press, 2008.
Kline, Mary-Jo, and Joanne Wood, eds., *Political Correspondence and Public Papers of Aaron Burr*. 2 vols. Princeton, NJ: Princeton University Press, 1983.
Koch, Adrienne. *Jefferson and Madison: The Great Collaboration*. New York: Oxford University Press, 1964.
Konefsky, Samuel J. *John Marshall and Alexander Hamilton: Architects of the American Constitution*. New York: Macmillan, 1964.
Kukla, Jon. *A Wilderness So Immense: The Louisiana Purchase and the Destiny of America*. New York: Alfred A. Knopf, 2003.

Kulsrud, Carl J. "Armed Neutralities to 1780." *American Journal of International Law* 29, no. 3 (July 1935): 423–447.

Lambert, Frank. *The Barbary Wars: American Independence in the Atlantic World.* Boston: Hill and Wang, 2005.

Lawday, David. *Napoleon's Master: A Life of Prince Talleyrand.* New York: Thomas Dunne Books, 2007.

Leiner, Frederick C. "The Charming Betsy and the Marshall Court," *American Journal of Legal History* 45, no. 1 (2001): 1–21.

Lesser, Charles H., ed. *The Sinews of Independence.* Chicago: University of Chicago Press, 1976.

Lillich, Richard B. "The Chase Impeachment." *American Journal of Legal History* 4, no. 1 (1960): 49–72.

Linklater, Andro. *An Artist in Treason: The Extraordinary Double Life of General James Wilkinson.* New York: Walker Publishing Co., 2009.

Lockhart, Paul. *The Drillmaster of Valley Forge: The Baron de Steuben and the Making of the American Army.* New York: HarperCollins, 2008.

Loth, David. *Chief Justice: John Marshall and the Growth of the American Republic.* New York: Greenwood Press, 1949.

Lukens, Robert J. "Jared Ingersoll's Rejection of Appointment as One of the "Midnight Judges" of 1801: Foolhardy or Farsighted?" *Temple Law Review* 70 (Spring 1997): 189–231.

Madelin, Louis. *Talleyrand: A Vivid Biography of the Amoral, Unscrupulous, and Fascinating French Statesman.* Translated by Rosalie Feltenstein. New York: Roy, 1948.

Magrath, C. Peter. *Yazoo: Law and Politics in the New Republic.* Providence, RI: Brown University Press, 1966.

Maier, Pauline. *Ratification: The People Debate the Constitution, 1787–1788.* New York: Simon & Schuster Paperbacks, 2010.

Malone, Dumas. *Jefferson the Virginian.* Charlottesville: University of Virginia Press, 1948.

——. *Jefferson and the Rights of Man.* Boston: Little, Brown and Co., 1951.

——. *Jefferson and the Ordeal of Liberty.* Boston: Little, Brown, 1962.

——. *Jefferson the President: First Term, 1801–1805.* Boston: Little, Brown, 1970.

——. *Jefferson the President: Second Term, 1805–1809.* Boston: Little, Brown, 1974.

Mapp, Alf. J., Jr. *Thomas Jefferson: A Strange Case of Mistaken Identity.* New York: Madison Books, 1987.

Marsh, Philip. "James Monroe as 'Agricola' in the Genet Controversy, 1793," *Virginia Magazine of History and Biography* 62, no. 4 (October 1954): 472–76.

Marshall, John. *The Life of George Washington.* Vols. 1 and 2. Philadelphia: C. P. Wayne, first published in 1804; reprinted, New York: Walton Book Company, 1930.

——. *An Autobiographical Sketch.* Edited by John Stokes Adams. Ann Arbor: University of Michigan Press, 1991.

Martin, Peter. *The Pleasure Gardens of Virginia: From Jamestown to Jefferson.* Princeton, NJ: Princeton University Press, 1991.

Mashaw, Jerry L. *Creating the Administrative Constitution: The Lost One Hundred Years of American Administrative Law.* The Yale Law Library Series in Legal History and Reference. New Haven, CT: Yale University Press, 2012.

Mason, Frances Norton. *My Dearest Polly: Letters of Chief Justice John Marshall to His Wife, with Their Background, Political and Domestic, 1779–1831.* Richmond, VA: Garret & Massie, 1961.

McConnell, Michael W. "The Story of Marbury v. Madison: Making Defeat Look Like Victory," in *Constitutional Law Stories,* 2nd. ed, edited by Michael C. Dorf. New York: Foundation Press, 2009.

McCoy, Drew R. *The Elusive Republic: Political Economy in Jeffersonian America.* Chapel Hill: University of North Carolina Press, 1980.

McCullough, David. *1776.* New York: Simon & Schuster, 2005.

——. *John Adams.* New York: Simon & Schuster, 2001.

McDonnell, Michael A. *The Politics of War: Race, Class, and Conflict in Revolutionary Virginia.* Chapel Hill: University of North Carolina Press, 2007.

Meacham, Jon. *Thomas Jefferson: The Art of Power.* New York: Random House Trade Paperbacks, 2013.

——. *American Lion: Andrew Jackson in the White House*. New York: Random House, 2008.

Merrick, Jeffrey, and Bryant T. Ragan Jr., eds. *Homosexuality in Modern France*. New York: Oxford University Press, 1996.

Miller, F. Thornton. "John Marshall in Spencer Roane's Virginia: The Southern Constitutional Opposition to the Marshall Court." *John Marshall Law Review* 33, no. 4 (Summer 2000): 1131–1140.

Minnigerode, Meade. *Jefferson, Friend of France, 1793: The Career of Edmond Charles Genet, Minister Plenipotentiary from the French Republic to the United States, as Revealed by His Private Papers, 1763–1834*. New York: G. P. Putnam's Sons, 1928.

Mordecai, Samuel. *Richmond in By-Gone Days: Being Reminiscences of An Old Citizen*. Richmond, VA: George M. West, 1856.

Morgan, Edmund S. *The Genius of George Washington*. New York: W. W. Norton, 1980.

——. *American Slavery, American Freedom: The Ordeal of Colonial Virginia*. New York: W. W. Norton, 1975.

——. *Virginians at Home: Family Life in the Eighteenth Century*. Williamsburg, VA: Colonial Williamsburg Foundation, 1952.

Mori, Jennifer. *William Pitt and the French Revolution, 1785–1795*. New York: St. Martin's Press, 1997.

Myers, Margaret Good. *A Financial History of the United States*. New York: Columbia University Press, 1970.

Nagle, John Copeland. "The Lame Ducks of Marbury." *Constitutional Commentary* 20 (2003–2004): 317–342.

Newmyer, R. Kent. *The Treason Trial of Aaron Burr: Law, Politics, and the Character Wars of the New Nation*. New York: Cambridge University Press, 2012.

——. *John Marshall and the Heroic Age of the Supreme Court*. Baton Rouge: Louisiana State University Press, 2001.

——. *Supreme Court Justice Joseph Story: Statesman of the Old Republic*. Chapel Hill: University of North Carolina Press, 1985.

Newton, Nell Jessup. "Federal Power over Indians: Its Sources, Scope, and Limitations." *University of Pennsylvania Law Review* 132 (January 1984): 195–287.

Noonan, John T., Jr. *The Antelope: The Ordeal of the Recaptured Africans in the Administrations of James Monroe and John Quincy Adams*. Berkeley: University of California Press, 1990.

Norgren, Jill. *The Cherokee Cases: The Confrontation of Law and Politics*. New York: McGraw-Hill, 1996.

Norton, Louis Arthur. *Captains Contentious: The Dysfunctional Sons of the Brine*. Columbia: University of South Carolina Press, 2009.

O'Brien, Conor Cruise. *The Long Affair: Thomas Jefferson and the French Revolution, 1785–1800*. Chicago: University of Chicago Press, 1996.

O'Fallon, James M. "*Marbury*." *Stanford Law Review* 44, no. 2 (January 1992): 219–260.

Oliver, Andrew. *The Portraits of John Marshall*. Charlottesville: University Press of Virginia, 1977.

Onuf, Peter S., ed. *Jeffersonian Legacies*. Charlottesville: University Press of Virginia, 1993.

Orieux, Jean. *Talleyrand: The Art of Survival*. Translated by Patricia Wolf. New York: Alfred A. Knopf, 1974.

Paul, Joel Richard. *Unlikely Allies: How a Merchant, a Playwright, and a Spy Saved the American Revolution*. New York: Riverhead Books, 2009.

——. "The Cost of Free Trade," *Brown Journal of World Affairs*, 22, no. 1 (Fall/Winter 2015).

——. "The Myth of Economic Interdependence," *Waseda Proceedings of Comparative Law* 11, no. 3 (Spring 2009): 293–303.

——. "The Geopolitical Constitution," *California Law Review* 86, no. 4 (1998): 671–773.

——. "Comity in International Law," *Harvard International Law Journal* 32, no. 1 (Winter 1991).

Pearson, Roger. *Voltaire Almighty: A Life in Pursuit of Freedom*. New York: Bloomsbury, 2005.

Perkins, Bradford. *Prologue to War: England and the United States, 1805–1812*. Berkeley: University of California Press, 1961.

Peterson, Merrill D. *The Great Triumvirate: Webster, Clay, and Calhoun*. New York: Oxford University Press, 1987.

——. *Thomas Jefferson and the New Nation*. New York: Oxford University Press, 1970.

Pflaum, Rosalynd. *Talleyrand and His World*. Afton, MN: Afton Press, 2010.

Pitch, Anthony S. *The Burning of Washington: The British Invasion of 1814.* Annapolis, MD: Naval Institute Press, 1998.

Pole, J. R. *Equality, Status, and Power in Thomas Jefferson's Virginia.* Williamsburg, VA: Colonial Williamsburg Foundation, 1998.

Pollak, Louis H. *The Constitution and the Supreme Court: A Documentary History.* New York: World Publishing Co., 1966.

Poniatowski, Michel. *Talleyrand et le Directoire, 1796–1800.* Paris: Librairie Académique Perrin, 1982.

Prakash, Saikrishna Bangalore. "The Appointment and Removal of William J. Marbury and When an Office Vests." *Notre Dame Law Review* 89, no. 1 (2013): 199–251.

Pryor, John H. *Geography, Technology, and War: Studies in the Maritime History of the Mediterranean, 649–1571.* New York: Press Syndicate of the University of Cambridge, 1988.

Pufendorf, Samuel. *De Jure Naturae et Gentium.* Translated by C. H. Oldfather and W. A. Oldfather. 2 vols. Carnegie Endowment for International Peace, 1964.

Rakove, Jack N. *Revolutionaries: A New History of the Invention of America.* Boston: Mariner Books, 2011.

———. *James Madison and the Creation of the American Republic.* New York: Longman, 2002.

———. *Original Meanings: Politics and Ideas in the Making of the Constitution.* New York: Alfred A. Knopf, 1996.

Remini, Robert V. *Daniel Webster: The Man and His Time.* New York: W. W. Norton, 1997.

———. *The Life of Andrew Jackson.* New York: Harper & Row, 1987.

Richards, Leonard L. *Shays's Rebellion: The American Revolution's Final Battle.* Philadelphia: University of Pennsylvania Press, 2002.

Risjord, Norman K. *Chesapeake Politics, 1781–1800.* New York: Columbia University Press, 1978.

———. "The Virginia Federalists." *Journal of Southern History* 33 (1967): 486–517.

Robertson, Lindsay G. *Conquest by Law: How the Discovery of America Dispossessed Indigenous Peoples of Their Lands.* New York: Oxford University Press, 2005.

Rossiter, Clinton. *1787: The Grand Convention.* New York: W. W. Norton, 1966.

Royster, Charles. *A Revolutionary People at War: The Continental Army and American Character, 1775–1783.* Chapel Hill: University of North Carolina Press, 1979.

Rudé, George. *The French Revolution: Its Causes, Its History, and Its Legacy After 200 Years.* New York: Grove Press, 1988.

Rudko, Frances Howell. "Pause at the Rubicon, John Marshall and Emancipation: Reparations in the Early National Period?" *John Marshall Law Review* 35, no. 1 (2001): 75–89.

———. *John Marshall and International Law: Statesman and Chief Justice.* Westport, CT: Greenwood Press, 1991.

Rutherford, Thomas. *Institutes of Natural Law.* Clark, NJ: Lawbook Exchange, 2004. Originally published in 1832 by William and Joseph Neal.

Satz, Ronald N. *American Indian Policy in the Jacksonian Era.* Lincoln: University of Nebraska Press, 1975.

Schama, Simon. *Citizens: A Chronicle of the French Revolution.* New York: Alfred A. Knopf, 1989.

Schiff, Stacy. *A Great Improvisation: Franklin, France, and the Birth of America.* New York: Henry Holt, 2005.

Schlesinger, Arthur M., Jr. *The Age of Jackson.* Boston: Little, Brown, 1946.

Schwartz, Bernard. *A History of the Supreme Court.* New York: Oxford University Press, 1993.

Scott, H. M. *British Foreign Policy in the Age of the American Revolution.* Oxford, UK: Clarendon Press, 1990.

Selby, John. *The Revolution in Virginia, 1775–1783.* Williamsburg, VA: Colonial Williamsburg Foundation, 1988.

Sheldon, Marianne Buroff. "Black-White Relations in Richmond, Virginia: 1782–1820." *Journal of Southern History* 45, no. 1 (February 1979): 27–44.

Sheridan, Eugene R. "The Recall of Edmond Charles Genet: A Study in Transatlantic Politics and Diplomacy." *Diplomatic History* 18, no. 4 (October 1994): 463–488.

Sidbury, James. *Ploughshares into Swords: Race, Rebellion, and Identity in Gabriel's Virginia, 1730–1810.* New York: Cambridge University Press, 1997.

Simon, James F. *What Kind of Nation: Thomas Jefferson, John Marshall and the Epic Struggle to Create a United States*. New York: Simon & Schuster, 2002.

Smith, Jean Edward. "Marshall Misconstrued: Activist? Partisan? Reactionary?" *John Marshall Law Review* 33, no. 4 (2000): 1109–1129.

———. *John Marshall: Definer of a Nation*. New York: Henry Holt, 1996.

Smith, Margaret Bayard. *First Forty Years of Washington Society*. Edited by Gaillard Hunt. New York: Charles Scribner's Sons, 1906.

Smits, Jan-Pieter, Edwin Horlings, and Jan Luiten van Zanden, *Dutch GNP and Its Components, 1800–1913*. Groningen, The Netherlands: N. W. Posthumus Institute, 2000.

Sparrow, Elizabeth. *Secret Service: British Foreign Agents in France, 1792–1815*. Woodbridge, UK: The Boydell Press, 1999.

Stahr, Walter. *John Jay: Founding Father*. New York: Hambledon and London, 2005.

Stern, Jean. *Belle et Bonne: Une Fervente Amie de Voltaire (1757–1822)*. Paris: Librairie Hachette, 1938.

Steward, David O. *American Emperor: Aaron Burr's Challenge to Jefferson's America*. New York: Simon & Schuster, 2011.

Stinchcombe, William. *The XYZ Affair*. Westport, CT: Greenwood Press, 1980.

———. "The Diplomacy of the WXYZ Affair." *William and Mary Quarterly* 34, no. 4 (October 1977): 590–617.

———. "A Neglected Memoir by Talleyrand on French-American Relations." *Proceedings of the American Philosophical Society* 121, no. 3 (June 1977): 204–207.

———. "Talleyrand and the American Negotiations of 1797–1798." *Journal of American History* 62, no. 3 (December 1975): 575–590.

Stites, Francis N. *Private Interest & Public Gain: The Dartmouth College Case, 1819*. Amherst: University of Massachusetts Press, 1972.

Stone, Geoffrey R. *Perilous Times: Free Speech in Wartime*. New York: W. W. Norton, 2004.

Story, William W., ed. *The Life and Letters of Joseph Story*. 2 vols. London: John Chapman, 1851.

Sydnor, Charles S. *American Revolutionaries in the Making*. New York: The Free Press, 1952.

Szatmary, David P. *Shays' Rebellion: The Making of an Agrarian Insurrection*. Amherst: University of Massachusetts Press, 1980.

Takagi, Midori. *Rearing Wolves to Our Own Destruction: Slavery in Richmond, Virginia, 1782–1865*. Charlottesville: University Press of Virginia, 1999.

Taylor, Alan. *The Internal Enemy: Slavery and War in Virginia, 1772–1832*. New York: W. W. Norton, 2013.

Treanor, William Michael. "The Story of *Marbury v. Madison*: Judicial Authority and Political Struggle," in *Federal Courts Stories*, Vicki C. Jackson and Judith Resnik, eds. New York: Foundation Press, 2010.

Turner, Kathryn. "The Midnight Judges." *University of Pennsylvania Law Review* 1909, no. 4 (February 1961): 494–523.

———. "The Appointment of Chief Justice Marshall." *William and Mary Quarterly* 17, no. 2 (April 1960): 143–163.

Tyler-McGraw, Marie, and Gregg D. Kimball. *In Bondage and Freedom: Antebellum Black Life in Richmond*. Chapel Hill: Valentine Museum and University of North Carolina Press, 1988.

Unger, Harlow Giles. *John Marshall: The Chief Justice Who Saved the Nation*. Boston: Da Capo Press, 2014.

———. *Lafayette*. New York: John Wiley & Sons, 2002.

Van Alstyne, R. W. *The Rising American Empire*. New York: W. W. Norton, 1960.

Vattel, Emer de. *The Law of Nations*. Béla Kapossy and Richard Whatmore, eds. Natural Law and Enlightenment Classics. Indianapolis, IN: Liberty Fund, 2008. First published in 1797.

Vaughan, Harold Cecil. *The XYZ Affair, 1797–1798: The Diplomacy of the Adams Administration and an Undeclared War with France*. New York: Franklin Watts, 1972.

Ward, Harry M. *Public Executions in Richmond, Virginia: 1782–1907*. Jefferson, NC: McFarland & Co., 2012.

Ward, Harry M., and Harold E. Greer Jr. *Richmond During the Revolution: 1775–1783*. Charlottesville: University Press of Virginia, 1977.

Ward, John William. *Andrew Jackson: Symbol for an Age.* New York: Oxford University Press, 1955.

Warren, Charles. *The Supreme Court in United States History.* Vol 1, 1789–1835. Boston: Little, Brown, 1926.

Wedgwood, Ruth. "The Revolutionary Martyrdom of Jonathan Robbins." *Yale Law Journal* 100, no. 2 (November 1990): 229–368.

Weddell, Alexander Wilbourne. "Samuel Mordecai: Chronicler of Richmond, 1786–1865." *Virginia Magazine of History and Biography* 53, no. 4 (October 1945): 265–287.

Wharton, Anne Hollingsworth. *Social Life in the Early Republic.* Philadelphia: J. B. Lippincott, 1903.

White, G. Edward. "The Marshall Court and International Law: The Piracy Cases." *American Journal of International Law* 83, no. 4 (October 1989): 727–735.

———. *History of the Supreme Court of the United States: Vols. 3-4, The Marshall Court and Cultural Change, 1815–1835.* New York: Macmillan, 1988.

Wiecek, William. *The Sources of Antislavery Constitutionalism in America 1760–1848* (1977).

Wilentz, Sean. *The Rise of American Democracy: Jefferson to Lincoln.* New York: W. W. Norton, 2005.

Wilkins, David E. *American Indian Sovereignty and the U.S. Supreme Court: The Masking of Justice.* Austin: University of Texas Press, 1997.

Williams, Frances Leigh. *A Founding Family: The Pinckneys of South Carolina.* New York: Harcourt Brace Jovanovich, 1978.

Wills, Garry. *Henry Adams and the Making of America.* New York: Houghton Mifflin, 2005.

———. *Cincinnatus: George Washington and the Enlightenment.* Garden City, NY: Doubleday, 1984.

Winik, Jay. *The Great Upheaval: America and the Birth of the Modern World, 1788–1800.* New York: Harper, 2007.

Witt, John Fabian. *Lincoln's Code: The Laws of War in American History.* New York: The Free Press, 2012.

Wood, Gordon S. *Empire of Liberty: A History of the Early Republic, 1789–1815.* New York: Oxford University Press, 2009.

———. *Revolutionary Characters: What Made the Founders Different.* New York: The Penguin Press, 2006.

———. *The Radicalism of the American Revolution.* New York: Vintage Books, 1993.

———. *The Creation of the American Republic, 1776–1787.* Chapel Hill: University of North Carolina Press, 1969.

Young, James Sterling. *The Washington Community, 1800–1828.* New York: Columbia University Press, 1966.

Zahniser, Marvin R. *Charles Cotesworth Pinckney: Founding Father.* Chapel Hill: University of North Carolina Press, 1967.

Ziegler, Benjamin Munn. *The International Law of John Marshall: A Study in First Principles.* Chapel Hill: University of North Carolina Press, 1939.

INDEX